Self-Mastery

(the way of the heaven born)

D1703749

FRONT COVER MATERIAL

Self-mastery introduces a series of lessons for the new age. As one begins to read self-mastery, he or she will began to realize that, even though Dr. Hutchison wrote many years ago; His lessons are just as relevant today as they were in times past. The work is divided into a group of four series.

The first series is Pathway to Personal Power. I personally, view this first book of enlightenment, as the ultimate self-help manual.

The second series is called The Way of Cosmic Enlightenment. The essential characteristic of this grade of imitation or realization. The student or knower begins to realize what Dr. Hutchison refers to as "Self-Consciousness". The knower becomes cognizant of the fact that he is an individual being distinct from all other created things or beings, and he also realizes his own thought—power, and he learns to develop this power.

The third group in the series of instruction is called the Reception. "The essential aim of this group of instruction is the attainment of that perfect annihilation of that personality which opposes his true self—he is predominately the master of mysticism, that is, his understanding is entirely free from external contradictions or external obscurity; Finally, he identifies himself with the impersonal idea of love".

The last of the series of lessons is called The Illumination or (The Path to Health, Wealth and Happiness). In this series, one is taught to recognize the attainment of mastership. This is what the rosecrucians refer to as cosmic-consciousness.

AUTHOR BIO

W. Gorge Bryant Ph.D. is a senior fellow of the academy of Philosophical Operational and Future Science where he is actively engaged in teaching and research. Dr. Bryant's professional interest focuses upon the interplay between science, philosophy, and religion in order to determine the highest truths of our physical world.

BOOK MARKETING STATEMENT

In the tradition of Anthony Robbins, Deepak Chopra, and Gary Zukoff. Self-Mastery offers a recipe for personal and spiritual development to the individual seeker.

FOREWORD

This work was first brought before the world by the now defunct American Bible Institute, and their chief adept, M.C. Hutchison. Legend has it that the work presented, in self-mastery is, many centuries old, being pasted down from the Seth priesthood to the Dravidian priesthood and finally to the Western adepts of the word.

The most important points of the teachings are becoming much more apparent, in our modern times, when we hear of the healing effects of prayer and meditation, the importance of diet, the effects of a positive mental attitude upon the mind-body system. Further, it has been shown by Marharshi Marhesh Yogi and others, that crime statistics goes down when significant numbers of mantric meditators are in a certain city of high crime rates.

One would wonder what is the mechanism behind such phenomena. It is nothing new. All the great teachers and masters of both east and west told us the same thing but they didn't leave us a "road map" or tell us of the reasons behind the process. Though certain clues are given in the words of the Christ Avatar:

1.) "The Kingdom of God is within you."

2.) "You are the temple of the living God."

3.) "Within you is hidden the treasure of all treasures."

In the second covenant in which the Christ came into the world to fulfill we are reminded of the promise of Yahweh, "I will write my Law or my spirit upon the hearts and minds of men and they will be my people and I will be their God." In essence what it says is that man doesn't need a priest or intermediaries to interpret the word of God because it is already inscribed within the individual seeker. We know this to be so because the primary mission of the Christ Avatar was to bring the knowledge of the over-soul to humanity. (see the keys of Enoch).

The soul has three components all of which are in a continuous state of development and are designated as Rauch, nephish, and Neshamah. We contend that, when Rauch, and nephish combines, this union becomes neshamah which is the inner spark of the Divine that merges with the over soul. This is a most important concept, that our modern day churches, don't teach or accept, mainly, because they have no reference for it, being literal interpreters of, biblical teaching. Even; the Septuagint translators erred in this point of fact (not having an inward reference from which to draw upon.).

Our second set of teachings in the self-mastery series gives us a road-map via the route the proper breathing exercises and mantric meditation, that leads to the development of our inner attainment. We practice the breathing exercises because in doing so we ingest energies into our Bio-electric mechanical computer we call our bodies, such that, we may attune our inner self with the cosmic vibrations of the over-soul.

This process is called Prana-Yama in the east. We have already discussed the importance of mantric meditation. We are also given the eastern mantric formula AUM-MANI-PAD-ME-HUM.

Again I would like to emphasize the importance of the over-soul in all our activities, as well as, the fact that the over self is not a new concept but has been taught throughout the ages. The eastern teachers call it the Atman. If you can't quite accept our word on this point perhaps, you will listen to those of Ralph Waldo Emerson's "Over Soul".

THE OVER-SOUL

There is a difference between one and another hour of life, in their authority and subsequent effect. Our

faith comes in moments; our vice is habitual. Yet there is a depth in those brief moments which constrains us

to ascribe more reality to them than to all other experiences. For this reason, the argument which is always

forthcoming to silence those who conceive extraordinary hopes of man, namely, the appeal to experience, is

for ever invalid and vain. We give up the past to the objector, and yet we hope. He must explain this hope. We

grant that human life is mean; but how did we find out that it was mean? What is the ground of this uneasi

ness of ours; of this old discontent? What is the universal sense of want and ignorance, but the fine innuen

do by which the soul makes its enormous claim? Why do men feel that the natural history of man has never

been written, but he is always leaving behind what you have said of him, and it becomes old, and books of

metaphysics worthless? The philosophy of six thousand years has not searched the chambers and magazines

of the soul. In its experiments there has always remained, in the last analysis, a residuum it could not resolve.

Man is a stream whose source is hidden. Our being is descending into us from we know not whence. The most

exact calculator has no prescience that somewhat incalculable may not balk the very next moment. I am con

strained every moment to acknowledge a higher origin for events than the will I call mine.

As with events, so is it with thoughts. When I watch that flowing river, which, out of regions I see not, pours

for a season its streams into me, I see that I am a pensioner; not a cause, but a surprised spectator of this ethe

real water; that I desire and look up, and put myself in the attitude of reception, but from some alien energy

the visions come.

The Supreme Critic on the errors of the past and the present, and the only prophet of that which must be,

is that great nature in which we rest, as the earth lies in the soft arms of the atmosphere; that Unity, that Over

soul, within which every man's particular being is contained and made one with all other;that common heart,

of which all sincere conversation is the worship, to which all right action is submission; that overpowering real

ity which confutes our tricks and talents, and constrains every one to pass for what he is, and to speak from

his character, and not from his tongue, and which evermore tends to pass into our thought and hand, and

become wisdom, and virtue, and power, and beauty. We live in succession, in division, in parts, in particles.

Meantime within man is the soul of the whole; the wise silence; the universal beauty, to which every part and

particle is equally related; the eternal ONE. And this deep power in which we exist, and whose beatitude is all

accessible to us, is not only self-sufficing and perfect in every hour, but the act of seeing and the thing seen,

the seer and the spectacle, the subject and the object, are one. We see the world piece by piece, as the sun, the

moon, the animal, the tree; but the whole, of which these are the shining parts, is the soul. Only by the vision

of that Wisdom can the horoscope of the ages be read, and by falling back on our better thoughts, by yield

ing to the spirit of prophecy which is innate in every man, we can know what it saith. Every man's words, who

speaks from that life, must sound vain to those who do not dwell in the same thought on their own part. I dare

not speak for it. My words do not carry its august sense; they fall short and cold. Only itself can inspire whom

it will, and behold! their speech shall be lyrical, and sweet, and universal as the rising of the wind. Yet I desire,

even by profane words, if I may not use sacred, to indicate the heaven of this deity, and to report what hints

I have collected of the transcendent simplicity and energy of the Highest Law.

If we consider what happens in conversation, in reveries, in remorse, in times of passion, in surprises, in the

and enhancing a real element, and forcing it on our distinct notice,—we shall catch
many hints that will broaden and lighten into knowledge of the secret of nature. All
goes to show that the soul in man is not an organ, but animates and exercises all the
organs; is not a function, like the power of memory, of calculation, of comparison,
but uses these as hands and feet; is not a faculty, but a light; is not the intellect or the
will, but the master of the intellect and the will; is the background of our being, in
which they lie,—an immensity not possessed and that cannot be possessed. From
within or from behind, a light shines through us upon things, and makes us aware
that we are nothing, but the light is all. A man is the facade of a temple wherein all
wisdom and all good abide. What we commonly call man, the eating, drinking,
planting, counting man, does not, as we know him, represent himself, but
misrepresents himself. Him we do not respect, but the soul, whose organ he is,
would he let it appear through his action, would make our knees bend. When it
breathes through his intellect, it is genius; when it breathes through his will, it is
virtue; when it flows through his affection, it is love. And the blindness of the
intellect begins, when it would be something of itself. The weakness of the will
begins, when the individual would be something of himself. All reform aims, in some
one particular, to let the soul have its way through us; in other words, to engage us to
obey.

Of this pure nature every man is at some time sensible. Language cannot paint it
with his colors. It is too subtile. It is undefinable, unmeasurable, but we know that it
pervades and contains us. We know that all spiritual being is in man. A wise old
proverb says, "God comes to see us without bell"; that is, as there is no screen or
ceiling between our heads and the infinite heavens, so is there no bar or wall in the
soul where man, the effect, ceases, and God, the cause, begins. The walls are taken
away. We lie open on one side to the deeps of spiritual nature, to the attributes of
God. Justice we see and know, Love, Freedom, Power. These natures no man ever
got above, but they tower over us, and most in the moment when our interests tempt
us to wound them.

The sovereignty of this nature whereof we speak is made known by its
independency of those limitations which circumscribe us on every hand. The soul

circumscribes all things. As I have said, it contradicts all experience. In like manner it abolishes time and space. The influence of the senses has, in most men, overpowered the mind to that degree, that the walls of time and space have come to look real and insurmountable; and to speak with levity of these limits is, in the world, the sign of insanity. Yet time and space are but inverse measures of the force of the soul. The spirit sports with time,—

"Can crowd eternity into an hour, Or stretch an hour to eternity."

We are often made to feel that there is another youth and age than that which is measured from the year of our natural birth. Some thoughts always find us young, and keep us so. Such a thought is the love of the universal and eternal beauty. Every man parts from that contemplation with the feeling that it rather belongs to ages than to mortal life. The least activity of the intellectual powers redeems us in a degree from the conditions of time. In sickness, in languor, give us a strain of poetry, or a profound sentence, and we are refreshed; or produce a volume of Plato, or Shakespeare, or remind us of their names, and instantly we come into a feeling of longevity. See how the deep, divine thought reduces centuries, and millenniums, and makes itself present through all ages. Is the teaching of Christ less effective now than it was when first his mouth was opened? The emphasis of facts and persons in my thought has nothing to do with time. And so, always, the soul's scale is one; the scale of the senses and the understanding is another. Before the revelations of the soul, Time, Space, and Nature shrink away. In common speech, we refer all things to time, as we habitually refer the immensely sundered stars to one concave sphere. And so we say that the Judgment is distant or near, that the Millennium approaches, that a day of certain political, moral, social reforms is at hand, and the like, when we mean, that, in the nature of things, one of the facts we contemplate is external and fugitive, and the other is permanent and connate with the soul. The things we now esteem fixed shall, one by one, detach themselves, like ripe fruit, from our experience, and fall. The wind shall blow them none knows whither. The landscape, the figures, Boston, London, are facts as fugitive as any institution past, or any whiff of mist or smoke, and so is society, and so is the world. The soul looketh steadily forwards, creating a world before her, leaving worlds behind her. She has no dates, nor rites, nor persons, nor specialties, nor men. The soul knows only the soul; the web of events is the flowing robe in which she is clothed.

After its own law and not by arithmetic is the rate of its progress to be computed. The soul's advances are not made by gradation, such as can be represented by motion in a straight line; but rather by ascension of state, such as can be represented by metamorphosis,—from the egg to the worm, from the worm to the fly. The growths of genius are of a certain _total_ character, that does not advance the elect individual first over John, then Adam, then Richard, and give to each the pain of discovered inferiority, but by every throe of growth the man expands there where he works, passing, at each pulsation, classes, populations, of men. With each divine impulse the mind rends the thin rinds of the visible and finite, and comes out into eternity, and inspires and expires its air. It converses with truths that have always been spoken in the world, and becomes conscious of a closer sympathy with Zeno and Arrian, than with persons in the house.

This is the law of moral and of mental gain. The simple rise as by specific levity, not into a particular virtue, but into the region of all the virtues. They are in the spirit which contains them all. The soul requires purity, but purity is not it; requires justice, but justice is not that; requires beneficence, but is somewhat better; so that there is a kind of descent and accommodation felt when we leave speaking of moral nature, to urge a virtue which it enjoins. To the well-born child, all the virtues are natural, and not painfully acquired. Speak to his heart, and the man becomes suddenly virtuous.

Within the same sentiment is the germ of intellectual growth, which obeys the same law. Those who are capable of humility, of justice, of love, of aspiration, stand already on a platform that commands the sciences and arts, speech and poetry, action and grace. For whoso dwells in this moral beatitude already anticipates those special powers which men prize so highly. The lover has no talent, no skill, which passes for quite nothing with his enamoured maiden, however little she may possess of related faculty; and the heart which abandons itself to the Supreme Mind finds itself related to all its works, and will travel a royal road to particular knowledges and powers. In ascending to this primary and aboriginal sentiment, we have come from our remote station on the circumference instantaneously to the centre of the world, where, as in the closet of God, we see causes, and anticipate the universe, which is but a slow effect.

One mode of the divine teaching is the incarnation of the spirit in a form,—in forms, like my own. I live in society; with persons who answer to thoughts in my own mind, or express a certain obedience to the great instincts to which I live. I see its presence to them. I am certified of a common nature; and these other souls, these separated selves, draw me as nothing else can. They stir in me the new emotions we call passion; of love, hatred, fear, admiration, pity; thence comes conversation, competition, persuasion, cities, and war. Persons are supplementary to the primary teaching of the soul. In youth we are mad for persons. Childhood and youth see all the world in them. But the larger experience of man discovers the identical nature appearing through them all. Persons themselves acquaint us with the impersonal. In all conversation between two persons, tacit reference is made, as to a third party, to a common nature. That third party or common nature is not social; it is impersonal; is God. And so in groups where debate is earnest, and especially on high questions, the company become aware that the thought rises to an equal level in all bosoms, that all have a spiritual property in what was said, as well as the sayer. They all become wiser than they were. It arches over them like a temple, this unity of thought, in which every heart beats with nobler sense of power and duty, and thinks and acts with unusual solemnity. All are conscious of attaining to a higher self-possession. It shines for all. There is a certain wisdom of humanity which is common to the greatest men with the lowest, and which our ordinary education often labors to silence and obstruct. The mind is one, and the best minds, who love truth for its own sake, think much less of property in truth. They accept it thankfully everywhere, and do not label or stamp it with any man's name, for it is theirs long beforehand, and from eternity. The learned and the studious of thought have no monopoly of wisdom. Their violence of direction in some degree disqualifies them to think truly. We owe many valuable observations to people who are not very acute or profound, and who say the thing without effort, which we want and have long been hunting in vain. The action of the soul is oftener in that which is felt and left unsaid, than in that which is said in any conversation. It broods over every society, and they unconsciously seek for it in each other. We know better than we do. We do not yet possess ourselves, and we know at the same time that we are much more. I feel the same truth how often in my trivial conversation with my neighbours, that somewhat higher in each of us overlooks this by-play, and Jove nods to Jove from behind each of us.

Men descend to meet. In their habitual and mean service to the world, for which they forsake their native nobleness, they resemble those Arabian sheiks, who dwell in mean houses, and affect an external poverty, to escape the rapacity of the Pacha, and reserve all their display of wealth for their interior and guarded retirements.

As it is present in all persons, so it is in every period of life. It is adult already in the infant man. In my dealing with my child, my Latin and Greek, my accomplishments and my money stead me nothing; but as much soul as I have avails. If I am wilful, he sets his will against mine, one for one, and leaves me, if I please, the degradation of beating him by my superiority of strength. But if I renounce my will, and act for the soul, setting that up as umpire between us two, out of his young eyes looks the same soul; he reveres and loves with me.

The soul is the perceiver and revealer of truth. We know truth when we see it, let skeptic and scoffer say what they choose. Foolish people ask you, when you have spoken what they do not wish to hear, `How do you know it is truth, and not an error of your own?' We know truth when we see it, from opinion, as we know when we are awake that we are awake. It was a grand sentence of Emanuel Swedenborg, which would alone indicate the greatness of that man's perception,—"It is no proof of a man's understanding to be able to confirm whatever he pleases; but to be able to discern that what is true is true, and that what is false is false, this is the mark and character of intelligence." In the book I read, the good thought returns to me, as every truth will, the image of the whole soul. To the bad thought which I find in it, the same soul becomes a discerning, separating sword, and lops it away. We are wiser than we know. If we will not interfere with our thought, but will act entirely, or see how the thing stands in God, we know the particular thing, and every thing, and every man. For the Maker of all things and all persons stands behind us, and casts his dread omniscience through us over things.

But beyond this recognition of its own in particular passages of the individual's experience, it also reveals truth. And here we should seek to reinforce ourselves by its very presence, and to speak with a worthier, loftier strain of that advent. For the soul's communication of truth is the highest event in nature, since it then does not give somewhat from itself, but it gives itself, or passes into and becomes that man whom it enlightens; or, in proportion to that truth he receives, it takes him to itself.

We distinguish the announcements of the soul, its manifestations of its own nature, by the term _Revelation_. These are always attended by the emotion of the sublime. For this communication is an influx of the Divine mind into our mind. It is an ebb of the individual rivulet before the flowing surges of the sea of life. Every distinct apprehension of this central commandment agitates men with awe and delight. A thrill passes through all men at the reception of new truth, or at the performance of a great action, which comes out of the heart of nature. In these communications, the power to see is not separated from the will to do, but the insight proceeds from obedience, and the obedience proceeds from a joyful perception. Every moment when the individual feels himself invaded by it is memorable. By the necessity of our constitution, a certain enthusiasm attends the individual's consciousness of that divine presence. The character and duration of this enthusiasm varies with the state of the individual, from an ecstasy and trance and prophetic inspiration,— which is its rarer appearance,—to the faintest glow of virtuous emotion, in which form it warms, like our household fires, all the families and associations of men, and makes society possible. A certain tendency to insanity has always attended the opening of the religious sense in men, as if they had been "blasted with excess of light." The trances of Socrates, the "union" of Plotinus, the vision of Porphyry, the conversion of Paul, the aurora of Behmen, the convulsions of George Fox and his Quakers, the illumination of Swedenborg, are of this kind. What was in the case of these remarkable persons a ravishment has, in innumerable instances in common life, been exhibited in less striking manner. Everywhere the history of religion betrays a tendency to enthusiasm. The rapture of the Moravian and Quietist; the opening of the internal sense of the Word, in the language of the New Jerusalem Church; the _revival_ of the Calvinistic churches; the _experiences_ of the Methodists, are varying forms of that shudder of awe and delight with which the individual soul always mingles with the universal soul.

The nature of these revelations is the same; they are perceptions of the absolute law. They are solutions of the soul's own questions. They do not answer the questions which the understanding asks. The soul answers never by words, but by the thing itself that is inquired after.

Revelation is the disclosure of the soul. The popular notion of a revelation is, that it is a telling of fortunes. In past oracles of the soul, the understanding seeks to find answers to sensual questions, and undertakes to tell from God how long men shall exist, what their hands shall do, and who shall be their company, adding names, and dates, and places. But we must pick no locks. We must check this low curiosity. An answer in words is delusive; it is really no answer to the questions you ask. Do not require a description of the countries towards which you sail. The description does not describe them to you, and to-morrow you arrive there, and know them by inhabiting them. Men ask concerning the immortality of the soul, the employments of heaven, the state of the sinner, and so forth. They even dream that Jesus has left replies to precisely these interrogatories. Never a moment did that sublime spirit speak in their _patois_. To truth, justice, love, the attributes of the soul, the idea of immutableness is essentially associated. Jesus, living in these moral sentiments, heedless of sensual fortunes, heeding only the manifestations of these, never made the separation of the idea of duration from the essence of these attributes, nor uttered a syllable concerning the duration of the soul. It was left to his disciples to sever duration from the moral elements, and to teach the immortality of the soul as a doctrine, and maintain it by evidences. The moment the doctrine of the immortality is separately taught, man is already fallen. In the flowing of love, in the adoration of humility, there is no question of continuance. No inspired man ever asks this question, or condescends to these evidences. For the soul is true to itself, and the man in whom it is shed abroad cannot wander from the present, which is infinite, to a future which would be finite.

These questions which we lust to ask about the future are a confession of sin. God has no answer for them. No answer in words can reply to a question of things. It is not in an arbitrary "decree of God," but in the nature of man, that a veil shuts down on the facts of to-morrow; for the soul will not have us read any other cipher than that of cause and effect. By this veil, which curtains events, it instructs the children of men to live in to-day. The only mode of obtaining an answer to these questions of the senses is to forego all low curiosity, and, accepting the tide of being which floats us into the secret of nature, work and live, work and live, and all unawares the advancing soul has built and forged for itself a new condition, and the question and the answer are one.

By the same fire, vital, consecrating, celestial, which burns until it shall dissolve all things into the waves and surges of an ocean of light, we see and know each other, and what spirit each is of. Who can tell the grounds of his knowledge of the character of the several individuals in his circle of friends? No man. Yet their acts and words do not disappoint him. In that man, though he knew no ill of him, he put no trust. In that other, though they had seldom met, authentic signs had yet passed, to signify that he might be trusted as one who had an interest in his own character. We know each other very well,—which of us has been just to himself, and whether that which we teach or behold is only an aspiration, or is our honest effort also.

We are all discerners of spirits. That diagnosis lies aloft in our life or unconscious power. The intercourse of society,—its trade, its religion, its friendships, its quarrels,—is one wide, judicial investigation of character. In full court, or in small committee, or confronted face to face, accuser and accused, men offer themselves to be judged. Against their will they exhibit those decisive trifles by which character is read. But who judges? and what? Not our understanding. We do not read them by learning or craft. No; the wisdom of the wise man consists herein, that he does not judge them; he lets them judge themselves, and merely reads and records their own verdict.

By virtue of this inevitable nature, private will is overpowered, and, maugre our efforts or our imperfections, your genius will speak from you, and mine from me. That which we are, we shall teach, not voluntarily, but involuntarily. Thoughts come into our minds by avenues which we never left open, and thoughts go out of our minds through avenues which we never voluntarily opened. Character teaches over our head. The infallible index of true progress is found in the tone the man takes. Neither his age, nor his breeding, nor company, nor books, nor actions, nor talents, nor all together, can hinder him from being deferential to a higher spirit than his own. If he have not found his home in God, his manners, his forms of speech, the turn of his sentences, the build, shall I say, of all his opinions, will involuntarily confess it, let him brave it out how he will. If he have found his centre, the Deity will shine through him, through all the disguises of ignorance, of ungenial temperament, of unfavorable circumstance. The tone of seeking is one, and the tone of having is another.

The great distinction between teachers sacred or literary,—between poets like Herbert, and poets like Pope,—between philosophers like Spinoza, Kant, and Coleridge, and philosophers like Locke, Paley, Mackintosh, and Stewart,—between men of the world, who are reckoned accomplished talkers, and here and there a fervent mystic, prophesying, half insane under the infinitude of his thought,—is, that one class speak _from within_, or from experience, as parties and possessors of the fact; and the other class, _from without_, as spectators merely, or perhaps as acquainted with the fact on the evidence of third persons. It is of no use to preach to me from without. I can do that too easily myself. Jesus speaks always from within, and in a degree that transcends all others. In that is the miracle. I believe beforehand that it ought so to be. All men stand continually in the expectation of the appearance of such a teacher. But if a man do not speak from within the veil, where the word is one with that it tells of, let him lowly confess it.

The same Omniscience flows into the intellect, and makes what we call genius. Much of the wisdom of the world is not wisdom, and the most illuminated class of men are no doubt superior to literary fame, and are not writers. Among the multitude of scholars and authors, we feel no hallowing presence; we are sensible of a knack and skill rather than of inspiration; they have a light, and know not whence it comes, and call it their own; their talent is some exaggerated faculty, some overgrown member, so that their strength is a disease. In these instances the intellectual gifts do not make the impression of virtue, but almost of vice; and we feel that a man's talents stand in the way of his advancement in truth. But genius is religious. It is a larger imbibing of the common heart. It is not anomalous, but more like, and not less like other men. There is, in all great poets, a wisdom of humanity which is superior to any talents they exercise. The author, the wit, the partisan, the fine gentleman, does not take place of the man. Humanity shines in Homer, in Chaucer, in Spenser, in Shakespeare, in Milton. They are content with truth. They use the positive degree. They seem frigid and phlegmatic to those who have been spiced with the frantic passion and violent coloring of inferior, but popular writers. For they are poets by the free course which they allow to the informing soul, which through their eyes beholds again, and blesses the things which it hath made. The soul is superior to its knowledge; wiser than any of its works. The great poet makes us feel our own wealth, and then we think less of his compositions. His best communication to our mind is to teach us to despise all he has done. Shakespeare carries us to such a lofty strain of intelligent activity, as to suggest a wealth which beggars his own; and we then feel that the splendid works which he has created, and which in other hours we extol as a sort of self-existent poetry, take no stronger hold of real nature than the shadow of a passing traveller on the rock. The inspiration which uttered itself in Hamlet and Lear could utter things as good from day to day, for ever. Why, then, should I make account of Hamlet and Lear, as if we had not the soul from which they fell as syllables from the tongue?

This energy does not descend into individual life on any other condition than entire possession. It comes to the lowly and simple; it comes to whomsoever will put off what is foreign and proud; it comes as insight; it comes as serenity and grandeur. When we see those whom it inhabits, we are apprized of new degrees of greatness. From that inspiration the man comes back with a changed tone. He does not talk with men with an eye to their opinion. He tries them. It requires of us to be plain and true. The vain traveller attempts to embellish his life by quoting my lord, and the prince, and the countess, who thus said or did to _him._ The ambitious vulgar show you their spoons, and brooches, and rings, and preserve their cards and compliments. The more cultivated, in their account of their own experience, cull out the pleasing, poetic circumstance,—the visit to Rome, the man of genius they saw, the brilliant friend they know; still further on, perhaps, the gorgeous landscape, the mountain lights, the mountain thoughts, they enjoyed yesterday,—and so seek to throw a romantic color over their life. But the soul that ascends to worship the great God is plain and true; has no rose-color, no fine friends, no chivalry, no adventures; does not want admiration; dwells in the hour that now is, in the earnest experience of the common day,—by reason of the present moment and the mere trifle having become porous to thought, and bibulous of the sea of light.

Converse with a mind that is grandly simple, and literature looks like word-catching. The simplest utterances are worthiest to be written, yet are they so cheap, and so things of course, that, in the infinite riches of the soul, it is like gathering a few pebbles off the ground, or bottling a little air in a phial, when the whole earth and the whole atmosphere are ours. Nothing can pass there, or make you one of the circle, but the casting aside your trappings, and dealing man to man in naked truth, plain confession, and omniscient affirmation.

Souls such as these treat you as gods would; walk as gods in the earth, accepting without any admiration your wit, your bounty, your virtue even,—say rather your act of duty, for your virtue they own as their proper blood, royal as themselves, and over-royal, and the father of the gods. But what rebuke their plain fraternal bearing casts on the mutual flattery with which authors solace each other and wound themselves! These flatter not. I do not wonder that these men go to see Cromwell, and Christina, and Charles the Second, and James the First, and the Grand Turk. For they are, in their own elevation, the fellows of kings, and must feel the servile tone of conversation in the world. They must always be a godsend to princes, for they confront them, a king to a king, without ducking or concession, and give a high nature the refreshment and satisfaction of resistance, of plain humanity, of even companionship, and of new ideas. They leave them wiser and superior men. Souls like these make us feel that sincerity is more excellent than flattery. Deal so plainly with man and woman, as to constrain the utmost sincerity, and destroy all hope of trifling with you. It is the highest compliment you can pay. Their "highest praising," said Milton, "is not flattery, and their plainest advice is a kind of praising."

Ineffable is the union of man and God in every act of the soul. The simplest person, who in his integrity worships God, becomes God; yet for ever and ever the influx of this better and universal self is new and unsearchable. It inspires awe and astonishment. How dear, how soothing to man, arises the idea of God, peopling the lonely place, effacing the scars of our mistakes and disappointments! When we have broken our god of tradition, and ceased from our god of rhetoric, then may God fire the heart with his presence. It is the doubling of the heart itself, nay, the infinite enlargement of the heart with a power of growth to a new infinity on every side. It inspires in man an infallible trust. He has not the conviction, but the sight, that the best is the true, and may in that thought easily dismiss all particular uncertainties and fears, and adjourn to the sure revelation of time, the solution of his private riddles. He is sure that his welfare is dear to the heart of being. In the presence of law to his mind, he is overflowed with a reliance so universal, that it sweeps away all cherished hopes and the most stable projects of mortal condition in its flood. He believes that he cannot escape from his good. The things that are really for thee gravitate to thee. You are running to seek your friend. Let your feet run, but your mind need not. If you do not find him, will you not acquiesce that it is best you should not find him? for there is a power, which, as it is in you, is in him also, and could therefore very well bring you together, if it were for the best. You are preparing with eagerness to go and render a service to which your talent and your taste invite you, the love of men and the hope of fame. Has it not occurred to you, that you have no right to go, unless you are equally willing to be prevented from going? O, believe, as thou livest, that every sound that is spoken over the round world, which thou oughtest to hear, will vibrate on thine ear! Every proverb, every book, every byword that belongs to thee for aid or comfort, shall surely come home through open or winding passages. Every friend whom not thy fantastic will, but the great and tender heart in thee craveth, shall lock thee in his embrace. And this, because the heart in thee is the heart of all; not a valve, not a wall, not an intersection is there anywhere in nature, but one blood rolls uninterruptedly an endless circulation through all men, as the water of the globe is all one sea, and, truly seen, its tide is one.

Let man, then, learn the revelation of all nature and all thought to his heart; this, namely; that the Highest dwells with him; that the sources of nature are in his own mind, if the sentiment of duty is there. But if he would know what the great God speaketh, he must go into his closet and shut the door,' as Jesus said. God will not make himself manifest to cowards. He must greatly listen to himself, withdrawing himself from all the accents of other men's devotion. Even their prayers are hurtful to him, until he have made his own. Our religion vulgarly stands on numbers of believers. Whenever the appeal is made—no matter how indirectly—to numbers, proclamation is then and there made, that religion is not. He that finds God a sweet, enveloping thought to him never counts his company. When I sit in that presence, who shall dare to come in? When I rest in perfect humility, when I burn with pure love, what can Calvin or Swedenborg say?

It makes no difference whether the appeal is to numbers or to one. The faith that stands on authority is not faith. The reliance on authority measures the decline of religion, the withdrawal of the soul. The position men have given to Jesus, now for many centuries of history, is a position of authority. It characterizes themselves. It cannot alter the eternal facts. Great is the soul, and plain. It is no flatterer, it is no follower; it never appeals from itself. It believes in itself. Before the immense possibilities of man, all mere experience, all past biography, however spotless and sainted, shrinks away. Before that heaven which our presentiments foreshow us, we cannot easily praise any form of life we have seen or read of. We not only affirm that we have few great men, but, absolutely speaking, that we have none; that we have no history, no record of any character or mode of living, that entirely contents us. The saints and demigods whom history worships we are constrained to accept with a grain of allowance. Though in our lonely hours we draw a new strength out of their memory, yet, pressed on our attention, as they are by the thoughtless and customary, they fatigue and invade. The soul gives itself, alone, original, and pure, to the Lonely, Original, and Pure, who, on that condition, gladly inhabits, leads, and speaks through it. Then is it glad, young, and nimble. It is not wise, but it sees through all things. It is not called religious, but it is innocent. It calls the light its own, and feels that the grass grows and the stone falls by a law inferior to, and dependent on, its nature. Behold, it saith, I am born into the great, the universal mind. I, the imperfect, adore my own Perfect. I am somehow receptive of the great soul, and thereby I do overlook the sun and the stars, and feel them to be the fair accidents and effects which change and pass. More and more the surges of everlasting nature enter into me, and I become public and human in my regards and actions. So come I to live in thoughts, and act with energies, which are immortal. Thus revering the soul, and learning, as the ancient said, that "its beauty is immense," man will come to see that the world is the perennial miracle which the soul worketh, and be less astonished at particular wonders; he will learn that there is no profane history; that all history is sacred; that the universe is represented in an atom, in a moment of time. He will weave no longer a spotted life of shreds and patches, but he will live with a divine unity. He will cease from what is base and frivolous in his life, and be content with all places and with any service he can render. He will calmly front the morrow in the negligency of that trust which carries God with it, and so hath already the whole future in the bottom of the heart.

Sincerely,

W. George Bryant Ph.D

Senior Fellow APofs. Org

SERIES

THREE

Lesson No. 1
THE PATH TO PSYCHIC RECEPTION

Third Gateway of the Temple Invisible—Being the secret Instruction Taught by The Masters in White, Whose Sublime Precepts are Now Exemplified in These Lessons.

METAPHYSICS: ADVANCED HEALING
TRUTH IS THE TOTALITY OF GOODNESS

> "To thine own self be true,
> And it must follow, as the
> night the day,
> Thou canst not then be false
> to any man."—Hamlet, Act l.
> Scene 3.

Passing now from the "Upper Room" of The Enlightenment, we lead you in vision into the silence of the mystic chamber, which was symbolized by the "King's Chamber" in the heart of The Great Pyramid at Gizeh.

Within this King's Chamber, the world shut out by thick walls of stone and silence, picture yourself seated with some two score or more of the Enlightened Ones before a triangular altar of white marble inlaid with gold. At the three points of the large triangle which forms the top of this altar, burn three large sacred candles.

Here, as One of The Enlightened, you will receive your secret instructions in true metaphysics, just as taught by The Masters in White, of whom Kyron, The Wise, our present proxy instructor is one. These occult doctrines of metaphysical knowledge will be imparted to you in a series of informal lectures by Kyron, our Teacher. In bringing to you these deeply metaphysical lectures by Kyron, The Wise, with your permission we shall continue to modernize his language, so as to be quite easily understood.

Let us understand that when Kyron uses the pronoun "I", he does not refer to his human or personal self as speaking, but rather that Soul-Self which walks with The Ascended Avatars.

Kyron, The Wise, rises and slowly gestures for silence, His greeting:

"Welcome, O Enlightened Ones, for unto thee is granted the Reception."

We begin our studies together this evening in the very great subject of true and applied Metaphysics with instruction in the basic truths of Advanced Healing as taught by The Illumined Masters

"Let us take as our underlying precept this evening the axiom that the perception of the allness of mind is also the perception of the totality of GOOD—and by "good" we also mean TRUTH. This perception wonderfully destroys mortal belief in the reality of human experience. This accomplished perception of Goodness-Truth is the "salvation" of every human being who reaches the realization in The Reception.

For each Enlightened One that development called "salvation" is a finished fact; all that we have to do about it is to perceive it. And while you are receiving, you will walk this earth in the glory of that Light until you reach the Illumination in which you see the perfect vision. Thus, Eternal God-Law has provided that you may possess the joy, the glory and THE HEALING of this message even before your mind is developed into perfect receptivity.

THE OCCULT SCIENCE OF METAPHYSICS

In these studies in Metaphysics, which is an occult science, we shall strive to make this tremendously important subject just as certain, just as useful and just as easily understood as the multiplication table of your school days.

Before you have advanced very far in the study of Metaphysics, you will realize that this occult science deals with the Creative God-Law, the Laws of Existence, the Laws of Cause and Effect, of Compensation and Retribution, and the Laws of Spirit and Soul, and the Laws which rule the Healing of Body and Mind.

This knowledge of the primary of basic Laws of Being, as taught in true Metaphysics will place at your command powers little known to the unenlightened. Very soon you are able to prove to yourself that through complying with these laws, you can attract to yourself whatever it is that you most greatly desire.

Metaphysics presents both an outer and an inner study. The outer study, is known as Soul science. Baptism by water as practiced by the early Christian mystics represents mental science to us, while baptism by fire (that fire which symbolized the 'Holy Ghost' to these early Christians) signifies Soul Science. Thus the awakening of the mind precedes and makes possible Soul consciousness.

The true science of Metaphysics is not new. Soul science has been taught throughout the ages, and this instruction is just as available today as in the past.. These Secret Schools of centuries and centuries ago are exemplified today in this land by their occult descendant, The American Bible Institute. Naturally, we guard their hidden teaching jealously, yet always we welcome the sincere student and are ever ready to share this priceless knowledge with our Initiates, when they are ready and willing to travel the PATH to the psychic reception.

Wisdom, Soul Consciousness, Immortality—all await us along this PATH.

HE WHO CONTROLS MIND CONTROLS NATURE

Every Soul is potentially divine, but each Soul manifests through Mind. Your great goal in this life, then is to demonstrate this divinity by controlling Nature, "matter," or the physical world around you. Self-mastery, victory over the world within you, gives you power over the outer world.

Let us together go back to the origin the nature and the development of the various faculties and powers of this great entity, the Mind, which is forever being evolved by humanity. We shall especially interest ourselves here in what are called the psychic faculties of powers of Mind.

From the dim and distant past orthodox religion, as represented by the various churches in this and other lands, has inherited a somewhat vague concept that this "psychic-mind" with its power to perform seeming "miracles" is a kind of subliminal and supernatural power bestowed upon certain historical persons by some super-being whom they call ("God') as a reward for the religious beliefs or the remarkable "piety" of these favored individuals.

We should also observe that certain psychic factors of the human mind seem to be shared by the 'minds' of animals and these factors enable animals to locate themselves in relation to their surroundings and to travel accurately to a goal hundreds and sometimes even thousands of miles away. Animals also seem to have an uncanny premonition of future events, for which they prepare, events which they could not know if they depended only on the physical senses. We are satisfied to explain this animal fore-knowing by the word "instinct"—but—does that word really explain? We think not.

May we not agree then that our friends the animals, share with us in the primary faculties of Mind, at least; Intuition, Premonition, the power of Orient, and Telepathy?

THE ANCIENT "GODS" OF MYTHOLOGY

The tremendous age of these strange powers of the Psychic Mind is indicated to us by those numberless traditions of a successive line of Masters and Avatars, often the "Gods" of ancient Mythology, who lived amond men in this world countless ages before the dawn of history. Also, there are the traditions of The Ancient Wisdom, long believed to be lost to mankind, and the traditions of vast civilizations ruled by The Masters which have vanished and the stories of great continents now buried beneath oceans.

In the light of both tradition and of history, we cannot doubt that the Initiates among the peoples of the world not only did possess and use this Ancient Wisdom and that they not only talked with Gods but were guided by these superpsychic-Minds.

In other words, these ancient peoples, through their Initiates, were in direct contact and guiding communication with super-endowed Beings, Masters or Avatars of such divine intelligence, of such psychic mind-powers, that they were called "Gods".

We cannot discard as idle dreams the numberless accounts in all ages and so widespread among the different peoples of the earth of men talking with "Gods," The Masters, the Avatars, angels or genii. Merely because these things are today beyond the perception of our physical senses, it does not follow that they cannot be psychic truths.

And psychic truths demonstrate through the physical.

MAN BECAME THE EQUAL OF THE GODS

Here Kyron paused for a moment, and Caddus asked:

"How is it then, O Master Kyron, if those certain ones among the peoples of the olden time were blessed with transcendent psychic minds, that we of today are not born with these psychic powers? Have these powers been lost—or are they only submerged?"

No, good Caddus, these strange powers of the Psychic Mind were never really lost to mankind but often— too often—they are submerged in modern life because but few today truly seek to develop and use this phase of mind.

Remember, to the undeveloped peoples of the ancient ages, the ability to reason, to think, to know and to apply the magical powers of the Ancient Wisdom to master nature and to control physical life was rare indeed and so to the masses of those ages this four-fold ability was in-deed "God-like." Thus, the Masters who alone know the secrets of attaining to the Psychic Mind came to be called "Gods.".

Also, during the ensuing ages two of these mental abilities which marked the "Gods" (the Masters), the ability to reason and the ability to think, were slowly developing, amont the peoples of the earth.

But, tracing the metaphysical story of the Psychic Mind, we are quite convinced that the masses of the peoples of the more ancient ages had not developed the power to think, to reason logically or to evolve connected plans. Instead, tradition and history tell us these people could "talk with the Gods," and the "Gods" (Masters) did their thinking, their reasoning and their planning for them.

We know that these peoples of the olden times built huge cities, erected imposing temples and created magnificent civilizations—but from both tradition and history, again we learn that all these were created under the supervision and the direct instructions of the "Gods," (the Masters) Not one plan, not one set of specifications, not one "blue print" came from the people. The Masters alone had the psychic power to create mentally, and the hands of the common, unthinking humanity of those days worked these mental pictures of the Masters into material form under exact direction.

Not until more modern days, when many men among the masses developed this psychic power to think and to create, did man's dependence upon the former guidance of "the Gods" begin to wane, for then man esteemed himself the equal of the Gods.

POTENTIAL POWERS OF PSYCHIC MIND ARE ELEMENTAL.

The potential powers of the Psychic Mind are as elemental as life itself. These Psychic, Powers are universal and are possessed by every human being, although in the great masses of humanity these transcendent powers are asleep, dormant and never recognized or used.

The powers of the developed Psychic Mind seem marvelous to us usually, especially when we encounter them in many inexplicable phenomena, simply because they are out of the ordinary, because they are unusual.

It is equally true that, although these marvelous psychic powers have become apparently submerged in the material advancement of the race, these gifts of the developed Psychic Mind are now being sought, attained to a degree and are manifesting among the Enlightened all over this land as never before.

The ancient traditions, which comprise the very heart of every root religion of earth, all agree in one symbolic statement, which each presents in a different form or ceremonial or parable. That statement is that man was originally of the divine estate of The Gods, but that "sin" caused pristine man to "fall" from his divine throne.

From this it becomes very evident that originally early man really possessed the developed Psychic Mind and that these psychic powers entitled him to the estate of the Gods. But according to these traditions, there came a time, when early man departed from "the voice of The Gods," (the voice within) and so left the realm of his divinity and plunged forth into the lower world of his animal instincts and his sensual passions, and his mind became saturated with the physical and the material.

In simpler words, man substituted the unreal for Reality.

This "fall" from divinity is not too hard to understand The Masters in White inform us that rarely can the Psychic Mind be developed in any man or woman whose life and body are subject to sensuality and to animal-ism—so rarely that it seems impossible unless that life and that body, are cleansed as if by fire. The grossly physical man or woman cannot become a true Psychic.

"THE DOVE OF THE TEMPLE"

The Psychic Mind is a primary phase of mind, and so it is not complex and difficult to understand, as are the faculties of reasoning and thinking for all primaries are simple. And yet even the primaries require study and understanding, if we are to use them.

As an illustration of this necessity for study and understanding of that great primary, the Psychic Mind, let us turn for a few moments to the life of Jesus, the son of Mary, to whom, because of his gentleness, tradition has given that beautiful name, "The Dove of The Temple."

You will remember that Jesus spent the larger part of his life until he was thirty years old studying under the great Masters in White of his time. From these Masters in White he learned the PATHWAY which leads to the attainment of the Psychic Mind and the laws which govern its powers.

According to all accounts, he attained to the Master-Degree of The Illumination and demonstrated his Avatarship under the name of The Christ by his 'miracles' of HEALING and his mastery over life and death.

In his teaching he plainly recognized them, as always, that every man had within him the possibility of becoming one of The Gods—just as the ancient Masters had become The Gods in the eyes of the undeveloped masses through their knowledge of The Ancient Wisdom.

"Jesus answered them (the Jews,) Is it not written in your law, I said, Ye are gods?."—(John 10:34).

Here Christ was quoting from The Psalm of Apaph (82nd Psalm, 6th Verse) wherein the psalmist, addressing the judges of the people of ancient Israel, says:

"I have said, "Ye are gods; and all of you are children of the Most High."

Does that concept stagger you—the concept indicated by the Christ-Avatar, that each one of you is a potential God. (Master)?

You are an uncrowned God—the crown is Mastery through the Psychic Mind.

LIMITLESS VISION OF THE PSYCHIC MIND

The Psychic Mind, with its single-eyed (focused) vision, sees farther into the spaces of the cosmic, unknown realms than the most gigantic telescope built by man can see into the material universe of the stars. This psychic vision penetrates far deeper beneath the surface of things than the most powerful microscope in the hands of the scientist.

The intelligent mind—the "knowing" mind—is material, it is mortal, by the Higher Psychic Mind reaches to immortality.

When you attain to the consciousness of the Higher Psychic Mind, then in the light of the cosmic rays which stream from that psychic centre your material, mortal, fear-haunted mind ceases to rule. Your mortal "knowing" is submitted in the rhythm of your immortal Soul-Life, for you have attained to a glorious harmony of vibration with your Soul-Self.

On the human side of life, this leads to a developed Individuality, an outstanding dynamic personality and endowment with an almost unbelievable HEALING power.

Was it not perchance of this kingdom of the Higher Psychic Mind ('heaven') that the Christ-Avatar spoke in his parable of the merchant man "seeking goodly pearls" and "Who, when he had found one pearl of great price, went and sold all that he had, and bought it."—(Matt. 13:45-46).

Consider for a moment these words from the inspired writings of Jacob Boehme concerning this "Glorious Pearl" (power) which he says in "the curse (the healer) of sickness:"

"Out of which, science all things grow, blossom, flourish and yield fruit, which Power lies within the Quint Essentia, and is a CURSE OF SICKNESS; if the Four Elements could be put into a temperature, then were the Glorious Pearl in its operation manifested."

By his quaint words of the middle ages, Jacob Boehme is here simply saying that divine harmony (which was the then meaning of that word "temperature," as he used it)—that divine harmony of the Higher Psychic Mind (Soul-Life) with the supreme Over-Soul (GOD) on the part of the Healer is the cure of every human ill, the remedy of sickness and disease.

"I SENT MY SOUL THROUGH THE INVISIBLE"

Probably the most powerful psychic understanding, and that which will become of the most biological value in your power to heal, is the realization of the nothingness of SIN. Sin is as impalpable as a shadow, for it is only a false mortal belief in the reality of limitation and of evil.

You will remember that Paul declares that "the wages of sin is death,"—(Rom. 6:23). Disease you will recognize as a partial concept of death.

And the Yiddish school of the prophets warned many ages before Paul's day: "Be sure your sin will find you out."—(Numbers 32:23). Probably each of you has heard that saying quoted time and again.

Was not this warning intended to frighten men (and women) into not sinning? But supposes that sin does "find you out" and that you are living in THE ALLNESS OF TRUTH—which is the totality or the sum total of all Good, what then? Why then sin would be shown as nothing. Let us remember that this statement—"Be sure your sin will find you out"—is both a warning and a promise. It is a warning IF YOU BELIEVE YOURSELF GUILTY, but it is a promise of supreme happiness IF YOU SEE YOURSELF AS ETERNAL TRUTH.

It is said that the Delphic oracle warned those who approached, KNOW THYSELF. In other words, don't wait for SIN—but find out yourself. For when you see yourself as Truth in the light of that Truth which is YOU, sin vanishes.

Again—be sure your sin will find you out—is it sin then which brings you self-knowledge? If sin be the great revealer of Truth (the shadows of night reveal the beauty of the stars!), what is sin?

Sin, figuratively, is an apparent belief in our inability to fulfill the requirements of our own estimates, our inability to obey natural laws, or to conform to ethics or ideals.

We dwell in the chambers of imagery. Christ, as did every other Illumined Master, came to show the unreality of illusions-of shadows-and to warn us of the bitter cost of giving reality to shadows by imaging sickness, diseases, hatred, jealousy, and lack or unsatisfied longings as being TRUTH or EXISTENT.

Instead, retire constantly and as often as possible into the alter-chamber of your Temple Invisible—the Higher Psychic Mind—and there behold in silent meditation THE CHANGELESS REALITIES of your endless immortality, of your abounding health, of your growing healing power, realize that divine love floods your life, and that happiness is forever yours when you LIVE its reality.

CROWNED BY THE LIKENESS OF GOD

To cease striving to manifest the likeness of men and to unfold our Soul-likeness to God consciously harmonizes us with undreamed of powers. Seen in the light of this nobler ambition, how vain and trifling are the many things in this unreal material world which have troubled us and which we have feared!

If we view our daily lives through the eyes of The Higher Psychic Mind, we see that we are dwelling in a world of vain show where the vanishing and unreal things are.

LESSON NO. 2
THE PATH TO PSYCHIC RECEPTION

Third Gateway of the Temple Invisible—Being the secret Instruction Taught by The Masters in White, Whose Sublime Precepts are Now Exemplified in These Lessons.

"I AM THE SPIRIT THAT DENIES"

Once again mentally see yourself as one of The Enlightened Ones amid the silence of that mystic chamber which was symbolized by the "King's Chamber" in the very heart of The Great Pyramid. With this goodly company of the Companions in White, you are seated quite comfortably before the altar, which is the sacred triangle of white marble inlaid with gold. Three large sacred candles are burning upon this altar, one at each point of the triangle.

And now you will receive another lesson in The Psychic Reception, just as taught in secret by The Masters in White in the ancient days, for Kyron, the Wise, our present proxy instructor, is pictured as one of these ancient Masters in reincarnate form, and, so that these deeper lessons may be more easily understood, we continue to modernize his language. (When Kyron is speaking, we omit quotation marks.)

Now, Kyron, The Wise, motions for silence, and greets us:

Welcome, O Enlightened Ones, for unto thee is granted the Reception.

Listen,—Kyron is reading from an ancient scroll the quaint words of one of the Masters:

"Thou shalt separate the earth from the fire, the subtile from the gross, gently and with much industry.

"It ascends from earth to Heaven, and again descends to earth and receives the force of things above and below.

"Thus shalt thou by this means possess the glory of the whole world, therefore all obscurity shall flee away from thee.

"This is the potent force, force of all forces, for it will overcome everything subtile and penetrates everything solid.

"So the world was created."

"'Two Souls, alas, reside within my breast."

You will remember that in your nineteenth lesson in The Cosmic Enlightenment, when you had reached and entered that "Upper Room" of The Arcanum, where you received the Enlightenment of Healing, I taught you how to summon the Infinite Power, known to us as 'Janadana,' the power that grants! And I told you that this power—the power that grants everything for men—is a power nearer to you than your hands or feet, just as near to you as is your heart or your mind.

I have sought to have you know that your Soul and the soul of every man and woman, bears much the same relation to this Eternal God-Power-Janadana—as the flowers of the field bear to the light of the sun above. Deprive the flower of light and it will sicken and die, and the soul deprived of this divine Spiritual Light may become degraded below that of the animal.

For it is the darkness of such a human soul—that soul which has shut out this effulgent Spirit-Light-of which I would tell you this night. As a symbol of this darkness, let us turn to the 'Mephistopheles' of Faust, in which that familiar spirit exclaims of himself, "I am the Spirit that denies."

Here we have a startling picture of that universal Spirit of Evil embodied in the symbolic Mephistopheles. We must agree that the promptings, the inner impulses, and the many seeming contradictions of human nature lead people either to the heights or to the depths, and perhaps no one understood this better than did Goethe. What a tremendous prototype he created in the character of the tempter, the tormentor, and the guide of this German doctor of old!

Be it said in the interests of truth, however, that the Germanic Doctor in this staggering tragedy was not always a willing follower. But Mephistopheles, clothed in the color of blood, and horned and hoofed, was forever alert to thwart and dominate every better impulse of his victim.

Here, Kyron, The Wise, paused and nodded to Heuroch, saying: Yes, good Heuroch, and have you a question?

MEPHISTOPHELES A SYMBOL UNIVERSAL

"Yes, O Wise Kyron," replied Heuroch, "after all, are not both Faust and Mephistocles just fictitious characters in a story which is limited to a fixed time and to a certain earthly locality?"

No, Heuroch, I feel that it would be very incongruous to limit these characters or this immortal masterpiece to such narrow meanings. Should we not rather interpret this ageless drama in the light of universal symbolism, and should we not credit Goethe with projecting on the screen of this drama exact world-materialism and symbolic Soul-darkness? And did not Goeth personify (personalize) these under the types of a truly human being and his evils...tempter?

Let us remember that Goethe, the learned metaphysician, the profound scholar, was most capable of projecting this great picture of universal human nature—in reality, a dramatization of the endless struggle which is life.

In this drama, which is built upon universal symbolism, let us read between the lines and when we do this we will realize that Mephistopheles is in truth a massive mirror which faithfully reflects the picture of not one, or two, or a few men and women, but indeed every human being. This ageless mirror reflects universal influences, emotions, and inner impulses, pictured in reflecting personalities.

INFLUENCES PERSONIFIED IN ALL AGES

Thinkers and writers in both ancient and modern times thus personify (represent as persons) powerful influences, and thus seek to make them vivid and understandable, and especially is this true of the sacred books and the religions of all ages.

(Here one of the Enlightened disciples signifies that he wishes to ask a question—pausing, Kyron, the Wise says):

Yes, Arondia, and what would you ask?

"If it pleases you, O Kyron, will you explain this matter of personification more at length, and perhaps give us some illustrations which will help us to know your meaning more fully?"

Gladly, Arondia, and as I talk, may we all together meditate upon these great Truths, these mighty but unseen powers, and upon these staggering occult concepts which are reflected in some of these pictures I shall bring to you from the most ancient archives of our order.

First, then, we turn to the Hebrew scriptures, where we find this metaphor in the Bible, which describes this same power or influence reflected in Mephistopheles—"He goeth about as a roaring lion, seeking whom he may devour."

According to the New Testament scriptures, and the history of the time of Christ, those poor human beings afflicted with little understood diseases were believed by the Jews, in common with the Greeks and Romans, to be possessed with DEVILS. This included such diseases as epilepsy, as we see from Matthew 17:115; and Luke 5:27.

In those days it was common to practice "exorcism" upon those persons thus believed to be possessed by "evil spirits" for the purpose of driving the "demons" but. According to our records, Jesus, the Illuminated, merely used the popular method of speech when he spoke of demonic possession, and healed these unfortunates without sharing this view which personified various diseases as "evil spirits."

THE WORD "SATAN" MEANS ADVERSARY

In the Hebrew scriptures, this word Satan is commonly used to refer to the "devil," who is personified as the enemy of God, Thus, the Bible pictures Satan as that great influence which is the tempter of man, the adversary of goodness, and the spirit of evil.

The ancient knowledge that man is a miniature universe and that he can rise to take his place among the Gathering of the Star Brothers is the sublime wisdom upon which all religions are built and which was symbolized in The Great Pyramid, The

House of Light, The Triangle Without a Peak—evolution limitless in universal symbolism.

In the far, far beginnings of our recorded wisdom, which has been handed down through the circling centures until today it is exemplified in our American Bible Institute, according to The Book of the Dead, in most ancient Egypt, the Initiate Worshipper personified himself by calling himself Osiris Neferu, meaning a being having all the symbolic powers of the sun.

The Egyptian Initiate also personified himself under each of the names of the seven gods, each of these names in his faith reflecting a different aspect of THE ONE GOD, known to him as the Hidden One— AMEN. This proves that the universal symbolism of Eternal Law is old beyond all reckoning. These most ancient Initiates knew that in man the universe reflects all of its powers, for they represented limitless evolution between everlasting growth and decay in their symbol of Eternity, which was a circle shedding rays between two lotus columns.

EGYPTIAN RELIGION PERSONIFIED POWERS

In that world-old Egyptian religion Amen is personified (Personalized) as The Supreme Ruler—the dual Mas Power, positive and negative, forever going out and returning, the Creator and the Destroyer, eternally creating anew from that which He destroys.

This most ancient religion teaches that Spirit Force, and Matter are the three (Trinity) which translate His will into effect. Those Initiates of tens of thousands of years ago knew (or personified) these three as Osirus, Isis, and Horus the Father, the Mother, and the Son. Each of these is represented as having supreme power upon its own plane of action; yet these three are One, and each pair of these forever create the third, thus demonstrating The Eternal Law in Change. But to each of these, on its own plane and in its own world, the other two are ILLUSIONS!

For example—to the purely physical Earth-Man, divine force and eternal spirit are illusions, for ONLY MATTER IS REAL TO THE MATERIAL MAN. But his power of thought and his endless urge to reach the stars are the gift of man's eternal spirit, and divine force—radio-active energy gives to his dense body the breath of life.

"...rest not, till the finished work has crowned me."

Thus, exclaims Faust, type of the ever-evolving Soul, referring to the eternally present "messengers of light" who enable us to oppose, yes, to conquer this "prince of darkness." For in this early life we must each one pass through the "valley of decision," where we sooner or later truly find ourselves between the devil and the deep blue sea.

Here Kyron pauses, for Vavania has signified that he, too, would ask the Master of Wisdom a Question.

Vavania speaks: "O Kyron, thou who art truly wise, will you tell us what the devil is, and tell us how this "prince of darkness" can help us to evolve, if he is but a destroying angel?"

First, my good friendVavania, know that life—all life—your life and my life—has a divine and a changeless PURPOSE, and that a very certain DESTINY is involved in your birth into this worlds, and that every power in the universe is working to help to fulfill that destiny. Now man's higher destiny is complete and perfect REALIZATION. Until that destiny perfects the physical, the mental, and the spiritual Self, the circle of creation cannot be completed. What you are really asking then, good Vavania, is, does the devil play a part in this process of self-realization (perfection), or WHO, WHY, AND WHENCE this "Satan," who, throughout the ages ruled by theology, has been represented as a malignant demon?

Now, let us just clear away all this superstitious fog, and proceed upon this basis of truth, if you will, that the devil is no more an entity, no more a being in reality than is darkness. Satan, then, we shall understand as a personified principle, for he so describes himself in his own words as Mephistopheles: "I am the Spirit that denies." Being thus the "adversary," this spirit (or principle) is squarely opposed by Janadana, the Spirit that grants.

Both of these are universal, so both are individual, also. It is very evident that both of these opposing "spirits" cannot occupy the same space in the same mind (or soul) at the same time. But may not both of these personified entities result from the operation of one and the same POWER—that Infinite Power which either builds or destroys, according to the direction which we ourselves give to it? We so believe.

MAN WALKS IN THE WAY HE HAS CHOSEN

After all, everyman makes his own choice, and we each walk the pathway we have chosen. Neither the Devil or God will force you to abandon that which you have definitely decided upon.

Perhaps this ancient proverb will help us to understand this matter more clearly: "Diablo est Deus Inversus" (The Devil is God reversed)!

Yes, my sister Signa—I perceive that you too would ask a question? Signa: "Justly so, O Wise Master, and this is my question—is this Mephistopheles, then, a personal devil?"

Yes, the Devil is a personal devil, but only as every man creates his own devil when he himself becomes the adversary of the Eternal Law of Universal Harmony, and by choosing the way that seems easiest to him and so hinders for a time his own evolving destiny. For we must realize, O Companions in White, that the grand, divine Plan behind the ALL is the individual evolution of the Soul-Self, so that the multitudes of mass-humanity may likewise evolve.

When he is faced with an alternative—a choice between two opposite lines of action—often, seemingly from within himself-every man sooner or later hears a voice whispering: "Just forget about right and wrong, take the easy way, and let the other fellow look out for himself." And that, my friends is the voice of Mephistopheles, and either we yield to this suggested evil or we oppose it, depending upon our own inner standards of values, But the voice itself is the voice of our own lower mind, a materialistic "spirit." And it is only the Fool who persists in yielding to that voice.

"THE FOOL"—(FROM THE DHAMMAPADA).

Just here let us turn to "The Dhammapada, or Path to Virtue," which is one of the Buddhistic Scriptures, for this is a canon which is proven to have existed before the Christian era, any scholars ascribe these utterances to Buddha himself, while others believe that it was compiled by Buddhist monks. Listen, then, to these striking words written more than twenty centuries ago in this Buddhist Scripture, from chapter five, which is entitled "The Fool":

"Long is the night to him who is awake; long is a mile to him who is tired; long is life to the foolish who do not know the true (Eternal) Law.

"If a traveller does not meet one who is his better, or his equal, let him firmly keep to his solitary journey; there is no companionship with a fool.

"Those sons belong to me, and this wealth belongs to me," with such thoughts a fool is tormented. He himself does not belong to himself; how much less sons and wealth?

"The fool who knows his foolishness, is wise at least so far. But a fool who thinks himself wise, he is called a fool indeed.

"Fools of poor understanding have themselves for their greatest enemies, for they do evil deeds which bear bitter fruits.

"That deed is not well done of which a man does not repent, and the reward of which he receives gladly and cheerfully.

"As long as the evil deed done does not bear fruit, the fool thinks it is like honey; but when it ripens, then the fool suffers grief.

"One is the road that leads to wealth, another the road that leads to Nirvana (Perfect realization)—"...

THE FOOL FOLLOWS MEPHISTOPHELES BLINDLY

The fool follows the "satan" that is his own lower animal nature blindly and unquestioningly.

Turn now to the Hebrew scriptures, we will find these significant words: "The fool hath said in his heart, THERE IS NO GOD."—Psalms 14:1.)

Pausing here Kyron nods to Eula, who has signified her desire to ask a question. Eula speaks:

"I would ask this, Kyron, for thou art wise, there is so much of the fool, so much of the lower nature, so much of the temptation to that 'easiest way' often in all of us—how shall we conquer this unseen Mephistopheles within?"

Eula, my good sister, your question shows that you realize the great power of habit, and that you perhaps have found how difficult it is for us to break a mould into which we may find ourselves formed, whether it be from environment, heredity, or our own blind choice. And no matter how much we may will or desire to break those bonds, Mephistopheles, the 'spirit that denies,' constantly urges us to take the line of least resistance.

Development, of course, always means change, change from the lower to the higher, and this onward and upward progression, or self-realization, creates a very real friction, and this results from a pull in two directions, from the old and the new mental attitude. These formative conditions may not always be happy, nay, may lead to periods of positive unhappiness. Yet, my good Eula, we must persist until that higher nature, Janadana, (SWF) 'the Spirit that grants,' dominates and rules without further conscious effort on our part.

"AND SATAN CAME...BEFORE THE LORD!"

In the Hebrew scripture (see Book of Job) there is a striking allegory in the ages-old story of Job which illustrates this teaching exactly:

"And the Lord said unto Satan (Mephistopheles), Behond he (Job) is in thine hand; but save his life.!—Job 2:6)

The ancient story of Job is everyman's story—read it, for it will interest you deeply, for this allegory has been or will be repeated in your life, just as surely as that life is worth while. In this enthralling story' Mephistopheles ("Satan") was deliberately challenged by God to test and prove for himself the faith and the loyalty of Job, of whom the Lord said: "Hast thou considered my servant Job, that there is none like him in the earth, a perfect and upright man, one that feareth God, and escheweth (avoids, turns away from) evil?"

By Faith Job triumphed over utter destitution, lack, and loss, for the price he paid for the "double amount of his former possessions" was simply the price of the conquering of SELF! And know this, O Initiates, each of you also will sooner or later be tested by this same Mephistophelian power, in greater or lesser degree for the same purpose.

But be of good heart, for if the Spirit that grants" is the ruling spirit of your higher consciousness, then the power or "the spirit that denies" disappears, just as the shadows dissolve before the morning sun.

Lesson No. 3 THE BIBLE IN STONE

(The Temple Eternal)

Transported silently upon the wires of thought, again you are seamed with The Enlightened Ones in that mystic "King's Chamber" in the heart of The Great Pyramid, which symbolizes to us "The Temple Eternal."

Before you gleams the beauteous altar of marble and gold, and upon it burn the three sacred candles, one at each point of the world-old triangle. The whole chamber seems suffused with a weird light, which glows from some hidden source. It is very still, for your Companions in White, like yourself, are in silent meditation.

Kyron, the Wise imaged as one of the ancient Masters in White, reincarnate, appears silently, and greets us:

Welcome, O enlightened Ones, for unto thee is granted the Reception.

(We listen as Kyron reads from another of the ancient scrolls of The Institute—this scroll contains the Vedic Hymns, old, indeed for the first of these are the most ancient Sanskrit writings in the world, and were intoned a thousand years before Christ was born. Kyron is reading that most remarkable of these Vedic Hymns, "To The Unknown God"):

"In the beginning there arose the Golden Child. As soon as born, he alone was the lord of all that is. He established the earth and this heaven:—Who is the God to whom we shall offer sacrifice?

"He who gives breath, he who gives strength, whose command all the living gods revere, whose shadow is immortality, whose shadow is death:-Who is the God to whom we shall offer sacrifice?

"He who through his might became the sole king of the breathing and twinkling world, who governs all this, man and beast:—Who is the God to whom we shall offer sacrifice?

"He through whose might these snowy mountains are, and the sea, they say, with the distant river; he of whom these regions are indeed the two arms:—Who is the God to whom we shall offer sacrifice?

"He through whom the awful heavens and the earth were made fast, he through whom the earth was established, and the firmament; he who measured the air in the sky;—who is the God to whom we shall offer sacrifice?

"He to whom heaven and earth, standing firm by his will, look up, trembling in their mind; he over whom the risen sun shines forth:—Who is the God to whom we shall offer sacrifice?

"When the great waters went everywhere, holding the germ, and generating light, then arose from them the breath of the gods:—Who is the God to whom we shall offer sacrifice?

"He who by his might looked even over the waters which held power and generated the sacrifice, he who alone is God above all gods;—Who is the God to whom we shall offer sacrifice?

"May he not hurt us, he who is the begetter of the earth, or he, the righteous, who begat the heaven; he who also begat the bright and mighty waters;—Who is the God to whom we shall offer sacrifice?

"Pragapati (God) no other than thou embraces all these created things. May that be ours which we desire when sacrificing to thee: may we; be lords of wealth!"

GREAT PYRAMID TEMPLE SYMBOL OF YOUR TEMPLE INVISIBLE

Thus (continues Kyron, the Wise) endeth the reading of the oldest of the hymns in writing in this world— the Vedic Hymn to The Unknown God. You will note that this hymn of our ancient Brothers in White agrees with the Hebrew scriptures that "He who alone is God above all gods, before whom heaven and earth stand trembling" in their mind "IS ONE GOD" and is unknown (to the world of material mind).

In their form and spirit these ancient Hindoo hymns resemble the Hebrew Psalter, the Psalms of David, and the lyrics of Pindar. These Vedas, in their inner or occult meaning refer to a Temple Invisible, sacred to the God above all Gods,"—The perfected human Soul. Many, many thousands of years ago the Initiates of Egypt caused to be builded near Cairo the Great Temple Pyramid of Gizah as an ever-or age-lasting symbol of this same Self-Realization of Oneness with "The Unknown God'—known to them as Amen—"The Hidden God."

At this time I wish us to consider together some of the unexplained mysteries of this stupendous Pyramid Temple in which we have assembled in imagination for these lessons in the occult Reception.

MYSTERIES OF "THE DIVINE RECORD"

To any intelligent man or woman who studies its construction, its measurements, and its symbolic meanings. THIS PYRAMID-TEMPLE of our Great Eternal White Brotherhood stands forth as the foremost wonder of the world. Some of our great scholars have called this Temple "The Bible in Stone," while others have termed it "The Divine Record."

Here, with Kyron's permission Sylvanus asks a question:

(Sylvanus:) "Good Master of the Wisdom pray tell us just what are some of these 'symbolic meanings,' of which you speak, and just how can this immense mass of stone be called a 'Divine Record?"

Have patience, my good Sylvanus, and I will try to answer both of your very apt questions, and gladly.

Sylvanus, would it surprise you very greatly if I tell you that, after so many thousands of years of mental lethargy, there are but a limited number of men and women in the world this day who can comprehend the tremendous significance that this Temple hides in its very form and measurements? That is why the Brothers in White have bequeathed this hidden knowledge to those chosen to follow these tremendously important teachings in this Aquarian Age. For each of your lessons is an occult preparation for the ever deeper mysteries that follow.

MODERN MAN CANNOT DUPLICATE THIS TEMPLE

Let us understand then plainly that those ancient Masters in White possessed a knowledge so vastly superior that modern man with all his inventive genius in material things cannot duplicate this tremendous Temple. For this vast monument is in reality and actually a divine record in stone of the history of the earth, of a changeless religion, and of the astronomy of the skies—all of which mankind just now is beginning painfully and slowly to RE-learn.

Personally, from certain secret light received from our ancient Akashic records, I believe that this Pyramid Temple was planned by, and built under the direct supervision of certain Descended Avatars, who were as "gods" to those ancient Egyptian people.

Here is a significant passage from "The Great Pyramid," by Louis P. McCarty:

"The Pyramid was built by a race of people with vastly more intelligence than we now possess...Before the people of earth will be able to duplicate the Great Pyramid they will have to re-discover the lost arts of perfectly hardening copper, overcoming gravitation, navigating the air, etc. Also, more perfect mathematics, measuring apparatus sufficiently correct at least to survey or measure the same object twice with the same results."

You will observe that this Pyramid is built mostly of lime-stone and granite. And as you see it today its sides consist of a series of steps. But before. 800 A.D., these steps or terraces were filled in with polished lime-stone "casing" blocks and these blocks fitted together with matchless perfection. Some of the problems of this construction can be gathered from the fact that many of these casing blocks were 12 feet long, 8 feet wide, and 5 feet thick!

With their rise to power, the Mohammedans used the Great Pyramid as a quarry, and they broke up these casing stones and carried them away to use in, building their mosques or temples. As I told you in Lesson 3 of your, first advanced course, this imposing of all Temples was.almost 500 feet high, and each side of its base measures 755 feet, so this Temple covers 13 acres of ground. Modern engineers estimate that when it was completed the Great Pyramid contained two million three hundred thousand blocks of stone, each averaging two and one half tons in weight!

Those wise Masters of old who apparently chose the exact spot upon which to build this greatest of Temples located it upon approximately the geographical center of the entire lands of the earth. Further, it is significant that the Great Pyramid stands upon a massive ledge of limestone and porphyry which has remained undisturbed since its first formation by any of the countless earthquakes which have devastated Asia Minor and the Mediterranean lands time after time throughout the ages of the past.

SYMBOLISM HIDDEN IN UNITS, PASSAGES, CHAMBERS.

If you will visit your library, doubtless you can find there a book dealing with the Great Pyramid (many such books have been published), and in such a book you will find diagrams and illustrations which will give you some working knowledge of this sacred message in stone from the world that was. To explain the symbology and the occult meanings of this ancient Temple would require many, many volumes and months, yes, years of study. In this lesson, however, I shall only tough upon a few of the highlights of these inner meanings. For these occult meanings will form the basis of future and deeper lessons which you will receive. THE OGP-

Here the disciple Eula signifies her desire to ask a question, and this is her question:

"O Wise Teacher, Kyron—why was this so-great Pyramid-Temple built, and what message does it bring to us?"

Know this, then, Eula, the ancient Masters in White foresaw that the peoples of the earth would later descent into intellectual darkness and into the obscurity of a crass and a gross materialism. So, these Masters (the "Heaven-born Ones") decided to perpetuate for future ages in enduring granite the knowledge of the Universal Eternal Law, of the inexhaustible wonders of the sky, and of the Religion of The One God, who, indeed, alone was their Grand Master.

This "Divine Record" dates back to times of which no other history exists, and this gigantic Sun Dial tells in mathematics the story of Astronomy and Astrology, for upon the symbolism of these man has from the beginning builded his Religion (no matter what name or outer meanings he gave to that Religion). This "Bible in Stone" gives us in symbolism the story of the world—from its beginning to its end—but we only have a few keys which unlock these symbols.

No man knows when this great Temple-Pyramid was built, whether 50,000 years ago, 15,000 years ago, or as some have supposed in the year 2170 B.C., basing this as the year of its completion because then the Pole Star, Draconis, shown directly down the small shaft set at a certain angle, which leads into the "Pit". According to astronomers, nearly 21,000 years must elapse from today before Draconis will shine down this passage again.

However, I would remind you that in modern times one of the great German astronomers, Prof. J. H. Maedler, discovered that Alcyone, (the brightest star in the cluster known as the Pleiades), is in reality the central Sun around which our universe revolves. Astronomers estimate Alcyone to be 10,000 times greater than our sun. Yet our secret scrolls inform us that the great White Masters in Egypt possessed this knowledge 50,000 years ago, and from it later they set the exact time for finishing their massive Pyramid-Temple. Our records show that exactly at midnight on the night of the perfect autumnal equinox 3733 B.C. the apex of this Great Pyramid pointed directly at this central Sun, Alcyone,—at that precise hour and minute!

PYRAMID AT GIZEH GREAT GEOMETRICAL WORK

For many, many years some of the greatest students and scholars of the world have studied the Great Pyramid at firsthand, and these have measured its base, height, vertical height and radius, areas, angles, declinations, chambers, passages and shafts, and all agree that it is the world's greatest geometrical work. Its own mathematical evidence proves, especially to those who know Astronomy and Astrology, not only that it was built by a wisdom supreme but that it is replete with mysteries which cloak both world history and world prophecy.

Yes, Kosmon, I see that you are perplexed—and what is the question you would ask?

Kosmon speaks: "Kyron, this puzzles me—are there not many other pyramids in Egypt? and if so, why does this greater one seem to be the only Temple-Pyramid—could it not have been a tomb?"

Yes, good Kosmon, there is indeed a veritable series of some sixty or more lesser pyramids, which were built during periods of thousands of years, in this mystic land of the Nile. Of these some 37 other pyramids were evidently built long after the Great Temple-Pyramid, and all bear the marks of being only crude imitations. Not one other pyramid has a perfectly square base line, not one of their angles slope at the same pitch, and not one of them is built entirely of stone. And no other pyramid has been found to possess the geometrical, chronological, astronomical, and religious meanings of The Great Pyramid.

Doubtless many of these crude pyramids, may have been used as sepulchres, but no intelligent student can for a moment think that the Great Pyramid was built as a tomb, for any Pharoah.

But let us now consider some of the symbolisms of this tremendous Temple. First, let us consider some of its mathematical symbolisms. Let us remember that Eternal Divine Law, as shown in the entire Solar system, is founded upon mathematical principles, as was in a later age demonstrated by Oenuphis, one of the priests of On, in Egypt, who taught Pythagroas the "True (religio-mathematical) System."

Located, as we have told: you, on the approximate center of the land of the earth, the great Temple-Pyramid was built exactly on the 30th degree of North Latitude at the 30th degree of East Longitude. There was a deep reason back of this enact location., for no other spot on earth could give this ancient Temple its wondrous mathematical and geometrical ratios and records of astronomy, and its prophetic messages from behind the veils of the ages.

IMPERISHABLE RECORDS REVEALED IN THIS AGE.

As you know, we are now living in the dawn of the Aquarian age, the sign of the outpouring of intelligence, after 2160 years of the Piscean Era, the sign of the fishes. During this Piscean period, man lost the Ancient Wisdom and sank to the depths of mental darkness and ignorance during those dark centuries following the advent of Christianity. During these darkened ages true Religion—that occult Religion whose Bible is to be found in the imperishable records of the everlasting Pyramid-Temple—was buried deep under the rubbish and the rubble of superstition, and man-made creeds, dogmas, and idolatry.

Now, with the opening of the Aquarian age, that sign of promise through which our Sun will proceed for 2160 years, we are on the verge of the most startling and wonderful discoveries the world has ever known, and not the least of these will come from the use of the keys we have found to the unanswered Riddle of the Sphinx hidden in these silent symbols of the Great Pyramid.

In deciphering the hidden messages of this immense Temple two basic measuring units are used, these are the Pyramid inch and the Hebrew sacred cubit. The Pyramid inch is just a hair-breadth longer than the English inch (to be exact it is 1.001). The Hebrew sacred cubit is 25 inches.

WISDOM AND SCIENTIFIC KNOWLEDGE IN SYMBOLS

Not only do the mathematical proportions and measurements of this Temple in stone tell us of an ancient wisdom now lost, but they also silently witness to a scientific knowledge unequalled today. As if done by the delicate skill of a master-jeweler, these stones are fitted together and polished by perfect workmanship, Of these stones, McCarty says: "If the different parts could be prepared, we could not place them in their present positions by any known process ,in this enlightened day, owing to their immense size and weight."

Did these ancient Masters in White know anything about. Eternal Natural Law? Let us see. The base line of the Pyramid we find measures exactly 365.242 (365 1/4 cubits), and this represents to a fraction the number of days in a solar year!

The height of the Pyramid is 232,520 cubits, and if we divided this figure by twice the base line, we have as a result the well-known mathematical formulae 3.1415, which is the number used in squaring the circle, also in finding the circumference of a circle.

Now, let us consider some of the significant measurements of that inner altar, room of this vast Temple, known as "The King's Chamber," Let us make the length of The King's Chamber the diameter of a circle, then we will find that a square of the same area as this circle has 365. 242 (inches) on each—(365 1/4)—again the length of the solar year.

Again, if the length of The King's Chamber is made the diameter of a circle, we find that a square of the same area as this circle has that magic 365. 242 (365 1/4) on each of its sides (number of days in the year).

Now, if we add the length and the height of The King's Chamber together and divide this by the breadth, once more we have the formula, 3,145, used in squaring the circle.

This sacred King's Chamber, in which we image ourselves as meeting for these lessons from time to time, is built on the fiftieth course of the Pyramid's masonry, and its content is twenty million cubic inches, and this gives us the exact number of cubits in the length of the polar axis of the earth.

In passing it is interesting to note that the height of the Pyramid (486 ft. plus), when multiplied to the ninth power of ten gives us 91,840,000 which is the distance in miles between the earth and the sun, as estimated by modern astronomers.

Another striking mathematical message is this: if the square of the Pyramid at the level of this King's Chamber be converted into a circle of the same area, we will find that its circumference equals 25,920, which is the exact number of years in The Great Cycle, the number of years, in other words, in the procession of the equinoxes—or the time it takes the entire solar system to complete its circuit of the Zodiac. (Of which, more later).

EACH CHAMBER AND PASSAGE SIGNIFICANT

Every chamber and every passage within the Great Pyramid speaks with symbolic and prophetic meanings. We find that "the Queen's Chamber" is built on the 25th, course of masonry in this most sacred Temple of Silence, and, contains ten million cubic inches, which is just one-half that of the "King's Chamber"—but strangely enough set in the east wall of the Queen's Chamber we find...the unchanging key to all of the temple measurements for here is a niche SET EXACTLY ONE CUBIT FROM THE CENTER, and measuring exactly one cubit, (or 25 inches), reflecting the Hebrew standard of measurement.

The greatest Temple known to man, ancient or modern, is the most stupendous Bible ever written by man, and it was "written in stone" in order to preserve inviolate that sacred Ancient Wisdom—thus to remain safe, unknown, and undiscovered by those who would destroy all such records throughout the countless ages until discovered by those who could rightly use the keys they left in such plain view.

Thus the mathematical philosophy of this most ancient Temple supplies us the perfect keys to all religions AND RELIGION. Truly, there is nothing new under the sun, and the deep truths of Eternal Divine Law, so well known to the ancient Magii and Masters, have been awaiting our re-discovery in this imperishable Record in Granite, which they builded upon the great fundamental laws of Astrology and her daughter, Astronomy.

LESSON No. 4 "THE BIBLE IN STONE"

(The Temple Eternal—Continued)

Once more you have mentally transported yourself to that mystic "King's Chamber" in the heart of The Great Pyramid, which is the imperishable symbol of

"The Temple Eternal," wherein you are now seated with the Enlightened Ones, before the magnificent altar of marble and gold.

At each point of the sacred triangle, which forms the top of the altar, burns without a flicker a sacred candle, for all is silence herein, for your Companions in White are stilled in meditation.

He whom we image as one of the ancient Masters in White reincarnate, Kyron, the Wise, seems to suddenly materialize before the altar—silently—but, listen, he greets us with his accustomed salutation:

Welcome, O Enlightened Ones, for unto thee is granted the Reception.

(Again we perceive that Kyron, the Wise, is about to read to us from still another of the ancient scrolls, he holds in his hand ("The Life of Buddha," written first in the form of a Sanskrit poem more than 19 centuries ago by the twelfth Buddhist patriarch, Asvaghosha, which was translated from Sanskrit into Chinese some three hundred years later, from which the translation was made from which Kyron read these words of Buddha):

One, Upaka, asks the Buddha:"...what then your noble tribe, and who your master?

Answering he (Buddha) said:

"I have no master, no honorable tribe; no point of excellence; self-taught in this profoundest doctrine, I have arrived at superhuman wisdom. That which behooves the world to learn, but throughout the world no learner found, I now myself and by myself have learned throughout; 'tis rightly called Sambodhi.

"That hateful family of griefs the sword of wisdom has destroyed; this then is what the world has named, and rightly named, the 'chiefest victory.' Through all Benares soon will sound the drum of life, no stay is pos-sible—I have no name—nor do I seek profit or pleasure.

"but simple to declare the truth; to save men from pain, and to fulfill my ancient oath, to rescue all not yet delivered. Wealth, riches, self, all given up, unnamed, I still am named "Righteous Master."

"And bringing profit to the world, I also have the name, 'Great Teacher'; facing sorrows, not swallowed up by them, am I not rightly called 'Courageous Warrior'?

"Seeing the wanderer, not showing him the way, why then should I be called 'Good-Master-Guide'? Like as the lamp; shines in the dark, without a purpose of its own, so burns the lamp of the Tagathatha (Buddha), without tine shadow of a personal feeling. All the Munis who perfect wisdom...They must first turn (follow) the Wheel of Righteousness."

So we conclude these few words of our Brother-Master of the Reception, Guatama Buddha (says Kyron, the Wise, as he again folds the ancient scroll).

GREAT PYRAMID TEMPLE OF ASTROLOGY AND ASTRONOMY

As you all know (continues Kyron) men have written many "bibles", but the first and the most stupendous Bible ever written by man is Astrology, the mother of Astronomy, the foundation and the fundamental source of Bibles was builded in the stone and granite of this Temple-Pyramid. For this was the great Pyramid Temple of Astrology and Astronomy.

Here we have the world's greatest Sun Dial and mark you, built, as I have told you, exactly on the 30th degree of North Latitude, at the 30th degree of East Longitude, for this is the only spot on earth where at mid-day (noon) on the equinoxes the elevation of the Sun would conforms exactly to the slope or angle of the sides of the Pyramid, which is the ratio of the diameter, to the circumference of the circle, that is 3.1415.

In your last lesson, I mentioned the Great Solar Cycle, or the precession of the equinoxes, as it is sometimes called. Let us seek a clearer understanding of this phenomenon, for its knowledge is plainly indicated in the Pyramid in its diagonal base measurements. For if we measure diagonally across the base of this Pyramid-Temple from Southeast to Northwest, and from Northeast to Southwest, we find the number of inches between these points in each of these diagonals to be 25,920 or the exact number of years in the great Solar Cycle.

For, you see, the sun by procession goes backward through the zodiac in just 25,920 years. This is because the sun in its annual cycle fails to keep its appointment (or fails to return to its exact starting point in the circle) by 50 seconds and this amounts to one degree in 72 years, so the sun goes backwards through one sign or 30 degrees of the zodiac (circle), in 2,160 years, or the' hole twelve signs in 25,920 years.

THE CLOCK OF DESTINY

As I have told you all the passages and chambers of this Temple-Pyramid not only have their symbolic meanings, but hidden in them scholars are re-discovering many prophecies. As you know, before entering the King's Chamber, we must pass through two very low passages—passages so low that we must stoop to go through them.

Measuring the first of these low passages in Pyramid inches, we find that this measurement would indicate a period of time running exactly from August 4-5, 1914, when England entered the First World War, to November 11th, 1918, the day the Armistice was signed.

After traveling through this first low passage, we reach the Ante-Chamber, in which we can stand erect, and where we find more strange features and more significant measurements. In pyramid inches, the measurements herein extend another prophetic period, which is indicated as running from November 11, 1918 to May 29, 1928, and Bible scholars claim that this indicates the period referred to in Matthew 24:22—"Except those days should be shortened, there should no flesh be saved: but for the elect's sake those days shall be shortened." (In the original, the word rendered here "elect" simply refers to the righteous or the goodly souls everywhere.)

ANTE-CHAMBER IS CALLED THE "TRUCE IN CHAOS"

This Ante Chamber has been named the "Truce in Chaos," and its symbolism is assigned by Bible Authorities as indicating the period from August 5, 1914 to September 15, 1936 because these students see in this the period referred to in the Bible as "the time of the end" (of a dispensation, or prophetic cycle). Our human minds can hardly imagine what would have happened to the world if the First World War had continued without the lull or the interval in hostilities until the time of the Second World War—so truly this "Truce in Chaos" was fulfilled literally.

The measurements of the second low passage are allotted as a prophecy of the period from May 29, 1928 to September 15, 1936, which is interpreted to symbolize the time of preparation for a final tremendous period of tribulation and destruction, the Second World War.

These interpreters believe that this final period of tribulation (Second Great World War) will result in the breaking up of the iron rulership of "Mammon," and will usher in the Kingdom of Love and Service foretold by the Christ—and this ancient prophecy, they, believe, points to the "battle of Armageddon" (warfare in the air) of Revelation, as being fought in this Second World War.

The prophetic Chronological (time) system as indicated in the Temple Pyramid measurements agrees strikingly with that of our Bible. In it we find indicated the Bible starting point of 4,000 B.C. and according to our symbolic measurements at the meeting point (or juncture) of the descending and the ascending passages, we find the Exodus (when the Jews fled from bondage in Egypt) very plainly indicated as being in the year 1486
B.C.

ADVENT AND DEATH OF MESSIAH INDICATED

According to One modern Pyramid student, Davidson, this Great Pyramid shows the birth of the Messiah (Christ) to have occurred Saturday, October 6, (Julian Calendar), in the year 4 B.C., and his crucifixion to have taken place April 7, in the year 30 A.D. (Davidson was an eminent English engineer.)

From the time of the Exodus of the Jews, indicated in Pyramid prophecy as 1486 B. C. they began to progress and to move upward as a people but from the time the Jews rejected the Christ as divine they moved on along a horizontal line, and this is symbolized in the passage which leads to the Queen's Chamber.

Bible scholars say that The Grand Gallery typifies or indicates the Christian Dispensation extending from the date of the birth of Christ to the year 1844, which is shown by the Great Step. According to the Pyramid message this year 1844 marks the opening of a new era or dispensation, and in the light of modern history we might well call this the dawn of the era of creative and mental sciences. For actually the beginning of the whole NEW THOUGHT movement was the year 1844, for in that year Prof. Quimby began teaching, and from his manuscripts Christian Science was born, at this time, also modern Spiritualism arose, and in 1844 "THE BAB," the founder of Bahaism, began preaching and teaching in Persia.

GREAT PYRAMID—SYMBOL OF SPIRITUAL ASTROLOGY

With our somewhat limited knowledge of the present time, we can of course but dimly discern the grandeur and the hidden messages of this Temple-Pyramid, but we do realize that more and more of its marvelous truths concerning The Eternal God-Law Plan will be brought to mankind during this Aquarian Age. And we do know that in this immense Temple, Astrology is demonstrated as Man's great Bible of the Skies, and that this vast monument perpetuates the Spiritual and mathematical knowledge of Astronomy of the Masters in White. There are no traces of Egyptian origin to be found in the Great Pyramid.

Is it not passing strange that the symbolism, the prophecies, and the symbolisms of this most ancient Temple have much that so exactly parallels the religion and the story of the Hebrew race? Turning now to Isaiah 19:19, I read you these significant words:

"In that day there shall be an altar to the Lord in the midst of the land of Egypt, AND A PILLAR at the border thereof to the Lord."

As an illustration of the universal symbolism of man's first Spiritual science, we might mention that, not only Temples but also in certain very old fraternities (lodges) such as Masonry, part of work of which is founded upon 'the ancient Magii and their deep knowledge of Astrology and of the Eternal Natural Laws, these sacred teachings are perpetuated and preserved often unknown to whose who unwittingly keep these symbols intact through the ages.

ASTROLOGY AND ASTRONOMY EXEMPLIFIED

Let those who have been 'raised' to such heights hear and understand. Throughout the world in Temple and in Lodge Room this symbolism is rigidly adhered to, and remains unchanged. In the East is the Master, or King Solomon (Solo-mon, meaning THE SUN), in the West the Senior Warden (Symbolism of the Moon), in the South the Junior Warden (Symbolism of Mars), and various other officers symbolical of the other planets, Mercury, Venus, Saturn, Jupiter—all shown in this old published chart of Ancient Masonry—and all are placed in the regular order and number, just as shown in every horoscope symbolizing Man.

For Man is the measure of all things in the manifested universe—Man, the Microcosm in the Great Macrocosm! Man, symbolized by the Pentogram, of the Ancient Mysteries—symbol of both material and Spiritual worlds!

Throughout every age of antiquity the Sun has been recognized as and held to be the symbol of the Deity, or God. The most ancient Masters realized, that behind the power of this physical sun was the Supreme Architect, that Divine Fountain from which all things spring into existence, just as the material Sun is the father and the source of all life on this earth, and these ancient ones recognized the Moon as the mother of life's manifestation, and they saw the earth as the womb of Nature, wherein gestation is completed, followed by the eternally recurrent cycles of birth.

This ancient wisdom, symbolized by Spiritual Astrology, and flaming forth in material astronomy, is forever the same to The Enlightened, whether they find its message in the Great Pyramid, the Mound Builders Tumulus, the Druidic Circle, the Pagan Temple, or the Christian Cathedral.

The Hebrew Bible, as you doubtless know, is filled with astrological symbolism from Genesis to Revelation. Limited time allows me to only refer to two or three examples, but these outstanding references can be multiplied many hundreds of times in this Book of books by the student. Let us, for instance, glance at one verse, Genesis 49:28—"All those are the twelve tribes of ISRAEL....'Is-ra-el' simply means the Sun-God of Egypt." "Is"-meaning Isis, the Sun; "Ra"-again meaning the Sun; and "El"-meaning Elohim, or God.

THE BIBLE OF THE SKIES

Hidden in the names of these twelve Sons or Tribes of Israel are the twelve SIGNS of the Zodias, or in other words, the twelve classifications of primary types of Mind.

Now, here are the names of the twelve tribes of Is-ra-el (the. Sun-God of Egypt) together with the twelve signs they, typify; God—Arias; Dan–Taurus; Issachar–Gemini; Zebulun–Cancer; Judah–Leo; Levi–Virgo; Simeon–Libra; Reuben–Scorpio; Benjamin–Sagittarius; Joseph–Capricorn; Napthali–Aquarius; and Asher–Pisces.

Sir John Herschel, who re-discovered the planet Uranus in 1871, wrote that the Zodiac is the greatest and the most fitting symbol of God in the Universe—that Zodiacal Circle which forms the apparent pathway of the Sun, surrounded by clusters of Stars so far from our world that even their disks cannot be seen by the most powerful telescope, for only their light is visible and here man's knowledge of them ends. Yet this Zodiacal Circle contains everything which can enter into the mind of man.

Here Kyron, the Wise, pauses and nods to Kosman, saying "Yes, O faithful Kosman, and thou wouldst ask yet another question?

(Kosman): "Pray explain more to us, O Kyron, for thou has wisdom, show us yet more of how this 'Bible of the Skies' of which you speak, is reflected in the words of our ancient Hebrew Bible."

Well and good, Kosmam, 1 see that you have the Hebrew Scriptures beside you— turn now to Revelation, the 44th chapter and the 7th, verse, and there we read that 'the first beast was like a Lion, the second beast was like a calf, the third beast had a face as a man, and the fourth beast was like a flying eagle.' Now, as you know, these represent the four fixed signs of the Zodiac; Leo, Taurus, Scorpio, and Aquarius.

And the "four and twenty Elders" represent the 24 hours of the day, which the Astrologer considers as being twelve "houses" (divisions) of two hours each in erecting a horoscope.

OPENING OF THE SIX SEALS

Now, we come to consider still deeper symbols in the Revelation of our Scriptures, symbols which for ages have puzzled the wisest scholars, because they had missed the simple key which we shall use. And let us remember; that here we encounter the same symbolism as to tremendous ages of time which are reflected in our great Temple-Pyramid.

Turn then to the 6th chapter of Revelation and there you read the mystical account of The Opening of the Six Seals,of the riders on the White, Red, Black, and Pale, Horses, about servants and kings, and about the moon becoming 'darkened'. For here we have in Bible symbols the Six Occidental Signs of the Zodiac very plainly represented; namely-Leo, Cancer, Libra, Scorpio, Virgo, and Sagittarius. And in this mystical language, these signs here are used as prophecies to refer to the different and following ages each of 2160 years— through which all mankind passes, marked by the "procession" of the Sun upon the face of the Gibantic clock of the Skies.

You all remember the story of the "three wise men, the Magii, (Astrologers also), the Masters in White, who followed the star or planet, Venus, to the birth-place of our Elder Brother, Ishuis, the Christ? Our ancient traditions tell us that the names of these three wise Magii were "Horus," for the sun, "Lun (a)" for the Moon., and "men" for Mercury.

And now, good Kosman, turn to the 22nd chapter of Revelation, and the 16th verse—"I, Jesus, have, sent mine angel to testify unto you these things in the churches. I am the root and offspring of David, AND THE BRIGHT AND MORNING STAR." Thus, you are the Hebrew and the Christian religions—the same as all other an even far more ancient religions—rest upon the same astrological and astronomical foundational symbolisms as do the mighty stones of the Great Pyramid.

MIGHTY PAGEANT OF THE SUN'S JOURNEY

The mighty pageant of the Sun's Journey through his vast orbit has been re-enacted each year since earthly time began. This story in symbolism is the course of all religious history and thus shadows forth upon the screen of the heavens that divine picture as presented in Christianity's story. This astrologically spiritual narrative begins at Christmas, December 27th, with "the Birth" when the sun is re-borne again at the period of its lowest declination, which is 23 1/2 degrees south of the equator, where it seems to stand still for a few days.

Then, on January 1st, the sun begins his northern Journey, and crosses the equator on March 22. Now, Easter (Resurrection) is observed on the first Sunday after the full moon's first culmination after the sun crosses the equator.

Next, at the Passover," in the autumn, the sun again crosses the equator: going south to his lowest declination, and then he is said to be "crucified" upon the autumnal cross, and then he enters into the tomb of winter, to be re-born again of a "Virgin" (new life) at Christmas. So reads the Bible of the Skies!

THE GREAT PYRAMID ILLUSTRATES SOUL'S HISTORY

And now I read you these striking words from "The Perfect Way" by Anna G.

Kingsford:

"This artificial 'Mountain of Stone' is, however, no other than a religious symbol, setting forth in its every detail from base to apex: the method of The Perfect Way...Outwardly its form denotes the ascent of the Soul, as a flame ever aspiring from the material plane to union with the Divine...

"Interiorly, the Pyramid is designed to illustrate, both in character and in duration, the various stages of the Soul's history, from, her first immergence in matter to her finial triumphant release and return to Spirit. In this view was constructed the complicated system of shafts, passages, and chambers...Of the two shafts, one, whereby the light from without enters the edifice, points directly to the Pole-Star at its lowest culmination, 2,170 years. B.C., the date given as that of the erection of the Pyramid. We must remember, however, that this exact position of the Pole-Star recurs each 25,920 years. (Kyron) By this is indicated the idea of the Soul as a ray proceeding from God as the Pole-Star and source of all things...

"Of this shaft the opposite extremity terminates in a pit lying below the center of the Pyramid. Constituting the only portion of the whole structure which is unpaved, this pit represents the bottomless pit of negation, and consequently final destruction. Descending thither the ray would become extinguished, and such is the fate of the Soul which, entering matter, persists in a downward course."

Lesson No. 5

THAT LABORATORY CALLED THE BRAIN (Temple of The Mind Invisible)

Again Kyron, the Wise stands before that gleaming altar of marble and gold, lighted by the steady glow of the three sacred candles, one at each point of the ceremonial triangle.

Again you are seated with The Enlightened Ones in the imagined King's Chamber within the silent depths of our mystic Pyramid-Temple, which to us is the changeless symbol of that Temple Eternal, wherein dwells the Soul.

Once more, Kyron, the Wise prototype of the ancient Masters in White, greets us in the salutation of the ritual:

Welcome, O Enlightened Ones, for unto thee is granted the Reception.

(We are all very still, for we see that Kyron the Wise, is ready to read to us from an old and worn scroll which he holds in his hands—and we perceive that he holds that Buddhistic Scripture known as the "Dhammapada, or Path to Virtue"—but, listen, Kyron reads):

"All that we are is the result of what we have thought: it is founded on our thoughts, it is made up of our thoughts. If a man speaks or acts with an evil thought, pain follows him, as the wheel follows the foot of the ox that draws the carriage.

"All that we are is the result of what we have thought; it is founded on our thoughts, it is made up of our thoughts. If a man speaks or acts with a pure thought, happiness follows him like a shadow that never leaves him.

"He abused me, he beat me, he defeated me, he robbed me"—in those who harbor such thoughts hatred will never cease.

"He abused me, he beat,me, he defeated me, he robbed me"—in those who do not harbor such thoughts hatred will cease.

"For hatred does not cease by hatred at any time: hatred ceases by love—this is an old rule.

"The evil-doer suffers in this world, and he suffers in the next; he suffers in both. He suffers when he thinks of the evil he has done; he suffers more when going on the evil path.

"The virtuous man is happy in this world, and he is happy in the next; he is happy in both. He is happy when he thinks of the good he has done; he is still more happy when going on the good path.

"The thoughtless man, even if he can recite a large portion of THE LAW, but is not a doer of it, has no share in the priesthood, but is like a cow-herd counting the cows of others.

"The follower of THE LAW has indeed a share in the priesthood."

(Kyron lays the scroll down, saying): And so, Good Friends and Disciples of the Reception, ends the reading of the wisdom of Buddha at this time.

We have completed our all-too-brief study of the greatest of all VISIBLE Temples known to man, the great Pyramid-Temple erected so many thousands of years ago under the supervision of those Heaven-Born Masters of our universal fellowship as a symbol, a mighty pillar of prophecy, and an earthly projection of that yet greater Temple, the Temple of the Soul.

So at this time it is logical to build upon this foundation of symbolism a still deeper Reception of The Ancient Secret Way in a series of lessons or lectures revealing the long-hidden mysteries of Mind, for Mind is the Divine Energy of The Eternal God demonstrating THROUGH YOU—and through every other human being.

First, then, let us consider the human skull, and the brain—for that which we call the "brain" is in reality the most wonderful chemical laboratory in the world, because its products are emotions and THOUGHT. And THOUGHT is the ruler upon the throne in this marvelous "King's Chamber!" The skull and the brain form this human Temple of the Mind invisible.

Now, Good Friends, exactly what is a human skull? Actually, is it not a box—a box made of bone—in reality, then a brain-box? Just so. Then the size if the "brain-box" determines the amount or the quantity of the brains it will contain, does it not'? Yes, of course, you will agree. Certainly, then if the length, the width, or the depth of this brain box is increased, its capacity for containing brains is increased also.

For instance, here is an every-day wooden box. This box, we will say, measures 10 inches wide, 10 inches high, and 20 inches long. It is very simple to find the entire capacity of this box, for all we have do do is to multiply its measurements together thus, 10 x 10 x 20, which gives us 2,000 cubic inches, which of course is its capacity.

So far we have been considering QUANTITY—or the capacity of the 'box as to holding contents. But should we not also consider the QUALITY and the VALUE of the contents of our box? If I should fill this wooden box with sawdust, we would have 2,000 cubic inches of sawdust—and the contents of the box are not very valuable, are they? But suppose, that instead of sawdust I could fill the box with Gold-dust—we still have our original 2,000 cubic inches of contents, but what a difference in the value! Again, let us substitute coal-dust and fill our box with that?— still we have the same amount as to capacity, but little value. But instead suppose we could fill this box with diamonds—what a difference in QUALITY AND VALUE! Yet science tells us that Coal-dust and diamonds are but different forms of the same basic substance, carbon.

Just so, all brain-matter is composed of the same basic substance. Yet what a tremendous difference we find in the ACTUAL VALUE AND QUALITY of various individual brains.

DEVELOPED BRAINS CHANGE SKULL-SHAPE

While mere size and quantity alone do not always indicate greater value or superior quality of the brain, here is a startling fact which experience in countless individuals has proven to be true. As you use your brain, as you develop your thinking capacity, as you develop your mind, the forehead changes its contour, and becomes somewhat higher, wider, and straighter, and the general shape of your "brain-box" will gradually change.

It is my desire at this time to help you to know and to understand character, personality, in a word, people, and to understand your fellow-human beings scientifically. First of all then, I should like you each one to realize that the real difference between the imbecile and the most brilliant scholar, between the thief or the murderer who seems utterly without conscience and the most charitable and kindly man or woman, that these startling differences depend largely upon differences of the brain and its ruler upon the throne within, the Mind. These vast differences are displayed in the variations of the weight, the health, the development, and the distribution of brain-matter.

The brains of most lower animals, birds, and rodents are quite smooth, but throughout countless ages The Eternal Divine Law, working through evolution, both larger brains and brains that are either wrinkled or folded DEVELOPED in the higher animals, most especially in man.

the human brain is subjected to more and more pressure at birth, and this pressure wrinkles the human brain and folds its surface. This process of folding the cortex (or surface) of the human brain gives it at least three times more Area than it would have if left smooth.

Now we must also understand that all mental power—the power of effective thought—depends first of all upon the gray matter, upon its quality, its quantity, its development, and its distribution throughout this "Temple Invisible."

So naturally, it follows that this increased surface of the brain enlarges the surface of the gray matter. Increased Gray matter carries infinitely more gray cells, and the greater the number there is of these cells the greater the number of nerve fibres, and these nerve fibres are the "electric wires" which connect with the great central "switch-board"—and this is the very center of that consciousness which is YOU—

the REAL YOU.

Should you dissect a human brain, you would find it to be composed of two main or principal substances— and these two substances are.the gray matter and the white matter. You would find the outside gray matter to vary from one quarter to one half an inch in thickness, and next just below this outer gray matter you would find the white matter, composed of countless fibres, and these white fibres all center in the medulla just as the petals of the rose meet and center in the heart of the flower.

The human Cregrum (main or larger brain) is divided so as to.form two halves, which appear to be practically identical alike, but you could not pull them apart with your hands, for they are connected by a very strong bridge of white fibres in the center—for while there is a deep groove between the halves, this bridge starts about one inch below the surface and unites the two halves into one machine, which is known as the Cerebrum, or brain proper.

NEXT, THE CEREBELLUM, OR "LITTLE BRAIN"

The "little brain" is also divided into two parts, although it is entirely unlike the "brain proper", or Cerebrum. Now, let us determine, if we may, the work or the exact purpose of this so-called "little brain." First, scientists tell us that the Cerebellum or "little brain", is the seat or center of the sex-emotions, and so is the source of the almost universal sex-urge we find everywhere about us. A well-developed and naturally active Cerebellum is the greatest factor in the loveliness of a beautiful woman, or a strong, magnetic man, for charm, strength, and magnetic personality are the products of the normal Cerebellum.

For in well-trained minds, minds which are normal and under the conscious control of the will, the Cerebellum impels love, marriage, and the established home. But in dull, subnormal, or uncontrolled minds, the Cerebellum only drives to immorality.

Your entire muscular system is also under the rulership of the Cerebellum or "little brain", and in this function it maintains perfect coordination between mind and muscles.

In the chemistry of the human laboratory (body)we find both acids and alkalis, and another part of the great work performed by the Cerebellum is to keep our blood sweet and pure, and to insure that it is always in health somewhat alkaline, not acid in nature.

THE MEDULLA—PETALS OF THE MENTAL ROSE

And now I want to call your attention for a brief minute to the Medulla. You will recollect that just a few minutes ago I compared the Medulla to the heart of the rose—and I told you how the white fibres from the gray surface cells of both halves of the brain all center and meet at the Medulla, just as the petals of the rose meet at its center.

Now for a moment imagine a line drawn through the head from the opening of either ear to the opening of the other sir, because such a line would go directly through the center.of the Medulla., and this little illustration will give you a very exact idea of the location of the Medulla.

Perhaps in connection with prize-fighting, you may have read or heard of the "solar plexus blow,"—a blow which, when properly administered, paralyzes its victim almost instantly, but of course, only for a time. Why is such a "knock-out" blow so paralyzing?

The answer is simple indeed. This sudden, powerful blow almost instantly compresses or contracts the abdomen, forcing the stomach upward and inward, and this shocks the entire sympathetic nervous system, and almost at once this shock reaches the Medulla, with paralyzing effect, and this in turn suspends the functions of the heart, the lungs, and the mental faculties—the victim falls unconscious, sometimes never to arise.

Because during all your lifetime the Medulla is sending forth a stream of nerve-energies (vibrations) to the heart, the stomach, the lungs, and to every other organ of your body, the Medulla is to your body actually what the storage battery is to the automobile. To waste these vital nerve energies is in reality a crime against yourself, and that is why. the Ancient Masters have taught us to RELAX to ENTER INTO THE SILENCE, and thus how to restore our vital life-forces.

THE HUMAN BRAIN IS SUPERIOR—AND WHY

In all the animal kingdom, man is superior and he is superior to all other creatures not because his brain is larger, but because of the superior development of his cerebral machine, in other words, because of the higher quality and the complexity of his brains.

But has man the largest brains, larger than the "lower animals?"

Not at all—for the brain of a full-grown elephant weighs from 4,000 to 5,000 grams or from 8.8 to 11 pounds. Now of course the weight of man's brain differs among different races, but I will tell you that a fair average estimate is about 1,417 grams, or three and one-eighth pounds. Two famous comparative anatomists, Bischoff and Chauvau, state that the comparative weights of brain to body in mankind falls in the ratio of one to. thirty-five or thirty seven.

Again, man is superior to all other animals because he not only is capable of receiving impressions but he also has the power to think about these impressions, to reason about these and to retain these impressions in the store-house of memory and, above all, man has the ability to decide upon a reasoned and a purposeful re-action to these impressions. And man alone has articulate communication with his fellow-men through speech.

MENTAL DEVELOPMENT INCREASES SKULL CAPACITY

It is a simple, a natural and an easily proven fact that the cranial (skull) capacity of any human race is appreciably increased by culture, by attainment, and by mental development, while on the other hand the cranial capacity of a defeated, decadent race decreases rapidly.

A striking proof of this fact is that the skulls of those Romans who lived nearly two thousand years ago, when the Roman Empire was at the height of her glory, skulls which were unearthed at Pompeii, are on the average much larger and of much greater capacity than the skulls of the Romans of today. And it is noteworthy that the skulls of those ancient Romans were much larger in the frontal region, denoting a superior forebrain, or intellectual capacity.

While it is generally true that the brains of great men—men who have made their mark in history—are usually larger and heavier than the average, still there are interesting exceptions, but these exceptions are simply explained by the fact that a large frontal (fore-brain) development, together with quality of brains, often found more than mere bulk and weight. In this connection, it is interesting to note that while Daniel Webster wore a size eight hat. Ralph Waldo Emerson wore a size six and seven-eighths hat.

HEADS CONTAIN BRAINS—NOT PHRENOLOGICAL "BUMPS!"

Because I have talked about skulls, brains, and cranial capacities, please do not jump to the conclusion that I am discussing "phrenology," or the idea of "bumps" on the human skull as denoting character. However, it is almost a self-evident fact that any enlargement of the skull in a particular area is the result of a corresponding development of that portion of the brain.

For after all, human heads normally contain brains, and within the brain is the mystical Temple of the Mind, and our studies of this Temple, simply seek to reveal the mighty, the invisible, the God-like powers of Mind, and lift us to a vision of the Astral or Soul Realm.

Here one Phylos signifies his wish to ask a question—and, Kyron obligingly waits. (Phylos): "But Kyron, O Master of the Wisdom, how may we learn the meanings of these many, many different shapes, sizes, and forms of human heads that we see everywhere around us—and how can we learn to analyze a ourselves?"

Wise indeed and searching is thy question, O Phylos, and many of the lessons to follow in your Pathway of the Reception will be devoted to imparting the exact knowledge which you ask.

LEARNING TO KNOW HUMAN HEADS

Indeed, Phylos, and you speak truly-for in the passing throng you will perceive wide heads, narrow heads, small heads, big heads, and some you will see that are high above the ears, and some that are flat or even appear hollow on the top. Here a head may be low and flat, and another that is a straight line in the back. And the next head may be fully rounded in the back. One head may be developed strongly from the ears forward and.upward, and another expanded downward and backward. The variations are many but each can be easily recognized with proper study, for these leading types recur constantly every day and everywhere you go.

In a word, learning to know human heads is. simply a study in comparison and relative proportions. Constantly compare heads as to since, shape, contour, and relative proportions.

You can always mentally locate the Medulla—the hub or center where all the fibres of the brain converge like the spokes of a wheel—by imagining a line drawn between the openings of the ears. Notice carefully the position of the ears, and with your eye measure the relative distances of the different areas of the head from the openings of the ears.

Let us always bear in mind the. ancient truth that the outer world is an image (symbol) of the inner world. At night when you look upward into the starry sky you are in reality beholding an external (outer) reproduction (image) of giant astrological processes taking place in the heavens beyond that are forever invisible to earthly eyes. Those mighty revolutions of the planets, stars, and suns which man can observe, are but outer symbols which reflect the tremendous spiritual powers of the Eternal God-Law operating throughout the universe. These great Spiritual powers vibrate in the human mind, whose symbolic Temple is the Human Head (skull).

LESSON NO. 6

DIVINE MIND-SCIENCE—MATERIAL BRAIN AND SPIRITUAL SUBSTANCE

Before the glowing altar of marble and gold, with its three symbolic candles burning at the points of the sacred triangle, once more we are in the presence of Kyron, the Wise, and we silently await his words, together with the rest of The Enlightened Ones.

For mentally we are all gathered within the silence of the inner depths of our mystic Pyramid-Temple, changeless symbol of that Temple Eternal, wherein dwells the Soul.

Listen—for Kyron greets us with the words of salutation from our ancient ritual:

Welcome, O Enlightened Ones, for unto thee is granted the Reception.

"All the Companions in White are very quiet, for again Kyron, the Wise, is about to read from the ancient scroll he holds, which is the same "Dhammapada," or the Buddhist "Path to Virtue"—Kyron now reads briefly from the chapter which is named "The Buddha—The Awakened"):

"He whose conquest cannot be conquered again, into whose conquest no one in this world enters, by what track can you lead him, the Awakened, the Omniscient, the trackless?

"He whom no desire with its snares and poisons can lead astray,. by what track can you lead him, the Awakened, the Omniscient, the trackless?

"Even the gods envy those who are awakened and not forgetful, who are given to meditation, who are wise, and who delight in the repose, of retirement from the world ("in The Silence").

"Difficult to obtain is the conception of men, difficult is the life of mortals, difficult is the hearing of the True (Eternal) Law, difficult is the birth of the Awakened (the attainment of Buddahood).

"Not to commit any sin, to do good, and to purify one's mind, that is the teaching of the Awakened.

"He who takes refuge with Buddha, the Law...he who, with clear understanding, sees the four holy truths; pain, the origin of pain, the destruction of pain, and the eight-fold holy way that leads to the quieting of pain:—that is the safe refuge, that is the best refuge; having gone to that refuge a man is delivered from all pain.

"A supernatural person (a Buddha—a (Master in White), is not easily found: he is not born everywhere, Wherever such a sage is born, that race prospers."

(Folding the scroll and laying it upon the altar, Kyron Says): So endeth the reading of the wisdom of the "Dhammapada."

And now let us continue our journey still deeper into the realms of the occult, the generally hidden or unknown Ancient Wisdom taking as our starting point, as always, the invisible, the unknown, and that which is called our "Material world."

For I use this term, "The Ancient Wisdom," advisedly, for the term is literally true. A history of these doctrines, or teachings, which I am imparting to you in these lessons, might well and truly begin with doctrines that were old when the land of Egypt was born. We find these same teachings in the most ancient papyrus manuscripts of Egypt, we find them voiced in the Vedic Hymns, the Dhammapada, the Zend-Avesta, the Upanishads, in the words of Buddha, in the mystic teachings of

Christ, and in the teachings of the philosophers.

"NEOPLATONIC PHILOSOPHY"

The Neoplatonic School of thought or philosophy was in reality founded by Ammonius Saccas, who lived about 190 A.D. His four greatest disciples were Plotinus, Errennios, Origenes, and Longinus.

Perhaps the best known, and the clearest thinker, among these was Plotinus, of whom you have learned something from some of your previous studies. Plotinus, as you may remember, was born at Lykopolis, in Egypt in the year 205 A.D., and he received his education at Alexandria. After serving in the war of the emperor, Gordianus, in Persia, Plotinus went to Rome, where he founded his school of Philosophy.

During the twenty-six years that he lived in Rome it is said that Plotinus did not have a single enemy, and that he attained to great renown—so great, in fact, that even the Emperor Gallienus, who was an utter villain, honored Plotinus.

I want to briefly acquaint you with the Neoplatonic philosophy of Plotinus for that philosophy of nearly twenty centuries ago bears the unmistakable imprint of the teachings of The Masters in White-the "Heaven-Born," throughout the ages from some unknown beginning far beyond the lost Atlantis.

ONE ETERNAL LAW—ONE DIVINE WISDOM

Because there is only One Eternal Law, there can be only One Divine Wisdom, or system of Divine Truth, and you can trace that Divine Truth (or "Ancient Wisdom") back through the history of each Great Teacher, each Master, each Avatar, known to mankind, till you reach that "First Initiator," in the day when "the Spirit of God moved upon the waters!"

One of these Great Teachers was Plotinus, and his life and his philosophy are perfectly illustrated in his words, spoken when the physician Eustachius, entered the room in which Plotinus lay dying—seeing Eustachius, he exclaimed with joy:

"I am now going to unite the God that lives within myself with the God of the universe!"

For the philosophy of the ancient Master, Plotinus, agrees with the ageless wisdom I am teaching you in these deeper lessons. You may ask, "But why should I study or seek to understand this Wisdom that is so old, I am living today, and the things I most greatly desire are the GOOD THINGS OF TODAY."

Granted, My Friend, you have rightly spoken, but I would have you realize very clearly that this same knowledge I am imparting to you, leads you straight to the Source of all Power—and we are leading you directly along the Pathway of Power from whence you will be enabled to obtain such a measure of success in realizing and possessing these GOOD THINGS OF LIFE AS MAY WELL AMAZE YOU, if you will only follow that Pathway. And after all, the WAY, is really quite simple.

LIFE IS A BATTLE—AND YOU CAN WIN

From our previous lessons, you have learned that the human head is a thin or thick box of bone, made to contain the brain. And within this box of bone is the "Inner Temple" where Mind rules supreme.

Now, here we approach the Source of all Power. We all agree, I am quite certain, that God (through the eternal God-law is the ONE foundation of all things in the universe, and in this world. So there is only ONE SUBSTANCE: and to us both Matter and Form are illusions, or shadows of Spirit-Substance.

The .God of Eternal Law, then is Pure Light, a Divine Unity, and YOUR MIND is the image of this Divine Light, or, May I say, the Image created by the Eternal Mind reflecting itself in the mirror of YOUR mind.

YOUR mind, then, is the vibration-in-activity of the Eternal Mind.

Also, we shall all agree that Life is a battle—but it is a battle wherein YOU can be the winner.

This battle of life everywhere around us is in reality a struggle between the FIT and the UNFIT—and these lessons teach YOU how to be one of the "FIT." On this earth the competition between the "strong" and the "weak" seems endless.

After all, "white-wash" it as we will, the "survival of the fittest" is a grim reality. In our vaunted "modern civilization" today the weak, the unfit, the UNTHINKING masses seem to exist largely to serve or to minister to those who are strong and fit because their MINDS ARE DEVELOPED, THINKING MINDS!

And these developed, thinking Minds control life and all of its good things—happiness, prosperity, fine homes, splendid cars, friends, secure incomes, appreciation, and love—because they reflect the power of Divine Mind—that God-Law-Light, which is primordial and changeless. Remember, the world of Mind is your inner world: and that world around you which you sense as the outer or material world is just the external expression of your own inner world.

YOUR MIND CREATES AND CONTROLS YOUR LIFE

Once again I repeat to you the simple secret of the ages—that simple Truth which makes you the Master of your own destiny and gives you Power to attract to yourself WHATEVER YOU WILL (that is humanly pos-sible)—your own MIND creates and controls your life.

Simply stated—your own mind and your own thinking can raise you from ignorance to knowledge, from poverty to wealth, from weakness to power, or from sickness to abounding health!

Please understand that I am now talking about your conscious Mind which I would simply define as Intellect on duty.

Because we want to show you how to work wonders in your life by the right use of this conscious mind, let me illustrate it by pointing out that your conscious mind is receiving the words of this lesson, and will perceive the meanings of this lesson by induction and reasoning, and will conceive the many ways in which to apply this lesson to your life.

I want to impress upon you again and again the tremendous importance to you of this conscious mind of yours—I want you to pause and realize that everything—both the living and the inanimate—ALL things in earth, and land, and sky, and sea, ALL other human beings, all "gods" and all "devils", all "heavens" and all "hells," that ALL these exist for you only as mental images upon the magic tissues of your conscious mind!

Remember, then, that which does not manifest itself within your conscious mind, anything which does not exist in your conscious mind, either as an image or a concept, DOES NOT EXIST FOR YOU.

"LEARN WHAT TO THINK AND THINK IT"

Wise indeed was the old sage who wrote: "Learn what to think and think it."

And here is the supreme test of this tremendous truth: choose a clear cut thought image of any good thing you want most in life, a clear VIVID DEFINITE IMAGE—love, happiness, healing, prosperity, or success for which you may long— let compelling desire create that image and hold that image in focus constantly, day after day, by your determined will-power, and just as surely, as you live that image will be eventually transformed into that very good thing which you have visioned in your own life and in your own possession—an actual reality in your own hands!

Make no mistake here—I'm NOT talking about mere, idle or wishful thinking, but I am talking about an image or vision of possession CREATED BY COMPELLING DESIRE and backed up by DAUNTLESS DETERMINATION, which will force you to go right out "in faith", believing," and CLAIM THAT THING YOU WANT MOST AND PAY THE PRICE.

For you have tremendous latent (sleeping) energies which are only awaiting your conscious demand to spring into life and action in making your "Heart's Desire" your own here and now. You have a Greater Self than you have ever been—and you can only know the power of that higher, that potential Self, when you learn to knock loudly and with simple Faith at the door of your subconsciousness. There are endless possibilities of learning and of achievement, of happiness and of prosperity for you, and for every one of us, and the riddle of human existence is simply to learn to use and focus (concentrate) the millions of brain and nerve cells in our bodies upon claiming and possessing those good things of life which we really desire. And it is my business in these lessons to help you to solve that RIDDLE for yourself.

AROUSE YOUR LATENT POWERS

The time to begin to arouse these latent powers of yours is today-and right now.

First of all, I want each of you to consciously plan on learning how to keep vibrantly alive, healthy, happy, and successful for a very great many years—banish "old age" from your thinking, for senility need never touch you.

Beginning right now, I want each one of you to get to work on yourself, and in dead earnest to arouse and to use these latent energies, which you have forgotten or over-looked, in this business of possessing the BEST THINGS IN LIFE FOR YOURSELF.

So, here is a brief outline of the program I shall teach you to follow in this and in the following lessons. The program is indeed quite simple, but absolutely PRACTICAL. We are going to aid you to rebuild your present life. Remember a NEW AND A HIGHER SELF is waiting to move into that brain and body of yours, which is the holy temple for the housing of that NEW SUCCEEDING SELF.

Thus to make the matter quite simple, we shall teach you EXACTLY WHAT TO EAT, HOW TO SECURE PERFECT SLEEP, and the various SECRET EXERCISES (breathing, mental, and physical) which will make your whole body vibrant with vigor, life, and health. We will show you exactly how to supply abundant oxygen and an even circulation of pure, rich blood to your entire body constantly— for thus you will keep every cell in your body ever alive and active, together with diligent attention to the elimination of waste matter.

For SUCCESS- THINKING, which is clear, straight inspirational thinking, comes when you learn to "Glorify God IN YOUR BODY and IN YOUR SPIRIT..."

LIVING THE ABUNDANT LIFE

Next, we must teach you how to LIVE RHYTHMICALLY, I must impress upon you the significance to you of the great systematic cosmic movements, and the lesson for us each one in the regular changes of the seasons, day alternating with night, and the regularity of the tides. The lesson is that we must each reduce our individual existence to a system of planned and orderly, events.

Now, you can see just what I mean by rhythm in the ABUNDANT LIFE THAT SUCCEEDS—simply an even and undisturbed recurrence of the main or fundamental work, plans and experiences of everyday life. By planned rhythm you will gain the momentum of alternating work and rest—of activity and relaxation—a momentum which will add mightily to your powers of achievement.

And third, we must teach you HOW TO just "let go" of your NEGATIVES—we shall show you exactly HOW to systematically banish the use of any word or any thought which in any way describes or even refers to any trouble, worry, mistake, fault or failure of yours, either real or fancied, no matter how real they may SEEM today. Facing each of these bug-a-boos once for all, you will declare your triumph over each, and then "let the past bury the dead." we shall show you how to win this victory quite easily.

For no man or woman can hope to do his or her best, while persistently thinking of the worst! And YOU are going to do your BEST from now on.

Because under our guidance you are going to bring up from the depths of your subconscious mind those slumbering Powers that will bring you Health, Happiness, Success, and Money, you must be helped to forever close the door to every NEGATIVE view, memory, or recollection of your past or present life. That is self-evident, is it not?

THEN...CHOOSE YOUR GOAL

Then, when you have followed your instructions and have renewed, re-built, and perfected your physical being, when you have re-arranged your daily round of work and relaxation, of duty and of recreation, to calm rhythm and entire smoothness, and when you have learned to close the door of your mental Temple against all your former NEGATIVE thinking—then your mighty latent energies are free to do your bidding.

Then only are you ready to choose your goal. Now I want each of you to prepare to be very, very careful in choosing your goal, your "Heart's Desire," your ideal accomplishment—so, let's get right down to brass tacks and do some serious thinking about this goal we are going to choose. For that is all-important.

Perhaps you are one of those who have done a great amount of reading about these subjects, or perhaps you have studied various presumably "occult courses" for a period of years, only to find yourself confused, bewildered, and disappointed. If so, then won't you just stop right here for a few brief minutes and mentally take stock of your studies and of your own life through the years? Now be fair and honest with yourself.

EXACTLY WHAT IS IT THAT YOU WANT?

In these "courses" you have taken, in all these studies in success or in the "occult," just what was it that you wanted, what were you hunting for ? Do you really know?

Perhaps you are like the many, many men and women who have admitted to us that they did not really know WHAT they wanted. Maybe, like them, you, too have just drifted, maybe you were attracted and intrigued by those glamorous stories of the amazing powers that attained to wealth, or fame, or a great romance, or to a miracle of healing, or to other marvelous phenomena...all of which seemed to point to some mystic or divine energy unknown to you.

Such stories literally enthralled you, didn't they? Of course, in all your reading or studies, you always honestly HOPED for Mastery, for Power, for some outstanding Attainment—but isn't it true that when it came to the patient persistent, and often gruelling task of striving day after day to develop these same powers in your-self, you really didn't have the courage or the energy to actually WORK FOR THIS HIGHER ATTAINMENT? Erreichung

In all this reading, in all your former "studies," then, you were really being merely entertained, weren't you? You need not answer—except to yourself. In some mysterious manner you hoped to find the one Teacher, or the one Lecturer, or the one set of "Lessons," that could and would DO YOUR WORK FOR YOU, didn't you? Remember, I am not blaming—I am simply explaining.

Because, in order to possess any of the GOOD THINGS OF LIFE, you must first know exactly what it is that you WANT. You, and only YOU, must decide definitely what this goal is for you.

No one, no Master, no Teacher no Book, or no Lesson can GIVE you miraculous powers, or success powers, or money or healing powers, or happiness powers, or those invisible powers that attract and sway people.

FOR YOU ALREADY HAVE THESE INVISIBLE POWERS

In these lessons it is our mission to help you to discover these invisible powers that are already within you, and to show you how to use them within you, and to show you how to use them wisely and effectively. But the Eternal Law is that YOU, must work to develop these powers, otherwise they slumber on unknown to you.

Do not expect to attain to mastery in controlling or working with your invisible forces overnight. There is no short cut to mastery. But once awakened—once you become conscious of your own inner powers—the world becomes your laboratory, and the people, and the things, and the circumstances about you are your substances to work with.

Each of your five previous lessons in this Second Advanced Course has been a progressed step toward your adeptship or mastery in the control and the direction of these tremendous invisible forces that are latent within you. In this supreme accomplishment of developing your hidden powers, you need no longer feel that you must work alone, for we are here to guide you and to help you, and if you study each of these lessons faithfully, and perform each simple exercise to the best of your ability, you will make some very great strides towards possessing your "Heart's Desire."

You have learned that The Great Pyramid was a gigantic silent symbol in stone, which typified The Temple Eternal—a tremendous monument to THE SOUL-MIND OF MAN—And it is God's plan today that YOU may attain to every good thing of life which you, make your unwavering goal. Behold the miracle of the cater-pillar and the butterfly—the Soul-Mind-Force which directs the growth of the caterpillar builds the beautiful body of the butterfly from the same substance of that more lowly body!

LESSON No. 7
ETERNAL LAW GRANTS YOUR SILENT DEMAND

Together with the, rest of-the white.-clad Enlightened Ones, once again you find yourself mentally in the presence of Kyron, the Wise, as he stands silently before the symbolic. altar of gleaming marble: and dully glowing gold. Once more imagery has transported.us to the Temple Eternal, dwelling place of the soul.

With hands outstretched in blessing, Kyron greets us with the ancient salutation of our ritual:

'Welcome, O' Enlightened Ones, for unto thee is. granted the Reception.

(It is very quiet now in the King's Chamber, for we all perceive that Kyron, the Wise, has chosen to read to us again words of wisdom from the ancient scroll of the "Dhammapada,"—Kyron now reads these few verses from the chapter entitled "On Earnestness":

"Earnestness is the path of immortality (Nirvana), thoughtlessness the path of death. Those who are in earnest do not die those who are thoughtless are as if dead already.

Having understood this clearly, those who are advanced in earnestness delight in earnestness, and rejoice in the knowledge of the elect.

"These wise people, meditative, steady, always possessed of strong powers, attain to Nirvana, the highest happiness.

"If an earnest person has roused himself, if he is not forgetful, if his deeds are pure, if he acts with consideration, if his deeds are pure, if he acts with consideration, if he restrains himself, and lives according to (the Eternal) Law—then his glory will increase.

"By rousing himself, by earnestness, by restraint and control, the wise man may make for himself an island which no flood can overwhelm.

"When the learned man drives away vanity by earnestness, he, the wise, climbing the terraced heights of wisdom, looks down upon the fools: free from sorrow he looks upon the sorrowing crowd as one that stands on a mountain looks down upon them that stand upon the plain.

"Earnest among the thoughtless, awake among the sleepers, the wise man advances like a racer, leaving behind the hack (The plow-horse)."

(Reverently laying the ancient scroll upon the altar, Kyron says): So ends our brief lesson on the power of earnestness from the wisdom of the Buddhists of old.

And now we continue our study together of the limitless powers of the Mind and the unmeasured possibilities that are before each one of us when, in absolute earnestness, we learn to concentrate IN THE SILENCE upon our Heart's Desire, our supreme goal, our ONE AND GREATEST DEMAND.

The subject of our study at this time is in that plain, flat, clear-cut statement which is the title of this lesson, "Eternal Law Grants Your Silent Demand."

In the very beginning of our lesson, let me say to you in all sincerity in that one great statement, composed of just six words, there is the universal panacea, the secret cure, for every ill which you may find that human life anywhere is heir to, whether that ill (or lack)be physical, mental, or financial.

Now, the power of this universal cure of panacea depends entirely upon the power of your silent demand. Nachfrage / Bedarf

And the power of this silent demand is generated in the absolutely EARNEST, the ENTIRELY SINCERE, the ONE-POINTED, FOCUSED INTENTION of each individual thinker who thus makes his or her demand in The Silence.

This is simply because our INTENTION always governs, controls, and directs our ATTENTION, and 100 per cent attention is 100 per cent concentration, and when your mind concentrates constantly upon any aim goal, or ambition, then you have solved the "secret" of THE SILENT DEMAND. For thus you transport inexhaustible supply from the realms of the invisible into your own smaller, visible world through the changeless law of sympathetic, harmonic attraction.

Your earnest, unwavering, faith-filled silent demand is the subtle cause and your new (or renewed), health, wealth (and I DO mean money), position, career, romance , or love, is your tangible, material effect, result, or "Answer".

AGAIN—WHAT IS YOUR AMBITION?

Now, in order to be effective, in order to become something more than wishful thinking, your silent demand must be the vision of your attainment of a great, a dominant, and a DEFINITE AMBITION.

I think that each of you will agree that to attain to the fulfillment of your greatest ambition is to realize success.

But it is not self-evident that when we speak about our desired health, or wealth, or our career, or our longed-for love or romance, or when we use any other words which denote either possession or a condition of mind or body, any one of which may mean "success" to us, that we must first understand exactly what is to be the measure of our individual "success"—because that standard will be the measure of our attainment.

For the measure that we each one of us mentally holds at this moment as our standard of success is very probably much different from the standard or measure held by every other person in this group. The thousand men and women would probably represent ten thousand different standards or measures of success, for when we realize that success is the realization of individual aspirations, the attainment of an individual, personal ambition, then we realize that success, attainment, or possession is entirely a personal, an individual matter.

In every walk of life, then, and in every human activity, we not only find different standards of success, but we find that success, whether that success be one of possession (such as money, wealth, property, fine home, dazzling jewels, etc.) or the success of mental or physical condition (such as intellectual attainment, mental power highly developed, or a renewed health and youth restored), whatever may be the standard of success, we find that all success is relative—or comparative—and that it is dependent upon the conditions surrounding each individual life.

ALL PERSONAL ATTAINMENT SUCCESS IS COMPARATIVE

We cannot standardize success, or the realization of personal ambition, because each is a matter of individuality, and, too, a matter of degree, and of comparative personal satisfaction.

Let's take a little trip mentally to a small town, say one of a thousand population. Here we may find a little, country newspaper, and a very successful editor—he has found his "place in the sun" just as certainly as has the editor or the great city daily, has he not? And may not this country editor be truly happy, respected, prosperous—and if so, hasn't his "silent demand" been abundantly fulfilled?

And in that same small town there is the "best" minister, the "best" doctor, the "best" lawyer, the "best" merchant, and perhaps a banker who is a success, and looked upon by the townspeople as a something of a "plutocrat"—even though the total capitalization of his bank is only $25,000!

From this we draw the simple lesson that each of these persons IS a success—each is the living example of his own "silent demand"—each is successful, respected; prosperous in the degree comparative to his surroundings.

BASE YOUR SILENT DEMAND ON YOUR OWN SUCCESS POSSIBILITIES

So, we begin now to realize that every man or woman cannot succeed in the same degree. But that fact does not rob success of its sweetness, its happiness, or its VALUE—far from it!

So, in making your SILENT DEMAND for the good things of life and that means success—let me warn you very kindly but very plainly that your first step must be an honest endeavor to learn your own personal success possibilities. Let us each be very careful not to under-rate these possibilities, and not to estimate them TOO highly—or we shall do ourselves a terrible injustice.

Remember, in this world, GENIUS is rare—after all, genius is rarely happy. We realize that every man who works upon a railroad cannot be an "Empire Builder,"—he cannot be a Hill, a Harriman, or a Gould—but, every railroad man (and woman) can succeed in direct ratio to his or her silent demand. Nor can every man in business be a Rockefeller, neither can every banker be a Morgan—every machinist cannot be a Ford, nor can every artist be a Raphael!

So far I have dealt largely in generalities, but you must grasp these generalities before you can understand fully their direct and personal application to you. Again let me remind you of a great and a most important truth, a truth which I have brought to your attention in previous lessons—every success in this life bears a PRICE-TAG. Eternal Law permits us to buy over Life's counter success in any form we choose—health, wealth (money), friends, romance, fine homes, luxurious cars, or Mind and Soul development—but there is always a price to be paid for each of these "successes."

Before you decide definitely just WHAT your Silent Demand shall be, learn something about how much you will be required to pay, and be sure that you are willing to pay that much in the coin of work, and of sacrifice. For we have to BUY the good things of life. And...set your mark YEARS AHEAD!

ETERNAL NATURAL LAW GOVERNS YOUR SUCCESS-SUPPLY

Eternal Natural Law governs your success-supply exactly the same as it controls the falling of a pebble thrown upward into the air.

Many of us may not have realized this stupendous truth because we have not studied the manifestations of that Eternal Natural Law in its relations to human destiny. Yet we will all readily admit that all matter is governed by unchanging Natural Law, and that basically the electrons, the atoms, and the molecules of different kinds of matter are related and inter-dependent.

But when we consider the Intellect, we mortals are often seemingly blind to the interdependence of Good Health, Good Fortune, and a Goodly Success-Supply and the Mind-Qualities, the Mind Direction, and the Mind-Thoughts of ourselves and the people around us.

This is supremely important, because the SILENT DEMAND I am now teaching to you is A MENTAL DEMAND—A MENTAL ATTITUDE.

(Here the disciple, Claudius, signifies that he would ask a question, and Kyron, the Wise, pauses—nodding in consent.)

(Claudius): "O Master Kyron, do you mean that our fortunes, good or bad, have been made what they are by our thinking? and if this be true, wilt explain to us how we can remedy these fortunes of ours?"

Claudius, my Good Friend and Disciple, I am very glad of your question, for in your fortunes, just as in your misfortunes, Thought is forever at work, like a carpenter who, is working in a house, and always either building up or tearing down. Because good Claudius, building a healthy, wealthy, happy life is just like building a handsome, strong, and lasting house—we must have correct and positive THINKING AND PLANNING before we can build either!

Why, Claudius, even your physical body is an exact reflection, the real expression, of your past thinking—not just your thoughts of yesterday, of last week, or of last year, but the composite of all the thinking you have ever done.

"...the Temple of the living God..."

You will remember that remarkable statement of Paul's in the New Testament scripture: "Know ye not that ye are the Temple of the living God and the Spirit of the Almighty dwelleth in you?"

If you will but fully realize and LIVE the Truth behind this one statement alone, in addition to your Silent Demand for the good things of life that you most deeply desire, will set you free from every thought of lack, of limitation, and frustration, and will help you to reach your goal in the shortest possible time.

So, make every thought you think, every word you speak, and every act of your life a positive, a constructive, an expectant thought, word, and action, and always in harmony with your Silent Demand, knowing that you are thus sowing the seed which the Eternal Law guarantees to multiply and to bring to you, the sower, an abundant harvest of its own kind.

Right now, and in your own life, stop seeing, or affirming, or thinking evil or imperfection, because when you see, or affirm or think of the evil, or the negative, or the imperfect, you are only sowing "dragon's teeth," and dragon's teeth will insure you a reaping, a harvest, of loss, lack, poverty, or sorrow.

Here you may ask, What is evil—what is sin? Nothing else than an incomplete mental vision of the perfect. We can learn much from the fact that the word "sin," as we find it in the Bible is derived from the Hebrew letter "Shin," or "U", which is never a complete circle-the circle always standing for the complete, the perfect.

THE NINE "DO MORES"

Your Silent Demand is a work of actual construction—because you are building with sound thoughts and positive concepts your complete vision of the good health, the good fortune, and the good goal which you have determined to possess.

So, you must DO MORE than ninety-nine people out of every hundred around you, who do not realize the dangerous seed they are sowing all the time in their imperfect, negative, and destructive thoughts, words, and actions—for mind-seed which is evil or negative multiples just the same as any other fruitful seed will multiply.

In building your Silent Demand, I want you to realize that there are certain concepts, thoughts, and, above all, certain activities with which you must construct your success, just as stones, bricks, and timbers are used in building a worth-while house. These I am going to call your "do-mores," and each of these must be "cemented" into its proper place in relation to all the other "do mores." These are the mental bricks of thought and action out of which you will construct your mansion of "good fortune."

Here, then, are your nine "do mores," (thanks to John H. Rhoades)—

Do more than exist: LIVE

Do more than touch: FEEL
Do more than look: OBSERVE
Do more than read: ABSORB
Do more than hear: LISTEN
Do more than listen: UNDERSTAND
Do more than talk: SAY SOMETHING
Do more than think: PONDER
Do more than plan: ACT

SILENT DEMAND TRANSFORMS INVISIBLE INTO THE VISIBLE

Everywhere, in this world and throughout the entire universe, we behold Eternal Law, through the power of the Silent Demand, forever transforming the invisible into the visible, and from subtle, unseen causes creating tangible, material effects. For instance, this stupendous power of the Silent Demand is expressed in the irrevocable Law of Attraction, that mighty Force which controls and guides the suns, planets, and stars in their circling orbits. In mighty, rhythmical periodicity all things in the universe obey this unseen Silent Demand in their evolutionary march before our often unseeing eyes.

This is the mighty force with which you, too, can work miracles in your own life and fortunes when you focus the concentrated power of your mind upon one supreme goal. And having •once achieved that "heart's desire," you will set your goal still farther ahead.

Believe me, Good Friends and Disciples, this Law of the Silent Demand, working to transform your life and your surroundings, is just as true, just as constant, and just as changeless as are all the other Laws of Nature known to man But you must actually and purposely put this Law to work in your life, and you must realize that the unending supply of the good things of life, which it will bring to you is measured entirely by the quality, the earnestness, and the intensity of thought with which you magnify your Silent Demand.

CHARGE SILENT DEMAND WITH DOMINANT THOUGHT

Charge your Silent Demand with dominant thought, because this is the shortest path to realizing any cherished desire which you hold. To make the matter quite simple, I am teaching you HOW to succeed in attracting your Heart's Desire by directing and focusing all of your pent-up powers of feeling (emotion), thought and will upon that ONE PARTICULAR OBJECT, excluding all others until you reach that objective. This simple method succeeds because your feelings (emotions) VITALIZE our thought and make it DOMINANT, then this dominant thought arouses the will or your determination, and it is your will which compels action and brings your reward in accordance with your inner thought-picture—Silent Demand.

So, true success in life your success in possessing the good things for which you long, simply depends upon your learning, to IDEALIZE your objective as perfection, then to visualize (mentally picture) that longed-for good fortune distinctly, and then through, your directed ACTIVITY to go right out and materialize your dominant mind-picture into the world of things that are for your, own happy possession and enjoyment.

You must realize first that every circumstance of your life and every possession of yours is determined, decreed, and attracted by the quality (depth) the persistence (faith), and caliber of your own feeling, thought, and determination.

TRANSFORMING (BAD LUCK(?)" INTO GOOD FORTUNE

So it is very plain that now, when you most deeply desire to bring about very real and very definite changes in your circumstances for the better, you must charge (electrify) your Silent Demand with INTENSE feeling, with a DOMINANT thought, and with an iron WILL-POWER. And when you blend these three mental attitudes you have created an irresistible, centered PULL floods your silent Demand with a power that is like magic.

This is the magic that before too long will either manifest your IDEAL YOUR HEART'S DESIRE, in your outer world, or else will give into your hands the material object of your vision. For thus only do we see and realize that our wealth or poverty, our happiness or misery, our health or sickness, our success or our failure, can be accounted to be the results of our own thinking and our own activity.

You will doubtless agree that everywhere is this orderly cosmos which we call the universe we find convincing proof of the eternal existence and the never-ceasing operation of an Infinite and Intelligent POWER—this Power we call God.

This GOD-POWER, Infinite, Eternal, Intelligent—is one and universal. This Cosmic Intelligence, then, we conceive to be UNIVERSAL MIND (Divine Mind of the Universe). We see this Intelligent Mind-Force as all-powerful, all-knowing, and ALL-PRESENT.

Yes, forever present in each individual mind—in YOUR mind, in my mind, in every mind—is this GOD-POWER-MIND, in potential form perhaps, but only awaiting YOUR WILL to become the kinetic Power in your life—demonstrating abundance, wealth, happiness, health, or healing.

For YOU—when you become THE THINKER—become a center through thought for this Infinite, Universal Mind. For thought is the matrix of power in your life; the center of God-Radiation, bringing into REALITY the conditions mirrored in your own Sub-conscious Mind!

LESSON NO. 8
YOUR TREASURE WORLD—WHERE RICHES AWAIT YOU

In that mysterious King's Chamber, deep within our symbolic Pyramid-Temple, again we sit with the assembly of The Enlightened Ones, awaiting the words of wisdom with which Kyron will impart our present lesson to us.

Once again Kyron, the Wise, standing before the magnificent altar of gleaming white and glowing gold, raises his hands in a gesture of blessing and greets us in the ancient form of our ritual:

Welcome, O Enlightened Ones, for unto thee is granted the Reception.

(All is silence now in the King's Chamber, for Kyron, is holding another of the ancient manuscripts, from which he is about to read. The ancient scroll which Kyron holds is an olden copy of the "Upanishads,"—a part of the Sanskrit Brahamic scriptures, the earliest of which were written about six hundred years before our Elder Brother, Christ Ishuis, was born—and now Kyron reads from that Upanishad which is entitled: "Knowledge of The Living Spirit":

"Prana, or breath, (spirit), is Brahman, thus says Kaushitaki.

"Of this prang, which is Brahman, the MIND is the messenger, speech the housekeeper, the eye the guard, the ear the informant. He who knows Mind as the messenger of Prana (spirit-life), which is Brahman (the divine), becomes possessed of the messenger. He who knows Speech as the housekeeper, becomes possessed of the housekeeper. He who knows the Eye as the guard, becomes possessed of the guard. He who knows the Ear as the informant, becomes possessed of the informant.

"Now to that prana, which is Brahman, all these deities, Mind, Speech, Eye, Ear, bring an offering, though he asks not for it, AND THUS TO HIM WHO KNOWS all creatures bring an offering, though he asks not for it. (The Silent Demand.)

"Prana, or breath (spirit), is Brahman, (divine), thus says Paingya. And in that prana, which is Brahman, the eye stands firm behind speech, the ear stands firm behind the eye, the Mind stands firm, behind the ear, and the Spirit stands firm behind the Mind."

As he lays the ancient copy of the Upanishads upon the altar, Kyron the Wise, says softly and reverently:

And thus ends our reading of these few lines from the old Sanskrit Brahamic scriptures, written by our Elder Brothers in white two thousand six hundred years ago, but in these brief lines there is a mighty message—a message across the centuries about the hidden powers of the living Spirit.

LIVING SPIRIT RULES TREASURE WORLD

For it is the "Prana" the LIVING SPIRIT, which is the psychic Power that creates, controls and unlocks your treasure world, where riches await you. Yes, a world of riches surrounds each and everyone of us, but we must each one learn how to reach out and receive our share. And it is my purpose in these lessons to teach you that secret vary plainly and simply.

Let us turn again to the latter part of the Upanishad from which I read, and see if we may just what those ancient Masters were trying to teach in these references to speech, to the eye, the ear, the mind, and the spirit (Prana).

Truly, the lesson they impart is simple, though it does lead us straight into the realms of the astral (or psychic) world, which is indeed our "treasure world." Here the Masters are quite plainly reminding us that speech is uncertain, and must be checked by the eye—the eye is also uncertain, perhaps mistaking something else for silver, and must be checked by the Mind, because if the MIND is not on duty (attentive), the ear does not hear—and finally, that the Mind depends on the spirit—for without Spirit there is no Mind!

THOUGHT—THE ULTIMATE PRODUCT OF MIND

In this world, then MIND is the supreme manifestation of SPIRIT, and as you know, thought is the ultimate product of Mind. As we have sought to impress upon you in our lesson on the brain—which is the temple of the mind—this "thought-machine" of man, his mind, is beyond all doubt the most marvelous, most sensitive, and most highly organized mechanism in the universe. No mechanical instrument in the world can weigh, measure and photograph as does the human mind.

By means of Thought, the ultimate product of mind, man can send vibratory impulses to Divine Universal Mind and can also receive messages and impulse-waves from the Supreme-Intelligence Mind.

Let us liken this seemingly mysterious system of communication between Supreme Universal Mind and our human minds to the comparatively new science of radio communication—broadcasting and receiving.

Now it is very certain that your radio receiving set does not create sound. No, your radio simply brings in (attracts) the myriads of sound waves that are pulsating through the ether, and by focusing ("tuning in") certain sound waves, gives you the power to select those you desire to hear.

Neither zinc nor copper can create electricity, but when properly arranged they conduct electricity, which is everywhere in the world, to a focused vibration, which manifests its power and, too, directs that limitless energy according to our desire."

Just so your mind is able to attract and gather together the invisible energy-thought-elements, which pulsate everywhere around us, and by focusing them into a conscious, thinking SELF, causes them to manifest AS YOU and THROUGH YOU.

Isn't that simple? Very well, then, let us proceed with our journey into the realm of

The Living Spirit, your real "Treasure World." This is of the greatest importance to us all, for it is in this "treasure world" that riches truly await every one of us, if only we will follow the plain laws of psychic (mind) power,

We all know that this conscious thinking/SELF, which is you, lives in a material "house," which we call the human body, and medical science tells us that this body is composed of sixteen known chemical elements, each element attuned to vibrate at a certain ratio, predetermined by Cosmic Law. Thus, the entire body and mind are primarily prepared, coordinated, and conditioned for the natural states of perfect health, abundant prosperity, and happiness.

UNIVERSAL MIND—GREAT GODHOOD OF ETERNAL LAW

When we focus ("tune in") our thinking and our bodily processes upon harmony ("at-one-ness") with Divine Universal Mind—which is the Great Godhood of Eternal Law—we are sustained, maintained, and granted Health, Happiness and Wealth by the Eternal Natural Law, which manifests through Universal Mind.

Here Kyron, the Wise, pauses, for one Sylvanus, has signified his desire to ask a question—nodding to Sylvanus Kiron says:

And now, good Sylvanus, what is it you would ask?

Sylvanus: "Wouldst thou explain, Master in White, HOW this Universal Mind is made manifest in us?

With gladness, O Sylvanus, and I would that each of you listen very carefully, for this is one of the secrets of the Ancient Wisdom, which we have taught through varying symbols throughout the ages. There are three phases of mind, which manifest Universal Mind in each normal human being.

First, then, there is your conscious or voluntary mind, or that portion or phase of mind which guides and controls your reasoning and by which you direct (and focus) your WILL and by which you determine (decide) your every coarse of action. When by negative thinking (mental attitudes of fear, anger, worry, lack, frustration, poverty-complexes, destructive thoughts, etc.) you misuse this conscious or voluntary mind, now impair the naturally perfect coordination of your body and mind, and result registers in your life as sickness, limitation or poverty, and unhappiness or suffering.

SUBCONSCIOUS MIND—STOREHOUSE OF MEMORY

And, second, the Universal Mind manifests in each of us through that phase of our mental world which we call the Sub-conscious mind. This sub-conscious mind is the monitor of every truly great influence in your life, and is also your hidden storehouse of memory. For herein is buried the perfect recollection of every individual experience through which you have passed, together with many of the imprints of the experiences of your ancestors, which all unknown to you influence much of your life through hereditary traits, talents, or faculties.

The third of these great mental phases through which Universal Mind manifests in man is what I shall call the deeper unconscious mind, or the SUBLIMINAL MIND. To the world this deeper or subliminal mind is shrouded in mystery, and always will be so hidden to the uninitiated. We, however, through our heritage of the Secret Wisdom, teach very plainly that this deepest unconscious mind IS THE COSMIC MIND—and by that we mean that this phase of mind KNOWS EVERYTHING, and is in direct communication with the world of living spirit, YOUR TREASURE WORLD.

This deepest, or subliminal mind, enters into the world of THE UNKNOWN through telepathy, clairvoyance, inspirational states of genius, deep somatic trance conditions, and the nuances of intuition.

Further, it is this subliminal mind which is the silent; unrecognized coordinator of the physical, the mental, and the spiritual worlds of each individual, and this leads us to the most important of all the revelations I have made to you thus far in these lessons. Now that I have revealed to you the existence of this deepest unconscious (cosmic) mind, I would further impress upon each one of you that your greatest problem is to learn how to focus this subliminal (cosmic) mind upon attainment of your Heart's Desire, and, further, and most important, you must use your understanding of this mystery to prevent both the conscious and the subconscious minds from interfering with the Cosmic Mind in its perfect control of your body, your intellect, and y our good fortune.

OUR "RESPONSE MECHANISM: TO ENVIRONMENT"

We call the conscious (thinking) mind, and its two great instruments, the brain and nervous system, man's physical "response mechanism"" to environment, or our bodily reaction to circumstances and surroundings. Unless we gain as much control as possible through the development of courage and will-power, this "response mechanism" may and can wreak havoc in our physical bodies through FEAR, TERROR, or SCHOCK. Let me illustrate this very simply.

When negative or fear vibrations from your seemingly very real danger, from circumstances or surround-ings—when these fear -vibrations strike through the brain and nerves, then the conscious mind instantly flashes these fear-messages to every part of the body, often with most harmful reactions in the body.

For example, suppose you are surrounded by a strange and dense forest and you are suddenly threatened by an angry tiger or some other wild beast. Your conscious mind comprehends this very real danger instantly and flashes its "fear-messages" to every part of your body through the system of your brain and nerves.

Every cell in your body responds to this "message," and your internal organs are either paralyzed as violently upset the normal functions of every part of your physical self. And why is this? The answer is simple—in those few moments the entire chemistry of your body has changed—your glands throw powerful poisons into your blood-stream, and these poisons are strong stimulants to give your body the power to combat or to escape from this outside enemy.

EMOTIONAL RESPONSE TO FEAR-SUGGESTION

In such a situation as I have pictured, we can begin to understand the human emotional response to fear suggestion. In the presence of danger (either real or even imagined) both the nerves and the brain are expending energy at a terrific rate, digestion stops, and the heart is over-burdened. Not only the work of body-building stops, but the whole physical organism is poisoned and weakened.

Here we have the picture of the emotional response of the human body to fear-suggestion, indeed, the picture of a most destructive process, involving both poison (self—generated) and disorganization of every normal function of the body.

So, we must protect.your bodies from every possible danger, both real and imagined, for, even "worry," (which is only fear of imaginary dangers which.continues), in time has the same destructive effects upon the body. Negative emotional responses DESTROY—either rapidly or slowly, but they destroy!

It was Dr. Alexis Carrel, of the Rockefeller Institute, who said: "The brain and nervous systems destroys us, or is the cause of death.

Yes, by negative emotional fear responses, the brain and nervous system do destroy us, and can and do cause death—yet let us remember that the correct positive use of the conscious protective powers of the brain and nervous system has saved mankind from being destroyed by environment, or by wild beasts, or by the storms and seasons of ice, or by starvation.

THE CONSCIOUS—KEY TO TREASURE WORLD

Now, I think it becomes quite clear that the key to your treasure world, where riches await you, that key which also unlock the door of Health, of Success, and of Happiness, is your control of your conscious mind. For thus you also control to a great extend the subconscious mind, which can also act destructively on your body, once you make it the reservoir of YEAR.

Thus, by controlling your conscious mind, and through it the subconscious, you free the third, or Cosmic (subliminal) mind to function naturally, protecting your body against the ravages of FEAR, TIME, and DISEASE, and attracting to you your desired share of the inexhaustible riches of your invisible treasure world.

By faithfully following the teachings of these more advanced lessons, you can develop the memory of your subconscious mind to a masterly degree, and by "intuition" you can call these memories to consciousness at will.

As you study these deeper metaphysical Truths, the truly complex, accurate, and sensitive development of your occult mental powers will astound you, no matter how skeptical you may have been. Remember that this accumulated "spiritual force," which I have named the "subconscious" and the "Cosmic" minds (in reality, phases of mind) is your submerged personality (THE REAL YOU), which thinks, reasons, loves, fears, believes, and draws its own conclusions beneath and seemingly independent of your conscious thinking.

Yet, these two deeper, or "transconscious" minds CAN BE CHANGED AT YOUR WILL but gradually. In this transmuting process, do not look for a miracle "over-night". And the secret of this transformation of your deeper minds is accomplished quite simply by a directed, constant stream of changed conscious thinking.

CONTROLLED THINKING CHANGES LIFE

Let us compare this simple process to a well into which a small, stream of muddy water has been pouring. for sometime. In fact, until all the water in the well is muddy. Now, divert the muddy water from the well, and in its place allow a stream of pure, clear water to flow into the well. Then in due time, of course, all the water in the well is gradually changed.

Just so, at any time you can begin by consciously directing thereto a stream of consciously pure, wholesome power-currents of thought.

And the power of the mind, that deeper power reached by control of the two great transconscious minds, that power is almost infinite, for it attracts and materializes what it most greatly desires, both from its environment and from the vast sea of cosmic consciousness which surrounds this earth,

But in order to gain this control your conscious thinking must pass the portals of the subconscious mind and through it, must unlock the closely guarded door of your Cosmic Mind. But here we encounter, at each of these entrances, a guardian/of the threshold who never sleeps. Before your own conscious mind can enter these magic realms, you must qualify as an initiate and the initiate must approach these gateways over that rough and rugged road known as SELF-MASTERY. (BEHOLD LIBERATION—)

"IN THE SILENCE"—MEDITATION, INTROSPECTION, CONCENTRATION

Control over the magic powers of the mind is gained "in The Silence"—through meditation, introspection, and concentration, as I have pointed out to you elsewhere in these lessons.

But now, Good Friends and Disciples, you are ready for a deeper understanding of this superb mental control which only comes through self-mastery, and yet the way is plain and simple, indeed to the initiate.

First, then, instead of idle fancies or "wishful thinking," let us understand by that word "meditation," the focused thinking which will plan your whole life-course in accordance with the Divine Light which shall guide you to the Happy possession of your Heart's Desire. This, you will accomplish by visualizing; your Great Desire IN THE SILENCE, casting out of our conscious mind every conflicting thought or doubt, and holding your conscious mind receptive to the cosmic minds. You will reach this receptive state in The Silence by completely relaxing every tension of your physical body and loosing your thinking mind from every active thought, for its condition must become passive—a condition similar to that which we sometimes experience between sleep and wakefulness, in which we sometimes "day-dream."

Introspection, by which I mean self-analysis should be concomitant with your meditation, and is equally important, because through introspection ("looking within") you will be made to realize imperfections or weaknesses, which might hinder your journey into your land of Heart's Desire. Thus, once you know them, you will free yourself from such hindrances. So step by step, you perceive the path straight ahead toward your goal, for so those greater "transconscious" powers of your Mind are realized by degrees to unfailingly guide you into that treasure world where riches await your claim.

TO ATTAIN SUBLIMINAL POWER, CONCENTRATE

Concentration is the Magic Key which unlocks the gateway to this treasure world to you. Each of the affirmations Which I am giving you in. these lessons is a focal-thought for your concentration, Once this secret is acquired, once you learn to) RELAX and so concentrate, the veil is lifted between you and the land of your fondest dreams. Then that which you most greatly desire of the finer things of life is revealed, not just as a vision, but as something real and within your grasp.

I have taught you much about The Silence and much about relaxing, because you can only enter into real or absolute concentration by constant exercise and under the proper conditions.

And great is the reward, for those who have developed the ability, to concentrate to a marked degree are known as the GENIUSES of the world; those who develop a moderate degree of concentration form the great "middle class" of "successful" men and women; while those who lack this ability entirely are the submerged "masses," the morons who make up the overwhelming majority of the peoples of the world.

Tension and friction, fear and negative attitudes are the most destructive enemies of the INNERSELF and of the human body. Everywhere around you is the living proof of this sad truth. But concentrate—relax perfectly In The Silence—and you sensitize, your mind And your body for the indelible, the divine impressions of Universal Cosmic Mind.

LESSON No. 9
MYSTIC ROAD TO ATTAINMENT-IMAGINATION

Once more deep within that mystic. King's Chamber of imagination, in the silence of our Pyramid Temple, you are one with the assembly of The Enlightened Ones, awaiting the unfolding of our present lesson by Kyron, the Wise.

Standing in quiet dignity before the beautiful altar of snowy marble and shining, gold, Kyron raises his hands. in blessing and greets us according to the ancient order:

Welcome, O Enlightened Ones, for unto thee is granted the Reception.

(Every one is very quiet now in the King's Chamber, because, as is his custom, we see that Kyron is about to read to us from one of the ancient scripts words from long-gone ages. We perceive that, Kyron holds an old copy of "The Life of Buddha" written almost twenty centuries ago by the twelfth Buddhist patriarch, Asvagosha, in ancient Sanskrit, another of the Masters in White of the ages gone who aided in the Great Work of the 'Wisdom-School of today by bequeathing to us his portion of The Secret Mission. Kyron reads briefly from the words which Buddha spoke to the king):

"There is a WAY of darkness out of light, there is a WAY OF LIGHT OUT OF DARKNESS, there is darkness which follows after the .gloom, there is a Light which causes the brightening of light. The wise man, leaving first principles, should go on to get more light; evil words will be. repeated far and wide by the multitude, but there are few to follow good direction.

"It is impossible, however, to avoid result of works, the doer cannot escape; if there had been no first works, there had been in the end no result of doing—no reward for good, no hereafter for joy, but because works are done there is no escape. Let us then practice GOOD WORKS, let us inspect our thoughts, that .we do no evil, BECAUSE AS WE SOW SO WE REAP...

"Only by considering and practicing the TRUE (ETERNAL) LAW can we escape from this sorrow filled mountain—

"Having found peace in FAITH, we put an end to all the mass of sorrows, wisdom can then enlighten us, and so we put away the rules by which we .acquire knowledge by the senses. By inward thought...following with gladness the directions of the "TRUE (ETERNAL)LAW," this is THE WAY."

Reverently Kyron, the Wise, lays the ancient scroll upon the candle-lighted Sacred Triangle of the altar, and softly says:

I have read to you, my beloved Companions, a few of the words of Buddha, another of the "Heaven-born" Masters—words of two thousand years ago—words which unerringly direct us to "The Way" and that WAY is the mystic road to attainment which I am teaching you in these deep yet simple lessons.

On this mystic road to attainment, there are many way-stations which mark your progress, and each distance you cover in traveling this road brings you nearer and nearer to those Heart's Desires, to the possession of those finer things of life which have been the objects of your voiceless longing. For "attainment" means POSSESSION.

THE MIGHTY POWER OF IMAGINATION

Each one of you to whom my words come can achieve perfect well-being (healing and abounding health), abundance (riches), and security (unbreakable good-fortune), and I want every one of you to actually possess all of these good things, so that you will enjoy life in all its inherent goodness.

Now, be assured, this is not merely a Utopian dream of mine, nor yet an idle wish; because YOU can actually realize, you can possess for yourself every one of these requisites of a happy, a worthwhile life. Remember, every one of these good things of life is simply the result or the outcome of certain specific actions and procedures on your part.

These specific actions and procedures on your part bring their astounding and bountiful results through the operation of LAW—Changeless, ETERNAL LAW. This Eternal Law is your unfailing compass which guides you along the mystic road of attainment. This compass—Eternal Law—when you fully understand it and rightly apply it, will direct you how to POSSESS health, wealth, love, and happiness just as unerringly as the mariner's compass guides his ship to its desired harbor.

From the very first of these lessons I have sought to impress upon you that tremendous yet simple concept which is the basis of every success in life, the foundation of attainment, the touch-stone of possession, and that concept is this:

THOUGHT IS THE KING UPON THE THRONE OF YOUR DESTINY

Imagination—thought pictures—rules the world, because Imagination is the child of thought, and as I have taught you in previous lessons, thought always seeks materialization. The thought-picture of the engineer is materialized in the complete, engine, or machine, or bridge, as the case may be, and the thought-pictures (the mental images—Imagination) of the architect is clothed in material form in the finished skyscraper.

So, your Soul's real world is that unseen world which, it has builded of its imagination (images); its mental attitudes, and its thoughts throughout the ages. Our heritage of "Free-will" (power to choose) gives each of us the power to build a mental world of beauty, health, and happiness or a mind—world which is filled with ugliness, sickness, and suffering. But the moment we intensely WILL to do so, we can begin to lift ourselves from this lower plane of lack, limitation, and sordid surroundings through determined "imaging" (picturing) of our Heart's Desire, through expectancy (faith), receptivity, and directed activity.

WAY OF ATTAINMENT——FROM IMAGE TO REALITY

Remember, in your own life, you and you alone hold the master-key which will unlock for you the treasure-world of possibility, yes, of possession—and that key is your power to transform your mental images (mindpictures in the "imagination") into material realities.

As each one of you knows, that giant airplane which wings its way above the clouds first existed as a mental image (an imagined picture) and because he WILLED to do so, because he proved his expectancy (faith), and his receptivity through his directed activity, man transformed (reflected) that airplane from a thought-pic-ture (produced by imagination) into a material reality.

By this same magic power of changing a mental image into a material reality man has assembled iron and steel, rubber and glass, copper and aluminum, gasoline spray and electricity and low! we have the modern automobile!

Through huge lenses of glass encased in great tubes of brass and steel the eyes of men now probe the heavens, and the mind of man weighs and charts the stars in their whirling orbits.

You, too, through this same power can re-make Fate and command those good things of life for which you long—today.

What a mighty power is imagination, the power to mentally picture!

For it is mentally picturing in the form of fear-images which transforms into reality the majority of the disorders and the diseases which afflict mankind and by the same token it is this same power which can banish them. For imagination either destroys or creates, it can either tear down or build up everything in human destiny. Imagination creates prophets and kings, priests and paupers, fathers bloody wars and destroys whole nations and civilization, and rebuilds other nations and civilizations upon their ashes.

EXACTLY LIKE YOUR MENTAL IMAGES

But what, you may ask, has all this to do with ME? Or with my desire to succeed, to have and to hold good fortune, good health, and real happiness" Just this. My Good Friends and Disciple your life is exactly like your mental images!

Day and night these changeless laws of the thought-world are constantly working to bring forth into reality in your own personal world the images you hold in your mind. Although they are generally unrecognized by you, still these mental images of yours are confronting you everywhere in your environment clothed with material bodies of form and substance.

Let us understand this one great, basic fact clearly right here; as I have intimated to you before, "thinking" is that magic process by which external (outer) impressions, together with emotions (your "feelings"), and sensory messages are transformed into mental pictures in your brain. So thinking is mental image-making. In all the world, I have found no better definition of thinking.

And here is a second stupendous fact for your reassurance—all the material things of life yield to the domination of intense, constant, and focused mental-picturing ("thinking"):

Every great fortune is just the prosperity-picture magnified many, many times in some intense, constant, and focused human mind. Pause here, and think that statement through. After all—simple, isn't it?

Here we have just three great, but simple factors; the visualized (pictured) thought, the magnetic (focused) thought, and the magnified thought—all intense, practical, and attainable mental attitudes, made so by "THE-WILL-TO-DO," "THE FAITH-TO-DO", and "THE ACTION-TO-DO."

MIND-PICTURES THAT ATTRACT REALIZATION

Now whatever it is that you most greatly desire to accomplish, to attain, or to possess, that will require you to make a very special effort, and that effort must be directed by understanding, for understanding MUST guide your WILL, your FAITH, and your ACTION.

When you speak of yourself, of your decisions, of your great Goal, cultivate the habit of always listening carefully to the INNER VOICE ("intuition"), for thus alone can you know if you are speaking from the soul-center, or from the superficial, physical senses.

That is one of the great reasons I have taught each one of you from the very beginning of these occult lessons to set aside at a certain time each day ten or fifteen minutes for your period IN THE SILENCE, so that during these sacred, hushed minutes you will sit in silent meditation, and simply WAIT receptive spirit.

For thus your mind-pictures attract reality to themselves and begin to materialize in your outer, personal world. Frankly, when you thus freely open the passive, receptive door of your mental nature to the invisible, infinite world of positive thought-currents, you are in reality engaging in the highest and most effective form of prayer.

Strange but tune, IN THE -SILENCE, to which you are advised to bring only a voiceless longing and tranquil waiting in simple faith, voiced in perhaps only a single affirmation, invisible powers from the psychic world spoken, of by the Christ as "The Kingdom," are attracted to you by the magnet of your concentrated (focused) faith.

CREATING EFFECTIVE MIND-PICTURES

Now let us turn once more to the HOW of creating effective mind—pictures, for now you are prepared to receive the deeper. instruction in this all-important work of mental visualizing. And yet I shall make this deeper instruction very simple indeed. First, your present thought-pictures are not under your proper control, because certain brain cells which you have shaped out of your past negative thoughts (or doubt or fear pictures) will often thrust these same negative pictures before your mind's eye unbidden and now unwelcome to you.

Yet you need not passively gaze upon these doubt-pictures or these fear-pictures—STOP DRIFTING!—grab the helm, man the oars, and change your course!

"But that is not so EASY," you may object. Quite true—but only dead fish drift WITH the current, the LIVE ONES are always going upstream. Live fish swim against the current, and here is where that "very special effort" I spoke about a few minutes ago is required, that effort which I told you must be directed by understanding.

And so that your understanding of this process of result-getting visualization will be complete, let us consider this process step by step. First then, upon entering INTO THE SILENCE, there is the state of, meditation in which often you are hardly conscious of yourself at all, you have become more or less absorbed in the Universal. In order to deepen this state of meditation, you can fix your. consciousness on that higher state of mind expressed in repeating that magic word "A-U-M" over and over silently or in a very low tone of voice." A-U-M, A-U-M, A-U-M..." You will remember this magic word from a much earlier lesson.

This carries you mentally away from the outer world to the DIVINE CENTER WITHIN YOURSELF, that center wherein dwells the Absolute, the king upon the throne of your destiny. Simple, so far, isn't it!

PICTURE THE UNFOLDING ROSE

Stop a moment here, and think of this—all of your life you have been unfolding your consciousness, you have unfolded your mind, your thoughts, your knowledge, your talents, from the center outward. You have been like the unfolding rose.

How does this rose unfold? From the center, of course, petal by petal. Now suppose the rose were to close itself up into the form of a bud; it would draw itself in petal by petal, beginning at the center, and wrapping up all the-petals close about it into the small bud-like form which they developed.

So you must now reverse this unfolding process of yours when you enter into The Silence, by meditation and concentration. I do not mean a drowsy, hazy condition, nor merely a state of day-dreaming, nor yet "wish-ful thinking." Rather, you are closing yourself into the CENTER of your consciousness, and you are very wide-awake in that center.

When you enter into your meditation-silence, think of our illustration of the rose, and then you will perceive the way to get into your CREATIVE CENTER mentally. And the nearer you get to this creative center within, the nearer you draw to the divine center to The Infinite—the creative, the Eternal-God-Law.

Here you have left behind the vain, the negative, the fear pictures of your physical sense-mind, for you are now within that "holy of holies," the realm of the CAUSE-LIFE, where new power flows into you from the vibrant radiations of the Divine Source of Health, of Healing, of Riches, of Love, and of Happiness.

So, in The Silence you step over the threshold of this doorway to the chambers of imagery, of creative conception, leaving behind for the time-being the outer world to form a background for your new inheritance of all the good, all the finer things of life.

For in this creative realm, your Soul shall be dominant, follow the guidance of the Soul, and soon your now limited mental horizon will broaden to embrace the All-consciousness of abundance!

LAY ASIDE BROKEN IDOLS—INFERIORITY A CHALLENGE.

Before you will be able in The Silence to fully inspire your spirit essence and transmute it into the soul-bea-con-light to light the way to your Heart's Desire in Abundance, 'Riches, and Happiness, outer appearances and your outer fear-thoughts must be stripped of every vestige of domination in your life.

As each of you now mentally surveys the glorious possibilities that are open to you, you will realize that right now your first decisive act must be to lay aside every one of your broken idols, every pet superstition, and the memory of every mistake you may have made in the past.

For, have you not learned a lesson from each of these'?—very well, then, they were necessary to your mental and to your soul unfoldment, and they have served their purpose.

Now you are striving for a consciousness of abundance, of well-being, and of joyous life that shall be as clear as crystal, and this consciousness must not be lessened or swayed by other and smaller minds. So—the Path-way of Silence—and In The Silence, you walk alone.

Here is truly a great secret from our hidden teachings which will hasten your attainment of your goal mightily, and yet it is very simple. Every night, when you retire, let your last walking suggestion to your deeper mind be this: "My Real Self—the Eternal "I"—is Spirit, and never sleeps; so while my body is taking its necessary rest, I shall be in constant contact with Universal-God-Mind, attracting to myself from that higher realm the splendid things of my rightful inheritance."

This training of your deeper consciousness begins with perception, continues through meditation into concentration (the state of being truly absorbed), and ends with the RECEPTION.

All outer perception (seeing) focuses your mind on gross matter, but your inner perception in The Silence connects your Real Self with that infinite realm. THE WORLD OF CAUSE. This spiritual perception of the within indraws your consciousness and thereby your mind attains to illumination.

"Every waking hour we weave, whether we will or no;

Every thought, act or word, into the woof must go."

Watch your weaving, Good Friend!

FACE YOUR "INFERIORITY COMPLEX" AS A CHALLENGE

Here one, Hakon, raises his. hand, desiring to ask a question—Kyron pauses. Hakon speaks: "Tell us, O Kyron, if it please you, what shall one do who feels always inferior—always as if he or she is somehow handicapped, for this is my sad case?"

A splendid question, good Hakon, and just to the point of my next proposition, which it brings out. The answer is simple—just face your "inferiority" feeling as a challenge, and so you can make it the cause, the spring board of a very great and real success. Yes, I know that nine out of every ten people permit this inferiority-complex (feeling) to rule them as a terrible tyrant, they think of their feeling of inferiority as a demon driving them to failure. How much better to weight this supposed inferiority, get a sound, reasoned conception of it.and no matter how bitter the fight, OVERCOME IT.

In every age, man has attained to mastery in spite of his handicaps, or even his inferiorities. Any man knows he is too weak to move ten tons from one end of the city to the other in a day. But man had domesticated animals; formerly he harnessed horses to move the ten tons, today he transports ten tons in a truck, for he has harnessed gasoline and electricity.

Let's take a good look at this weakness-inferiority complex, for we shall find it fine driving force behind all human progress. Man cannot run as fast or as far as an ordinary alley cat—but man moves more swiftly today than any other creature on earth!

Inferiority only beats us in life's game, when we feel we are beaten at the start, lay down, and refuse to seek a way out.

A lad of twenty, say, contracts consumption—then these defeatists say, "too bad—too bad—his life is ruined at the very beginning—too bad." Perhaps. But do you happen to remember the marvelous work Robert Louis Stevenson did before he was vanquished by the "white plague"? Haven't you heard of one-armed ball players? or blind poets? or great music written by one stone deaf ? or have you ever read about Helen Keller. Of course you have. And what drove each of these on to victory? Inferiority feeling, to be sure. But...they met the challenge.

EYES AND EARS OF YOUR MIND NEVER SLEEP

After all, Good Friends and Disciples, we determine our own fate. Universal-Divine-Mind (God-The Over-Soul) is waiting for us each one IN THE SILENCE, in all places, everywhere, and under all circumstances-just as near to you as your own thought.

LESSON NO. 10
MYSTIC ROAD TO ATTAINMENT—MAGNIFY YOUR THOUGHT

Again all is silence deep within that hidden King's Chamber of our retreat from the world, in the midst of our great Pyramid Temple, where you are welcomed among The Enlightened Ones, and where we quietly await the words of Kyron, the Wise.

Once more before the shining mystic altar of marble and gold, Kyron imparts his blessing with upraised hands, and welcomes us with the ancient greeting:

Welcome, O Enlightened Ones, for unto thee is granted the Reception.

(Again Kyron reverently holds that scripture, entitled "The Life of Buddha," handed down to us from the ancient Sanskrit writing of Asvagosha, that twelfth Buddhist saint of two thousand years ago—and now Kyron reads from the words of Buddha and of the great Brahma):

"Buddha for those seven days, in contemplation (In The Silence) lost, his heart at peace—Now resting here in this condition, I have obtained,' he said, 'my ever-shifting Heart's Desire, and now at rest I stand, escaped from self.' The eyes of Buddha then considered 'all that lives'...much he desired to bring about their welfare, and how to gain for them that most excellent deliverance from 'covetous desire, hatred, ignorance, false teach-ing...by...thoughtful silence.

"Great Brahma (Messenger of God)—(speaking)—"What happiness in all the world so great as when a loving Master meets the unwise; the world with all its occupants, filled with impurity and dire confusion, with heavy grief oppressed, or in some cases lighter sorrows, awaits deliverance, the lord of men, having escaped by crossing the wide and mournful sea of birth and death, we now entreat to rescue others—those struggling creatures...the world indeed is bent on large personal gain, and hard it is to share one's own with others. O let your loving heart be moved with pity towards the world burdened."

"Thus having spoken"...he turned back (returned to) the Brahma heaven. Buddha...rejoiced at (in) heart..."

Quite reverently laying the ancient tome upon the Sacred Triangle of the Altar, Kyron says:

My companions and Disciples, so ends the reading of the mystical words of Buddha and Brahma—words which seek to teach us that on our WAY of attainment, "crossing the wide and mournful sea of birth and death," when we have attained to Mastery, our mission is in turn to rescue others "with pity towards the world burdened."

Let us first of all remember that we see that in reality that world which "with all its occupants filled with impurity and dire confusion, with heavy grief oppressed.. waits deliverance" is but an.outer world of seem-ing—a world of "the unwise" who have chosen to make negative seeming into grim reality for themselves.

My great mission is to teach you that your REAL SELF is an inseparable individuality forever linked to that divine life which reaches from the everlasting to the everlasting. To this REAL SELF of yours there is in reality no sickness and, no limitation, no pain, and no poverty. That REAL INNER SELF that is you will remain untouched by even the wreck of matter and the seeming crash of worlds. For your REAL SELF dwells, in realm beyond the cloud-land and the shadows.

Because of this stupendous truth I have taught you to enter into The Silence regularly, for there you can reach that unseen realm of reality, and there, where the human and the divine blend, you can attain to perfect harmony ("at-one-ness") with Infinite Universal Mind. In that Divine Presence, in The Silence, you will find your sure refuge from the world's tumult and confusion and from that Divine Presence you will be endowed with a new strength, and you can go forth with a living power that will transform your life.

FROM DESIRE TO ATTAINMENT-BY ETERNAL LAW

Everything in this world, and in the universe, works by Natural Eternal Law. Human fortunes, good or bad, are never exceptions to this great fact. You will remember that primitive man was quite sure that anything which he could not understand was the work of "magic." And the phenomena of today, which the uninitiated call "miracles," are simply the result of subtle and higher forms of The Eternal Law, which their minds cannot understand.

No, man can set aside or change one "jot or tittle'" of Eternal Natural Law, but we can learn to use and to control the inexhaustible forces subject to and in accordance with The Law, and so attain marvelous results.

So, now we come to the next great step in your Mystic Pathway from desire to attainment—MAGNIFY YOUR THOUGHT PICTURE!

Now, having chosen with the utmost care those good things in We—that supreme goal, that greatest Heart's Desire—which you most deeply desire to bring into material existence in your life, your entire attention must now be directed towards magnifying your mind-picture or pictures.

First, begin today to live in harmony with that mind-picture. just act and plan exactly as if that mental image was already a reality.

Remember the Words of the Master-Teacher, Christ:

"Therefore I say unto you, What things soever ye desire, when ye pray, believe that ye receive them, AND YE SHALL HAVE THEM.—Mark 11:24.

So, banish all thoughts of doubt or uncertainty about the matter. And shun—just as you would shun a plague-anybody whom you feel to be negative, or who show any doubt in their attitude toward you.

In working with the forces of The Eternal Law, avoid long or sustained vigils in The Silence, power in magnifying your mind-picture comes more from repetition, and your mental visioning must not become mental drudgery. Escape mental monotony by recreation and by change of thoughts, but always return at regular intervals to that mental picture of your Heart's Desire.

This way your mental image will be magnified gradually, and as you return to The Silence from time to time, before very long you will begin to see evidence in your material, outer world that your "dream" is coming true!

FIRST—THAT CLEAR CUT MIND-PICTURE

You must have that "one big idea," that Heart's Desire, that clear cut mind picture to build into reality, or of course you will fail utterly. But now you are creating that "major dream" in your material, personal world day by day, and all your physical forces and your mental energies are focused at the command of your will upon that objective.

But you may wonder, "Although you have told us about the importance of imagination, suppose that we each have chosen the thing or things we want most from life, and we each form a 'mind-picture' of our Heart's Desire, how can those mind-pictures, which are after all held in the imagination, be changed into the real things we want most in life?"

That, My Good Friends, is exactly what I propose to teach you in this lesson, and in various lessons to follow.

By way of illustration, let us take a look at the power of negative (or evil) mind-pictures, for their results are everywhere about us, I have told you, and now I want you to hold this truth in mind, thought (pictured images) always seek materialization.

Medical annals (and even the streets about you) are crowded with the sad examples of the disastrous effects upon the physical life of the negative thoughts (mental-pictures) of fear, anger, jealousy, worry, hatred and greed. Almost everyone today will agree that such negative thought-pictures, held for any length of time, actually pull down, disintegrate, and paralyze the physical forces and the nerve centers, and so cause most of the disease and suffering in the world. Pride, selfishness, pessimism, and all these other negative thoughts (mental Pictures) of fear, harm digestion, acidulate the blood and tend to dry up the normal secretions of the physical body.

YOUR IMAGING OF ABUNDANCE IS CREATIVE THINKING

Although the destructive power of wrong (negative) thought-pictures seems to be quite generally understood, isn't it strange that the corresponding opposite—the wonderfully upbuilding effects of abundance-imaging—has been so long ignored by people in general?

Always remember that your imaging (mental-picturing) of abundance, of good fortune, and of happiness, is creative thinking. People who fail are those who assume that they have no control over their thinking (thoughtpicturing) and so of course their thought-motor drifts in a helpless craft, tossed about by every current and eddy. Self-limitation is ignorance and weakness, and gives reality to every morbid negation and inversion of truth that passes before the distorted gaze of its victim.

But you are steadily progressing straight toward your goal of realization, of possession. Answering your query about the power of imagination to materialize objects not yet present to the senses, but existing only as mental pictures, if you will but pause to think you will realize that imagination has led every step in the progress of mankind from the cave to the palace.

For it was imagination that gave us art, music, and religion—imagination wrote our every book, painted every picture, blue printed every sky-scraper and conceived every city on earth!

Never hesitate to act upon your vision, for now doubt, uncertainty, and fear are strangers to you. So, just by the act of having faith, simple belief in YOURSELF, and you will attract to yourself greater confidence and courage with every step you advance upon this pathway of creative thinking. Every obstacle you conquer will stimulate your imagination to new life and power.

MAGNIFY YOUR DESIRE—PICTURE BY OBSERVATION

Consciously, we live in two worlds. Deep down in your consciousness (awareness) there is that inner world wherein is enthroned the REAL YOU—that self which is independent of space and time, and as I have told you, that self is indissolubly linked with the Infinite, Entering this sanctuary, where God and Soul blend, IN THE SILENCE, you can invoke that mighty Power vibrating there to aid you to realize your Desire-Picture.

But, remember, the threshold of this inner realm is constantly guarded, and no one shall enter this realm except he enter through the door of The Silence, and first he must free himself from the shadow of doubt and fear, thus proving his implicit faith in the wisdom and the power of Eternal, Divine Law.

By this inner power you can rise superior to every adverse influence, you can master every circumstance, and reach the goal of your Heart's Desire. In The Silence, you abide not in the world of sense, but in the realm of Soul, of Spirit, and there the Infinite Intelligence will lead you.

Then there is that outer, physical world which surrounds each human being everywhere. I want you each one to realize very clearly that within this OUTER material world you build your own personal world. This is because everything OUTSIDE of your inner world exists for you in the form of mental pictures drawn from the impressions that are brought to the REAL YOU by your physical senses.

Your developed power to OBSERVE is a tremendous aid in magnifying your Desire Picture, because every one of your mental pictures is vital, vibrant, and true to life in exact proportion to your ability to observe— no more, and no less. So, to be effective all mental imaging (mind-picturing) requires first of all keen observation.

According to your of ability to observe, to really perceive, this outer world is great or small, beautiful or ugly, vivid or colorless. Honestly now and you need answer this question to yourself alone–just how big or how little is your treasure of fact and fancy, of form and color, of outline and of detail? How many "mindperceptions" (definite mental images) of the wealth of beauty and the. wonders of this outer world around you have you made your own through observation, and filed away in the storehouse of your conscious mind?

Because it is only from this material—from these vivid mental impressions which you have gained from observation—Imagination can paint with the magic colors of conception those desire-mind-pictures which your deeper consciousness silently transforms into material health, riches, and happiness day by day.

BE A KEEN OBSERVER—and you give both size and substance to your mental desire-images.

MARKET PRICE OF YOUR HEART'S DESIRE

Make no mistake, there is always a price-tag attached to success.

In the storehouse of life you can buy according to the price you pay. And in speaking of price, I am not talking abut money, but rather of time, faith, enthusiasm, concentration, magnified thinking, and directed, determined activity.

Too many people are paying grievous prices for spurious goods. As I have pointed out to you before, most of the men and women around you have never grown up mentally. Their minds are like the minds of children. These undeveloped minds are ruled by those terrible negative-images—fear, superstition, anger, jealousy, inferiority, and failure-complexes. Of course, these undeveloped multitudes are blind to their self-imposed bondage, and The Eternal Law, entirely impersonal, cannot rescue them from the poverty, the failure, and the wretchedness which they attract to themselves by holding these negative images.

But you are no longer walking blindly, and you are gladly paying the market price of your Heart's Desire. The entire system of these courses in the hidden Wisdom is designed to rest upon this great, this all-important fundamental fact—the real difference between those men and women who stand head and shoulders above the forgotten millions in this world is simply the difference in the DIRECTION, the REALITY, the ENERGY, and the SIZE OF their thoughts.

YOUR MOTTO: "MY PLACE IS AT THE FRONT!"

I want to give you a new slogan—a personal motto for you—keep this slogan always in your mind and it will change your thinking from mediocrity to that of a distinctive personality:

"From now on my place is at the front. Where the failures in life halt, there is where my path begins. The best positions in life are many of them empty yet—and one of them belongs to me, and here is where I claim the best things in life."

That is what I am teaching each one of you, My Good Friends, to become a distinctive personality, for then and then only you ATTRACT every good fortune that life has to offer, Health, Love, Wealth and Happiness. I say this to each disciple, for I know that if you have pursued these studies this far, you CAN become THAT OUTSTANDING PERSONALITY WHICH ALWAYS WINS. Exactly the same inner Power to picture success and to attain to importance that was used by those who stand head and shoulders above their negative neighbors, IS VIBRATING WITHIN YOU THIS MINUTE. That Power is yours to USE, for it was born with you, but YOU must develop it, direct it, and focus it upon a positive, an intense Heart's Desire.

In your first course of Lessons, I taught you something about personality—let us review that word for just a few moments. What is personality? Briefly, your personality is your own, individual WAY of thinking and acting. And to have a distinctive personality is to live above and beyond the false and negative opinions or thoughts of everybody around you. In other words, you are free, you are independent, you are true to your own higher, inner thought-picture of yourself and of your rightful place "at the front."

Thus you can "dream fine dreams, "and you can build your own fine dreams into the finest realities in your life. It was hard" headed Andrew Carnegie who once said: "Be as kings in your dreams. Say to yourself, "My place is on TOP!" I would not give you a penny for a young man who does not imagine himself to be the head of a world famous concern."

History tells us that Napoleon inspired his armies to heroism by this powerful suggestion:

"Every mother's son carries the baton of a marshal in his knapsack!"

DISTINCTIVE PERSONALITIES LEAVE LENGTHENED SHADOWS

Distinctive personalities and great thoughts live forever.

Emerson wrote: "The man Caesar is born, and through centuries afterward we have the Roman Empire."

Every great religion, every great philosophy, every great university, every great factory, and every great modern corporation—each of these is but the lengthened shadow of some man who magnified the power of his dynamic thought-picture.

The monastic system; the shadow of Erima Antonius—The Reformation; the shadow of Martin Luther— the power of Rome; the shadow of Scipio—this great, independent Nation; the shadow of George Washington—freedom from slavery here; the shadow of Abraham Lincoln.

The world of history is a series of stories about distinctive personalities—and each of these stories deals with the inner thought (the "dream") of some human Mind, which was magnified a thousand fold.

That is the lesson I am giving to you now, straight from the shoulder—when you learn to MAGNIFY YOUR THOUGHT (image), you are drawing upon an invisible cosmic Power, which magnified both your, thought-image and the thinker, yourself, beyond all measure in the world of outer reality.

DISTINCTIVE PERSONALITIES EVERYWHERE: TODAY

Potentially great, potentially distinctive personalities are living everywhere around us today—you meet them every day—you are looking at one, of these potentially distinctive personalities whenever you look into your mirror!

But these distinctive personalities are potential-sleeping-unknown and unrecognized because they are simply not DEVELOPED, and probably that includes you yourself.

But remember, you, too, can develop that great, that distinctive personality that is now sleeping within you, if you will only arouse and mobilize all the latent (dormant) powers within the citadel of your MIND and stop wasting your precious time and effort seeking outside for that "magic" which you will find only WITHIN YOURSELF. This is not a power—which can be given to you by someone else—it is within your own being, but you alone can awaken it.

My mission is to teach, and in teaching you the Ancient Wisdom which has been handed down through the ages to be exemplified in these days in this philosophy, I am of a truth teaching you from an occult fountain of knowledge unsurpassed in all the world. Yet I must warn you that the greatest teacher in the world, even though he open to you this occult fountain of the sublime knowledge that has been kept secret from the beginnings of time—that teacher cannot transform you, nor can this hidden knowledge alone transmute your life from lack to abundance.

I can but show you how to unfold your REAL SELF, and our instruction teaches you HOW to awaken the illimitable powers within you.

Just as the gardener may provide every necessary condition of soil necessary to the rose, and he may lavish every care upon the rosebush, but he cannot make the rosebud unfold its petals to the sunshine that power is WITHIN the bud itself. The gardener can only help to free the rose to fulfill the Eternal Creative God-Law of its own being—and this teaching simply frees you to bring into material reality the inherent Eternal God-Law of your own, unfoldment.

Our Nazarite Master in White, Christ, referred to this unfoldment as "the kingdom of God"—said he: "But rather seek ye the kingdom of God; and, all these things shall be added unto you." Luke 12:31. And where is this unfolding kingdom? He said: "For behold, the kingdom of God IS WITHIN YOU." Luke 17:21.

LESSON No. 11
FOCUSED MENTAL—AND THE LIVING BREATH

Once more we are gathered with The Initiates in that hidden King's Chamber, deep in the midst of our imaged Pyramid Temple, "the world forgetting by the world forgot," and again we wait in silence the unfolding of yet another lesson in the occult wisdom by which The Masters in all ages have led their disciples to the psychic Reception.

And now Kyron, the wise, standing before the symbolic altar of purest marble and dully gleaming gold, with hands upraised in blessing, welcomes us with his mystic greeting:

Welcome, O Enlightened Ones, for unto thee is granted the Reception.

(Once more Kyron, holds that sacred tome, "The Life of Buddha," and waits to read to us from those words of the ancient wisdom, as recorded by Asvagosha twenty centuries ago—Kyron speaks):

My good Friends and Companions, two thousand years ago this ancient record tells us that Buddha was teaching the attainment of the Psychic Reception by what he spoke of as "THE ONE TRUE WAY," and in these words he referred to the powers of focused mental vision, and the way of the living breath. In the words I shall read Buddha is warning against the way of "the foolish masters"—both those practicing austerities (selfpunishment and those who live to gratify their senses, and he shows how both greatly err. Listen. "Neither of these," he (Buddha) said, has found the way of highest wisdom...The emaciated devotee by suffering produces in himself confused and sickly thoughts, (negatives), not conducive even to worldly knowledge, much less to triumph over senses!

For he who tries to light a lamp (filled) with water, will not succeed in scattering the darkness, and so the man who tries with worn-out body to trim the lamp of wisdom shall not succeed, nor yet destroy his ignorance or folly...

"But to indulge in (sensual) pleasure is opposed to right; this is the fool's barrier against wisdom's fight. The sensualist cannot comprehend the Sutras (sacred wisdom)...

"I, then,. reject both these extremes; my heart keeps in the middle way. All sorrow at an end and finished, I rest in peace, all error put away; my true (mental) sight greater than the glory of the sun, my equal and unvarying wisdom, vehicles of insight—right words as it were a dwelling place—wandering through the pleasant groves of right conduct, making a right life my recreation, walking along the right road (THE PATHWAY) of proper means, my city of refuge in right recollection (mental imaging), and my sleeping couch right (silent) MEDITATION; these are the eight even and level roads by which to avoid the sorrows of birth and. death."

Gently laying the ancient book upon the Sacred Triangle Kyron, the wise, quietly says:

I have read briefly My Good Friends and Disciples, from those words of Buddha in which he, another of the Masters in White, the unforgotten teacher of the ancient days, commends to us the mystic PATHWAY to attainment through focused mental vision, in The Silence of meditation, and wherein in beautiful imagery he indicates to us the "eight roads" by which to escape sorrows, frustrations and failures.

COMPLETE AND JOYOUS LIFE

Happiness—by which I mean a complete and joyous life—is without doubt the great quest, the supreme goal of every man, an every woman in the world, whether consciously or unconsciously. And this happiness will be the reward of your courageous efforts to possess the one thing—that Heart's Desire—which means the most to you.

To attain to the great wants of life, Health, Happiness, Love and Abundance, you must center, and you must focus your mental vision, your spiritual and physical attention and activity upon each of these great objectives.

And this process My Good Friends, is very simple indeed and very easy to understand. There is nothing mysterious at all about it. The first step, as have explained to you before, toward the triumphant self toward the complete and joyous life, is self-belief, self-confidence, which after all is self-determination for it is your determination, your unwavering will-power which focuses your mental vision and your energies upon your goal. It was good old Dr. Tilley who once said this same thing in these words: "Every man carries within himself to a great extent his own destiny, undaunted will, unflinching energy, ever and everywhere make their mark and bring success."

Thomas Buxton wrote even more pointedly: "The longer I live the more I am certain that the great difference between men, between the great and insignificant, IS ENERGY, INVINCIBLE DETERMINATION, an honest purpose once fit, and then death or victory. The quality will do anything in the world; and no talents, no circumstances, will make a two-legged creature a man without it."

"To endure as seeing invisible Divinity is to become one-pointed—"Only the one-pointed succeed,' said the old Buddhist priests."

So we see that the complete and joyous life results from the focused (one-pointed) mental vision, together with energy directed toward that desired goal by "invincible determination."

GOOD FORTUNE IS CREATED IN THE MENTAL WORLD

When you constantly and intently focus your thoughts upon good fortune, riches, abundance, healing, or any other objective you create that objective thing in your mental (your four-dimensional world)realm. Now the more focused thought you add to this mental image (mind-picture) the clearer and the stronger that subjective picture becomes.

Soon you will find that you have reached the stage where even if you wanted to, you cannot will, successfully NOT to think about this chosen good thing; because even to will DENIAL of its existence brings its vision into focus in your mind instantly. Your Heart's desire thrives, prospers and grows into reality according to the extent to which you give to it your focused attention.

Here Kyron pauses, for the disciple, Heuroch, has silently signalled—his wish to ask a question—Kyron nods assent and Heuroch speaks):

"Good Kyron, permit me to ask this—how can I overcome or erase.unworthy desires, or doubts, or fears— fears of failing—all those ugly discords which are in my mind sometimes, for methinks they will cheat me of the good things I do deeply desire?"

There is but one way, my dear Heuroch, to destroy all these noxious discords, doubts or fears, and that way is very, very simple—for these evil things are subject to the same mental Law which I have just told you governs the good desires and the good goals in your mind; they thrive and grow strong to the exact extent that you give them conscious attention, which, after all is only another phase for focused thought.

Each of these evil discords will disappear when you stop giving it thought-nourishment! When you fear a thing, good friend Heuroch, you keep its image before your mind's eye, and the accompanying emotion (fear) nourishes it.

EMOTIONS ADD CREATIVE ENERGY TO MENTAL PICTURES

Whether the image (picture) you hold in your mind is good or bad, constructive or destructive, abundance or lack, whatever emotion is aroused by this image, joyous expectation, happiness or abounding faith, fear, anger, mental misery or discordant doubt, that emotion charges the mental image with energy and power. And this energizes myriads of thought-calls within the conscious, the Noetic, and the Subliminal departments of Mind and directs is these invisible powers to attract that pictured thing into your life.

When, through focused mental vision (thoughts) and a powerful DESIRE you tune your inner self completely to one "frequency" of thought-vibrations, this, of course, automatically cuts you off from others. Just the same as when you turn the dial of your radio set to "tune in" a certain program broadcast by one certain station you eliminate ("cut-off ") the reception of all other programs, for they are broadcasted over different rates of vibration ('frequencies"). So naturally the best way to escape undesirable mental influences, emotions and pictures is NOT TO FIGHT THEM—which would in reality only "tune in" your mind to their "frequencies" or rates of thought-vibration-but instead to constantly "tuned-in" by the thought to your higher, happier Heart's Desire!

FOCUSED MENTAL VISION—THE "FOCALIZER"

Now, I am going to explain to you what I am pleased to call "the Focalizer", which is a simple but tremendously important device to enable each one of you to attain focused mental vision by means of certain exercises, exercises to be followed in private, of course.

Permit me to assure you that these simple exercises will not only develop focused mental vision, but will train the muscles of your eyes to absolute control, and in due time will impart to your eyes that look of magnetic power that speaks of quiet mastery. Further, if your eyes are somewhat impaired and you wear glasses, these exercises should only strengthen your eyes, and perhaps later the glasses may even be dispensed with.

Now to prepare your "Focalizer," which you will find a very simple matter. Procure a piece of white cardboard, or a piece of heavy white paper, about 8 or 10 inches square, perhaps you will find the larger size better. Now with a sharp lead pencil draw a faint line with a ruler or straight-edge from the upper right hand corner to the lower left hand corner, and another faint line from the upper left hand corner to the lower right hand corner. Thus you have two diagonal lines which cross at the exact center of your card-board or paper.

Now place a 25 cent piece as nearly as possible over this central point and draw its outline there with your pencil. Then you can either fill this outline with black ink, or you can make a round disc with black paper the exact size of the 25 cent piece (by again outlining same) and pass this black disc neatly over the center of your paper. Next erase the faint diagonal lines you have drawn to find the center, and your "Focalizer" is complete... (Note: you will find black parts in many newspaper or magazine advertisements).

EXERCISE IN FOCUSING MENTAL AND PHYSICAL VISION

When you are ready for your first work with the "Focalizer", and being alone in The Silence, (during your regular period of concentration), pin your Focalizer on a blank space on the wall where the light will fall or shine upon it fully, making sure that the center black circle is precisely level with your eyes when you are seated.

Now, seat yourself in an ordinary straight backed chair in about the middle of the room, exactly in front of and facing the Focalizer. Sitting quietly relaxed, hands-palms down upon your knees, each foot flat on the floor(not crossed), fix your eyes upon the black spot, but without straining. You should be now quite relaxed, with your vision very clear, so without blinking just quietly look at the black disc for one minute, then just look away and rest your eyes for a couple of minutes.

Don't become alarmed or worry if the first few times the black spot becomes blurred to you, and should your eyes fill with tears, just let the tears run from the outside corners of your eyes by tilting your head to one side, but try not to lose sight of the black spot until the minute is up.

You are to repeat this one minute, period of gazing at the black spot in the center of your Focalizer four times, then gently wash your eyes in cold water, softly stroking the closed kids toward the nose.

For the second part of this "exercise, place your chair about three feet to the right of your first position, which was you remember, directly in front of the Focalizer. Now sit down directly facing the wall upon which your Focalizer is pinned, and without turning your head quietly gaze at the central black circle four times, each period being for one minute, resting your eyes for one or two minutes between each focusing period.

Next put your chair three feet to the left of your first position, which was directly, in front of the Focalizer. Now repeat the four one minute exercises in just the same way you did when you were seated three feet to the right of the centralized Focalizer, resting your eyes between each one minute period just as before, and then wash the eyes in cold water as directed before.

INNER VISION AND MAGNETIC POWER
CONCENTRATED

Repeat this focalizing exercise at least once daily for five days, and then continue the exercise each, time you enter your 15 minute period of quiet meditation in The Silence just as 'described, except that after the first five days you will increase each period of fixed or focused gaze of the black inner spot by one minute. , Follow, the directions faithfully, and in due time you will be able to hold your penetrating' gaze upon the small black, disc for the entire 15 minutes. (Do not follow the exercises for more than 15 minutes).

Before long, as you follow these exercises faithfully, simple as they are, you will begin to notice some remarkable results. First, you will note that your field of vision is growing larger and larger in the world around you, as your gaze becomes steadier and steadier, and focused as never before.

I want you each one to realize something of the tremendous importance of these really simple exercises with the Focalizer, because they not only give you a new and strong magnetic power in your trained physical eyes, but by the same exercises you are training your mind to concentrate your inner mental vision. We leave the Focalizer with you now but I shall return to this same simple device with some startling developments in our next lesson.

THE LIVING BREATH—NEW LIFE FOR YOU

Again and again in these lessons, I have taught each one of you that the secret which you seek—the secret of Power, the secret of Success, the secret.of Abundance and Leadership—that secret is WITHIN YOU YOURSELF. That secret is simply mental and magnetic ENERGY, which men and women everywhere sense in its possessor, and which they instinctively obey.

This unlimited energy is latent (sleeping) in every normal, healthy man and woman, and The Great Work of These teachings is to arouse and to help you each one to focus and direct this limitless Power to attain the greater life and happiness which you desire.

Knowing what each of you know about modern radio, we can realize that the leaders of men everywhere, both the great and the small, have radiated (and do radiate) this invisible mental power to those whom they desire to influence or control. We all know the literal truth of these teachings , that a strong, focused, visual thought, held in a developed mind will transmute itself into some direct action (or reaction) by those who have received this thought more or less directly from the thinker. How many times have you yourself been thinking about some certain thing, only to have this subject of your thoughts spoken of by someone present? That "someone" was simply mentally attuned to you.

Now this, and many other possible illustrations, prove that we (generally unconsciously) use some finer force which can be broadcast, and which can, be received by the minds of other men and women. We teach that this force, is an intelligent energy and that usually this energy is conveyed by and acts through the nerves. However, in cases of great emergency, or when the developed WILL is focused in its power, this same invisible intelligent force is often radiated from the physical body (remember the "aura") just as waves of energy are projected from a central broadcasting station.

UPANISHADS PICTURE LIVING SPIRIT IN BREATH

Here I want to repeat to you a few lines from a passage from The Upanishads—written 600 B.C. in Sanskrit—a very brief extract from a passage of this Brahmanic scriptures which I read to you before:

"Prana, or breath, is Brahman, (which means the living spirit, the last cause of everything), thus says Kaushitaki. Of this Prana, which is Brahman, the MIND is the messenger, speech the housekeeper, the eye the guard, the ear the informant. He who knows MIND as the messenger of Prana, which is rahman, becomes possessed of the messenger..."

So you see that almost two thousand six hundred years ago those Masters of the Ancient Wisdom were teaching how to attain to a vastly intensified life through this same limitless energy which they symbolized as BREATH—"Prana"—or LIVING SPIRIT, which they pictured as "Brahman" (The Divine Power) of which, they tell us, (MIND is the messenger)."

And there has been bequeathed to us, from that same dim, distant and almost forgotten past; from those ancient Elder Brothers and Masters of The Way, certain methods by which we can today begin to arouse, to control, and to direct this living Spirit-Prana-Force—this 'intelligent energy' which can transform both body and mind from weakness and even inferiority into strength and dominance.

And these certain methods which I shall give to you very simply are not difficult or complicated, and will take only a few minutes every day. Already you have each been given the cosmic urge to hasten your development and advancement, or you would not be following these intensely practical and advanced lessons in the Secret Wisdom of our Great Work.

But in order to awaken, develop and control this force effectively, there are a few necessary conditions. Your body must not be in a weakened condition, and you should have no organic or mental derangement—you should not be hysterical, impatient, or unable to control your mind in the ordinary affairs of life—in other words, you should be just a normal man or woman.

TAUGHT BY MYSTERY SCHOOLS OF EGYPT AND CHALDEA

So far as we can trace them these simple but secret methods of arousing and controlling this mysterious but

potent focusing force of the entire mental and nervous system were first taught in the ANCIENT MYSTERY SCHOOLS of Egypt and Chaldea. These ancient Masters taught that the most dynamic force of life is breath—not the mere mechanical act of breathing, but they mean that VITAL ENERGY which vibrates in the proper, scientific breathing which they impart to their disciples—their initiates.

From your study of physiology in your school days you will recollect that you learned that the vitality, the health, and the very life and longevity of all the cells and tissues of your body depend upon the circulation of the blood and lymph, and that these circulations, together with the heart action itself,—each of these depends equally upon breathing. Only by combustion in the lungs during the process of breathing are the black and white corpuscles, and in this breathing-process—when correctly practiced—is generated powerful currents of human electricity, abounding in health and magnetic force. For thus, according to the ancient teachings, we attract to ourselves currents of the universal energy which vibrates everywhere around us.

DYNAMIC PERSONAL MAGNETISM CAN BE YOURS

In our next lesson I shall impart to you quite fully and in quite simple words these marvelous exercises which, if you will follow them faithfully, will prove the truth of these ancient teachings, for if you follow the simple instructions implicitly, in just a few days you will begin to see a wonderful change in yourself. You will feel alert and alive in every part of your being, and, too, you will know for yourself that you are acquiring a renewed, a dynamic personal magnetism.

These same simple exercises which I will impart to you are known as "Prana-Yama," or literally translated, Controlled Breath, and over a period of years these carefully guarded secrets of the ancient Masters have proved their amazing value and transforming power in the lives of many thousands of people in this country, and thousands more are faithfully following these power-giving instructions today.

This hidden energy, of which I have spoken so often in this and in other lessons is already within your body and within your nervous system, in almost unbelievable amounts, and only awaits your awakening command and your direction to work its wonders IN YOUR LIFE.

LESSON NO. 12
THROUGH PRANA YAMA TO THE GREATER LIFE

Sitting once more in that symbolic King's Chamber, hidden in the midst of our imaged Pyramid Temple. Amid the peculiar glow that floods down from an unseen source, again the wait for the unfolding of another and still deeper lesson in that ancient wisdom which awaits only our Psychic Reception to endow us each one with renewed power and the greater life.

With hands now upraised in his customary blessing, Kyron, the Wise, standing before the mystic altar of marble and gold, now greets us with the" words of the ancient ritual:

Welcome, O Enlightened Ones, for unto thee is granted the Reception.

At this time I will read to you, as an introduction to our present lesson teaching the Pathway to still greater life, a few brief extracts from a very ancient ritualistic prayer. This prayer I will read from the Zend-Avesta, which is the sacred book of the Parsis, which represents the religion of Zorostrianism. This religion reigned over Persia until the overthrow of the Sassanian dynasty about 642 A.D. Today the Parisi are the ruins of a people, and their sacred books tell of a religion forgotten now, but of a past splendor, which is reflected in reflex in The Gospels, the Talmud and the Zuran (Koran).

This prayer is dedicated "to the bountiful immortals" and here are some striking passages from this ancient ritual, the ritual of a people who worshiped God under the symbol of LIGHT—

"I would worship these with my sacrifice...and this One especially I would approach with my praise, Ahura Mazda (God of Light). He is thus hymned in our praise songs. Yea, we worship in our sacrifice that Deity and Lord, who is Ahura Mazda, the Creator, the gracious helper, the maker of all good things.

"And I would declare forth those (institutions—laws) of the Ahura Mazda, those of the Good (God) Mind...and the good and pious prayer for blessing against unbelieving (doubting) words.

"And these we would declare in order that...we may be as prophets...holy men who think good thoughts, and speak good words, and do good deeds...That he (Ahura Mazda) may approach us with the Good (God) Mind, and THAT OUR SOULS MAY ADVANCE;—Yea, 'how may my soul advance in good? let it thus advance.

Closing the ancient Zend-Avesta, Kyron, the Wise now lays the book upon the altar, and says: I have read a few passages from this very old prayer from the Zend-Avesta, My Good Friends and Fellow Initiates, because some twenty-five centuries ago these Parsis worshiped God as LIGHT—and if you will turn to the New Testament scriptures, in John 8:12 you will find these significant words: "Then spake Jesus again unto them, saying, I am the Light of the World: he that followeth me shall not walk in darkness, but shall have THE LIGHT OF LIFE."

THE MORE ABUNDANT LIFE

In all the great root religions God is Symbolized throughout the ages as both Light and as Life.

"I am come," said the Christ (John 10:10), "that they might have LIFE, and that they might have it (Life) more ABUNDANTLY."

At this time Good Friends and Companions, we shall advance toward the greater life, the more ABUNDANT LIFE, following the ancient pathway of Prana Yama (controlled-breath-energy) and each one of you who follows this Pathway faithfully will find it is the Pathway of rejuvenation (restored youth) for you. You who begin to feel the weight of your years, and you younger folk who would retain your springtime powers and who would add to these powers an energy that is truly amazing, each of you will find that this Pathway of Prana Yama leads straight to the true "fountain of youth."

With the awakening and the control of the new and startling energy, you will find that Life becomes vastly intensified. This strange energy is so great you will find that you are able to do twice your usual amount of work practically without fatigue, and you will experience a wonderful feeling of lightness in your body, a feeling often as though your body had no weight.

Just imagine for a moment how much you could accomplish if your powers are multiplied ten fold or even a hundred fold! And that is exactly what this time proven method will do for you, if you will only practice it regularly and faithfully.

CONCENTRATION (FOCUSED THOUGHT) COMES FIRST

Concentration—the power to focus your thoughts—is our first step in developing this energy. Again and again in these lessons I have stressed the supreme importance of concentration—the "one-pointed" mind, and in your last lesson you will remember I very carefully explained to you the construction and the use of the "Focalizer," which you will find to be a marvelous yet simple mechanical aid to your development of concentration, and which we shall use surprisingly in lessons to come.

WHY YOUR MIND WANDERS—CONTROLLING THOUGHT

If you have not used to the best advantage your many really wonderful natural gifts, it is largely because you have not learned HOW to control your mind—how to concentrate. That one among you who thinks he or she is the weakest of all, by actually concentrating upon any one great and single objective, will sooner or later reach that objective (goal) if it is humanly possible, while the strongest and most gifted men and women may fail to accomplish anything worth while by scattering their forces.

Let us face this question quite frankly and quite honestly, because it is of such supreme importance in the Prana Yama method of attaining to the MORE ABUNDANT LIFE, which I shall reveal to you a little later. Your mind wonders from your great, your real objectives in life because you are interested in too many other things—and most of these other things are really trivial. The degree of mental "one-pointed attention" (concentration) which you bestow upon any subject or any goal in life depends upon the degree of personal interest you have in that subject or goal. Yet by a conscious use of your WILL, power you can learn very easily to direct or focus your attention upon any subject, just as completely as though you were interested in nothing else on earth.

So, first, you can secure sustained attention upon any subject by your mind by stimulating and increasing your personal interest in that subject, and, second, by simply removing your personal interest in the things you find not worth thinking about.

Here is a simple but effective method of training your mind not to wander. Suppose you are concentrating upon a certain subject—you have laid out a road for your thoughts to follow—when you find your thoughts straying, your mind wandering from the road you have decided upon, just shut your eyes for a minute and mentally trace your line of thought back to the exact point where it strayed from your original direction. This way you will quickly discover the "how and the why and the where" of your mind-wandering, and the next time this happens you will almost instantly recognize this danger-point, and to stop your thought from leaving the "road" you have chosen for it.

DON'T HESITATE—PUT ON THE BRAKES

Until we train our minds, our thoughts tend to flit here and there aimlessly. This is true of everybody. When you catch your thoughts wandering, or when you find yourself "day-Dreaming", snap out of it, close your eyes a moment, and by sheer will-power bring your mind back to the objective YOU have chosen.

Your thoughts will be sure to wander again, for this is probably a habit by now, but the very instant you become aware that your thoughts are running away again, put on the brakes, and bring those thoughts back into the road to your goal again. If you have never done this before it will not be easy at first. But make up your mind that the next time those thoughts will stop right where they strayed before. The second time you will find it very much easier. Until you will gain almost complete control over your thoughts, for you see, you have established a new HABIT—and habit is powerful!

Suppose that you were in the midst of noises of all kinds, confusion all around you, and distractions on every side—could you concentrate your thoughts—could you do collected focused thinking? Yet I should like, each one of our initiates, and disciples to purposely drill himself or herself in focused thinking, amid just such noise and confusion. I want each of you to learn to be your own companion, and thus cultivate the ability to become to a great extent oblivious of your surroundings in developing your focused and collected thinking, and each one of you can develop this faculty by persistent self-training.

EXERCISES THAT DEVELOP THE FOCUSED MIND

To illustrate the mental powers of concentration which can be attained by persistent practice, Ellingwood tells us this in his "Engineering Marvels."

"Recognizing the value of inner concentration I have drilled myself to write important letters and make the most of my electro-mechanical designs in the midst of the roar and thundering noises of big machinery. Most of my earlier successful inventions originated in this way. Later I conversed with some other person and attended to my correspondence. These gymnastics of the will, or as some may call it, concentration drills, enabled me to talk aloud and at the same time write an article for a trade journal."

To perform such feats as the above, we must develop almost perfect mental focus by becoming as it were deaf and blind to our surroundings, for our great aim is to be able to withdraw our attention from everything that does not serve our immediate purposes. Here are a few very simple drills which will wonderfully aid you to awaken and control this marvelous focusing power of your mind which has simply been dormant (sleep-ing)within you.

(1) True concentration results from your close and vivid attention to the object or the subject of your centered thoughts. Take some simple object—no matter how uninteresting it may seem to you—and try mentally to get thoroughly acquainted

with it. Very well, let us say you have chosen your watch, or fountain pen, or what not, it makes no difference just what it is that you choose. Fasten your attention by purposely willing to do so, upon this one simple (?) object; don't let your thoughts wander; focus them upon this one object only. Observe this object from every angle, study it carefully for ten minutes. Ask yourself questions mentally about it; what is its shape? its size? its value? its origin? its actual-purpose? its material? its color? its relation to other objects? in brief, ANALYZE this object thoroughly, together with its every meaning to you.

.(2) Here is a simple drill for gaining muscle control-just stand still, motionless, for as long as you can without strain. Relax every muscle, and do not move at all, even a fraction of an inch. Repeat this simple drill every day, trying to increase the motionless period each time until you can hold this position for ten minutes.

.(3) Try to think at will—your WELL—upon one certain subject, or some certain objective of your own. Allow me to suggest that you select a convenient time tomorrow for this test, and that you attempt to "concentrate" on the word "determination," the power to decide things for yourself. The ability to WILL every action of yours. But I am quite certain that at first you will find your will to concentrate quite helpless.

Though you will find that it is extremely hard to think upon that one word—determination—for even a single minute, don't be discouraged, this is only the beginning, and this should only prove to you how much you need this drill. Now try a calm impersonal relaxed meditation upon this word, and withdraw your attention from every other thought. Of course, the first days your attention will waver, and your attention will wander and your WILL may even try to "balk," but keep right on trying and you will acquire this thought-control, and with it a new and wonderful self—confidence and reserve energy.

Once you are master of two minutes of concentration (focused thinking), increase this period to as many more minutes as possible, even ten or fifteen. Of course, these same simple drills can be applied to any other word, subjects or objects which may mean the most to you and your Great Desires In Life.

FOCUSED MIND PICTURES DEVELOP POWER OF PRANA YAMA

Your faithful daily practice in concentration (focused thinking) in due time you will also find that you have gained the ability to make your mind almost perfectly blank by not allowing any thought or sensation to enter your consciousness. Also, through your constant practice, you have acquired the power to focus your thoughts upon a desired thing or a chosen object or subject for five or ten minutes.

When you have reached this degree of mental control, and not until then, you are ready to develop the power of Prana Yama through focused mind pictures.

While it is true that each of the exercises I shall impart to you in the ages-old science of The Controlled Breath—Prana Yama—is quite simple, each must be followed implicitly and faithfully, for your reward is both certain and abundant. Now if you have practiced until you can hold your mind focused on one thought or one mind picture, you are ready to begin your first exercise in what we shall call for the present "RHYTHMIC breathing."

Open your window to insure fresh air, and sit perfectly erect with the backbone really straight. Now this exercise is very simple indeed, but it is tremendously effective. Just practice breathing rythmatically, INHALING through the nose while you mentally (and slowly) count eight; now hold the breath without strain while you mentally count four, then EXHALE the breath slowly while you mentally count eight.

Isn't that simple—and easy? Now each time continue this exercise for a few minutes and soon you will establish the rhythm perfectly. Repeat this simple exercise every day, and preferably several tunes a day, (if possible), for seven days.

Then following this week's exercise, taking your thoughts away from everything else as much as possible, sitting erect as before, with your window open, follow the same routine of RHYTHMIC breathing, except that you place the forefinger on the right nostril, closing it, and inhale through the left nostril while you count eight, (mentally), hold the breath just as before while you count four, and then, exhale (breathe out) through the right nostril, which you release for that purpose. Now, reverse this process, closing the left nostril, with the forefinger, inhaling through the right nostril, etc. with the same counts as before. Continue this latter exercise three times a day for ten days, always being careful to keep your breathing slow and regular.

After a few days of this last exercise you will begin to feel a new and vibrant energy throughout your body, very soon you will notice that your nerve-reactions are gaining speed, and that a new force seems to radiate from you.

"SENDING" BREATH-ENERGY TO THE NERVE CENTERS

After faithfully following these two periods of the different exercises for the time I have specified, you are prepared .for the following more advanced routine, which combines the RHYTHMIC breath with focused mind-pictures (visualization), or Prana Yama.

In these more advanced exercises, you will "send" the Breath—(Spirit)—Energy to the visualized (mentally pictured) nerve centers of your entire body, and remember, with this invisible Breath—(Spirit)—Energy you are sending healing, power, and rejuvenation (renewed youth).

Here is your simple, secret method of directing this transforming current of healing and youthifying energy to the different nerve centers of your body. Seated as before, comfortably erect, with plenty of fresh air in your room, withdraw your mind from everything else and establish the regular breathing rhythm as in your first exercise, inhaling with both nostrils during eight counts, holding your breath for four counts, and exhaling for eight counts.

After two or three minutes of this, pause, and fix your thoughts upon the lower part of your spinal column ("Back-bone") and picture a great nerve center as located there, which is actually true. Try to visualize this central nerve station (this nerve plexus) and picture it as a center, like a disc, radiant with light and energy, and vibrating with NEW LIFE.

Focus your thoughts upon this nerve center, just shut everything else out of your mind, and picture (imagine,) your thought as going down that long flight of many steps which is your spine, go down steadily from step to step (slowly now) until your mind reaches that lowest spinal nerve center.

AWAKENING GREAT NERVE CENTERS AT BASE OF SPINE

Now, when your thought has reached this great nerve center at the base of your spine, just stop, and mentally try to "feel" with this focal plexus, this nerve center, or, in other words, picture (visualize) it as becoming in-tensely active and focus your "mind's eye" upon it until you can actually "imagine" that you really do feel its renewed energy vibrating there. Now you can readily see why I have given you various drills in "concentration," and ' why we have tried to develop your imaging (picturing) power to a high degree.

Practice this exercise just as I have given it to you herein every day for ten or fifteen minutes at a time for ten days. After this ten day period of preparation you are ready for the second and more advanced part of this marvelous exercise.

In this, you again establish your RHYTHMIC breathing; again through the right nostril first (closing the left nostril); inhale while you could eight, as before, but now while you are doing this I want you to picture your breath as a narrow ray of light-like a focused beam of white light—which you are drawing through this right nostril and which you are directing downward through the inner spinal canal into that great nerve center at the base of your spine where it is awakening the life-giving, healing, renewing energy which is stored there.

After you have thus sent the breath (spirit) energy by your mind, see (visualize) it being drawn up again through your spinal canal, and being sent out through the other (left) nostril as you exhale for eight counts, having held it the usual four counts.

Next as in your previous exercise, just reverse this process, inhale through the left nostril (closing the right, send the breath-energy-spirit, visualized as the ray of concentrated white light, down and into the lower spinal nerve center, then exhale through the right nostril, seeing just as vividly as possible the breath as light being drawn up through the spinal canal and passing invisibly into the air.

For two weeks at least, or longer, if you desire, practice this simple but marvelous routine once or twice a day, ten complete breaths to each, nostril, using first one and then the other.

At first sight these exercises may seem complicated to you but I assure you that if you will just follow my directions implicitly until this system of Prana-Power breathing becomes a habit, you will realize how very simple the whole process becomes to you.

Further, there is nothing illusive or "mystical" about these exercises, for their results are intensely practical, and you can prove these results in your own life. For once you succeed in awakening this boundless nerve-energy in that center at the base of your spine you have a marvelously powerful "electric storage battery" at your command.

And this "battery," when its energy is at your command, will furnish more Power, more Abundant Life, more Healing than you ever dreamed could exist in your body. For when you awaken this energy you will find it difficult to use all the power that is at your call. Once you "feel" this energy in that basal nerve center, it is yours to command.

Lesson No. 13 BUILDING DYNAMIC LIFE BY BREATH, FOOD AND GLAND CONTROL

Again we are transported upon the wings of, thought to our accustomed place amid the white robed Initiates, and together with them we are seated within our symbolic Pyramid Temple. We wait quietly within the golden glow that suffuses all, awaiting still another incomparable lesson from the words of Kyron, the Wise.

Standing now before the mystic altar of glowing gold and gleaming marble, Kyron raises his hands in the blessing given in our most ancient ritual, and softly speaks the words which have come down to us through the ages:

WELCOME, O ENLIGHTENED ONES, FOR UNTO THEE IS GRANTED THE RECEPTION

(Kyron, ;the wise, continues):

My Faithful Companions, once again l have chosen to open our lesson by reading to you a few sentences from the words of Buddha, as written twenty-five centuries ago by that great and wise patriarch, Asavaghosha, as recorded in this ancient book from our archives.

Let us not listen idly to these words, for, as a religious teacher, Buddha is the most revered and powerful name in the history of Asia. Many, many , ages ago the religion taught by Buddha traveled from the valley of the Indus to the valley of the Ganges, and from Ceylon to the Himalayas; from there this teaching traversed China, and in each of these lands it has remained permanent.

We are struck by the fact that the religion taught by Buddha so greatly resembles pure Christianity in that both combine mysticism with asceticism, both seek to combine practical rules of the highest conduct with the mystery of the transcendental.

That Buddha, Gautama, was one of the Masters in White is shown by these words of the patriarch, from this ancient book:'

"Thus did he complete the end of self...Thus, he had done what he would have men do; he first had found the way of perfect knowledge. He finished thus the first great lesson...light burst upon him; perfectly silent and at rest, he reached the last exhaustless source of truth; lustrous with all wisdom..."

And these are the inspired words of Buddha himself that I wish to read to you, Good Friends—"The way superlative of life immortal I offer now from accumulated deeds comes birth, and as the result of deeds comes recompense. Knowing then that deeds bring fruit, how diligent should you be to rid yourself of worldly deeds! how careful in the world your deeds should only be good and gentle. Fondly affected by relationship or firmly bound by mutual ties of love, at end of life the soul goes forth alone—then, only our good deeds befriend us.

Infinitely quiet where the wise man finds his abode (In The Silence); no need of arms or weapons there.

"Subdued the power of covetous desire and angry thoughts and ignorance, there's nothing left in the wide world to conquer! Knowing what sorrow is, he cast away the cause of sorrow...he casts off fear and escapes the evil ways (results) of birth."

"THE WAY SUPERLATIVE"—BUILDING DYNAMIC LIFE

In our last lesson (continues Kyron, the Wise, as he again reverently lays this sacred book of the East upon the candle lighted triangle of the altar), We learned from the ancient wisdom that breath—and especially that controlled breathing taught in the ages-old system called Prana Yama—is the most dynamic force of life. The ancient masters laid the stress upon this most effective method of building a dynamic, forceful, healthful life.

But, as I have pointed out to you, Prana (breath) means something infinitely deeper and greater than mere breath, for it really means the vital spirit-energy represented as Life in the breath.

According to our ancient archives, the priests Buddha, the priests of Shinga, the more ancient Pedandas of the East Indies, down to the Hindoo Yogis of today—all taught this simple but marvelously effective system of Prana Yama, or the controlled RHYTHMIC breath.

Accumulating life force, or building a reserve of magnetic power, simply means building a reserve of nervous energy, for your nervous system furnishes the governing energy of your body. To a great extent, the strength of your muscles and of your physical organs depends upon the health of the nerves which act upon them and which control them.

I need hardly point out to you that today as never before, we are living in an era`of great nervous strain. This "mile-a-minute" life we are now living makes unusual demands and unnatural strains upon our nervous system. Reckless expending of your nerve force has the same weakening effect upon your body as would a constant draining of your blood.

BREATHE DEEPLY—RHYTHMICALLY- REBUILD NERVE FORCE

Breath represents the vital fire—life of your entire body, and your breath is controlled by what is called the "gastric plexus" and this plexus also embraces the solar plexus, and this is probably the greatest of all the nerve centers of your body. Your breathing must be deep, RHYTHMIC, and controlled, so that you can secure and build up a constant supply of nerve force (or nervous energy) sufficient for every need of your body and of your brain. (It is understood that you should always breathe through the nose).

Perhaps it will surprise you to learn that the brain, in the work of its various functions, uses up one half of all the oxygen that is absorbed by your lungs, and yet this is true. And, as you probably. already know, oxygen is the great building of all human nerve force. Further, each one of your nerve cells consumes four times as much oxygen as any one muscle cell.

So in your work of building up dynamic nerve force and in acquiring supreme brain power deep, controlled and RHYTHMIC breathing is the great factor.

Naturally, the deeper you breath, the MORE OXYGEN you inhale, the clearer and the more active your brain, the more healthful and developed your entire nervous system, and the more effective your will-power. While, of course, exercise IS necessary in order to develop and to maintain strength and must not be neglected, still three to ten minutes of deep, controlled Prana Yama breathing will do more to strengthen the body and the nerves than a whole hour of tireless exercises.

And now I shall give to you the deeper and more advanced routines (methods) of the Prana Yama system, in a series of simple exercises which will cover a period of five weeks, and after that, I trust that you will continue them throughout your lifetime. It is understood that you are not to strain or become tense during any of the Prana Yama exercises which I impart to you herein. Instead I want you to always be sure that you are comfortable and entirely RELAXED. The best position is lying down upon your back, with a pillow raising your head a little higher than your body.

INDRAWING NEW LIFE FORCE AND MAGNETIC POWER

Prana Exercise—First Week:

Lie down comfortably upon your back with the outer clothes removed, or at least loosened so that you can breath quite easily. Now inhale, draw in a long deep breath, while you count nine very slowly. As you do this your abdomen will gradually swell, and your diaphragm will go downward, as your lungs slowly fill with this long, deep inhalation.

Now hold your breath while you again count nine slowly, and then during the next count of nine very slowly and steadily exhale (breath out) every last part of this changed air which is now filled with the waste of your lungs. Thus following this method, one complete "Prana" breath cycle takes twenty-seven counts. This exercise is not quite so easy as it may seem from reading about it, but each time you repeat it this controlled breath will become easier and easier. But I would caution you never to hurry, and don't breathe oftener than I have indicated.

Repeat this exercise in controlled Prana Breathing for at least ten and not longer than twenty minutes at any one period during the first week, and take this exercise at least once each day.

In the beginning, it is very likely that you may tire, or even feel a little dizzy. If either of these symptoms occur, don't stop or give up, because these feeling only show that your system needs more oxygen. Almost immediately after beginning this exercise you will notice that your life forces seem renewed and you can sense a renewed magnetic power, and soon every unpleasant little symptom will vanish.

I want you each to learn "by heart"this mystic triangle affirmation of the ancient Masters of Prana, and mentally repeat these words as you breathe—for thus you transform the "'words" from spirit into physical health. So repeat mentally: (While you inhale)—

In my breath I am drawing New Life Force and Magnetic Brain Energy.

(While holding the breath)

While I hold this breath I am drawing from it every particle of its spiritual-oxygen-power."

(While you exhale)—

"While I slowly send out all of this used and deadened air, I am purifying my lungs and my blood to hunger for still greater life."

And right here let me warn you that the WAY in which you EXHALE (breathe out) is indeed very important, for there is where many beginners in this system of Prana defeat themselves, because their great temptation is to hurry. In order to intensify its marvelous effects, you must control the exhaling of your breath to the slow count of nine, for this control and this slowing down of the exhaling multiplies the amount of magnetic life force you will gain from it many, many times.

CONTINUING THROUGH PRANA TO PSYCHIC POWER,

Prana Exercise—Second Week:

Your second week's Prana Breath exercise should continue for twenty minutes each day. The method for your second week's routine is this: inhale (breathe in) while you count eleven, but now you press the right nostril closed with the first finger of your right hand, and you inhale the breath ONLY through your left nostril. Now when you have inhaled ten breaths through this nostril, holding each breath while you again count eleven, and exhaling it while you count eleven, then after these ten complete breaths change nostrils, again inhaling, exhaling and holding each breath while you count eleven, only this time through the right nostril, keeping the left closed. This way, you see, the complete cycle of one breath extends through 33 counts.

If you have difficulty with this exercise, give yourself ten minutes longer for practice, and continue faithfully for the entire week, and you will perform the exercise quite perfectly.

Prana Exercise—Third Week:

Your Prana Exercise for the third week is similar to that of the second week, except that now we are going to increase your time of inhaling to fourteen counts, then you will hold your breath while you count ten, and exhale while you count fourteen. After each ten complete breaths change nostrils as before, closing each one alternately. When you exhale, breathe out slowly and control the rhythm firmly. Again, twenty minutes each day should be devoted to this exercise.

Master this exercise thoroughly, as this is a sure method of developing the keenest mind power and also renewing the cells of your body. It may seem strange, but still it is true that the degree of inflowing brain energy is almost entirely controlled by the WAY you breathe. So, cultivate the habit of breathing in certain rhythms all the time, mentally counting and timing your breathing to the counts—try this often when you are walking, and often at your daily work. It will transform you.

Prana Exercise—Fourth Week:

During the fourth week, count twenty while inhaling, count ten while holding your breath and count twenty while exhaling.

Change nostrils after each complete breath cycle, alternately closing one and then the other nostril. Again devote twenty minutes every day to this exercise. By this time you are beginning to enjoy your reward, if you have faithfully followed these simple routines, for now this RHYTHMIC, period Prana Breathing is becoming a habit so that even while you are asleep this Prana breath will begin to assert its effect by vitally charging your mental physical organisms with new life and power.

Prana Exercise—Fifth Week:

After the fourth week of these simple Prana exercises, you will realize within yourself a surprising increase in your health, and an abounding increase in your mental and physical energy. If you have faithfully followed each simple exercise, you will now feel an inflowing dynamic life and strength such as you never dreamed possible for you before. Every.part of your body will seem renewed, and your eyes will sparkle with the magnetic light of mental mastery.

You see, simple though it is, prolonging the periods of in-breathing and out-breathing (in-haling and exhaling) each week, and somewhat decreasing the periods of holding the breath as you have progressed, have so greatly strengthened your abdomen and the lungs that now they are more than equal to the greatest tasks.

Never stop these exercises, just follow there throughout life, and you will not be alone in this-for everywhere in this country there are thousands of Initiates who never miss one day without having spent at least twenty minutes (and often a full half hour) in these simple Prana exercises of the controlled -breath—routines which are in reality LIFE-CELL-BREATHING.

DEVELOPED PRANA BREATH GENERATES POWERFUL PERSONAL AURA

In your former lessons, in a preceding course, I told you something about AURA, which is a field of magnetic influence extending from and surrounding the physical bodies of all the people you meet, to a greater or lesser degree.

Simply stated, in the life-spirit forces which vibrate in the act of breathing, there is generated in the human organism a magnetic "field" something like a fluidic, generally invisible out-going radiation, which is called the "aura:" Only to certain trained and super-sensitive eyes is this aura ever visible as what might be called light.

Every human being radiates this aura, in either strong or weak waves (generally rather weak) to a distance from the body ranging from two or three inches to several feet.

Coming into actual contact with this "field" of influence, this aura, in different persons you will always experience a re-action, often unconsciously, and this explains your likes and dislikes in your attitude to the people you meet, for in one the personal aura may be strongly magnetic and attractive, while another person's aura may be very obnoxious (repellent) to you. A very large number of people have such weak and negative auras that they are neutral, and make little or no impression upon you.

Now if you have become sensitive to these finer forces, which you doubtless have under our training, there will he times, perhaps often, when you can actually feel this fine magnetic force being drawn from you when you are in the presence of certain men and women. In such cases, let me warn you to move away to some distance from any person whom you feel drawing your magnetic forces from you, for such a person, whether you realize it or not, is in reality a sort of "vampire," feeding upon your accumulated energy.

In this connection I should like to point out to you that many invalids and sick persons have this peculiar ability to draw strength from those who have abundant energy and health, in fact these ailing persons are often like sponges when it comes to absorbing your own health-forces.

You must protect yourself against such persons. I want you to know that the left side of your whole body draws in this invisible, magnetic force, and that your right side sends it out; and so always be somewhat careful as to WHO is seated at (or next to) your right side.

THESE WONDROUS LIFE-POWERS ARE YOURS-KEEP THEM!

As you have followed them faithfully, the wonderful yet simple Prana breathing exercises which I have given you have created for you and stored up in your body a great reserve of these wondrous Life-Powers, so now I urge you to keep them, guard them, protect them from those who, like "vampires" would either knowingly or unconsciously rob you of them.

Bear in mind that these invisible life-forces not only leave your body through the pores of your skin, but also your hands send these powers forth in great and strong currents. So, unless you have the use of certain Healing Powers in mind, or unless you are using your hands to impress others, you will do well in the presence of others to clasp your hands together, or to lay one on top of the other, and also to keep your feet slightly touching. For these simple precautions close the magnetic circuit of your body, and retain and protect your magnetic life-currents.

FOCUSED VISION SEES AURA AND CENTERS THOUGHT FORCE

When you have attained to the focused vision you will be able to see this personal aura very often.

If you have faithfully performed your Prana breathing exercises, by now you should have accumulated a very strong and vibrant personal aura, forming a field of electro-magnetic influence which surrounds your body to a distance of three to four. feet on every side. In other words, your body should be like a great storage battery now filled to overflowing with energy.

Now, if this be true, if you will follow these simple directions very carefully you will be able to see this aura-energy emanating from your hands, for instance, at night. Light an ordinary white candle, and then extinguish all other lights in your room, being alone, of course.

Now place the candle on a table, some three feet behind your chair, and seat yourself comfortably in the chair. Have a square piece of black cloth (any kind of material will do) ready, and cover your lap with the black cloth.

Then rub the palms of your hands together for just a few minutes, not too hard. Next, hold your hands about two inches above the black cloth upon your lap, with the palms downward and the elbows lowered; with the tips of the second fingers of each hand touching one another, elbows outward and level with your hands.

Now spread your fingers apart, and slowly draw your hands away from each other without lowering or raising them. Then focus your eyes upon the space between your hands, just look steadily without straining your eyes, and strangely enough you will distinctly see the bluish-purple or often violet emanations of faint magnetic light (emanations of your magnetic aura) glowing from your hands!

I want each of you to realize that in the transmission of thought, mental vibrations do not leave the sender by way of the cranium—thoughts do not penetrate through the bones of the skull, but instead are transmitted in the breath and in the emanations of the personal aura.

LESSON No. 14 BUILDING DYNAMIC LIFE BY BREATH, FOOD AND GLAND CONTROL (CONTINUED—2ND SECTION)

Once more we are seated mentally in our accustomed place among our fellow initiates, all robed in white, deep within the mystic King's Chamber, within the depths of our symbolic Pyramid Temple. Yes, once again we are quietly awaiting a still more advanced lesson on the Psychic Reception from that Master-Teacher, Kyron, the Wise, whom we have received as one reincarnated from the hosts of the "Heaven-born."

Silently he stands a few moments before the mysterious altar, with its golden glow and its marble sheen, then Kyron raises his hands in the ancient gesture of blessing, and again softly speaks the words of greeting which have been bequeathed to us in our ancient ritual:

Welcome, O Enlightened Ones, for unto thee is granted the Reception.

My Faithful Friends and Disciples, once more I have selected to read to you in beginning our lesson a few sentences from one of the most ancient books included in the canon of the Buddhist scriptures, named The Dhammapada, or Path to Virtue, and I may say to you that a great many scholars agree in ascribing these utterances to Buddha himself, words that were recorded before our Elder Brother, Christ, The Nazarite Master, was born.

Because that is what all the world is seeking, I want at this time to read to you these ancient words of this great Master in White about Happiness. He says in part):

"We live happily indeed, not hating those who hate us! among men who hate us we dwell free from hatred!

"We live happily indeed, free from ailments (sickness) among the ailing! among men who are ailing (sick) let us dwell free from ailments!

""There is no fire like passion; there is no losing throw like hatred (the negative);...there is no happiness higher than rest.

"Health is the greatest of gifts, contentedness the best riches; trust (faith) is the best relationships, Nirvana the highest happiness.

"He who has tasted the sweetness of solitude and tranquility (The Silence), is free from fear and free from sin...

"He who walks in the company of fools suffers a long way...company with the wise is pleasure, like meeting with kinsfolk.

"Therefore, one ought to follow the wise, the intelligent, the learned...the elect; one ought to follow such a good and wise man (teacher), as the moon follows the path of the stars."

Closing the tome of the Buddhist philosophy, Kyron lays it reverently once again upon the triangle of the glowing altar and proceeds with our present lesson.

CENTERING YOUR THOUGHT-FORCE—POWER AFFIRMATIONS

By focused self-suggestion you can both develop wonderful will-power and actually transform your life. But .first you must understand this suggestive thought force, and then you must be able to direct and to control it. Self-suggestion is simply the photographing, we might say, of self-chosen ideals and goals directly upon the cells of your brain, both through your senses of sight and the sound of your own voice.

Auto-suggestion is simply a suggestion originating within the individual—within yourself. This may be either a suggestion from your conscious self to your subconscious self, or you can narrow the field to one idea by holding a chosen thought and reading and repeating constantly a short suggestion (affirmation) upon which you focus your mind, excluding all other thoughts.

Remember, each and every one of you CAN develop the power to choose and to control your thoughts, and that is just what these lessons are teaching you to do. Fortunately, every earnest effort that you make along these lines makes your task that much easier.

After all, life is simply a series of experiences and habits, and I want to impress upon you right now that every one of you has it in his or her power to determine, to choose just what that series of habits shall be. Because of your wonderful reflex nervous system, whenever you do a certain thing in a certain way, it is far easier to do the same thing in the same way the next time, and the next, and the next, until finally you are doing that thing with scarcely no effort—because you have established a habit.

As I have told you before, what you are is built by long continued habits of thought—good, fortune depends upon each himself or herself we create or choose the conditions which make the Heaven or the Hell in which we live.

THE GRAY MATTER OF YOUR BRAIN IS PLASTIC

Now, before you receive the further secret exercises for centering your tremendous thought-force, and before you receive the power-affirmations which will follow, I should like you to fully realize that the gray matter of your brain is actually plastic, and may be fashioned (formed) according to your will.

I mean exactly what I say when I state that each of us can mould our own brains (so to speak), so far as special mental functions and aptitudes are concerned. It is only necessary for us to have normal intellects to see the far-reaching advantage this gives us, and then to cultivate enough will-power to practice, practice, practice, guided by our lessons, and we cannot fail. For then not only does the will-stimulus organize the brain centers to perform these new functions but it will also project new (connecting) "association fibres" which will make the nerve centers work together marvelously.

According to the ancient wisdom which is our heritage from the Masters in White of our ageless fellowship we teach that the spiritual, mental and moral, together with the physical forces are real substances, and that all demonstrate eternal divine Law. For example, your thoughts are generated by mental activity, energy, and this forms the pictured words, phrases, and sentences in your mind. It is the work (energy) of cell fibre which produces them, nothing else than the transmutation of material substance into mental energy or force, and though rarefied and invisible, still a material substance.

And here WILL, determination, is the important thing. Without the conscious direction of your WILL, no collected, purposeful thought and no concentration is possible to you. A powerful WILL, such as you are developing as you follow this WAY enforces its commands; whole all around you, you see weak wills overcome by foolish and fleeting desires.

or an event which you can recall by memory which images the proper words.

I have taken great pains to explain these matters in detail, so that you would clearly understand the truly great, though simple, exercises in "auto-suggestion," and the power-affirmations I shall give you in this new and advanced set of exercises. Because I want you to form absolutely clear concepts, you will repeat each of these power-affirmations aloud, as you see them before you.

Now that you realize fully, I hope, the utmost importance of the WILL, the determined mind, in this Great Work—transforming of life—always be careful to follow each exercise -in "dead-earnest," never approach one of these exercises with. that_ weakness of WILL which stamps itself as failure by saying "I'd like to...or I wish to...," because such words are never translated into vivid, effective action.

Instead, your resolve must be accompanied by immediate action—for that immediate ACTION is the great essential in training your WILL. Never let your resolve—your determination—be without ACTION, and take no action not sanctioned by your resolve.

FOCALIZER AND POWER AFFIRMATIONS REBUILD WILL

If you have mastered the previous lessons in our instruction, the following exercise will show amazing results in rebuilding your WILL-POWER, and will help you to be master of every situation. No matter how simple these routines may seem to you, follow them out to the letter, and in a comparatively short time they will aid you in developing a will powerful beyond your fondest dreams.

Your first step now, then is to carefully cut twelve pieces of white writing paper each about the size of four by five inches, then I want-you to write or print with very black ink or with a soft black lead pencil on each of these pieces of paper one of the following power-affirmations, which I have numbered. The purpose of this exercise (which follows) is to deeply impress each of these power suggestions upon your inner subconscious-ness-so deeply that you will never really forget them. Thus they will work consciously and also upon your subconscious mind, arousing your WILL to the power and the rulership which is its rightful heritage.

Here are the twelve Will-Power-Affirmations which you are to copy:
1.   1. I can have a dynamic Will-Power!
2.   2. I am determined to have unbreakable Will-Power!
3.   3. My New Will-Power makes me Master of myself!
4.   4. Because I so will it, nothing escapes my piercing vision!
5.   5. Nothing can make me nervous or afraid because my Will-Power protects me!
6.   6. Already my strong Will-Power has cast out all fear!
7.   7. No ordinary human power can resist my Will right now!

8.   8. I am already Success—so others obey my Will!
9.   9. Because my Will is Master, I can control myself and those around me!
10.   10. Because I am master of my own will, every word I speak is a command!
11.   11. My road to Success is right in front of me, and Because I WILL IT, everybody will help me along that road!
12.   12. Because I myself am the living Power of Will, I alone control my thoughts, my actions and my fortunes!

Now, having fastened the Focalizer upon the wall at the proper height, as I have previously instructed you, with a common pin in each upper corner of the white piece of paper, pin slip number one upon the Focalizer so that the upper edge of this slip of paper is just about two inches lower (below) than the black center spot of the Focalizer.

First remove all objects which would be in your line of vision, or anything else which might distract your attention, seat yourself comfortably in the middle of the room, opposite the Focalizer. Now, focus your eyes quietly upon the Focalizer for ONE MINUTE, then read out loud softly and slowly the words on the slip below the black center spot for one full minute.

Next, once again focus your glance upon that magic inner black spot for one minute, then once again read the power affirmation aloud. Now once more center your glance upon the inner (center) spot of the Focalizer for one minute, then read the power affirmation aloud for two minutes, and continue the exercise on from there by alternately as concentrating upon the center black spot for one minute and repeating (reading) the power-affirmation for two minutes until you have spent a total of about fifteen minutes on this exercise. Repeat this auto-affirmation exercise, if at all possible, twice each day for three-days—using the slips as numbered in succession, changing at each session. Thus you will use the first six in your first three days. Each time be careful to analyze the meaning of the affirmation as you repeat its words, and let that meaning sink into your mind. I want these thoughts to become second nature to you.

CONTINUE EXERCISE, ANALYZING EACH AFFIRMATION

Now, continue your exercise twice each day for three more days, in which you will use the following (last) six numbered slips in the same manner.

When you have finished this preliminary drill of six days I want you to take your first four slips for the next fifteen minute exercise, which you will take once each day, preferably in the evening. Pinning slip number one, center your glance on the Focalizer's center spot for one minute, then turn your attention to the words on the slip and repeat (read) them slowly for four minutes—then continue with slip number two, with one minute's concentration upon the Focal spot, and four minutes reading of the affirmation, and so on until you have used the four slips in your fifteen minute period. The next day, do the same with your second series of four slips, and the third day, use your last four numbered slips.

It is well to repeat this process with each of the numbers in succession, just as I have outlined it, with alternate one minute periods of centralizing upon the center black spot of your Focalizer followed by four minutes concentration upon its affirmation for a period of several weeks:

You will positively be amazed at the almost unbelievable personal Power that these seemingly simple exercises will bring to you, and soon you will begin to observe with surprise its almost uncanny effect upon your friends and associates. When this is true you are ready for still higher grades of power, which we shall impart to you later. But again, I must warn you to keep sacredly secret these studies, and all the experiments which we shall give you, together with every occult exercise. Even your most intimate friends had best know nothing about these potent developments of yours, not only because others might hinder and thwart your work, but because the uninitiated are afraid of any hidden things which they cannot understand. Protect yourself by silence.

FOOD-THE FUEL OF BRAIN POWER AND NERVE ENERGY

The food you eat is the fuel of your brain power and of your nerve energy—the quality of your mind itself depends upon what foods you furnish to establish that quality. If we lead animal lives and if we cherish animal desires and sensual lusts, we are forced to desire animal foods. If we destroy the desire for animal food, we must also exclude animal indulgences. The higher life is entirely a matter of personal choice.

Not only does the quality (and kind) of the food you eat decide the quality and the power of your mind, but it is just as true that the quality and the power of your mind largely controls your stomach, that marvelous laboratory where your food is prepared for your brain, your nervous system and your mind. Each is dependent upon the other. If, for instance, you eat food that you know is of the quality best suited to your needs, and you eat that food with a happy and a contented mind, that food through the processes of the stomach—will renew your brain, and so produce thought of a much finer quality. But sad the results when the wrong fuel (food) is forced upon this body of ours.

PROPER FOOD REBUILDS BLOOD, GLANDS AND NERVES

Proper food is vitally important to your body, as it is to your finely attuned nervous system and to your brain, wherein dwells the mind. You must, of course, take into your body nourishing foods and the correct foods if you wish to be healthful and abounding in vigor. Yet, it is true, that on the other hand, over-eating brings laziness and inability to work efficiently.

In all this the circulation and the purifying of the blood is most important, for these again depend upon proper sustenance—In this sustenance ,-enters in not only correct food,—but also pure air, liquids, light (sunshine), even weather (climatic) conditions play their part, and also the social conditions play their part, and also the social conditions play a most important part.

Also, in these lessons you will find still another tremendous secret—a secret you will find known only to our initiates—the method of rejuvenating (restoring youth) to your glands through the use of proper foods, which I shall explain to you in detail and in plain and simple words. Through a previous lesson on the brain, you are already somewhat familiar with the functions of the brain glands.

Other previous lessons in this course have given you a working knowledge of those other glands of the body, known as the Endocrine glands, some of which we may consider as "relay- stations" under the direction of the Pituitary Gland (a main "power station"), such as the tonsils, the Thyroid and the paraThyroid (located near the bronchial tubes), then we have the Thymus above the heart, the Adrenals above the kidneys, the female gonads or Ovaries located in the pelvis of women, also the male gonads, and Prostate Glands, and Interstituary Glands in the lower pelvis of men, to name but a few.

In every man and in every woman the glands are the great and basic factors of personality. Not only is the "personality-pattern" of every human being dependent upon the natural or the abnormal functioning of his glands, but even his peculiarities are almost entirely the product of his glandular activities.

HERE'S THE SECRET—GLANDS DEMAND CERTAIN FOODS

The great food secret of the ages is that the glands demand certain, select foods, upon which they thrive and become vital, and that other foods harm them beyond measure. The value to the glands of these certain foods depends upon the fact that in these foods there are certain vitamins, hormones, and enzymes. Now, as you know, some of the most important glands, such as the Thyroid, the Pituitary, the Gonads, and also the Adrenals hold within themselves a form of chemical energy (in rarefied substance) called the Hormone. Our studies of that chemical laboratory called the brain have taught us what this energy or substance IS.

Now, a word as to vitamins, of which you have doubt.less heard and reed much. Vitamins are the most elusive and refined of the food elements so much so that I shall refer to them as the "spiritual substance" of the foods you eat. A very small amount of the proper vitamins, rightly, assimilated can work wonders for and in your body, for they act like the electro-magnetic "substance" of the hormones in powerfully helping the chemical reactions with-in your body. Eventually both vitamins and hormones are transformed into human, spiritual substance through transmutation in the Brain organism.

CONCENTRATED FOOD (FLUID) SUBSTANCES FINALLY ENERGIZE THE PINEAL GLAND

After the food substances; have reached their most highly refined (and fluidic) form of mastication, digestion and assimilation, they are conveyed in fluid form, now highly concentrated, by the blood and the capillary vessels from the body to the brain, and here in the cerebellum and the cerebrum these fluid substances are transformed into highly charged human electro-magnetic fluids.

These fluids—which pulsate with the secret of life—are positive and negative—masculine and feminine.

Now, from both hemispheres in the brain these concentrated life-fluids are next transferred to the Pineal Gland—not directly, for there is no direct path open to this all-important ductless gland, but rather by absorption, via electro-magnetic induction, to the PINEAL GLAND. Here and once again these highly charged fluid-food-substances are re-elaborated by Alchemic vital processes.

This last process transmutes, these vital fluids into the most subtle life force, which we have named the "PNEU-MO-PSYCHIC."

To use this word represents the two-fold quality of Spirit or SPIRIT-SOUL, which is a conscious, duality of power, for from this is drawn the sperm or germ of both male and female sex potency, the most subtle spirit-force, life power, or potency known to mankind. This is living force the concentrated spirit of life itself—for when it descends from its throne in the human brain it has power to give, yes, to become life, when united to that of the opposite sex.

In our next lesson, we shall continue still more deeply into the mysteries of the Pineal Gland, and teach you how to control the Endocrine glands of your body.

LESSON No. 15 BUILDING DYNAMIC LIFE BY BREATH, FOOD AND GLAND CONTROL (CONTINUED - 3RD SECTION)

Transported once again upon the wings of imagination, we find ourselves now seated in our usual places among our fellow initiates—a white robed company that fills the mystic King's Chamber, deep within the heart of our symbolic Pyramid Temple. We wait in hushed silence for our next enthralling lesson which shall reveal to us still deeper mysteries, as we shall listen to the inspired words of our Master-Teacher, Kyron, the Wise.

Kyron stands before the magnificent altar of the Sacred Triangle, beautiful with its glow of dull gold and its gleam of purest marble, and now Kyron raises his hands in that ages-old gesture of blessing, and gain he softly speaks the words of greeting prescribed by our ancient ritual.

Welcome, O Enlightened Ones, for unto thee is granted the Reception.

Kyron holds in his hands quite reverently one of the ancient volumes of the Sanskrit Brahamic Writings, this being an old and yellowed copy of the Upanishads, writings so old that they date back to six hundred years before the Christ was born. If we lay aside for the doctrines of metempsychosis and of reincarnation in these early sacred writings we will find in them a scientific transcendentalism as deep and as pure as if written yesterday, and we will find in the metaphysical subtlety of these ancient writings the strongest argument against materialism.

But listen! Kyron is now reading the words of Indra from the Upanishads—Indra is speaking of Life and Consciousness:

"I am prana (breath, spirit, life), meditate on me as the conscious self, as life, as immortality. Life is prana, Prana is Life. Immortality is Prana, Prana is immortality. As long as Prana dwells in this body, so long surely there is life. By Prana he (the Initiate) obtains immortality in the other world, by knowledge—true conception. He who meditates (in The silence) on me as life and immortality, gains his full life in this world, and obtains in the Svarga world (higher realms) immortality and indestructibility (changeless, because "Heaven-born".)

"Thus it is indeed, "said Indra.." Man lives deprived of speech, for we see dumb people. Man lives deprived of sight, for we see blind people. Man lives deprived of hearing, for we see deaf people. Man lives deprived of mind, for we see infants (and the insane). But prana alone is the conscious self, and having laid hold of this body, it makes it rise up (live). Therefore it is said, 'Let man worship it alone as uktha (the divine). What is prana—self consciousness...of that, this is the evidence, this is the understanding. When a man, being thus asleep, sees no dreams whatever in the trance-like state, he becomes one with that prana alone.

"Then speech goes to him, when he is absorbed in prana, with all names, the eye (filled) with all forms, the ear with all sounds, the mind with all thoughts. And when he awakens, (returns from The Silence), then, as from a burning fire sparks proceed in all direction, thus from the (higher) self the pranas proceed, each towards its place: from the pranas the gods, from the gods the worlds."

Quietly closing the ancient tome in his hands, Myron now lays the sacred book, which has been our heritage of the ages, reverently upon the mystic triangle of the altar—and begins our present lesson, saying:

We will now take up the thread of our last lesson) just where we left off, and you will remember that I was considering with you those mysterious processes by which concentrated foods in fluid form reach their great electromagnetic energy in the brain and finally in the Pineal gland. You will recollect that I taught you that this latter process transmutes these vital life fluids into that most subtle life force which we have named the "PNEUMO-PSYCHIC."

GLANDS PRODUCE CONCENTRATED SPIRIT OF LIFE

In these human bodies of ours it is the Endocrine glands which produce the concentrated spirit of life itself which pulsates within us. Most important of these glands, and perhaps the least understood is the "Conarium" or Pineal Gland, which functions from its own voluntary energy alone. within this small gland are focused the living forces of life and of thought.

"Every faculty of the brain, of which there are forty-two, and their functions, throw their influences and forces toward and into the central cell (the Pineal Gland), and its vortex." Yet an other authority has said, "And both Nature and super-Nature have their terminal points in this central cell."

There are some seventy-five substances, essences, or so-called "elements" in the human body, and the concentrated essence of these reach the Pineal Gland through electro-magnetic induction. Here these essences mingle in the greatest activity. From this mysterious activity comes our every mental and Psychological function. We teach and believe that every mental or spiritual phenomenon and every so-called "Miracle" are the results of the demonstrated powers of the Pineal Gland.

When we dissect the Pineal Gland, we find that its transparent fluids and its solid contents are in concentrated form the same substances from which the physical body and the material brain are created. But we know that this substance is the mental and physiological conscious life-essence, most refined and subtle, ready to descend into the physical body when called by sensual thought.

CORRECT FOODS MAGNIFY MENTAL ABILITY

It is very essential that your diet be adjusted so that you not only sustain the bone and muscle structure of your body, but also that you properly nourish the forty-two brain faculties which are yours. The keen thinker— the alert mentality—is always in demand at a high price, and each one of you can realize your ambitions when you acquire still greater mental ability. And remember, correct foods magnify mental ability—but this secret is so simple that but few people realize its supreme importance.

First, then, we must realize that no two human beings are alike, and in our studies in nutrition we must always bear this in mind. People are divided into distinct TYPES, and each type has its different needs...and peculiarities. I should like to help each of you to find out with certainty just what type you yourself are. For example, what we call the Calcium Type could not possibly thrive upon a diet correct for the Sulphur Type, for he could not assimilate these foods properly. Foods which build muscle in one man might very possibly mean anemia to another type of man.

For while the general physical make-up and appearances of people may seem much the same to you, still the quantities of certain chemical combinations. vary greatly in different persons. We teach that thought is a generated substance (highly rarefied) and this (thought) substance is generated energy transformed from the chemical elements of the foods we eat. This being true, if we furnish the brain but little of certain necessary elements to work with, we can only expect an inferior grade, a poor quality, of mental output (thought).

FUNCTIONS OF IMPORTANT CHEMICAL ELEMENTS IN THE ORGANS OF YOUR BODY

And now I am going to give you in plain and simple words the functions of the important chemical elements, all of which you can derive from foods, in the organs of your body. I should like each Initiate to study quite carefully each particular chemical element, together with its relation to the chemical elements of other foods. This will be followed by our secret chart listing in short form the principal foods for building a super-brain energy. Certain foods not listed in the chart you will find under these chemical functions in the following sections.

PHOSPHORUS—NECESSARY TO EMOTION, INTELLIGENCE AND THOUGHT

Phosphorus is the true agent of life and growth in the human body, and is a basic element most necessary to emotion, intelligence, and growth. This element is the great brain and bone builder, and during the process of active thinking large quantities of phosphorous are consumed in the brain. The philosopher in his audience spell-bound, the famous lawyer sways the court by his brilliant handling of his case—each is using phosphorus in great quantities!

When phosphorus is lacking in the diet the brain slowly decays and intelligence finally leaves. This is the subtle element that multiplies the number of red corpuscles in your blood, nourishes your brain, feeds your nerves, and gives you magnetic power. Every thought you think uses up its certain amount of phosphorus, and you must see to it that sufficient phosphorus foods are in your diet each day. Plenty of foods containing phosphorus enables your mind to act quickly and brings out mental brilliance you never dreamed you possessed. Also, these foods nourish your entire nervous system, as no other foods can.

IRON INCREASES CHARM, BEAUTY, AND MAGNETISM

If there was no iron in your blood your body could not absorb life-giving oxygen through the lungs, and you would very soon suffocate, your life would be gone the same way that fire goes out when its supply of oxygen is cut off. Iron directly stimulates the sexual system, and increases charm, beauty, and magnetic attraction. Plenty of iron in your blood makes you magnetic, makes your blood rich and strong, and makes you attractive to the opposite sex.

But when there is a marked deficiency of iron in the body of any person, you will find a host of serious symptoms and weaknesses, such as mental dullness, unreasoning fears, outbursts of petty anger, self-pity, melancholia and failure of memory.

IODINE STIMULATES THE GLANDS TO GREATER ACTIVITY

Iodine is highly important, because it promotes Oxidation within the brain, and stimulates the intellectual processes in general. Iodine also marvelously stimulates all the glands to greater activity, and this is especially true of its action upon the thyroid gland, and the secretion of the thyroid gland is absolutely necessary to normal brain functioning. We must remember that the thyroid gland must constantly pour into the blood a certain essence which accelerates the vigorous assimilation of Chlorine, Silicon, Calcium and other chemical salts by the blood.

But when the thyroid gland does not secrete enough iodine into the blood stream these necessary salts cannot be properly assimilated. This is the direct cause of defective metabolism, as well as of goiter. And even more important, iodine neutralizes the poisons (toxins) due to decomposition and putrefaction that enter into the blood stream from the intestines. Thus, by its neutralizing action, iodine protects the brain, the nerves and the vital cells from these poisons.

If you do not eat foods rich in iodine, but live largely on starches, fats, meats, eggs or albuminous foods in general, you rob and weaken the thyroid gland. In this case, not all of these toxins (poisons) are neutralized by the iodine of your thyroid gland; so some poisons enter the brain and accumulate in the blood streams and this results in autointoxication (self-poisoning) of the brain, or body, or both. Iodine we may well liken to the sanitary police officer of the body, and the guard of the brain.

This sanitary officer has his headquarters in the thyroid gland, where his duties are not only to guard your brain by destroying the poisons that would harm it, but also to increase the assimilation of the necessary chemical salts, and to promote oxidation within the brain, the underlying process of thought.

CALCIUM—ANOTHER GREAT BRAIN FOOD

Calcium is another food-element which directly imparts more mental energy, makes the acquiring of knowledge easier, adds brilliance to genius, and makes mental concentration more highly efficient. Calcium in abundance helps you to develop a more perfect memory, and also helps to banish fear in every form, and is the basis of persistence, courage and will power, Two of the most highly charged calcium foods, which are not given in our food chart which follows, are buttermilk and halibut (fish).

SILICON—HELPS RESTORE LOST POWERS

A diet rich in silicon has a marvelous rebuilding influence upon your whole nervous system and upon the brain. Silicon has remarkably good and curative effects upon those who suffer from impotence, and from nervous sexual debility. A diet rich in this important element, silicon, will enable the brain worker to accomplish ten times more work with less fatigue than ever before.

CHLORIN—THE BODY'S GREAT DISINFECTANT

Chlorin as found in the foods I will list in our chart which follows is the great, the active disinfectant of your body. It counteracts intestinal infection and prevents bacterial formation in the body, and also it keeps the tissues firm but elastic. Chlorin magically aids in the absorption of new blood material, and removes waste products from the tissues and the blood. When a man works hard physically and perspires, chlorin passes out of his body through the skin, and this is equally true of those who do heavy brain work. To off-set such losses, you must keep a constant reserve of such chemicals by eating the foods which contain them. So, you must know what you are eating—and you must know WHAT to eat. Additional chlorine foods, not given in our chart, are salt, ox blood, ham, and salt fish.

SULPHUR—FORMATIVE LIFE-CHEMICAL

Sulphur acts in your body as one of the greatest of all the formative life-chemicals. We find this life-support-ing element in liberal quantities in the essences of reproduction, and without sulphur the phosphorus present would soon burn out the brain. Sulphur forms the magnetic medium of thought, action, nerve-impulses, emotion and intelligence. One great food source of sulphur not listed in our chart is shrimp.

FLUORIN PROTECTS BONE AND TISSUES

Fluorin maintains the growth, repair and strength of the bones of the body, and not only is the greatest preventive of dental decay, but also protects the life and health of the bones and the tissues. It also constantly rejuvenates the brain glands. Here are additional foods rich in fluorin: Roquefort Cheese, cod liver oil, egg yolk, black bass, garlic, goat's milk, sauerkraut, spinach and watercress.

POTASSIUM GIVES POWER AND FORCE

Potassium, when supplied to the body in the proper foods, is a great source of muscular power, adds to your resistance, gives you greater vitality, and greatly aids your executive powers and your forcefulness. Added foods rich in potassium (not listed in our chart) are chickory, dandelion, dill, sage, bitter (strong) tea and mint.

MAGNESIUM RELAXES, COALS AND PURIFIES

Magnesium—Relaxing, cooling and purifying—magnesium in your body counteracts gases, poisons and acids, and purifies the intestines. While it increases the magnetic impulses of the body, this chemical food-element soothes the nerves, and magnesium-rich foods should be eaten regularly by every person who is too impulsive, highly nervous, too emotional and excitable. Rich magnesium foods (not listed in our chart) are smelt, sole, frog legs, tender chicken, shoulder of lamb, rice flour , apples and grapes.

CARBON—NECESSARY, BUT HARMFUL IF EXCESSIVE

Carbon does a very necessary work in metabolism and in the cell organisms, but too much carbon in the body is extremely harmful, for carbon ruins more nervous systems than any other food element known. So I must advise that you eat foods rich in calcium, iron, potassium, silicon and sodium so as to reduce the carbon content of your body, and eat sparingly of the carbon foods. The carbon foods are the starches and sugars, found in all white floor products, gluten, graham flour, potatoes, white rice, white sugar, candy, syrup, molasses. etc.

HYDROGEN, GREAT CREATIVE AND PURIFYING ELEMENT

Hydrogen is one of the principal elements which most greatly promotes well-being of the whole body, soothes the nerves, regulates the temperature of the body, carries away impurities and prevents inflammation. Without hydrogen, all creative processes in the body would stop at once. There could be no elimination, no perspiration and no procreation—without hydrogen there would be no music, no song, no baby voices, no activity, in fact, no life. Foods most filled with hydrogen are all tender vegetables, all juicy steaks, fowl, liver, juicy fish, all dairy products, berries, melons and all sweet fruits. Each of these foods contain more than 50% of water.

SODIUM acts upon those convolutions of the brain which control the metabolic functions, sodium salts are naturally found in the saliva and in the bile. Sodium acts as a solvent upon the calcium in the body, and is absolutely necessary to health. Celery, Okra and watercress are excellent sources of sodium, together with the other foods listed in our food chart.

OXYGEN stimulates the muscles, vitalizes the circulation, increases the iron supply in the life-processes, and keeps the creative fires burning in the body. Rhubarb, tomatoes, radishes, horseradish, onions, and most cereals are rich in oxygen.

NITROGEN is a great vitalizer and tissue builder—one fifth of our human bodies is nitrogen, which we obtain largely from meat and vegetables. Meats furnish an abundance of nitrogen, also this is true of sturgeon and mackerel, beans, peas, all dairy products and nuts.

MANGANESE is perhaps our greatest protective agent against putrification, because of its powerful germicidal properties, and constantly helps us to battle against germ life and septic ailments. Parsley, peppermint leaves, watercress, egg yolk, endive, almonds, chestnuts and California walnuts are all rich in manganese.

Let me remind you that nuts are extremely important in your diet, for they are a highly concentrated food, and they contain chemical salts invaluable to your muscles and arteries.

CHART—FOODS THAT BUILD BODILY HEALTH AND BRAINPOWER
(NOTE: "R" TO BE EATEN RAW: "C" TO BE EATEN COOKED: "B" TO BE EATEN BAKED: "S" TO BE EATEN SMOKED)

PHOSPHORUS FOODS

Sweet Almonds, R. Beechnuts, R. Whole-wheat, C-B. Whole rye, C-B. Wild rice,' C-B. Whole oats, C. B. Whole barley, C. B. Green Peas, C. Yellow-peas, C. Lentils, C. Beans. C. Egg yolk, R. Corn, C-B. Trout, C. Red cabbage, C-B. Haddock, C. Salmon, S. Clams, C. Crabs, C. Lobsters, C. Oysters B-C.

FOODS RICH IN IRON

Asparagus, C. Beet juice, R. Blackberries, R, Blueberries, R. Wheat bran, C=B. Whole barley bread, B. Black and Red currents, R. Egg yolk, R. Dried figs, R. Concord grapes, R. Head Lettuce, R. Lentils, C. Oxblood, R. Bartlett pears, R. Prunes, R-C. Raisins, R. Spinach, C 3 minutes, Strawberries, R.

IODINE

FOODS Turtle, C. Irish Moss, R: Cod liver oil, R. Crabs, C.
Clams, C-B, Crawfish, B Lobster, C. Mushrooms, C. Salmon,
S. Oysters, R. Scallops, C. Carrots, R-C Artichokes, C. Frog
Legs, C. Grapes, R. Garlic, R. Pineapples,
R. Pears; R. Shrimp, C.

SODIUM FOODS Sodium and

Silicon are combined in foods shown in capital letters, and so are MOST desirable.
Sweet apples, R. Asparagus, C. Beets, R-C. CARROTS, R. CELERY, R. Coconuts,
R. Cucumbers, R Egg yolk,
R. Figs, R. Fish, C. Chicken GIZZARDS, C: Gooseberries, Lentils, C. Cow's milk, R. Goats, Milk, R. ALMOND NUTS, R. PISTACHIO NUTS, R. OATMEAL, C.OKRA C. Prunes, R. Radishes, R. SPINACH,
C. Rutabagas, C. Turnips, C. STRAWBERRIES, R.

LESSON NO. 16
SECRETS OF GLAND CONTROL AND MYSTIC MASTERY

Again you have taken your accustomed place amid your Companions in White in the mystic King's Chamber—that marvelous chamber of Imagery—hidden away from the outer world within the very center of our great Pyramid Temple, Symbolic of the ancient temple schools of the Initiates. Together in silence we wait for the inspired words of Kyron, the Wise, who in this another great lesson will lead us still further along our Path, which thus prepares us each for our several missions.

Standing now before the glowing altar of the Sacred Triangle, with upraised hands Kyron imparts his blessing and welcomes us in the words of our secret ritual:

Welcome, O Enlightened Ones, for unto thee is granted the Reception.

We perceive that Kyron holds reverently one of the great sacred books of the East, the Life of Buddah, translated from the Sanscript of Asvaghosha, who wrote this worshipful volume nearly twenty centuries ago.

And now, softly and clearly Kyron reads:

"Buddha, perceiving that the, whole assemb)y was ready to receive the (Eternal) Law, spoke thus...

"Listen now an understand The mind, the thoughts, and all the senses are subject to the law of life and death. This fault (illusion) of birth and death, once understood, then there is clear and plain perception...

"'Knowing oneself, and understanding how the senses act—then all the accumulated mass of sorrow, sorrows born from life and death, being recognized as attributes of body, and as this body is not 'I' (the Soul) nor offers ground for 'I', then comes the source of peace unending. This thought of (physical) 'self' gives rise to all these sorrows, binding as with cords the world, but having found there is no 'I' that can be bound, then all these bonds are severed. There are no bonds indeed—they disappear—and seeing this there is deliverance.

"The world holds to this thought of (the physical) 'I', and so, from this, comes false apprehension. Of those who maintain the truth of it, some say the 'I' endures, some say it perishes, taking the two extremes of birth and death, their error is most grievous. For if they say the 'I' is perishable, the fruit they strive for, too, will perish; and at some time there will be no hereafter; this is indeed a meritless deliverance.

But if they say the 'I' is not to perish...(that) which is not born and does not die, if this is what they call the 'I' then are all things living ONE—for ALL have this unchanging self—not perfected by any deeds, but self-perfect (Soul).

Gently Kyron closes the ancient and sacred Buddhist volume and lays it upon the Mystic Triangle of the altar, and begins our present lesson in these words:

CONSCIOUS, SUBCONSCIOUS AND SUBLIMINAL MIND

Good Friends and Initiates, in this lesson I shall seek to reveal to you in words so plain and simple that all can understand those amazing secrets of gland control and of mystic mastery guarded as our heritage from the Masters in White.

You will remember that in former lessons you have learned much about the tremendous importance to each human life of the Endocrine glands, also known as the ductless glands. You will recollect that these are named the pituitary, the pineal, the thymus, the parathyroics, the thyroid, the adrenals, and last, but perhaps most supreme in the human body, the sex glands.

But before I impart to you these secret methods for energizing and controlling these Endocrine glands, upon which your very life, your health and your happiness depends, I want to impress upon each of you that back of every such mechanical method and each secret exercise there must be the mystic mastery of Mind—conscious, the subconscious and the subliminal Mind—that divine 'I' which does not perish of which Buddha spoke in the words which I have just read to you.

So as a safe and sure basis for these secret methods of gland control, and of mystic mastery which I shall give you in this lesson, let us once more consider together still deeper truths in this inexhaustible field, MIND—SPIRIT—SOUL—the real 'I.'

First, we realize that today men of "science" are still floundering in the deceptive quicksands of materialism. But we who have learned of the philosophy, are after all the wiser. For we go for guidance to the Great Oracle—that imperishable Inner Mind—which perceives clearly with a single eye, an eye that needs no man made instrument to perceive the TRUTH as Eternal Divine Law. We shall hold fast to this

TRUTH, knowing that as long as we do, the pestilence, the famine and the terrors that fly by night cannot come nigh unto us.

HUDSON'S "LAW OF PSYCHIC PHENOMENA"

Much of the so called "modern" new thought in Psychology in this country can be traced back to the work of Thomas J. Hudson, who, after observing different kind of psychic phenomena, concluded that man possessed, in addition to his everyday ordinary consciousness, hidden mental powers and mental processes of which he was entirely unaware.

So, some sixty year ago, in his "Law of Psychic Phenomena," Hudson set forth this theory, and demonstrated by many examples of their workings, that each human being has two minds (or phases of mind). The everyday mind, of which we are normally and ordinarily conscious, he called the Objective Mind. The other mind or phase of mind, the one of whose processes we are usually unaware, he called the Subconscious Mind.

Now, while great credit is due to Hudson for his theory of the Sub-conscious Mind, and the logic with which he explained its workings, we must remember that this DUALITY OF THE MIND is not a modern conception, for indeed it is very ancient.

Two thousand eight hundred years ago Homer, in ancient Greece, when he wrote those imperishable legends that have come down to us, showed that he, too, understood this duality of mind quite well indeed, and his Greek information on this subject was derived from the teachings of the Masters in White in the still more ancient Chaldea.

These ancient Greeks had highly developed artistic expressions, and, so, the occult knowledge that was theirs instead of being stated as a series of dry facts was generally clothed in the beauty of legend or the grace of wondrous sculpture.

THE GREEK LEGEND OF CASTOR AND POLLUS

In the immortal Greek legend of Castor and Pollus we have an allegory in which the two chief characters are used to represent THE TWO MINDS the objective and the subconscious, or the mortal and the immortal. Doubtless you will remember the story told in this ancient Greek legend—and this seemingly simple story becomes deeply significant to us when we realize that to the early Chaldeans, just as to our modern astrologers, the Zodiacal sign, Gemini, ("The Twins") RULED THE MIND. This section of the zodiac is yet today pictured in the sky by the constellation of GEMINI, the chief stars of which are named CASTOR AND POLLUX.

According to this Greek form of the world-old legend Castor and Pollux were TWINS, and they engaged in battle with certain rivals for the hands of two fair maidens. During this fierce combat Castor was killed. Now Pollux, who was himself immortal, so deeply loved his brother that he was not willing to live without him, and so he plead with the god Zeus to restore Castor to life. Zeus consented to grant this petition, but with the condition that only one of the brothers should be permitted to be on earth at a time, the other to be detained meanwhile in the underworld.

Thus, 2800 years ago Homer expressed it in these words:

"By turns they visit this ethereal sky, and live alternate, and alternate die."

And so, in this way, the ancient Greek Masters of the occult wisdom, passed on to future generations the occult knowledge of the Mind which they had in turn gained from the Chaldean Masters in this legend, picturing Pollux as immortal, the imperishable "I" that could not be slain.

Here we find their deeper meaning—that there is a MIND (Soul or Personality) which forever retains its identity, and cannot be destroyed.

In the person of Castor, who was slain, they picture the objective Mind which is vulnerable and so perishes.

WHILE OBJECTIVE MIND RULES, SUBCONSCIOUS IS DORMANT

It is just as true today as it was nearly thirty centuries ago when Homer wrote, that while the Objective (waking) Mind is actively ruling the Subconscious Mind has small chance to express itself through the physical, for it remains in "the underworld." But when the Objective Mind sleeps, or from some other causes is no longer active in ruling our physical lifes, then the Subconscious Mind takes charge, and becomes the living, active ruler.

So when the Objective Mind (represented by Castor) relinquishes control and rulership to "brother" Pollux (the Subconscious Mind), under his direction we continue to breathe, the heart keeps right on pumping blood through the arteries, digestion and assimilation proceed as usual, and we still have mental experiences, some of which we call "dreams."

Perhaps two of the greatest of modern physical researchers were Sir William Crookes and Sir Oliver Lodge, both of whom had gained worldwide fame in the field of physical science. Applying rigid and exacting laboratory methods to their tests, they believed that they had demonstrated what the ancient Chaldeans and Greeks believed, that there is an Immortal Mind which does not die with the physical body.

They also reported that there is a phase of the human Mind which functions marvelously, though often unrecognized, even as Hudson described it but these two eminent scientists gave it a different name, joining the Latin limen, meaning threshold, to sub, which means under, to form the word Subliminal, thus meaning those states (or phases) of mental activity or consciousness that are below the threshold of everyday awareness.

UNWARRANTED IDEA THAT SUBLIMINAL MEANT SUBLIME

Until the time of Freud what Hudson called the Subconscious Mind was currently called the Subliminal Mind, and certain metaphysical writers advanced the unwarranted idea that this term meant sublime.

According to these misguided writers, but not to scientific men, there were delete three minds: the Objective, the Subconscious, and what they imagined to be the godlike mind, the Subliminal.

But with the work of Freud, and the vast number of books on "Psycho-analysis" which followed him, new names were adopted, and today all "three" of these minds are commonly known to psychologists as the Unconscious Mind. Although these former writers had drawn the rather unwarranted idea of the Subliminal Mind as meaning the sublime mind, in a way they were nearly correct, for while there is really but a single mind, within that mind reside all the higher powers and all the possibilities of attainment which any individual can ever realize.

Your physical body is composed of countless physical cells and each of these cells has an independent consciousness. And the 'thought-body,' (your mind) also functions through countless brain cells, each having its independent consciousness. Thoughts and emotions are the foods which nourish your mental body, so you are today the sum total of all your past experiences, as these have become organized as cells in the structure of your mental and physical self.

And because you are constantly acquiring NEW experiences your thought cells and your body-cells are undergoing constant change. These changes you can greatly control, for the mental body which you build, either consciously or without knowing it, determines the conditions which will be attracted to you in the future.

So now you are ready to learn how to demonstrate abounding health and happiness through the power of self-directed thought to gain control over your Endocrine Glands, and mystic mastery over your body, through these very simple exercises.

SECRET METHODS OF ENERGIZING YOUR GLANDS

First, I want you to realize that these time-tested methods of arousing into healthful activity the thyroid gland, the prostrate gland, and adrenals, the sex glands, etc., if you will but follow them faithfully will positively transform and rejuvenate your bodily, your mental, and your spiritual cell-structures. You will easily perceive this change for the better yourself, because from the very first day you will begin to feel stronger, more vital and vigorous in every way. As you keep on with the exercises your mind will become clear and keen, you will begin to sleep soundly, and your appetite will be renewed. Your stomach and digestive organs will improve wonderfully. In a word, you will be transformed.

ENERGIZING THE THYROID. Stand perfectly straight, hold your head erect, now bring the chin backward and inward as far as you can, without either raising or lowering it. When done properly, this movement will arch the upper part of the chest; the chest will come forward and upward. This will also slightly arch the neck.

Now turn your head to the right. Next extend your chin forward; next pull your chin in and backward. Now bring your head back as far as you can; then turn your head to the left. Repeat the former movement. Tense the muscles of your back as you perform these exercises for energizing your thyroid gland. Repeat the entire exercise ten times.

ENERGIZING THE SPLEEN, ADRENALS AND SEX GLANDS

Stand erect, and consciously pull your abdomen (stomach) in and up. Now press the buttocks (the fleshy part you sit on) very tightly together, at the same time tensing the muscles of the small of your back and upper legs. While doing this, exhale (breathe out) every bit of stagnant air from your lungs. Then inhale (breathe in) strongly, slowly, and deeply, at the same time relaxing all the back and rear muscles. After this, exhale again and once more tense the back and rear (buttock)muscles, and again pull your abdomen in and up. Repeat this complete exercise ten times.

After you have learned this exercise perfectly, you can combine this energizing exercise with the thyroid exercise, which will hasten the wonderful results that will follow.

When you energize the glands by these simple methods, you will very soon realize for yourself that you are wonderfully stimulating the healthful activity of every tissue and of every part of your spinal column, as well as the small of the back, together with all the ligaments, muscles and nerves in the pelvis. By this gland; nerve, and general stimulating effect, you are helping to bring renewed health and restored youth to every part of your body.

By these simple methods of energizing, you circulate greatly increased supplies of vitally rich and nourishing blood to every organ of your body. By these exercises, simple as they seem, you electrify and stimulate the Endocrine as well as all other glands. In turn, and because of this stimulation, the glands manufacture their secretions more rapidly and in much large quantities and secrete them into the blood stream, and this energizes all the nerves, all the organs and all the structures of your body—all of which draw their life and health from the circulation of your blood.

Thus, for example, when you so greatly increase the healthy activity of your thyroid gland,`by our simple method of energizing, through that most important gland, the thyroid, you are sending new strength and renewed health throughout your whole body. For the wondrous spinal nerves carry these stimulating impulses to the heart, the lungs and to every organ which plays a part in changing the food you eat into nutrition and vitality for all the body cells. And this process helps to renew life by a stronger elimination (getting rid of), the food debris and waste products.

Further, the brain, with all of its marvelous functions, is powerfully stimulated by these energizing exercises. Persistent energizing by these simple exercises is a powerful aid to the heart, the lungs, stomach, pancreas, spleen, in fact, to all, of the alimentary organs. In due time, this means true and real rejuvenation.

TRANSMUTATION—AND INSTANT CONTROL OF SEX GLAND'S

Each of us should learn to control our affections—but our passions, however, we MUST conquer, and this we can do by sublimating them to higher desires and purposes. Thus Paul Wisely advises in Romans 6:12: "Let no sign reign :in your mortal body, that you should obey it in the lust thereof."

According to science, the true life forces of men and women are the sex essences. These essences are the highest product of the human body, for the seed is the ultimate, the highest product in any form of life or existence. Now when these sex essences reach their highest development through their circuit in the body and the brain, we teach that they assume the form of conscious, spiritual (thought) entities. These thought or spirit entities inhabit the cells of the brain and body—and their central place of assembly is in the hidden recesses of the brain,

Through sensual propagation these entities are transmitted, and each such transmission is a LOSS OF ENTITIES TO THE transmitters. Herein is the real, the basic cause of mortality (death). Such loss by transmission also causes loss of health, of vigor and youth, of nerve-power and of length of life.

Yet sensuality (sexual passion) proves extremely difficult, if not almost impossible, to govern to all those who do not possess the simple methods of sex-gland control which I shall impart to you as Initiates. Those who try to struggle against sensuality mentally only are usually waging a losing battle, for to combat physical passion by thought alone usually only makes its hold stronger upon its victim. To overcome this, we must use strategy; we must cease to think of the sensual by substituting higher, nobler, spiritual thoughts and desires.

This substitution of spiritual thought, desire, and nobler activity is what we mean by sublimations, and these mental weapons WILL conquer the enemy. Remember, your mind can concentrate upon only ONE line (or subject) of thought at a time, and when it is flooded by higher thoughts and absorbed in spiritual interests, like a full vessel, it can hold no more, and there is no room for this baserel ement.

We must learn to cleanse ourselves from sensuality—its mere suppression through will alone is in vain, for it is not permanent.

MASTER METHOD OF SEX GLAND CONTROL

Here is the master method of sex gland control, it is very simple, and its first step is a firm and absolute determination that you will demonstrate your mastery over these purely animal elements in your mental and physical life. So, when you are tempted by the opposite sex, or by lewd thoughts or portrayals in any manner, shape, or form, meet such temptation first by this firm and absolute RESOLVE.

Then, instantly use the spear and helmet of "guardianship" by mentally affirming:

"Supreme Spirit, cleanse me this minute, for thy habitation keep me pure, for I am one of thy Heaven-Born!"

While holding this sublime thought-sentence, by repeating it over and over, TAKE A LONG, DEEP, SLOW BREATH. During this inhaling of new air into the lungs, the diaphragm descends, thus it automatically pushes down the stomach, the intestines, and exerts pressure upon the sex glands.

Now exhale (breathe out), until you have expelled every bit of the changed (impure) air from your lungs. While you do this the diaphragm will be drawn upward, and the abdomen will flatten out. ASSIST THIS MOVEMENT BY CONSCIOUSLY PULLING YOUR ABDOMEN INWARD, especially the lower abdomen.

Also, hold your breath while thus drawing the abdomen inward and upward while you slowly count ten. Now resume your slow and rhythmic breathing again, but keep your abdomen pulled inward and upward.

Men and women both can use this master method with equal results—IT NEVER FAILS, for it gives you absolute mastery over your sex glands and over sensual or animal desires.

LESSON NO. 17
DEFEAT OF FEAR AND MASTERY OF THOUGHT WAVES

Once more we are transported upon the wings of imagery to that mysterious King's Chamber, deep within our symbolic Pyramid Temple, and again you are in your usual seat, with your Companion Initiates. And so now we quietly await another still deeper and more advanced lesson from our Teacher, Kyron, the Wise, he who shall speak to us from the Ancient Wisdom of the occult, which is his mission as One of the Masters in White.

Standing before us, just in front of the softly gleaming altar of the Sacred Triangle, Kyron imparts his blessing with upraised hands and welcomes us according to the ages-old form prescribed in our hidden ritual:

Welcome, O Enlightened Ones, for unto thee is granted the Reception.

Again, softly and clearly, Kyron reads to us from that same ancient volume, sacred in the East, the Life of Buddha, handed down to us through the ages from the Sanskrit original.

(Buddha, speaking to his father, the king):

"In this world, there is rupture of family love in another life it is sought again; brought together for a moment, again rudely divided, everywhere the fetters of kindred are formed. Ever being bound, and ever being loosened! who can sufficiently lament such constant separations; born into the world, and then gradually changing, constantly separated by death and then born again.

"You desire to make me king, and it is difficult to resist the offices (offers) of love; but as a disease is difficult to bear without medicine (healing remedy), so neither can I bear this weight of dignity; in every condition, high or low, we find folly and ignorance, and men carelessly following the dictates of lustful passion; at last we come to live in constant FEAR; thinking anxiously of the OUTWARD FORM; the spirit droops, following the ways of men the mind resists the right; but the conduct of THE WISE is not so.

"The sumptuously ornamented and splendid palace I look upon as filled with fire, the hundred dainty dishes of the divine (palace) kitchen as mingled with destructive poisons; the lily growing on the tranquil lake, in.its midst (center) harbors countless noisome insects; and so the towering abode of the rich is the house of calamity; THE WISE will not dwell therein.

"I reject the kingly estate... This then would be the consequence of compliance; that I, who, delighting in religion, am gradually getting wisdom should now quit these quiet woods ("The Silence"), and returning home (to the palace), PARTAKE OF SENSUAL PLEASURES, and, thus by night and day increase my store of misery,...Far better dwell in the wild mountains and eat the herbs..."

Slowly Kyron closes the ancient Buddhist Volume from which he has read these illuminating words recorded as spoken so long ago by Buddha Gautema, and returns the book. reverently to the altar of the Sacred Triangle once more. And now quite simple he speaks to us, and leads us mentally, gradually deeper into, the practical and the occult truths of our present lesson. In this lesson Kyron is to teach us how best to defeat FEAR, and the secret of the MASTERY of thought-waves. But listen, for Kyron, the Wise, speaks:

THE GREAT SECRET—HOW TO ATTRACT WHAT YOU WANT

My Good Friends and Fellow Initiates; right now I want to talk with you and think with you about one of the greatest secrets that our incomparable...teachings is seeking to impart to you in everyone of our carefully. guarded lessons. In everyday words that secret is simply HOW TO ATTRACT WHAT YOU WANT. In this great work of ATTRACTING to yourself what you want...what you most deeply desire—there are two most important steps; first, you must know HOW to defeat FEAR,,and second, you must attain to the MASTERY OF. THOUGHT WAVES.

Now, as the result of our previous lessons, I am sure that each Initiate here realizes, and understands that you DRAW TO YOURSELF thought waves, persons, surroundings, and circumstances which harmonize exactly with your own REAL and your own-INNER THOUGHTS.As I have taught you before LIKE always attracts LIKE both in the world of thought and in the material world of things.

For, again I repeat, thoughts are THINGS, and they are ruled by The Eternal Law of things just as truly as are all material things. In other words, if you permit yourself to think thoughts of FEAR, of failure, or of despair you will inevitably draw to yourself the thought currents (thought waves) of everyone around you who is thinking these same thoughts of defeat, and in turn these waves of fear or defeatist thought will greatly increase and hasten your own failure and defeat.

When you succumb to fear-thinking, to gloom and discouragement, you not only draw to yourself a goodly share of the failure thought-waves from the mental atmosphere about you, but you will also attract to yourself many other defeated and gloomy persons, failures and useless people.

Not only will you thus attract undesirable companions but also unfavorable environments and unfortunate conditions, and these in reacting upon you only deepen and intensify your original non-success and your own fear-thoughts.

YOU GET WHAT YOU EXPECT—WHAT YOU THINK ABOUT MOST

Generally we get what we look for, and what we think about MOST. For example, have you ever noticed that a man or a woman with hatred or anger uppermost in his or her mind so often draw to themselves situations in which hatred or anger inflicts irreparable damage upon their own lives?

Like Job, countless men and women can truthfully exclaim: "The thing I greatly feared hath come upon me!"

On the other hand, the good things of this world, the finer things of life which you constantly EXPECT and which you demand from Life in all faith will surely come to you in due time. In short, "As a man thinketh in his heart (inner mind), SO IS HE." Just as the Fear Thinker attracts fear-thought-waves, failure, and gloom, so when you are actively cheerful, filled with energy, hope, and constant FAITH, you attract to yourself similar thought waves from others, and successful people who will help you and conditions which favor your success.

You will note that the truly successful men and women of the world around us do not allow their minds to DWELL upon thoughts of fear, failure or discouragement, but who always keep before their "mind's eye" pictures of HOPE, SUCCESS AND SELF CONFIDENCE.

SUCCESS PICTURES IMPRESSED UPON SUBCONSCIOUS.

These mental pictures (mental images) of Success, of Hope and of supreme Faith (Confident expectation) must be impressed upon your subconscious mind and you must confidently command your subconscious mind to produce these things you want most.

Different schools of thought and different philosophies, both ancient and modern, have different names and different theories for this same Law of Attraction, which is an inherent part of the great, changeless Eternal Divine Law, and perhaps these various names and differing explanations may have puzzled you in the past. You may have even given up in despair some particular courses of occult study because of these many and often conflicting explanations.

And that is exactly where this system of instruction is incomparable, for we seek to use quite simple words in order to avoid confusion. For I tell you frankly here and now that no matter what method is employed or what theory is advanced, in every occult or religious teaching THAT GETS RESULTS, the subconscious mind's the active principle which produces the results in response to the METHOD, and in spite of the THEORY.

I repeat again that which I have taught you from the first of our lessons, your subconscious mind has unlimited control over your physical functions;it also has a strange power of telepathic communication and psychic influence over the minds of other persons who may be distant or near-by. And your subconscious mind is also the unseen power that moulds and fashions your inner character—the REAL YOU—and that same invisible power can transform YOU into just the man or the woman that you most greatly desire to BE. Never forget this, the very heart of our philosophy, that your subconscious mind also has the miraculous power that, can materialize and objectify YOUR IDEALS AND YOUR INTENSE DESIRES.

SUBCONSCIOUS MIND ONLY OBEYS CONFIDENT COMMANDS

You will remember that when Peter, in answer to the call of the Nazarite Master, essayed to walk upon the waters, "he was afraid; and beginning to sink, he cried, saying, Lord, Save me."

"And immediately, Jesus stretched forth his hand, and caught him, and said unto him; O thou of Little Faith, wherefore didst thou DOUBT? -Matt. 14:30-31.

Just so, your subconscious mind obeys no commands that you give in DOUBT. Any mental command, which you give to your subconscious mind must be given with the authority that confidently EXPECTS that command to be obeyed.

In previous lessons I have taught you how to VISUALIZE each thing you want most, and have also explained that you must KNOW EXACTLY WHAT YOU WANT, that you must INTENSELY DESIRE that thing with your whole heart, mind-and soul, and that you must FOCUS your thought upon that Heart's Desire, constantly.

Then your subconscious mind will ATTRACT that finer thing which you intensely desire to you, or you to it, just as Nature's invisible Law leads the root of the tree to the distant water, its source of nourishment, or just as instinct leads the animal to the place where its food can be found. In the animal world the subconscious manifests as instinct. And when you use your subconscious mind purposely, consciously and with understanding, it,WILL attract to you without fail that which you most greatly desire from the outer world around you.

POWER OF WILL CONQUERS NEGATIVE EMOTIONS

Negative emotions and negative (bad) habits are the arch enemies of all success, of all happiness and of your ability to attract to yourself those finer things of life for which you long. Habits rule our lives, and whether these habits are good or bad depends largely upon whether we cultivate positive or negative emotions and, thoughts, and also many habits are largely the result of our environment, the conditions under which we live.

All negative or harmful habits, whether mental or physical, can be conquered by the POWER OF WILL— determination—for thus alone we gain self control. Will-power alone is the counter-poise of habit. Through your own determination, through your instructions, and through choosing your own proper environment, you are developing mastery over every negative emotion and every harmful habit.

Habit-actions, and habit-thinking, whether positive or negative, good or bad, are performed by the average man or woman almost instinctively, because in following the habit we are prone to do so unconsciously, too often we never think about the consequences of our habitual lines of action or of thought. Many of these; insistent and unconscious mental impulses (habits-compulsions) which to us act as slave-drivers, may have arisen within us gradually and almost unnoticed, often having their origin in hereditary tendencies.

These habits of thought and of action manifest themselves for good or ill in our talents, our motives, our emotions, our likes and dislikes, our customs and in the failure or success of our brains and nervous systems to adapt themselves to our various activities and accomplishments. When negative habit thinking becomes the entire character of any person, and manifests itself in pride, vanity, envy, jealousy, greed, egotism, anger or hatred (all negative emotions,), that person is SELF-DEFEATED.

Everyone, at some time or other, is subject to attack by these evil (negative) emotions, and everyone must face the temptation to fall prey to harmful habits. The Intelligent Initiate can nullify these negative emotions by focusing his mind consciously and purposely upon the positive emotions, which are the exact opposite.

CONTROLLING EMOTIONS AND CONQUERING FEAR

Whenever you feel certain or various habits taking form in your consciousness, just sit alone in The Silence and picture to yourself (and weigh fully and fairly) all possible happiness or personal advantages which may, result from yielding to them; and then after that, seek carefully for any evil results which they may produce in your life. When you thus honestly weigh one set of results against the other, you will generally decide that they are very unequal, and then you will choose wisely THAT WHICH IS BEST FOR YOU.

As I have taught you in previous lessons, FEAR is the greatest obstacle you will ever encounter in attracting to yourself success, happiness, prosperity all those finer things of life which you want most. Every negative emotion is your enemy but among the negative emotions- FEAR is your most dangerous foe. Now because this is eternally true,. I shall now impart to you the secret system FOR THE ABDOMINAL CONTROL OF THE EMOTIONS, and this simple secret, method will enable you to control and to master each negative emotion at will and quickly.

The abdominal "brain" is truly the powerhouse of wonderful energies—this abdominal brain is in reality a tremendous and automatic nerve center, called the "'Solar Plexus." This, great center of nervous energy lies behind and a trifle above the stomach and consists of an interwoven network of well nigh countless nerve ganglia, and these, like the wires from a central telephone station, connect the abdominal brain to the vascular systems, the arteries, the veins and the glands of the body.

Thus, for example, these out-branching nerves, surround the arteries like a sheath and run parallel with them, and these nerve-wires extend to every part of the human body along the walls of the blood vessels. The caliber, (size) of the blood vessels, more especially the smaller ones, is controlled by these fine strands of nerve (wire). By this action of control these nerves produce the scarlet flush (capillary dilation)which we see as the rosy blush of health, or the marble paleness (capillary contraction) of fright.

We might make this comparison—the orders from the cranial brain (brain within the skull) are direct, active and reflex and cease after the desired action is accomplished; but the orders from the abdominal brain, which presides over the glandular system also, are continuing orders, holding the balance proper between the normal blood stream and tissues, and the substances for nourishment and those ready for secretion.

SECRET OF NEUTRALIZING EMOTIONAL STORMS

Let us approach this important subject by laying a sure groundwork for your understanding. First, then, it is the elasticity of the covering of our glands which makes it possible for them to send out by rhythmical motion under varying circumstances their all-important secretions to the nerves and into the flood stream. Now, if the proper muscular control is established and maintained, an order from your cranial brain to your abdominal brain will be obeyed.

Let us understand that just as long as the natural processes of life—such as assimilation, circulation, respiration, secretion, etc.—continue undisturbed your abdominal brain remains a silent, a steady, a ceaseless guardian, always on the job. But once being even slightly unbalanced by negative or irritating upsets and emotions, that abdominal brain very quickly resents such emotional upsets, and you pay the price in suffering.

While it is true that the ganglia (nerve-wires) of your sympathetic nervous system are entirely beyond the direct control of your will-power, yet there is a way which your will can assert control. Your determined MIND—mind that WILLS—can in time of emotional storm send out an order for what I may term a counter revolution" in your abdominal region, AND SO NEUTRALIZE THE HARMFUL EFFECTS OF EMOTIONAL STORMS. This order, or balancing message is carried along the sensitive lines of communication through the cerebro- spinal axis - and its countless wires of nerve-extension.

In this lesson I shall teach you just HOW to enter into this neutralizing state of perfect repose and self-repair—but the secret is that this state of controlled rebuilding can only be attained when you know how to contract the capsules of the glands and then strongly massage them by certain successive INTERNAL MOTIONS. Thus, at will, you induce a state of activity, followed by a condition or state of nerve-relaxation, repose and repair.

NOW TO CONTROL FEAR AND EMOTIONAL STORMS.

In order to control fear or other negative emotional upsets, you must first NEUTRALIZE those negative forces which are creating these disturbances in your physical system. It is also very essential that the method you use should not be apparent to those who may be around you.

So, whenever the necessity for this emotional control arises, take a long, slow, deep breath, thus thoroughly expanding your chest and at the same time contracting the abdomen; consciously pulling it IN and UPWARD, Now HOLD YOUR BREATH while you count ten slowly, contract your chest and draw it inward as much, as you can, and by this motion push your diaphragm and your inner organs DOWNWARD AND OUTWARD, thus you enlarge the abdomen and force it outward. Still holding your breath contract your abdomen once more and expand your chest again.

Alternately expand the chest and contract the abdomen six times in succession, taking the long breath and holding it each time. Wait half a minute and repeat this procedure. Repeat this entire routine, six breaths, four times. That is all. But if you will pay close attention while you are performing this simple method of control, you will know for yourself how powerfully it influences your abdominal brain, or solar plexus, by immediately restoring order and quelling your emotional storm.

During this exercise, repeat the words of this affirmation to yourself mentally: "Now I am MASTER of myself; this emotion shall NOT control me; my WILL gives me complete control right now." It seems almost unbelievable but speedily your fear, or any other negative emotion will VANISH into thin air, and in its stead you will experience a glorious feeling of relief, of power, and of a deep and peaceful calmness.

DO SOME MENTAL HOUSE CLEANING

Remember that we are all fated to encounter moments or even hours of despair, when things go wrong for us and the whole world around us seems determined to balk our ambitions. Times of gloom, of doubt, and the feeling of engaging in a futile search for an elusive truth come to even the strongest among our Initiates. The more powerful you may feel yourself to be in this work the greater in proportion your doubts may become in these testing times.

For such assaults upon your ideals and upon your attainments ARE tests sent by the Unseen—perhaps by your own higher consciousness, that you may feel the spur of fiery enthusiasm and thus spurred, rise to ever greater heights.

When these spectres of doubt, of seeming futility, or of discouragement come to haunt you, that's the time for you to do some MENTAL HOUSE CLEANING! For these are just the negative emotional storms which I have taught you how to conquer in this lesson.

Never forget, nor neglect, my former teaching—so oft repeated.—take at least a few minutes—better a half-hour—to be absolutely alone—in The Silence. Center your entire attention upon the GREATER MIND within you...tell it exactly WHAT you want...AND...Listen!

LESSON NO. 18 MENTAL DOMINION—HOW TO ATTRACT POSITIVE AND REPEL NEGATIVE THOUGHT-WAVES

Here again we find ourselves in phantasy deep within our symbolic Pyramid

Temple, and again you are in your accustomed place amid your Companion-Initiates within that mystic King's Chamber. We wait in silence for the inspired teaching of Kyron, the Wise, as he once more prepared to unfold to us still more of the deeper occultism of the ancient wisdom.

But see—with upraised hands Kyron is now imparting his silent blessing, and he greets us in the prescribed words of our secret ritual.

WELCOME, O ENLIGHTENED ONES, FOR UNTO THEE IS GRANTED THE RECEPTION

Kyron holds an ancient volume open in his hands, and we see that it is that same Buddhistic Scripture, called the Dhammapada, from which he has read for us many words of a wisdom little known to the outer world. Slowly and reverently Kyron reads from this canon of old, sacred to this day in the far East:

(Selections from Chapter 3 of the Dhammapada, the title of which is THOUGHT.)

"As a fletcher makes straight his arrow, the wise man makes straight his trembling and unsteady thought, which is difficult to guard, difficult to hold back.

"As a fish taken from his watery home, and thrown on the dry ground, our thoughts trembles all over in order to escape the dominion of Mara, the Tempter.

"It is good to tame (rule) the mind, which is difficult to hold in and flighty, rushing wherever it listeth; a tamed (controlled) mind brings happiness.

"Let the wise man guard his thoughts, for they are difficult to perceive, very artful and they rush wherever they list; thoughts well guarded bring happiness.

"Those who bridle their mind, which travels far...and hides in the chamber of the heart (the Inner self), will be free from the bonds of Mara, the tempter.

If a man's faith is unsteady, if he does not know the true (Eternal)Law, if his peace of mind is troubled, his knowledge will never be perfect.

Whatever a hater may do to a hater, or an enemy may do to an enemy, a wrongly-directed mind will do him greater mischief.

"Not a mother, not a father, will do so much, nor any other relatives; a well-directed mind will do us greater service."

Quietly laying the ancient volume upon the altar of the sacred, glowing triangle,

Kyron begins another marvelous lesson with these words:

The alchemists of old, another title for the Masters in White, taught under the guise of symbols that the mind must be developed and sublimated by the three fundamental substances, which they hid in the symbols of sulphur, mercury and salt. Under these three great occult influences they taught that man could consciously apply the emanating spiritual forces (currents) which alone could enable him to walk the CREATIVE PATH—the "WAY" of the Masters.

SYMBOLIC KEYS TO THE GRAND ARCANUM

According to the occult wisdom of these ancient Alchemist-Masters, I Sulphur, (Symbolized by the eagle), represents divine inspiration. Mercury symbolized in the ancient temples by Man-Woman, standing on a cube, and crowned with flame) represented divine fatherhood and motherhood, the male (positive) and the female (negative) elements, also the blood and lymph coursing within along the three nervous systems of the human body.

Many, many centuries later we find these same symbolic keys to the Grand Arcanum plainly reflected in the legend of the Greeks of Pegasus, who, when he had slain the Gorgon Medusa and cut off its head, mounted into the air on wings given him by Mercury and sped homeward carrying the awful monster's head. And according to this Greek story it was the blood dripping from this monster's head falling into the ocean (the waters) that is, imagination vitalized by emotion, from which the fabled Pegasus sprang, a powerful steed whose other name is INSPIRATION.

The third great element used in their occult teaching of the ancient Alchemists was Salt, and by Salt (symbolized by the Dragon) these masters symbolized the selfish lower nature which would keep imprisoned the precessional force—that force which would destroy the lower nature and exalt the Higher—or Soul-nature— by releasing the Christ-Spirit to reign upon the throne of the Inner Self. SULPHUR—MERCURY—SALT

MENTAL DOMINION AND THOUGHT-WAVES

Now we are ready to consider the problem of our present lesson, which is simply the attaining of mental dominion—the power to attract and to focus psychic force—the method of drawing to ourselves positive thought-waves, and of repelling the negative mental currents around us.

First, then, I want each of you to realize that the laws which govern mental dominion and positive psychic energy are just as definite and just as changeless as are the laws which govern chemistry and physics. Each Initiate who has advanced this far in the WAY can learn and can apply these laws with transforming results.

You will agree that today we live in a society (the herd) in which the instinctive, the sense mind rules. Our whole civilization is built very largely on the lower intellect, blindly ruled by the sense-mind.

You will further agree that your mind is constantly sending forth thoughts and is always receiving thoughts from others. This constant stream of outgoing and incoming thoughts is like the action of an electric battery when in operation, for it, too, constantly sends forth its forces...and must be replenished from time to time.

While you are speaking, as in conversation, or when you are writing, you become a positive magnet because you are generating thought-force. But when your mind is not actively occupied, you lapse into a passive state, and become as it were a negative magnet. It is when you are in this passive or negative state that you become receptive to thought-waves—carrying thoughts that may be either highly beneficial or terribly harmful to you, depending upon their nature, for we teach that thoughts are material substances, although highly rarefied.

And the great danger lies in the fact that, although you may be entirely unconscious of it, your mind unguarded appropriates or absorbs these thoughts in much the same way as the body absorbs food. There is a very real danger that, while you are in a negative or passive (receptive) state of mind, if you are among people whose minds are vibrating with fear, anger, jealousy, or any other destructive emotion, their thought-waves will affect your own mind with the same harmful vibrations.

PROTECT YOURSELF BY POSITIVE THOUGHT

So it is highly important for you to be able to cultivate awareness of the mental attitudes of those around you, because unless you protect yourself by assuming positive mental attitudes (by positive thinking) you may absorb the poisonous emanations of some or many emotionally disordered minds.

For example, if you visit a sick-room, or a hospital, or attend a funeral, or any other place where there is a gloom that taxes your nervous system, in these negative atmospheres of worry, of disease, or of sorrow and despair, if you then allow yourself to become negative or receptive, you are almost certain to be overpowered by these negative emotional waves.

When you are tired in mind and body, should you happen to become one in a crowd of either excited, angry, or despairing people you will almost inevitably take on the mental attitude of that crowd; unconsciously, unless you are on guard, you will begin to feel as they feel, to think as they think. Thus the negative emotions of the crowd around you supplant your own faith, your own hope, your own magnetic Power of attraction.

Let us suppose that you have carefully planned to engage in some line of business—a line which you know and which you like—a plan which you know offers you every opportunity for success and prosperity. But you are surrounded by people with negative, discordant minds—people who only criticize your proposed venture and who predict the worst for you—if you accept these destructive thought-waves, you are lost. For then you will see only failure ahead of you, you have exchanged your own former courage for the fear that is inspired by these discordant minds.

So, instead of carrying out your own plan that would have carried you on to great success you hesitate, lose confidence in yourself and finally abandon your plan entirely, and perhaps in desperation, and allowing yourself to be influenced by the negative minds around you, you allow yourself to embark upon a plan suggested by someone else, a plan that later proves to be disastrous, to your sorrow.

We live in a world filled with thought emanations, and you cannot guard yourself too carefully from becoming a way-station for receiving negative thought-waves. because they are always destructive. For as you have learned in your early lessons, negative mental attitudes always spell failure, poverty sorrow and despair.

So if and when you must mingle with the crowd, or with people whose thoughts are negative, critical and destructive, do so only when you are in a POSITIVE mental attitude (frame of mind).

FORTIFY YOURSELF BY POSITIVE AFFIRMATION

The great secret of mental protection is to fortify yourself by positive affirmation BEFORE meeting others or mingling with the crowd.

POSITIVE men and women succeed in what they undertake because they are both leaders and (more or less subtly) drivers—such people are going somewhere, but always their goal is a very DEFINITE SOMEWHERE.

Of course, we must use due discretion in this matter, for there are logical times for receiving valuable lessons, ideas, truths, and constructive instruction which we gain from others. We must not build walls of positivity around our mental reservoirs, because of supplying these reservoirs of ours, for they are constantly being drained.

Your own good judgment must rule in this, always remembering that the negative or passive state of mind is the RECEIVING state, for you can receive to the point of congestion. The danger in this is that when you are swayed by this opinion and that, your mind refuses to act consciously. And if your mind is at the beck and call of others always, it will accomplish little or nothing.

In your dealings with other people, you must always be POSITIVE. Suppose a boxer should assume the negative (receptive) attitude before his opponent, wouldn't he lose the contest? He surely would. And it is just as necessary for you to cultivate a positive mental attitude when you are dealing with the business or the social affairs of life.

Here is a seeming paradox: if you would render the greatest assistance to the unfortunate, in most cases you must restrain your sympathy, somewhat. For when, by being over-sympathetic, you ABSORB the misfortunes, the troubles and the sorrows of another you may thus unfit yourself to render him or her any worth-while help. Have you ever noticed that those men and women who are least accessible to the crowd exercise a vastly greater power than those whose privacy is like that of a gold-fish bowl? For people who have no privacy permit themselves to become the victim of every passer-by, and as they absorb the negative emotions of others they become powerless to help others—or themselves. When you understand the Eternal Law that governs thought-waves (mental vibrations), then you will know why I teach you to withdraw yourself from the passing crowd. Sooner or later you must learn from experience that the PATHWAY TO POWER, to Mastery and to Happiness leads through the FREEDOM OF SECLUSION.

AVOID INFERIOR AND NEGATIVE PEOPLE

When you constantly associate with any person or persons of inferior or negative personalities, you are endangering your own success, your own magnetic powers, and your own happiness. Always avoid as you would a pestilence any close association with any person who is habitually "nervous", irritable, excitable, always worried or hurried; in a word, one who is emotionally negative.

For if you do persist in such an association you will sooner or later pay a grievous price for your folly, no matter how good your intentions may have been. Somewhere along the way, when you are passive or receptive, you will unconsciously absorb that negative person's emotional or mental attitude which will handicap you beyond belief.

How can you avoid this danger? You simply guard yourself mentally. Stop robbing yourself of success and happiness by such a mentally close association with such negative, emotional bankrupts. Your intentions may all be very fine—you are being so "noble", so "sympathetic," so "helpful." But you may little dream at what a terrible cost to yourself. Because when you make such a negative person the center of your thoughts, you may, it is true, send to him or her a current of thought-force which will perhaps help them to achieve a temporary material success which you) yourself may not now achieve, for you have parted with a great deal of your own actual Life Force and Vitality, a part of your own Capital Stock of Mental Power which you should use for yourself.

The crude mind of a negative person can, at best, use only a small part of the Force which you are sending out to them in your own well meant thought-waves, the rest of this power from you is just wasted; but in' return that very person whom you have mistakenly tried to bless, may send out to you the poisonous (negative) thought -currents from which disease and disappointment results.

The only associates whom you can really afford to cultivate are the happy, healthful, magnetic men and women—people who possess a POSITIVE personality. Only in this way can you be helped to really enter that higher mental dominion to which you aspire.

MENTAL DOMINION IS MIND CONTROL

Let us each understand clearly that mental dominion is simply mind control, and let us realize that this mental control—the hall-mark of a positive personality—is used every day, either knowingly or unknowingly, by countless thousands of successful men, professional and business men and women everywhere. Whether it is skill, training, service, merchandise or personality, every one of us is "selling" something—we are all salesmen and saleswomen in one way or another.

To be more specific—doctors, lawyers, merchants, ministers, priests, and people in every occupation and in every walk of life, all are using this mental influence—this mind control power—either knowingly or unknowingly.

Now we all know that the perverted use of thought force—through thought-waves of hatred, envy and strife, as shown in those murderous struggles which we call "wars,"—has many, many times almost wiped out the inhabitants of many nations. This sowing of the evil forces of hatred, the dragon's teeth that rend life's finer forces, the destruction of spiritual goodness on earth—all of these fill the very atmosphere around you with malicious influences, with evil and poisonous suggestions.

Our teachings show that only through enlightened REASON, only through the knowledge that comes to the Initiates, can we find and possess the invisible spear and helmet which will guard us from these unseen streams of (mental) malicious influences. For you remember that we have learned that a strong SUGGESTION whether it be good or whether it be evil which is sent out with great force and which is constantly repeated, will eventually control that recipient for whom it is intended and to whom it is directed.

The freedom or the enslavement of your mind and your life by any suggestion, good or evil, is determined entirely by your acceptance or your rejection of the thought-waves which carry that suggestion.

GUARD THE DOOR OF YOUR MIND AGAINST INTRUDERS

We live in a world which is ruled by suggestion. I have taught you much about the powers of suggestion in your earlier lessons, but now we shall study this subject still further. For now it is my purpose to teach you how to guard in the door of your mind against intruders—and by intruders I mean unwanted, negative or harmful suggestions. Let reason and your wisdom guard you and guide you in closing your mental doors against these unwanted, negative influences.

You cannot prevent suggestions from reaching you—because suggestions of every kind are all around you— but you CAN make harmful suggestions powerless by refusing to entertain them, by denying them any place in your thoughts. Carefully EXAMINE every suggestion, ask the WHY of each one, and beware of each new suggestion until it has passed the test of your reason, and examine each in the light of your teaching.

For a very long time, in fact throughout the ages, our Masters in the Mystery Schools have known and have taught their Initiates that a determined mind, backed by a strong will, always finds it possible to influence them, even when there is no visible communication by either written or spoken words, and even at sometimes great distances.

This is perhaps made clearer when we understand that telepathic communications can be conveyed by means of IMPRESSIONS, the recipient feeling what she or he often calls a "hunch," or an "intuition," or "message," which they often think comes from some other world.

Remember that a swinging pendulum which is suspended from a solid support will start into harmonic vibrations another pendulum hanging from the same support. A tuning fork or a violin string tuned to another will impart its vibrations to another fork or another violin string. Strike any key on a piano and its vibrations will set into motion the corresponding wire of another piano in the room. In the same manner strong mental vibrations emanating in the form of thought-waves from you can be invisibly communicated to another person whose vibrations are in harmony (in tune) with your own.

When your brain is intentionally active—when you WILL to send forth thought currents—these thought-waves travel in a straight line direct to the person to whom you direct them. You have powers of which you little dream and I shall teach you HOW to use these powers consciously.

SECRETS OF CONSCIOUS THOUGHT-PROJECTION

You can project (send) your thoughts and your purposes to other people by the ACTIVE POWER OF YOUR WILL. When you have a determined mind and a trained WILL, you can very easily transmit your thought-message to another person. There is a definite magnetic attraction between the brain centers of every human being and this attraction becomes powerful indeed when human vibrations are in tune (in harmony) with one another.

Suppose you have an object to be attained through another person—you are now the "SENDER", and you must focus the object firmly in your mind, and you must POSITIVELY EXPECT ("faith") that person to help you attain that object. In your own mind PICTURE exactly what you are mentally commanding this other person to do. Picture this desired action as being done now, or as already forming in the other person's mind.

Remember, through your conscious determination (WILL) you are bringing the psychic forces of yourself, the sender, and of the other person, the receiver, into MENTAL HARMONY. According to the degree of mental power and the determination (WILL) which you expend will be your success in attaining to this mutual rapport, but when you succeed the other person will believe that he has acted upon his own ideas.

Your firm determination, your resolve, and your absolute expectation that the other person will ACT ACCORDING TO YOUR DESIRES is your conscious method of bringing into working harmony the vibrations of your own unconscious brain centers with those of this other person.

In sending forth your waves of psychic (thought) force take as your motto these five words from the Apostle Paul: "This ONE THING I do." These significant words embody all that I have taught you about concentration. Make this motto your own, obey it to the letter, AND YOU WILL SUCCEED.

LESSON No. 19

MENTAL DOMINION—TRANSMITTING DESIRE, THOUGHT AND HEALING

Once more mentally picture yourself in your usual seat before the gleaming altar of the Sacred Triangle in that far-away King's Chamber, hidden deep within our occult Pyramid Temple. And around you are seated your familiar Companions, those other Initiates in White, and all within this mystic chamber are together waiting in the silence for another inspired lesson from the wisdom of our leader and guide, Kyron, the Wise—so named because he is the living exemplar of that deeper knowledge which the Masters in White have hidden from the outer world throughout the ages.

Kyron now imparts to us his silent blessing with upraised hands and then greets us in the words of our most ancient ritual.

Welcome, O Enlightened Ones, for unto thee is granted the Reception.

And now once again Kyron reads to us softly and clearly from that one of the Buddhist Scriptures which is named of old The Dhammapada. (From Chapter 6, of the Dhammapada, which is entitled "The Wise Man."

"If you see a man who shows you what is to be avoided, who administers a reproach; and is intelligent, follow that wise man as you would one who tells of hidden treasures; it will be better not worse, for him who follows him.

"Let him admonish, let him teach, let him forbid what is improper—he will be beloved of the good, by the bad he will be, hated.

"Do not have evil-doers for friends, do not have low people for friends the best of men.

"He who drinks in the (Eternal) Law lives happily, with a serene mind; the sage (the-wise) rejoices always in the Law as taught by the elect.

"Well-makers lead the water wherever they like, flecshers bend the arrow; carpenters create from a log of wood; wise people fashion (mould and control) themselves.

"Few there are among men who arrive at THE OTHER SHORE (Become Arhats; Initiates or Masters); the other people here run up and down the shore.

"A wise man should leave the dark state of ordinary life, and follow the bright state of the Bhikshu (the Masters)...

"Those whose minds are well grounded in the seven elements ("degrees") of knowledge, who without clinging to any (material) thing, rejoice in freedom from (sensual) attachment, whose appetites have been conquered, AND WHO ARE FULL OF LIGHT ("the Enlightened"), THEY ARE FREE EVEN IN THIS WORLD."

Kyron slowly closes The Dhammapada, and reverently lays the ancient volume upon the altar of the Sacred Triangle.

MENTAL DOMINION EXPRESSES THE HIGHER CONSCIOUSNESS

In seeking the higher powers of psychic energy, our first problem is discrimination as to our mental, subconscious and spiritual states of being. These states of being range all the way from simple animal lethargy to the highest spiritual inspiration—and we will soon discover that there is a natural rhythm in all states of consciousness.

As you increase your higher vibrations through concentration and meditation in The Silence, and in the various occult exercises which you are learning in this incomparable instruction, then you are able to express your higher psychic self, or state of being, because this mental dominion which you are attaining expresses your higher consciousness.

You must understand that we cannot transmute the entire substance of consciousness ("thoughts are things") all at once, so it is but natural that on the WAY you will fluctuate through or among many and different rates of vibration. These fluctuations or changes in your vibration from time to time as you advance result from the transforming of your etheric mental and astral "bodies", and also from the higher relations which you have formed with group karma, and this, of course, affects all of your contacts with environment or the outer world.

The next step in our Great Work, then, is to coordinate and to harmonize our outer and our inner lives, for unless we do a serious conflict will follow between the man or the woman we ARE and the man or woman we APPEAR TO BE. The whole problem of mental dominion according to our teaching—the great WORK of receiving and TRANSMITTING psychic energy, in the form of desire, of thought and of healing, lies in our ability to transform our lives so that we can BE and EXpress in our personality that which we really ARE in the higher consciousness itself.

ETHERIC ENERGY MANIFEST IN YOUR PHYSICAL BODY,

In this world, we live in the midst of a sea of invisible etheric force. In its highest apparent form, this etheric energy manifest itself in the organic life of your physical body. For in your physical body for the first time in nature chemical action comes under the direct influence of the mental, the astral and the spiritual SELF that is the Real You. Here, in these human bodies, we see constant changes in gross matter wrought by the power of mind and thought. Your human brain through its etheric counterpart, registers as THE IMAGE OF GOD.

Once you realize that the ETHERIC WORLD is the world of reality you no longer react blindly to the visible and tangible outer world which is your environment. Thus you release a tremendous volume of psychological energy from the heavy burdens of the material senses. This psychological power you can then use to develop your mental and astral "bodies", and to harmonize them with the Light Eternal that we call God.

Now perhaps for the first time we begin to understand the mighty lesson of our higher consciousness, when it is organized and controlled from WITHIN and we realize that WE CAN BE MASTERS. Then you realize, apart from all theories and abstractions, that YOU are a series of states—conditions—a body of thought and of spirit over which the world has no rulership (except that you give it) and that you have within your grasp absolute MASTERY.

Your next step in attaining to the mastery of psychic energy—mental dominion— is to realize that you are in reality a series of (mental) states. In all situations which arise in life, this means that you must deal with these mental or psychic states just as if they were objective realities. In doing this you are to discover the interrelation of your various states; you are to measure and transform your material sense-knowledge according to your higher consciousness. For this way you will be able to maintain your higher spiritual development in spite of every obstacle that circumstance and destiny may seem to place in your pathway.

For remember you are surrounded literally and always with a boundless sea of spirit force, and there is no time or place in your life where these tides of psychic energy may not carry you upward to the Universal Light. For as someone has said, "The truest end of life is to know the Life that never ends.'

TRANSMITTING (DIRECTING) DESIRE, THOUGHT, HEALING

Desire, Thought and Healing (or currents) are all mental products, and are all to be controlled only in accordance with certain basic, eternal laws. These laws you must understand, and so I shall devote some time to explaining these laws very simply and in words easy to understand.

First then, for your currents of desire, thought or healing to be effective, to be result-getting, these streams of mental force must be of unbroken continuity. The more continuous, the more constant your focused determination, and your conscious sending forth of these currents of magnetic force, the more powerful your desire, your thought, or your healing waves become, For we teach that each of these thought currents is actually substance, invisible, spiritual substance. For this is a palpable psychic force, generated in your mind by the direct action of your WILL, your determination. Continuity (constancy) of thought magnifies its power a thousand-fold. This truth throws a great light upon the Biblical admonition, "Pray without ceasing."

Pay no attention to the "distance" of the person to whom your thought currents are directed, because in the thought-realm there is neither time nor space, for you can think of a friend no matter how far away that friend is in the twinkling of an eye, and in the very next second your thought can return to someone sitting next to you; So neither time nor distance can be an obstacle to desire, thought, or transmission.

Transmission of these thought-currents can be cultivated and developed to the utmost success by each Initiate here, once you understand the methods I shall reveal to you in this lesson. And the requirements are few and simple: First, persistent practice; second, mental control through willpower; third, mental and physical balance, fourth, freedom from worry and DOUBT.

PERSISTENT PRACTICE GAINS MIND CONTROL

Perfect faith casts out fear from any mind, and doubt is just another form of fear—so your FAITH must be strong enough to eradicate all doubt from your mind. True, I realize that this is not easy, nor is it easy to concentrate your thought upon any one object or person without a break in its continuity, so your motto here must be "persistent practice," for persistent practice gains mind control for you. For, where there is a WILL there is a WAY, and constant practice is the WAY.

I have spoken repeatedly of continuity of thought, because this is absolutely essential to the power of potency of any mental transmission of psychic force. And when your WILL enters fully into this practice, you may be surprised to find that such mental activity does not result in fatigue. Instead you will find enjoyment and recreation in this Great "Work."

In order to prove to yourself by results that you can transmit desires, thoughts and healing with success it is not necessary that you understand all of the complexities of mental law or psychic science by which these ofttimes miraculous effects are obtained. But the first and greatest essential is that you maintain a faith and a belief so positive and so absolute that there is not even the shadow of a doubt in your mind, for through doubt fear creeps in, and fear is fatal to your success.

As I have pointed out, without continuity of thought the power to focus thought persistently—mental potency and psychic force are impossible. But the great secret is that you can acquire this continuity of thought-currents by PRACTICE. For by means of practice mental continuity becomes a habit.

As we all know, the transmission of the IDEA is the primary, the fundamental element in telepathy. The process of transmitting thought-currents is after all rather simple. In this process of transmitting Ideas, Desires, Emotions, Motor Impulses or Healing, you, the sender, must hold the particular entity you are sending as a mental image in your own mind, absolutely expecting AND WILLING that it shall be received clearly by the recipient.

REDUCE YOUR MESSAGE TO IDEAS AND IMAGES

Probably you have often heard or read of cases where two persons were in harmony, or closely bound together by affection, and Ideas, emotions or mental messages were consciously sent by one mind and almost instantly received by the other person's mind.

In beginning this work, at first your transmitted thought may make such a slight impression as to be merely "felt" by the person to whom you direct your effort, and may result only in a "feeling" of uneasiness. But don't be discouraged, for this is a really fine beginning.

This is true because just as surely as you persevere, your persistent WILLING—DRIVING psychic force can make this impression so much deeper and so much more intense that a vision or a definite thought of you, the sender, or of the scene from which you send the message, may form within the mind of the recipient, and appear as very real to him or her. As a result of your occult work in thought-sending, close friends of yours or loved ones at a distance may often mentally "see".your face, or see you wearing familiar clothes. The reason for this is simple—the waves of mind-energy which you are sending forth strike the mind of the recipient when in a passive mood, and your message is interpreted by this person in the light of his or her own recollections of you.

One of the first requisites in this work is to acquire mental composure, balance, relaxation. You will acquire this by first constantly relaxing all the voluntary muscles, and by purposely withdrawing your thought from other objects. For this work you will find a place of quiet, of silence, very essential, especially in the beginning. Now with the body comfortable and entirely relaxed, and with the eyes closed, practice deliberate reflective reverie—meditation—this you will find to be the very greatest help in acquiring the proper mental attitude.

You must control your attention, so as not to disturb the correct mental attitude, or condition, when you have acquired it. This correct mental attitude is very much like the state we call "day dreaming," and your magic affirmation, which you will repeat softly over and over is this:

"Now my entire body, muscles and mind are relaxing, relaxing, relaxing."

SECRET OF VISUALIZING THE MAGIC TUBE

Now, with body and mind relaxed, visualize (picture)yourself as sitting at the open end of a very long tube, like a long, circular tunnel and see yourself as quietly looking into this tube. This tube or tunnel shuts everything out of your vision—except the one, certain person whom you "see" as stationed at the other end of this long tube, for this is the one person who is to "receive" your vibrating thought-wave. Probably it will require a number of sittings before you will be able to clearly picture this long tube, and "see" only that one other person through the tube. At first you will mentally see a bluish haze in the tube, but after a short time this will change to a haze or misty violet color. Then you will find that you are beginning to "see" (visualize) that person at the other end of the tube quite distinctly.

When you have attained to this state of development in your exercise, when the visualized image of the other person at the far end of your mental tube has become clear-cut and well defined, you will be amazed to find that your magic tube is seemingly becoming shorter and shorter. In other words, you are mentally drawing the person to whom you are directing your thought-waves nearer and nearer to yourself. Now you must hold the thought of expecting FIRMLY, together with the mental attitude of entire certainty (absolute FAITH) that what you WILL to bring to pass will occur. During this process of visualizing, keep your mind focused upon the one great thought-image of exactly WHAT you desire this person at the other end of your magic tube to do, to feel, or to experience.

ESTABLISHING MENTAL RAPPORT BY THE PSYCHOSCOPE

I have named this imaginary thought-tube which I have described to you, and which I want you to use, the Psychoscope, because through it you can establish rapport (mental harmony) with any person you choose, be they near or far. But always remember, the great secret in this work is that you must clearly picture the action, the emotion, or the effect you desire the recipient to manifest as actually taking place WHILE YOU CONCENTRATE AND SEND PSYCHIC POWER THROUGH THE PSYCHOSCOPE.

According to the amount of silent thought-force which you expend in attaining to this condition of rapport of mental harmony of vibrations. When you have established this state of harmony between your mind and that of the recipient, then you can really and actually transmit (send) your Desire, your Emotion, or your

Healing Power to that person whom you have mentally pictured mat the other end of your Psychoscope. However, you must understand that when these thought waves are RECEIVED, when you have; attained this unison of minds, the person who receives if he does not KNOW you are sending will almost always regard this desire, this emotion, or this Healing effect as his own accomplishment.

Of course, as I have told you so often throughout these lessons, concentration is the first requisite in using and directing the marvelous powers of your mind. Everywhere around you there is the "scatter-brain", who wastes brain power and never accomplishes anything. But you, if you focus your Desire-waves your Emotion-waves or your Healing waves through the Psychoscope, can purposely penetrate and ATTRACT the thoughts of any person upon whom you concentrate, sooner or later—and usually surprisingly soon.

According to the ancient wisdom, however, I must warn you that there is a very real danger in attracting an excess of thought-waves or the WRONG KIND of thought-currents to yourself. You must be careful to guard against promiscuity in thought attraction, take care to attract only those thought-forms from others which will be of the greatest advantage and help to you.

You will remember that I have previously taught that the human brain is a chemical laboratory, the most wonderful in all the world, and that I have also taught you that BREATH IS LIFE—("prana")—and I want to add to this another startling fact, thought-waves are discharged (sent out) only in the process of breathing.

We attract the thought-waves of other persons when we INHALE (when we draw the breath inward), and we discharge or send forth our own thought-waves when we EXHALE (send the breath out). Now, this being true, you can readily see that the deeper and the more thorough is your breathing when you inhale and when you exhale the greater is your power to attract or to repel thought-waves.

Also, we have learned that not only we breathe with our lungs, but with the skin as well, In other words, the nerve endings at the surface of the skin are also senders and receivers of mental-currents. Of course, this receptivity of the skin surfaces is most intensive wherever these tiny nerve endings are most numerous. Normally the left side of the human body, and the left hand especially are receivers of mental currents (thought-waves), while with the right side of the body, and the right hand particularly, we send out thought currents (Psychic force)

PINEAL GLAND TRANSMITS—THE PITUITARY RECEIVES

Now, more than ever, you will appreciate the supreme importance of these two greatest gland centers of your whole body, when I point out to you once more that in all thought transmission, the Pineal Gland is the concentrated SENDING POINT, or center, and the Pituitary Gland is the central RECEIVING STATION IN YOUR brain.

Again, so as to make this process doubly clear to you, thought waves, or psychic force, is sent forth from your body on the vibrations of your breath, and I mean the breath which you exhale or send out not only from your lungs but also from the capillary nerve endings of the skin surface. And these same invisible thought vibrations are taken into the body when you inhale your breath, and likewise drawn in by absorption by the skin.

This principle is most simply stated so that you can remember it always in these words, "Breathe IN, receive thought waves; breathe out, send or transmit thought currents."

You DO NOT send forth thought waves through your skull—but you transmit them on your breath, so you see we are all thus constantly charging the atmosphere around us with your own mental currents. Now you can easily understand our PERSONALITY, whether weak and negative, or powerful and magnetic, depends entirely upon WHAT KIND OF THOUGHT- VIBRATIONS WE SEND FORTH.

In our next lesson, Lesson 20, we will take up the question of MENTAL DOMINANCE, the art of Mastering your Secret POWERS. I am sure you will find this to be most Thrillingly Interesting and Helpful to you in achieving that higher accomplishment, your Heart's Desire, toward which you are so earnestly striving. I leave you now with the assurance that the richest blessings of Allah are yours to command, once you have learned the secret of using your latent (sleeping) Powers that are your Divine Birthright.

LESSON NO. 20
THE PATH TO PSYCHIC RECEPTION

Third Gateway of the Temple Invisible—Being the secret Instruction Taught by The Masters in White, Whose Sublime Precepts are Now Exemplified in these Lessons.

MENTAL DOMINANCE—MASTERING YOUR SECRET POWERS

Far away from the tumult of the outer world, again we are quietly sitting before that beautiful glowing altar of the Sacred Triangle within the mystic King's Chamber, hidden in the depths of our symbolic Pyramid Temple. Together with all the other white-robed Initiates, now your familiar Companions, all are awaiting our next lesson from the matchless teachings of Kyron, the Wise—that mysterious Master in White who represents the occult wisdom of the Mystery Schools of the ages.

But listen—as Kyron with hands upraised in blessing once more welcomes us in the ritualistic greeting:

"Welcome, O Enlightened Ones, for unto thee is granted the Reception."

And now in clear and vibrant tones Kyron reads to us our evening lesson, these passages from Chapter 5 of that ancient volume, The Life of Buddha, as translated first from the Sanskrit into Chinese in A.D. 420 by Dharmaraksha, and later translated from Chinese into English by one, Samuel Beal. These are the words of Buddha.

"Therefore the wise man ought to practice pure behavior; passing through the wilderness of birth and death, pure conduct is to him a virtuous guide. From pure behavior comes SELF-POWER, which frees a man from many dangers; pure conduct, like a ladder enables us to climb to heaven.

"Those who found themselves on right behavior, cut off the source of pain and grief; but they who by transgression destroy this mind (wisdom), may mourn the loss of every virtuous principle. To gain this end first banish every ground of "self " (selfish pride), this thought of "self" (false pride) shades every lofty aim, even as the ashes that conceal the fire, treading on which the foot is burned. Pride and indifference shroud the heart, too, as the sun is obscured by the piled-up clouds...

"As age and disease waste youthful beauty, so pride of SELF destroys all virtue; the Devas and Asuras (evil or negative spirits) thus from jealousy and envy, raised mutual strife.

"As I am a conqueror amid conquerors, so he who conquers SELF is one with me. He who little cares to conquer self is but a foolish man; beauty, or earthly things, family renown and such things all are utterly inconstant, and what is changeable can give no rest.

"Covetous desire is the greatest source of sorrow, appearing as a friend, in secret is our enemy...The Fire which fiercely burns the desert grass dies out, and then the grass will grow again; but when the fire of (sensual) lust burns up the heart then how hard for true religion there to dwell! for lust seeks worldly pleasures, these pleasures add to an impure karman (karma) by this evil karman (karma) a man falls into perdition, so there is no greater enemy to man than lust."

Again closing this sacred book of the Buddhists Kyron gently replaces it upon the Sacred Triangle altar, and proceeds with our present lesson upon the greater mastery of our secret powers and the deeper attainments of mental dominance.

THE "LIVING FIRE" OF ZOROSTER

Each student should know and understand that throughout all the ages of the past our Masters in White-those great Initiates of the ancient wisdom who have bequeathed to us their secret knowledge—that these, the "heaven Born," have had from the beginning a thorough understanding that within the pulsating nerve-fluids of the brain, the heart, and the Endocrine glands`is to be found the master key to the mastery of our tremendous secret occult and mental powers.

For countless ages ago these vibrant nerve fluids were called the "Universal Solvent." the "Azothe," and the "Quintessence" by the alchemist, they are the "Living Fire" of Zoroster, the "Teloma" of Hermes, the "Generative Fire" of Heroditus, the "Ignis Substillisimus of Hypocrates, the "Astral Light" of the Kabala, the "Spirit of Life" of St. Thomas Aquinas, the "Subtle Matter" of Descartes.

Every student to whom this "Key" or knowledge is revealed can now scientifically understand the many phenomena which until now have been unexplainable, and by the use of this Master Key of psychic power will be enabled through development to perform "miracles."

Again and again I have stated very emphatically and very plainly that each and every one of you who has progressed into a working knowledge of our Great Work in this School is endowed with latent, hidden powers which will amaze you once you put them into active use. Mental dominance is the birthright of every true student.

So here and now, and in this lesson, we shall proceed to get right down to the fundamentals of using these hidden or secret powers of yours, and right down to the basic practical work of "cashing in" on your mental dominance.

You will recollect that in our last lesson I told you that when you are transmitting thoughtwaves, these mental vibrations DO NOT LEAVE YOU—THE SENDER—BY WAY OF YOUR CRANIUM-that thought does not penetrate through your skull and flesh on its way from there. Instead, I explained to you that THOUGHT IS TRANSMITTED ON OR IN YOUR BREATH. Further, I pointed out to you that thus you are constantly charging the atmosphere around you with your mental vibrations, either positive or negative, either powerful or weak and wavering.

HUMAN HANDS POWERFUL TRANSMITTERS OF PSYCHIC FORCE

And now you are ready to receive another startling revelation about the sending forth of thought currents, and that is the fact that human hands your hands—can be used as powerful transmitters of psychic force.

For since time immemorial when treating the sick, the afflicted, the suffering victims of disease THE HEALER has released and set forth his Healing Power through his hands, and especially so from the palm and the fingers of his RIGHT hand. As of old he completes the magnetic circle and replenishes his life-giving and often miracle working vital force by drawing in fresh supplies through the left side of his body and through the left hand. But through the determined direction of the WILL, the left hand can also be caused to send forth these magnetic, invisible, healing thought currents (or vibrations).

So you see you actually have the power dormant in your own hands to transmit your thoughts and your mental vibrations—if you will only learn and use this so-strange power by the simple methods I am revealing to you.

You are the transmitter (the sender), or perhaps it is more nearly correct to say that your WILL is the dynamo that energizes or endows with power your thought transmissions. For example, when transmitting desire, thought, or psychic messages of healing, or any other messages, through THE PSYCHOSCOPE word your message very simply, using short, strong, forceful words, and use the fewest possible words.

Now repeat your message again and again; each time striving to send it direct to the recipient with more and more force, and visualize ("see") yourself as sending your thought waves in a straight line through The Psychoscope (your "thought tunnel") by the sheer power of your own WILL. So when the Psychoscope seems to you to grow shorter and shorter, as it will with practice, and when the other person at the far end has thus been mentally brought close to you, then you will use your hands for added power. Stretch forth both hands, fingers extended and close together, and palms slanting somewhat upward and outward toward the other Person, whom you are visualizing (mentally picturing).

At the same time breathe regularly, deeply and slowly, and with each breath hold the thought of absolute expectancy—you must feel, you must believe, you must KNOW that the recipient whom you have chosen WILL GET YOUR MESSAGE. Just as surely as you are persistent and just as certainly as you follow this simple method you will be rewarded with amazing results.

BIBLE TELLS OF POWER OF UPRAISED ARMS AND HANDS

Recalling to your memory the histories of Moses, Joshua, Elijah, and other Old Testament leaders favored of the Lord, is it not significant that we find that they were continually reminded by Jehovah to raise their hands high above their heads, and to also stretch them forth? You will remember that during the wars that Israel fought, the priests, the leaders and the warriors, we are told by the scriptures, supported the upraised arms of "the chosen of the Lord." According to these accounts, as they held their arms and hands upraised, as these certain chosen ones did during battle, some invisible, some mystic Power seemed to insure them victory. But according to these scriptures, when the arms and hands of these chosen ones dropped to their sides, the battles were lost by Israel, or went sorely against them.

It is interesting to know, in this relation, that when the modern minister rabbi or priest raise the arms and the hands and extend them over their followers-when bestowing their "blessing" that this gesture (The "Mudras") is simply the modern version of one of the oldest religious customs in the world. Even the most ancient "pagan" religions used this same gesture, and always and in every land the original meaning was the same—the sending out of "spiritual" (occult) power in thought waves. But today this formerly sacred and significant gesture has little if any effect or meaning, for it has become an empty symbol.

But in your life, if you faithfully follow our methods and our secret instructions, the great and good results you most earnestly desire will soon begin to manifest themselves. Day by day you will find that the power of your brain cells to transmute your thoughts into very real material blessings is increasing, often with results almost beyond belief. For with each directed thought, each conscious breath, and with every heart beat you are building up a new mental force, you are creating new brain "substance," you are attracting new and finer conscious conditions through new and finer thoughts.

Thus you consciously transmit "new" thoughts (new only to the changing mind of the recipient) subtly break up and destroy opposing negative thoughts in the mind of the person who is unconsciously RECEIVING your stream of directed thought—waves. Because this change in his thought-forms is imperceptible to the person receiving them, he will not know that this change is due to the conscious effort of your intellect, or that YOUR WILL has worked this "miracle" in his life (unless you should so inform him at some later date).

STRUGGLE FOR SUCCESS IN BUSINESS WORLD IS MENTAL

Look about you in the business world, and everywhere you will find that the battles for success and for supremacy are mental battles that are fought in the private offices of the executives. The weak points in their own organization and in that of their competitors are carefully investigated and weighed by these executives, and when their decisions are made and their "battle plans" are completed, subordinates carry out their instructions. Thus, the actual work, the effective work that carries any business to success is MENTAL WORK, so you can see that the mind of the executive must be strong and alert, able to solve the many difficult problems that arise daily.

Just so you, as a student, when you successfully master the simple instructions which I have given you in the preceding lesson and in this lesson: on the method of transmitting your thought waves of your mental messages, will find that this strange development of new mental power has endowed your mind with a greater vitality, a more vivid outlook, and a renewed psychic virility.

As you demonstrate success in transmitting thought waves, desires, healing, etc., and as your concentration grows stronger and stronger you will find that your entire personality is being renewed and transformed, changed from weakness to power, your eyes become magnetic, your voice more expressive, and you will gain a marvelous control over your .breathing.

When, through faithful practice, you learn how to use The Psychoscope (the "Astral Tube"), so that you are able to bring the image of the person to whom you are directing your thought waves seemingly almost at arm's length from you, then you have mastered the great secret of THOUGHT CONTACT.

But once again I would repeat that in order to successfully experience the wonderful results of this great secret of thought contact you must eliminate all DOUBT from your mind. When your mind is burdened with.doubt, your desires are dull, dormant, sleeping. While it is true that both doubt and desire are thought "substances" (or products), we must remember that they are of exactly opposite natures. These two can never blend, for doubt cancels desire. Desire can rule your life only when you have banished doubt. When you have cast out doubt, then through FAITH your desire assumes shape in your material world.

SIMPLE EXPERIMENTS IN THOUGHT CONTACT

To help you in banishing your doubts—to prove to your self that YOU CAN establish thought contacts, that right NOW you can transmit mental messages and SEE their result, here are three very simple experiments for your practice. And if you will follow these simple methods persistently, the results will prove more to you than volumes which I might write.

First: Suppose that you happen to find yourself about ten feet behind some person on the street who is going your way—in this experiment keep about this distance behind this person and fix your gaze intently upon the back of this person's neck, at the base of the brain. Now at the same time purposely WILL and DESIRE (mentally command) that this person shall turn and look at you. You will be surprised often to find that it may take only a few moments or a very few minutes of intense, concentrated WILLING on your part to succeed in this experiment. As a rule, even in the beginning of this occult experiment fifty percent of your trials should be successful.

Second: Here is another simple experiment which you can carry out secretly when riding in a street car, a train or in any other public place where people are sitting. Pick out some man or woman at random, one who is sitting either at your right or your left, or is seated across an aisle from you. Now without looking at the person whom you have chosen., strongly WILL (command) that he or she shall turn and look at you. Simple, isn't it? Yet that person will generally in a few moments suddenly turn and look at you as if you had actually called him or her by name. .

Third: Suppose you are meeting another person as you are walking, DO THIS—as you approach him, look straight at him, fixing your gaze on the root of this person's nose (right between his eyes) and purposely, strongly WILL (comman) that he pass you either on your left or your right side, whichever one you choose. You will be amazed to find that this little-experiment is casually successful.

I am giving you these simple experiments because they are of tremendous value to you in PROVING to you that you can establish thought contact when YOU WILL, that you can silently and consciously dominate others and too, these experiments will aid you beyond measure in developing your POWER OF WILL, and the visualizing of your CLEAR-CUT DESIRES upon the mind-screens of other people.

PRACTICAL DIRECTIONS FOR MENTAL DOMINANCE

In your occult work of establishing thought contacts and acquiring mental dominance by thought-vibrations which you send as "messages" through the pictured Psychoscope, or Astral Tube, you must at ways be practical, and make the work just as easy as possible for yourself. For instance, when you have chosen some certain person to be the recipient of your thought-waved message, choose as the time of your "sending" an hour in the day when it is least likely that disturbing conditions will prevent your mental message, desire, command, or healing current from being most clearly received.

Decidedly it is most practical that you avoid endeavoring to complete thought contacts or thought circuits during this person's dinner hour (or any meal time) and especially the hour that follows dining.

This rule applies equally to you yourself, because when your stomach is busy digesting the food you have eaten, your mind becomes sluggish, your brain slows down and so it is not in the proper condition to send out strong intense thought waves. Instead, choose a time when your stomach is inactive, or at rest.

Now as your first step in transmitting your mental messages or your psychic influence to the person whom you have chosen, write out on paper in the form of very short sentences exactly WHAT you desire this person to DO, or exactly WHAT you wish him or her to FEEL about you, or the exact HEALING EFFECT you desire to impart through the Psychoscope. Far example, write similar sentences to these:

"I deeply desire that A. be attracted to me."

"I absolutely demand that B. Send me the money..."

"With all my Soul, I intensely WILL that C. be HEALED."

Make each sentence as brief as you can, and express each mental message clearly and concisely. Use white paper, of course, a separate slip for each sentence, and cut these slips to the size I gave you in our previous lesson on the use of The FOCALIZER.

Now once more you are going to use your FOCALIZER, but this time in combination with the PSYCHOSCOPE (the Astral Tube). Choose which sentence-message you are going to concentrate upon, read it over out loud to yourself several times, then read it over and over mentally, thus imprinting it upon your own mind.

Now attach this chosen slip of paper just below your Focalizer which you remember is to be upon your wall, just at the level of your eyes when you are seated. Now, sitting in a comfortable chair directly in front of your Focalizer, relax your body completely, and breath deeply and slowly for two or three minutes.

THE FOCALIZER CONCENTRATES—THE PSYCHOSCOPE SENDS

Then for a few moments fix your eyes upon the center black circle, of the, Focalizer. Now concentrate your attention upon the desire, the demand, the command, or the healing affirmation written upon the slip of paper which you have attached to the wall right below the Focalizer. Next, close your eyes and "Look" through your imaginary Psychoscope, or Astral Tube picture ("see") the person whom you have mentally placed at the other end of this imaged tube, picture the object, the action, or the effect which you are sending by WILL-Power to this other person as already taking form, taking place, or taking effect in the other person's mind, or feelings, or physical body, as the case may be.

With due practice, I assure you it will not be too long before you will be able to see quite clearly the mental picture of the thing, the objective, or the event you are WILLING as actually forming and taking place, then you will know that you are well on the road to success.. When you are thus able to image your desire clearly, still with the eyes closed, stretch out your right arm and hand, and, as you exhale your breath, make a number of slow passes upward and downward with your hand over this objective image which you mentally "see" before you. At the same time, strongly WILL (command) that your entire desire shall be fulfilled completely.

Meantime keep your mind focused on the act, the event or the effect which you picture as taking place. As a matter of fact, the thought-picture you create must be a LIVING THING, and not just a meaningless series of words. You must "SEE" your mental picture in shape and form as something already happening.

The principle involved in this occult sending of mental or psychic currents of force is simple—when your mind is focused upon the creating and the sending of the thought image to this particular person, the vibrations which you thus send forth will sooner or later objectify that image into reality.

In order to illustrate the use of your personal power in direct contact, suppose you meet some person upon whom you would impress your desire, your demand or your Healing Power without even speaking of such an intention. Suppose that you shake hand's with him; as you withdraw your hand from his, let your thumb and fingers firmly but lightly drag across the palm and back of his hand, as you pull your hand away slowly. Naturally, while shaking hands you will be talking to him, so at the same time looking at him, focus your eyes on the root of his nose, and during this somewhat brief but intent glance you must SUGGEST MENTALLY (silently) and STRONGLY THE RESULT YOU DESIRE.

Also during your conversation, extend the right arm, palm outwards, towards him in some gesture, for thus your thought-waves are projected through the countless never endings at your palm and fingers. As you do this, INTENSELY WILL that the exact results you desire shall be attained—and you may be amazed to see your desire so quickly realized.

Always bear in mind that your hands are MAGNETIC, and that your thought currents are sent forth from your hands while you are EXHALING your breath. Not only are you able to project your psychic force through your hands, but remember also that mental contact is more easily established while shaking hands. So, while shaking hands, just AFFIRM strongly (and silently) the desire you wish this person to help you to realize.

LESSON NO. 21
THE PATH TO PSYCHIC RECEPTION

Third Gateway of the Temple Invisible- Being the secret Instruction Taught by The Masters in White, Whose Sublime Precepts are Now Exemplified in these Lessons.

YOUR DYNAMIC MENTAL POWER—ADVANCED TRAINING

Once more, with our Companion Initiates in White, we are gathered in the magical

King's Chamber, far within the depths of our imaged Pyramid Temple.

Before us an eerie glow bathes the beautiful altar of the Sacred Triangle, as we quietly await the further and deeper lessons to be given us by Kyron, the Wise, for now he has promised to reveal to us still greater and undreamed of depths of our dynamic mental powers, and to grant to us still more advanced training in the mental magic which has been hidden from the vulgar eyes of the world through the ages by the Masters in White.

And now, with hands upraised in blessing as always, Kyron bids us welcome in the words of our most ancient ritual:

"Welcome, O Enlightened Ones, for unto thee is granted the Reception."

From that ancient Buddhic scripture, the "Dhammapada, or Path to Virtue," Kyron now reads to us the evening lesson from Chapter 4, which is entitled "Flowers." In clear, well modulated tones Kyron reads to us the flowing words of this sacred old book wherein; strangely enough, Epicurean philosophy and the faith of the devout Buddhist find a common meeting ground. Listen:

"Who shall overcome this earth, and the world of Yama, the lord of the departed, and the world of the gods? Who shall find out the plainly shown path of virtue, as the clever man finds the right flower?

"He who KNOWS that this (physical) body is like froth, and has learnt that it is as unsubstantial as a mirage, will break the flower-pointed arrow of Mara, and never see the king of death.

"Like a beautiful flower, full of color, but without scent, are the fine and fruitful words of him who ACTS accordingly.

"The scent of flowers does not travel against the wind, nor that of sandal-wood, or of Tagara and Mallika flowers; but the odor (vibrations, atmosphere) of GOOD people travels even against the wind.********

"As on a heap of rubbish cast upon the highway the lily will grow full of sweet perfume and delight, thus among those who are mere rubbish the disciple (Initiate) of the truly enlightened Buddha shines forth by his knowledge above the blinded worldling."

Closing the ancient Dhammapada, Kyron now lays the volume reverently upon the altar of the Sacred Triangle, and begins the present lesson thus.

SYMBOLS AND PARABLES USED TO CONCEAL— ANCIENT WISDOM

In every root religion throughout the ages and in almost every course of instruction yet today which purports to develop dynamic and occult mental and spiritual power the practice always is to conceal the Ancient Wisdom behind symbols and parables. So in teaching you these hidden powers which seem magical to the uninitiated, we purposely present our occult lessons in plain and simple words, and avoid as much as possible allegories or symbols that may be confusing.

When the first dawn of occult "Light" shines within the mind and soul of our students, many of whom are just emerging from the shadows of an orthodox or materialistic viewpoint, it is very natural that the first interest aroused is in the possibility of attaining to "magical" powers, such as clairvoyance, thought-transmission, miraculous healings, etc.

Too often the Occult Advancement through the various degrees of these lessons in the Ancient Wisdom may mean to the disciple in the beginning ONLY these seemingly "magical" powers. This, of course, is a somewhat mistaken impression of our marvelous instruction, because it is too limited. For while your development, as and if you faithfully follow our teachings, will result in powers which seem like magic to the outsider, but in themselves even these powers are not the chief result to be obtained.

True self-development is the goal to which we point every student, and this is the great aim of every student of the Ancient Wisdom within our ranks, from the beginner to the Elder Brothers or the Masters in White. Yet we must warn you that we do not use or allow any "hot-house" methods of forcing premature or one-sided development of your psychic powers, for this would of only result in loss of balance and would actually retard your real development. So, our instruction comes to you in carefully graduated lessons, which insure you the possibility of a mature, a complete, a fully rounded understanding.

DEVELOPMENT OF YOUR "MAGICAL" POWERS

As I have intimated before, through the ages our Masters in White have often been forced to conceal the simple and beautiful truths of the Ancient Wisdom, in order to transmit them to us, behind obscure phrases, symbols, and seemingly meaningless forms. This we find especially true in the centuries of religious hatred and persecution, when to even mention any occult or higher teaching meant a quick trip to the torture chamber or to the stake.

A knowledge of the derivation and the true meaning of some of these obscure words, many of which are in common use today, will remove many of our misapprehensions. As I have just spoken of things magical, for instance, let us take the word MAGIC as an example. Looking up this word in the ordinary desk dictionary, you will find it given as a synonym for "sorcery, necromancy and supernatural powers."

But as a matter of fact, these meanings are the result of centuries of misused words, indifference and ignorance of the people in general. Now if you will consult a complete dictionary, one which gives the derivatives and the roots of words you will find that our word Magic comes from the Persian word, MAGI, meaning wisdom! So, in its true sense this word Magic does NOT mean, sleight-of-hand nor trickery, but is a word denoting WISDOM, or a deep knowledge of Nature's Eternal Laws.

So according to this, the true meaning of the word MAGIC, which is the meaning of this word as I am using it in these lessons, each of you has the power and the ability to become a magician. Further than this, you are a magician in so far as you USE these latent and undeveloped powers which we are now teaching you now to demonstrate in the material world.
understanding of the layman and utterly bewildering to the ignorant.

To the savage, for instance, ignorant even of the existence of these inner laws of Nature these modern inventions are a source of wonder and of terror. And our own estimable (?) but ignorant ancestors would have burned Edison, Bell, Marconi and the Wright Brothers at the stake for being in league with the "devil" even as they sacrificed Gallil, Bruno, and numberless others for possessing "magical," forbidden knowledge!

Just as it is with the word "magical", so it is with the word Occult, the one meaning that which is hidden, and the other meaning the NEW KNOWLEDGE. For these words represent that deeper knowledge (the "Ancient Wisdom") for which the ignorant either do not search, or only search superficially and then say it does not exist. The truth is of course that such knowledge DOES NOT EXHIST FOR THE IGNORANT.

That is why it is given unto you, as an Initiate, to know these "hidden" things. ALL of Nature's eternal fundamental laws, whether of chemistry, of electronics, atomic energy or of healing, of thought-transmission, or of Soul-powers, ALL are hidden deeply—hidden always EXCEPT to the "IN-SIGHT" (the inner vision) of the scientist or the Initiate. I can illustrate this profound truth most clearly by repeating for you once more this striking passage from the ancient Chandogya Upanishad:

"Just as those who do not know the spot might go over a hidden treasure of gold again and again, but not find it, so do all creatures here go day by day to the Brahma-world, but do not find it, for truly they are carried away by what is false."

The "Brahma-world" as I have taught you, is the world WITHIN OURSELF— your inner Self, that is the "golden treasure" hidden ("occult") WITHIN YOU." As an Initiate, you are taught the hidden laws of this innerworld of SELF, and I am but striving to help you to find for yourself its inestimable treasures.

HOW TO AWAKEN YOUR OCCULT POWERS

Before you can awaken and master the almost unbelievable powers WITHIN yourself, you must understand your own entire organization as a LIVING BEING lest you, too, be "carried away by what is false."

The average, uninitiated person roughly divides man into what he calls "body and soul," or perhaps "matter and spirit," usually not even understanding what he means by these words.

However in the first few lessons of your first course, you were taught that a more complete and subtle division of this wondrous organism that is YOU is necessary that you may understand that even your physical body is a precise and marvelous instrument reflecting the "image" (stamp) of the Divine.

Perhaps, like many of our other Initiates, in seeking the higher development of your "magical" powers, or in searching for the occult (hidden) mysteries of The Ancient Wisdom, you, too, may have tried to follow the mazes of either Hindu or Theosophical writings. If so, very probably you have become lost amid Sanskrit terms, symbols, or allegories, which though you are exquisitely subtle and accurate, are indeed difficult to understand unless you have the guidance of a Master.

On the other hand, many of our Initiates have formerly sought to unlock these mysteries by the study of psychoanalysis according to Jung and Adler, or perhaps Freud, only to find that they are merely approaching the edges of the analysis of that intricate; human-divine SELF that we call Man.

But it must be remembered that you are living IN and functioning UPON the material plane in this present life, and that because you are living IN and demonstrating THROUGH a physical body, whatever under— standing of the hidden powers WITHIN that work "miracles" must come to YOU through that body, or through its organs. How amazingly perfect your brain can become, when your body is trained and purified by our simple methods until it is able to both receive and to transmit vibrations (thought waves) from superconscious or astral planes—that brain-mind perfection is the purpose of this "Mystery School."

PERSONALITY—RESULT OF YOUR THINKING AND MEMORY

In your earlier lessons you learned that Personality is the most important one thing in your life. Also you learned that your personality is your characteristic behavior, or the every-day ways in which you express in your physical life the habit-patterns of your mind AND of your memory.

As I have intimated previously in this lessons YOU are individual Divine Life, YOU are individual Divine Mind, YOU are individual Divine SELF manifesting in, by and through a material, physical body. So all of your particular identifying ways (characteristics) by which you manifest your personal existence to other human beings, all of these are the direct or the indirect results of the thinking you have done and of your power of Memory, for MEMORY is the great recorder of thought, of sensation, of experience.

In this connection, let us realize the wonder-working power of memory. Simply stated, that YOU which you now exhibit in Life's shop-window to the passing crowd is moulded by your thinking, true, but it is only perfected by a powerful memory, and sadly marred by undeveloped or poor memory.

As you have already learned from your previous lessons, within the depths of your own mind are all the vital elements necessary to work the "miracle" of transforming your life from failure to success, from sick ness to health and from useless existence to abounding happiness. And the WAY to that success, to that health and to that happiness—the WAY that leads to that transforming miracle is the Path to strong, developed, positive personality.

Never forget that within you the great dynamo of your subconscious (deeper) mind awaits your conscious command to connect your life with those mighty, invisible currents of cosmic energy which can transform both YOU and your entire material world. If your personality has been neutral, weak or negative, it is because you hAve trusted to some "trial-and error" method of personality-growth, and so this radiant energy which is rightfully yours has been perverted, repressed or disconnected entirely.

HAVING EYES, SEE YE: NOT?" ASKED JESUS

Nearly twenty centuries ago Jesus, The Nazarite Master, asked three keenly pointed questions Lions of the rabble about him who had condemned themselves to nonentity, to failure and to servitude—and the answer to their plight is plainly intimated in the question themselves. These are the three significant questions:

"...perceive ye not, neither understand?...Having eyes, see ye not? AND DO YE NOT REMEMBER?

Probably you long ago realized that the five senses-seeing, hearing, smelling, tasting and feeling—are the only possible ways by which impressions of the outer world can be transmitted to your mind. And it is from these outer impressions that have been brought to the Inner Self by these five senses that your whole mental world of ideas, mind-pictures and thoughts has been created.

And as long as you live you must always create your inner world of ideas, images and thinking from your sense-impressions of the outside world, the material world around you. Now if a great many of these numberless sense-impressions have been confused, hazy and weak in their reception, then from these you can only acquire a more or less confused, hazy and weak personality.

So, to MAGNIFY your inner, mental world, you must first MAGNIFY YOUR SENSE IMPRESSIONS and, because MEMORY IS THE REGISTER OF THE

MIND, you must imprint upon memory clear-cut, vivid and distinct impressions.

This is the simple lesson contained in Christ's three pregnant questions.

YOU can acquire a strong, unfailing, outstanding memory by the quite simple methods which I shall reveal to you presently. Plainly, the first step is to TRAIN YOUR EYES TO SEE! From this day forth I advise you never to be satisfied to "see" objects or people as merely hazy, indistinct images. Begin right now to FOCUS your attention upon the object or the person you desire to observe by the conscious direction of your WILL. In this way you will see clearly, sharply and distinctly, and very soon you will realize that your MEMORY has improved wonderfully.

YOU WILL REMEMBER WHAT YOU REALLY SEE

With personal interest, with focused attention and by the conscious demand of your Will, your mind will register accurately what you SEE with your eyes—and you will REMEMBER.

Whatever you see, or hear, or taste or smell or feel, everything in life that you experience, every emotion, every thought is imprinted upon your mind as an impression. And each impression alters or changes the cells or corpuscles of our brain substance, entirely apart from any consciousness on our part. An absorbing interest in any subject, object or thought, will deepen these impressions, but without our being aware of it the brain receives the impression of each passing thought, emotion, subject or object.

The basis of a powerful memory is in a distinct, clear, intense impression. Each such impression that you want to be able to recall at will must be registered consciously by thought in such a way that it will be easy to recover by you, just as letters, bills, legal papers, etc., are filed in an indexed filing system.

Remembering that the future recalling, recollecting or remembering will be done at the direction of your WILL, so your will must be directly concerned with the storing of the material which you will file or store away in your memory.

Whether you ever recall it or not, each recorded impression which reaches the brain is INDELIBLE as long as the cells of the brain—substance last. Your brain, being normal, well-nourished and healthy, takes in and "files away" a vast number of ideas, emotions, thoughts and impressions every day. These countless records which are stored away in your brain-cells constitute the physical basis of your memory. Now in the process of remembering, your WILL switches on a current of mental force which vibrates through your brain-cells in directed activity, and especially in a trained memory the result is an almost instant reproduction of the desired impression (idea, object, emotion or thought) which you previously registered in your brain.

ASSOCIATION OF IDEAS—CHAINS OF CONNECTION

Ideas, emotions, experiences and thoughts which have a strong similarity or likeness to one another, also those which reach the brain at the same time, are generally chained together (connected), just as though their impressions were recorded on the same mental tablet, or traced on the same sensitive cell surface. Psychologists call this similarity the association of ideas, and when the impressions reach the brain at the same instant it is called "conassociation."

Now an impression, once it is lodged (filed) in your mind (and "brain substance") may remain dormant (sleeping) for an indefinite length of time, until at the direction of your WILL, mental force (or psychic energy) brings into activity that particular layer of brain-cells which are stamped with that certain recorded impression. So if for instance you have purposely, consciously focused your mind upon some particular set of conceptions thus recorded, as, let us say, your studies, this conscious study (concentration) will create for you a special chain of connections.

Thus those subjects or things which you have most thoroughly studied and analyzed for yourself will be most easily remembered. For thus you have laid a sure track of communication along which your WILL to recollect or remember such subjects or conceptions will travel easily and will swiftly restore them to your conscious grasp.

Now you can readily see, in connection with this and the following lesson on memory development, the tremendous, yes, the priceless value of the instruction and the methods I have given you on concentration. And now I would most strongly advise that you turn again to our teachings and our methods of concentration and review them carefully, if you have not made these exercises a part of your daily routine.

In our next lesson we shall give to you in plain and simple words some marvelous methods by which you, too, can develop a great, a powerful and an unfailing memory.

Further, we will reveal to you HOW the myriad impressions we receive from the outside world are kept "on file" in the brain. Also, we will explain the marvel through which, despite your never-ending inflow of NEW impressions, the old impressions are neither erased or lost in the background. The result will be, with our simple training, your memory becomes the UNFAILING register of your mind.

LESSON NO. 22
THE PATH TO PSYCHIC RECEPTION

Third Gateway of the Temple Invisible—Being the secret Instruction Taught by The Masters in White, Whose Sublime Precepts are Now Exemplified in these Lessons.

DEVELOPING MIGHTY MENTAL POWER OF MEMORY

Again you are mentally far removed from your everyday Surroundings, for as if in response to your touch upon the Alladin's lamp of imagination you find yourself in your familiar seat amid the mystery of the King's Chamber, the center of our occult Pyramid Temple.

Around you in quiet meditation sit your Companion Initiates in White, and before us shimmers the effulgence of our symbolic altar of the Sacred Triangle. In the silence—which is so soothing and so restful—we wait for the words of our Teacher, Kyron, the Wise, words which shall reveal to us still greater lessons in acquiring and developing those mighty powers of MIND and MEMORY, mighty powers which create and control life.

Now, with upraised hands, Kyron imparts to us his silent blessing, and as always he welcomes us in the ancient words of our ritual—words descended to us from the long-gone ages of those other Mystery Schools:

"Welcome, O Enlightened Ones, for unto thee is granted the Reception."

"And now Kyron opens once more The Dhammapada, one of the oldest of the Buddhist scripture, and in tones that are soft but clear he reads to us a few brief passages selected from Chapter 20 of this old volume— the chapter which is entitled "The Way."

1.   1. "The best of ways is the eight-fold: the best of truths the four words; the best of virtues passion-lessness; the best of men he who has eyes to see.

2.   2. This is THE WAY, there is no other that leads to the purifying of intelligence (wisdom). Go on this PATH! This (path) is the confusion of Mara, the tempter.

3.   3. "If you go on this WAY you will make an end of pain...

4.   4. You yourself must make the effort. The Rathagatas (Buddhas) are only teachers. The thoughtful (wise) who enter the WAY are freed from the bondage of Mara.

5.   5. All created things perish", he who knows and sees this becomes passive in pain...; this is the WAY that lead to purity.

6.   6. "All created things are grief and pain", he who knows and sees this becomes passive in pain; this is the WAY that leads to purity.

7.   7. "All (physical) forms are unreal", he who knows and sees this becomes passive in pain; this is the WAY that lead to purity.

8.   8. "Watching his speech, well restrained in MIND, let a man never commit any wrong with his body! Let a man but keep these three roads of action clear, and he will achieve the WAY which is taught by the WISE (THE MASTERS).

9.   9. "Through zeal (intense interest) knowledge is gained, through lack of zeal knowledge is lost; let a man who knows this double path of gain and loss thus place, himself that knowledge may grow...quickly clear the WAY that leads to Nirvana.

EACH SINGLE BODY-CELL HAS ITS OWN CONSCIOUSNESS

Every single cell in your body has its own consciousness, and is like a complete little world in itself. Does it seem strange to you that so tiny a thing as a human body-cell has a consciousness of its own? If so, stop and consider this analogy! just as we can think of your physical body as being one cell in the Universal Allness, so does one cell in your body express completeness within itself.

If it seems a bit difficult for you to vision a single cell of your body as receiving and acting upon impressions, remember that here we are dealing with MIND. So many confusing names are given to the functions by summing them up under the one word, consciousness.

As you now realize from your former lessons, Mind—absolute MIND—is everywhere and in everything manifest in the universe. Because this is true the cells of your body must react in Mind, and are endowed with a consciousness of their own apart from the brain. Further, these cells do respond to thought-currents and TO MEMORY, for they also are instruments of both thought and memory.

Proving that the cells of the human body are endowed not only with a consciousness of their own but also that they possess instinctive intelligence QUITE APART FROM THE BRAIN, I quote this dispatch which was issued by The Associated Press on August 18, 1935:

"BOY WITHOUT BRAIN LIVES 27 DAYS: ACTS NORMALLY"

"New York—A baby boy lived 27 days after birth with only fluid in the cranial cavity (brain-cavity) instead of a developed brain, it was revealed today after an autopsy.

"The child was born July 21 and died Saturday morning. A member of the St. Vincent's Hospital staff, who declared the case was rare to medical science, said that for his first six days of life the infant was apparently normal.

"Despite the belief that behavior is dictated by the brain", he said, the child ate regularly, cried lustily, and moved his limbs freely. As remarkable as anything else about the case was that the infant reacted to pain tests."

"After the child died we removed about 10 ounces of fluid from the cranial cavity," the physician said.

He asserted an X-ray after birth showed a partial collapse of the lungs, but "there was no outward indications of an abnormality until the seventh day".

EVERY CELL A RECEIVING SET

So, as we consciously understand that each cell of our bodies has a "brain" or consciousness of its own, we perceive that every cell has an intelligence that causes it to perform its own particular work in the body in just the right way, and at just the right time, without conscious direction from the brain.

When we realize that each cell in the human body is actually a "receiving set" complete within itself, then we understand that the brain is not the main or most important part of the body, but is only a necessary part of the physical being, as long as that being manifests in and through a physical body.

Now if every cell in your body is a "receiving set", is conscious, has intelligence, is imbued with mind—IS mind—and if you fully realize that YOU are the controlling power which can rule mind, then you can adjust any inharmony in your life or surroundings, you CAN HEAL bodily ills, and YOU can develop MIND-POW-ERS within yourself that are marvelous.

Again I would remind you that this process of power-attainment, or power-rebuilding, starts from WITHIN. To Yourself YOU, whether you have realized it or not, ARE THE CENTER OF THE WHOLE UNIVERSE. What you hold in your consciousness—whatever is focused in your mind constantly—YOU ARE!

If you would change that which you ARE, or have been, simply change that inner consciousness, picture in your mind a NEW and an IDEAL SELF, focus your mind upon that IDEAL YOU, LIVE that IDEAL YOU within yourself—and lo! you will become that IDEAL!

As your occult teacher and your instructor in the Ancient Wisdom, in these lessons it is not my purpose to fill your mind with mere affirmations or denials, but rather to explain to you what YOU can do, and to reveal to you our time-tested methods for attainment. Our great work in this course of instruction is to help you to unfold the Eternal Law within yourself in such a way that you will understand all natural laws and know how to use them scientifically both for yourself and for others.

MEMORY—IMPRESSIONS FILED IN BRAIN CELLS

Our ability to keep on file numberless single impressions so that they can be mentally arranged and connected, and safely stored for future reference we call MEMORY.

For example, in the process of perceiving the rate of vibration, the quality and the duration of sound (as in speech, song, instrumental music, etc.) or our almost instant impressions of the union of single letters in words, the words united in sentences, the sentences into paragraphs (as in reading, writing, etc.) this process is only possible through our use of many and various mental faculties.

Just how is it possible for us to recall ("re-collect") certain impressions even after many years? That word "recollect" is the key to the answer. We "re-collect" when we endow or unite that which seems forgotten with the same sense-impressions with which or through which it first entered that inexhaustible filing system which we call "memory". In other words, we remember when we cause or compel any certain organ through which the original impression was received to REPEAT (though more faintly) the original process through which we received that impression. Suppose you have heard a shot fired, when you remember that shot, the shock which your ear received through hearing that shot must be repeated, and thus the entire telegraphic nerve process is RENEWED. Of course, in memory the shot will be repeated with greatly diminished force, as on a fainter scale.

Remembering is simply a repetition by the proper senses of that event, experience, or occurrence which we recall or "re-collect". The great difference between the actual occurrence and its repetition in memory is that the reflection or the "echo" we thus capture by nerve-processes is dimmer, fainter, or weaker than its actual first cause. Unless we have a trained memory of any occurrence.

Through intensive training and by constant practice YOU can develop a great, an unfailing, yes, a truly marvelous memory. The very first step is to LEARN TO OBSERVE and to see CLEANLY everything which you desire to remember. Pay close attention here, for your first impressions are tremendously important, see that each impression is distinct and analyze each impression carefully.

After this, the means of attaining your chosen goal of a marvelous memory is simply practice, practice, prac-tice—remember, by repeating again and again you can make any impression, fact, event, or experience your life-long possession. By constant repetition old impressions can be forever renewed.

THE KEYS TO MEMORIZING ARE SIMPLE

After all the keys to memorizing are simple, and you will find these keys in the methods which I will outline for you so very plainly that you will find them very easy to acquire. First I must remind you that the faculties which constitute our mental power, including the power of memory, are arranged in the normal human brain in groups so that each group completes some one mental attribute, as for instance, Individuality, Form, Size, Weight, Color, Order, Number, Tune, Time, Eventuality, etc., the complete list of attributes numbering 42, according to psychologists.

Now, this being true, in order to memorize successfully we must bring as many of these groups or mental faculties as we can into active operation in making an indelible, an intensive imprint of that image, object, experience, or thought upon the tablets of the mind.

It is surprisingly easy to memorize almost anything in which we are really, deeply, and personally interested, especially when we consciously WILL (determine) to analyze each and every particular thing, object, person, or subject you desire to remember. In order to focus your attention, to arouse your interest, and to bring every possible faculty into play, just make it a habit to question yourself concerning everything with which you come in contact. Make these questions to the point— what is the cause of this thing? What is its direct origin? _ What of its individuality? Its history? What are its distinguishing marks, signs and characteristics?—In your own mind, what interesting facts, sounds, or places are connected with it? And what will it DO, or what will it LEAD TO, and what are its PURPOSE and its FUTURE?

When you have answered these questions, when you have found out everything you can about it, the object of that mental image is yours—in memory it has become your possession—and you will not forget it. Forever after you can recall that imprinted image at will by calling into action one or more of these faculties you used in making your observation in the first place and in a flash the entire situation, experience, picture, person or names and facts you want to "re-collect" will appear before your "mind's eye"! Keen observation, actual personal interest, and an insatiable curiosity are the very foundation stones of a magnificent memory.

MEMORIZING FACES AND NAMES

Suppose you are introduced to some stranger, and it is important that you remember his name. Here is your method. First, you spell his name to yourself, letter by letter, and make a mental picture of that name, and stamp that name mentally right across his forehead or face. Next, focus your attention upon any peculiarities of his face,—notice closely his lips, eyes, nose, and ears, all of this only requires one scrutinizing glance—and during this glance, spell out his name once more.

With seeing eyes observe his forehead, his eyebrows, chin, teeth, and throat, and again mentally repeat the image of his name and stamped across or upon his face. Notice also the way he holds his head, take note of his chin, and how he walks, and talks and gestures. What is his complexion? The color of his hair? His approximate size and weight?—Make a mental note of the surroundings where you meet him, and the circumstances of the meetings.

In short, you are to study, analyze, and classify him, at the same time focusing your mental gaze upon his name as stamped upon his face by you. While it takes time to explain his method to you, remember in practice it takes but a few moments, especially with training, and training comes from practice.

And when you see this man again, one or more of these faculties which have registered him in the vast files of your memory will suddenly recall the picture which you have thus imprinted upon your brain-cells, and with lightning-like speed will summon all these "associated" memories, giving you his classification as you made it, his individuality, and his name!

MEMORIZING HOUSES, BUILDINGS, PLACES, ETC.

As the first step, suppose you go outdoors and look carefully at the house or building you live in, together with its' surroundings. Now if you will focus your attention closely upon this house or building, you will notice many, many different details which have escaped your eyes before. Perhaps you will now observe some memorable peculiarities about the walk which leads to the entrance; the walk may seem to you a little too narrow or too wide, or you might note if it is composed of blocks, anything noticeable about their arrangement, or their condition, etc.

For example, ask yourself, what is the color of this house or building, and of what material is it constructed, wood, brick, or stone? What is the condition of the outside of this house—if wood, is the siding uneven, narrow, or wide? If it is of brick or stone, is the mortar washed out anywhere, leaving empty crevices? Is there a porch with pillars, or of what form is the front entrance? This house or building in which you live, do you really know it? For in order to remember anything, you must first KNOW that thing.

Here again your practice with the FOCALIZER will prove to have been a priceless training, because this training has given your eyes that wonderful, penetrative gaze which sees things as they are IN DETAIL.

MARVELOUS METHOD OF MEMORIZING FIGURES

Memorizing figures (numbers) becomes 100% easier to you when I explain to you that you memorize numbers by exactly the same mental process (of visualizing) which I taught you to use in memorizing NAMES and FACES.

The only difference is this, instead of mentally spelling out the name and picture it has stamped upon the face of a person, you will mentally write out the number or numbers to be remembered, and in your mind connect each number with its surroundings, associate each number with its related event, or sounds, or purpose or the measure, weight, color, and form of an object that is related to such a number or numbers.

Just be sure to always keep your mental image of these numbers in their proper order, stamp these mental-number-images upon the face of the related facts. Stamp these numbers upon your mental impressions at the time of reception, and picture these numbers as blazing forth distinct as lightning at your command against this background of associated facts and impressions.

HOW TO MEMORIZE SENTENCES, PARAGRAPHS, POEMS, ETC.

The first thing to remember in memorizing sentences, paragraphs, poems, etc. IS TO READ EACH SENTENCE ALOUD AS OFTEN AS POSSIBLE AND TO ANALYZE EVERY POSSIBLE MEANING. The sound of your voice helps greatly to record each word.

Now, to prove to you how easily you can memorize sentences, I want you to copy in pen and ink on a sheet of white paper the first sentence (paragraph) which I read to you from The Dhammapada in opening this lesson beginning with the words— "The best of ways is the eightfold..." etc.

Next, place your copy in front of you, where you can easily see and read it. Now slowly and clearly, read this complete sentence five times aloud. Then analyze to yourself each clause in this sentence—seek to find their associated meanings. For instance ask yourself what is it that Dhammapada here describes as "the best of ways"? ("the eight-fold") Next ask yourself what is said here to be "the best of truths"? ("the four words") And what "is the best of virtues?" ("passionlessness") And who is said to be "the best of men?" ("he who has eyes to see")

Now mentally tie these clauses together by association, and picture each meaning as distinctly imprinted upon your memory. Thus you make a complete series of "seeing pictures" by analyzing and classifying the meanings conveyed by this sentence. Now you are to slowly read this complete sentence once more, recalling or recollecting in its proper order each meaning which you have analyzed. Then turn your paper face down, and recite the words of the sentence aloud. If you find that you really seem to have forgotten a word, or a clause, turn the sheet of paper over and refresh your memory, and repeat this little exercise until you have memorized this sentence perfectly. Again, before you retire tonight, repeat this same exercise with this same sentence.

Second day: Add two more sentences from this same passage and study them in the same manner that I have outlined above, until you can recite all three sentences from memory.

Third Day: Repeat your exercise of the second day, reciting it slowly from memory, and add the three next sentences from the same passage—practice until you can recite all the lesson thus far studied.

Fourth day: Repeat the sentences you have learned in the preceding three days—reciting them slowly from memory—and then add the next four sentences—then recite from the beginning all the sentences you have memorized.

Fifth day and following days: Repeat slowly from memory twice all the sentences you have learned previously, and then add as many new sentences from this same passage as you have been practicing this exercise in days until you have memorized this passage completely.

If you will follow this method faithfully, you will be amazed at how quickly and how powerfully your memory will develop under this training. Remember, always memorize one sentence perfectly before starting on on another—"make haste slowly"!

Lesson No. 23
THE PATH TO PSYCHIC RECEPTION

Third Gateway of the Temple Invisible—being the Secret Instruction Taught by the Masters in White, Whose Sublime Precepts are Now Exemplified in these Lessons.

SUPER-INTELLECT—YOUR UNFOLDING GOD MIND

Far removed from the turmoil, the worries, and the endless strife of the outer world, now you are once again mentally amid the peaceful beauty of The King's Chamber, sitting in your old, familiar place among your Fellow-Initiates in White.

Silence reigns, as each Companion sits in quiet meditation, and the soft light that glows throughout the mystic Chamber deep within the very heart of our imaged Pyramid Temple seems to blend with our thoughts.

For now we are again awaiting yet another and deeper lesson in our, present Psychic Reception degree from our reincarnate Master in White, whom we know as Kyron, the Wise, but look! and Listen!—for there before the sacred altar of the Sacred Triangle he stands with hands upraised in ,sing, and again with clear and musical tones he welcomes us in that ageless greeting of the ritual:

WELCOME, O ENLIGHTENED ONES, FOR UNTO THEE IS GRANTED THE RECEPTION

We perceive that Kyron again holds in his hands The Dhamapada, the most ancient Buddhist volume, and now for our evening lesson Kyron reads to us certain brief passages from the chapter entitled "The Bhikshu," the Initiate, the Wise):

"He who controls his hand, he who controls his feet, he who controls his speech, he who is well (self) controlled, he who delights inwardly, is collected, who is solitary and content, him they call Bhikshu.

"He who dwells in the (eternal) law, delights in the law, meditates on the law...that

Bhikshu will never fall away from the true law.

"A Bhikshu who, though he receives little, does not despise what he has received, even the gods will praise him, if his life is pure, and if he is not slothful.

"He who never identifies himself with name and form, and does not grieve over what is no more, he indeed is called a Bhikshu.

"Without knowledge there is no meditation, without meditation there is no knowledge: he who has knowledge AND meditation is near unto Nirvana (immortality).

"And this is the beginning here for a wise Bhikshu; watchfulness over the senses, contentedness, restraint under the law; keep noble friends whose life is pure, and who are not slothful.

"As the Vassika plant sheds its withered flowers, men should shed passion and hatred, O ye Bhikshus!

"The Bhikshu whose body and tongue and mind are quieted (in The Silence), who is collected (self-controlled), and has rejected the baits (vain desires) of the world, he is called Master.

"For self is the lord of self, Self is the refuge of self, therefore CURB THYSELF as the merchant curbs a noble (spirited) horse."

YOUR "MILLION DOLLAR" MIND—SUPER-INTELLECT

My Good Friends and Companion-Initiates, how truly the ancient words of Buddha, which I have read to you as our evening lesson impress upon us the mighty fact that ONLY when self-discipline, self-control, is acquired, only then can the Great Work of self-evolution endow us with the super-intellect of the true Bhikshu, or Initiate.

Great thinkers everywhere have more or less clearly seen the light of this stupendous truth. For example, speaking before the Academy of Medicine in Paris in October, 1928, Dr. Charles Mayo, one of the most eminent of America's surgeons of that time, said:

"We are using only a small part of our brains today; the untouched parts are unlimited. As we learn to control our glands and habits, A RACE OF SUPER-INTELLECTS WILL BE DEVELOPED!"

By this control of glands and habits the good doctor also infers self-discipline, the control of feelings, emotions, and of thoughts. For further medical proof along this line, let us turn to a lecture delivered almost twenty years ago before the Institute of Hygiene, London, by Dr. Charles S. Thompson, who said among other things:

"Anger and storms of passion can shake the nervous system to pieces!" Saying that "ambition and pride, and aesthetic and intellectual emotion" rarely affect the body adversely, Dr. Thompson pointed out that the coarse negative passions, such as anger, hatred, jealousy, fear, and lust cause most dangerous physical reactions.

Do not jump to the conclusion from these facts that emotion in itself is necessarily a devastating force to be always repressed at all costs—far from it. On the contrary, emotion—and I mean positive emotion—is our most powerful agency for good when rightly directed and controlled, stormy emotions produce diseased physical bodies, we must realize that it is equally true that harmonious, constructive, positive emotions are the most powerfully HEALING forces known to man, producing their corresponding harmonies of physical health.

This matter of harmonic, controlled emotion was not overlooked by Dr. Thompson, who further said:

"The whole point of educational training should be to establish control of feelings (emotion), WHILE DEVELOPING ABILITY TO EXPRESS ALL FEELINGS (EMOTIONS) IN THE MOST SPIRITUAL WAY."

MASTERY OF BODY, MIND, AND EMOTION

This close inter-relationship of mind and its thoughts, of the Inner Self and the emotions, and each of these with the human body, has been taught by the Masters in White from the dawn of history as the necessary vision of SELF-MASTERY, which must precede that phase of self-evolution from Man to Super-Man, from Student or Initiate Master.

For the full flowering of the beauties and the power now hidden within your inmost Self will come only after you have learned to control and master those two greatest instruments of mind, your physical body and your emotions, for it is through these instruments that the divine energies (psychic thought-waves) of your God-Soul must manifest in this material world.

The most powerful, creative, harmonic emotion known among men is LOVE—for the simple truth is that LOVE is the eternal life-giver of the universe. No matter how material you may have thought this world to be, LOVE is the one tremendous emotional force which cannot perish, and which cannot be destroyed, because without this God-Force nothing else can long exist. And the Pathway of LOVE is the only WAY that leads you to mastery of your body, your mind, and your negative emotions.

Twenty centuries ago another of our Masters in White, Ishuis, or Jesus the Christ, voiced this tremendous truth in these simple words:

"Thou shalt love the Lord thy God with all thy heart, and with all thy soul, and with all thy mind.

"This is the first and great commandment.

"And the second is like unto it. Thou Shalt love they neighbor as thyself.

"On these two commandments hang (depend) all the law and the prophets."—Matt. 22:37-40.

"IF GOD SO LOVED US…"

Again, turning to 1st John4: verses 8 and 11, we find the Beloved Disciple uttering these words, which may explain something of that divine mystery, which we call "Love":—

"He that loveth not, knoweth not God; for God IS LOVE."

"Beloved, if God so loved us, we ought also to love one another."

That individual YOU, endowed with all the mysteries of spirit, and with all the untold powers of thought, is one UNIT of the COSMIC BEING—GOD—and as such you can develop an independent GOD-Mind with unlimited possibilities, and by that word "independent" I simply mean not dependent upon this material world spiritually. Your great mission upon earth is to glorify this supreme Cosmic Intellect, otherwise the penalty is that one by one you lose your God-given endowments. For as you evolve, as you develop, as you unfold the God-consciousness The Eternal Law endows you to glorify the Cosmic Creator,

Let us revert in thought to that far-away lime when this earth was born as a "fiery mist," because that is the time when, our soul first radiated into this world-to-be in their virginal purity, like divine sparks from the Eternal Anvil, and each of us endowed with the tremendous power to attain and return to the OVER-SOUL. That is what The Masters in White have meant in every age by their teaching that through myriads of lives we over attained these cycles of RETURN, and will continue this age-lasting round until we have each fulfilled our Great Mission.

So, looking upon nature, and life, and "death" in this light we can readily understand WHY and HOW physical "death" is a mere transition, Medical science shows us that this same process of life and death is going on within our physical bodies every day—a constant katabolic catalysis Yes, we die daily, that we may LIVE more abundantly!

THE COSMIC RULER IS NONE OTHER THAN LOVE

For the Cosmic Ruler, whom we call "God," is Love, and Love is the gigantic urge creating all LIFE.

Just as the sunshine is interwoven with warmth, and heat, and creature force, so is love interlocked with our bodies and our lives. This portion of The Eternal Law is very clearly demonstrated in chemistry, for instance, for here we see chemical "affinity" at work when one element shows its love for another by UNITING with it. As an example, when you mix sulphuric acid with water, the resulting, union causes heat. Now we know that the "desire" (attractive force) of these two elements to UNITE WAS AND IS ETERNAL, and in no way limited to the age of man upon this earth. This desire, or attraction, or affinity, of chemicals is transformed into force, energy, or both creative and destructive power. In this tremendous energy is the unseen hand of the Cosmic-God-Will in the instant of chemical union, just the same today as during the aeons of the "fire-mist."

From our great luminary, the sun, as well as from each of the sub-luminaries, we unconsciously draw the cre-ative forces, which construct and maintain our human bodies. We must realize that all force is born of Eternal Design, and the name of the great DESIGNER is Love.

Yes, LOVE vibrates in every heart-beat, in every corpuscle, and every cell of your body, for this is part of the work involved in the Great Design. Now, at times we may think that we, with our puny hands, can thwart or change some part of this

Great Design, which does not suit us, or that we can cheat our fellow-beings of some advantage without punishment. But no! The Eternal Verity, working through the laws of compensation and retribution will soon or late even things up with a vengeance, and these laws are just as sure as that law which causes the apple to fall.

LOVE OF OFFSPRING IS LOVE OF IMMORTALITY

Hidden within the center of each seed on earth is the unconquerable desire for continuing LIFE, just as the love of immortality is implanted deep within each human heart, and this love of immortal life is manifested in the human family by our love of our offspring. Had this magnificent gift of Love from the Divine God Law not been granted to this world, every form of animal, human or plant life would have vanished from the earth like a passing shadow. But the Love and—life desire implanted in every seed is over-flowing, boundless, and wonderful.

But wondrous as is this life impelling love of the seed, yet it is mother-love which comes nearest to being Divine. A true mother will unhesitatingly sacrifice her own life that her child may live—no price is too great for her to pay for the continued life of her offspring. And this mother love is manifest also throughout the animal kingdom. From the dust-covered history of the sixteenth century comes the story of the Spanish vivisectionists, who in one experiment blind-folded female dogs and by a Caesarean operation removed from several the unborn puppies, placing them in a row side by side. When, in due time, the mother dogs were brought to the puppies, they looked them over, and then each mother dog caressingly licked her own puppies AND NO OTHERS.

Of course, we call this "animal instinct," or implanted love, or some students might choose to call it "group spirit" manifestation, but call it what you will, this continuing love of life is universal all through Nature.

Love is the one great primordial attribute, and every one of our passions is closely linked with love, and each of our emotions is but a sub-division of this primordial element. If you direct any of these passions or any of your emotions into the wrong (negative) channel and Love takes wing, because if you direct hatred against love, or negative forces against life, then love AND life will both disappear, leaving but the empty forms to disintegrate.

WORLDS AND ALL THINGS CREATED FROM THE INVISIBLE

Far beyond the beginnings of "time"—even as dimly perceived in the rituals of the ancient fire worshippers— eternally heat, light, radiant energy, and electrical force— all have been forms of ONE GREAT ENERGY, convertible one into another. Back of all these forms, divisions, or sub-divisions of ENERGY we find the emanation or sending forth of WILL ("THE WORD"), and so we conceive that in the gigantic drama of The Creation before even the "fire-mist" there was this mystic WILL or "WORD" emanation from a great nebula, resulting in what we know as sun radiation.

In Hebrews 11:3, Paul writes these inspired words touching upon this creative conception.:

"Through faith we understand that the worlds were framed by the WORD (WILL) OF GOD, so that these things which are seen were not made of things which—do—appear."

Substance or matter is spirit on its way to solidification. For example, in the newly born tortoise (turtle), the life-spirit crystallizes or solidifies an armor from a liquid substance. Another familiar instance of this is the hen's egg.

So, chemical science teaches us that all matter can be caused to retrograde from solids to liquids and to gases, and thence into the world of the invisible, called by some the world of "negative spirit." Yet forever WILL and LOVE remain as the supreme life-giving forces.

These lessons teach that the whole universe was originally ("in the beginning") composed of ONE substance, and that today we, you and I, 'live and move, and have our being' in that same substance. Materially, we find that under the piercing eye of the cathode ray all the atoms of each different chemical element resolve themselves into different aggregations of THE SAME PRIMORDIAL SUBSTANCE.

SPIRIT OF MAN MANIFESTS SUPREME OVER-SOUL

We further teach that the spirit of each man and woman is a direct, individual manifestation of THE SUPREME SPIRIT back of the vast spiral nebulae.

It may enlighten your thinking to know that the Ancient Mystery Schools recognized, just as we teach today, among the many phases of man's make-up, two spirits (positive and negative), three bodies (physical, nervous, and mental), and one soul. However, in our Lessons for simplicity we use the word "man" to represent the one complete being.

If you have followed these lessons carefully, many of you will have reached that advance stage of "The Reception" where you can conceive of matter as constantly retrograding into its primordial state, and emerging countless times in numberless created forms. Likewise, now you can begin to comprehend the tremendous conception of the soul burying itself invisibly in matter for untold aeons of time.

This is not teaching that the entity itself can be annihilated, or that the soul sinks into positive oblivion, or is "lost" in some realm of spiritual chaos—for none of these things are part of the concept, far from it.

For until our finite minds are able to apprehend the fourth, as well as other yet unknown dimensions of space, we can only understand LOVE, LIFE, WILL, and ENERGY as the ONE great merger or combination of spirit with matter. This combination we see as manifested to us and in us as a continuing existence of creative advancement, of development, of construction.

LOVE AND LIVE—CREATIVE AND CONSTRUCTIVE

Love and Life are forever creating and constructing—they are the two greatest forces that are eternally building and giving life to the world around us. You can observe these mighty processes every day in the four great divisions of LIFE: namely, the growing stone, the green plant, the pulsating animal, and MAN, the "Living Soul." Your life is a living force—an invisible stream of positive spirit vibrations, which unites with negative, (spirit) matter to form your individual SOUL LIVING IN PHYSICAL MATTER.

Strip man of his physical embodiment, and the Soul-Entity still remains, with its endowments of Love, Will, intelligence, and wisdom—for these love-forces can never perish. Science tells us that nothing can really be destroyed, and we hold these invisible attributes of man to be more enduring than even the hardest granite.

Again I repeat that what seems to us to be dead matter is actually negative spirit in retrograde motion. And remember back of all motion, all force, all energy in this universe is intelligent, creative DESIGN. There is no life, as we know life, in a seed, but within the newly laid egg and within every seed countless cells purposely so arranged as TO INVITE LIFE TO ENTER UNDER PROPER CONDITIONS.

As you know, in the spring the sap courses up the tree, drawn upward by what we call capillary attraction. Each tree, each plant, each animal, and each human being has a life—spirit or a life tone (purpose) peculiar to itself. This tonal or life-spirit of the tree, plant, animal, or human being RULES with a fixed and an intelligent purpose (or design), and it clings to that set design with a tenacity beyond comparison.

WISDOM OF UNTOLD AGES IN YOUR BODY-CELLS

Every cell within your body, together with every corpuscle and every tissue, has the wonderful wisdom of untold ages within it. This wisdom reaches you as an endowment from COSMIC MIND, and it is LOVE that directs this wisdom.

All about us we see the constructive plant and animal life which manifests The Supreme Spiritual Intellect—that Divine Intellect back of our physical sun and vibrating throughout the entire solar system. And even each tiny atom of matter is surrounded with a cushion of ether, and is ruled by the love-desire-spirit which forever broods over and within it!

The IMMUTABLE WILL back of all creation is LOVE, and so this is the "vis a tergo," (the force from behind").

LOVE—human love—is always creative, if not constructive, DESIRE, but when human "love" runs "amuck," riots beyond control, it becomes a DESTRUCTIVE passion. And destructive (negative) passion reaps the whirlwind of destruction, disease, and death, whether it be in men or nations. Remember, ungoverned negative passions "create" wars.

True Creative-Love-Desire is the process of becoming consciously AWARE of those better things which you may have forgotten, by ceasing to be conscious of them—Love, Wealth, Health, and HAPPINESS! For too often we are like one in a balloon too heavily laden.

We have tried to carry a too heavy load of the wrong kind of ballast—hate, fears, doubt, worry, greed, or malice. Your Desire—Love directs your hand in Faith to pick up these evil sandbags and throw them overboard; as you throw these evils out, your balloon will rise. So, through Desire, Faith, and love you rise into the consciousness that these better things ARE YOURS.

Lesson No. 24
THE PATH TO PSYCHIC RECEPTION

Third Gateway of the Temple Invisible—Being the Secret Instruction Taught by The Masters in White, Whose Sublime Precepts are Now Exemplified in these Lessons.

SECRET DOCTRINE OF THE GRAND ARCANUM

Amid the stillness of the King's Chamber once more we find escape from the worries and the cares of the material world, as again you find yourself surrounded by your faithful companions, each wearing the white robe of the Initiate.

For now we are mentally transported to this mystic inner shrine hidden in the far depths of our symbolic Pyramid Temple, and we quietly await our last lesson in the degree that is know as THE PSYCHIC RECEPTION to each Initiate.

For now our Master of THE WAY, Kyron, the Wise, stands before the altar of the Sacred Triangle and with upraised hands silently imparts his blessing to us—but listen as Kyron bid us welcome in the ages-old words of our ancient ritual:

Welcome, O Enlightened Ones!, for unto thee is granted the Reception.

And now Kyron reads to us softly and clearly from that ancient Buddhist volume, The Dham-apada, certain short passages from the chapter which is entitled "The Brahmana"—

"If the Brahmana has reached the other shore in both laws, in restraint and contemplation, all bonds vanish from him who has attained KNOWLEDGE.

"Because a man is rid of evil, therefore he is called Brahmana.

"Him I call indeed a Brahmana who does not cling to sensual pleasure...

"Him I call indeed a Brahmana who, even here, knows the end of his own suffering, has put down his burden, and is unshackled (free).

"Him I call indeed a Brahmana whose knowledge is deep, who possesses wisdom, who knows the right way and the wrong, and has attained the highest end (mastery).

"Him I call indeed a Brahmana from whom anger and hatred, pride and hypocrisy have dropped like a mustard seed from the point of a needle.

"Him I call indeed a Brahmana who in this world has risen above both ties, good and evil, who is free from grief, from sin, and from impurity.

"Him I call indeed a Brahmana who has traversed this miry road, the impassable world, difficult to pass, and its vanity, who has gone through, and reached the other shore, is thoughtful, steadfast, free from doubt, free from Attachment, AND CONTENT.

"Him I call indeed a Brahmana who, after leaving all bondage to men, has risen, above all bondage to the gods, and is FREE from all and every bondage.

"Him I call indeed a Brahmana who knows the destruction and the return of beings everywhere...who is AWAKENED (as Buddha).

"Him I call indeed a Brahmana who knows his former abodes (lives), who sees heaven and hell, has reached
the end of births, is perfect in knowledge, a sage, and whose concepts are all perfect."

THE ANCIENT WISDOM FOREVER SECRET

The ancient wisdom must remain forever secret to the uninitiated, for they have no keys by which they may understand our sacred symbols and allegories.

All of Nature is an expression of THE Eternal Law as TRUTH, but few there be who can recognize TRUTH as expressed in the universe about us. External study and investigation can only deal with outer things; but all outer forms are merely reflections or shadows to the Initiate, because he recognizes through the power of his trained spiritual perception the TRUTH which the form (the shadow) represents.

Wisdom as an abstract principle is inconceivable until it becomes manifest in the WISE, and then only the wise can recognize it. Thus, if you would know the TRUTH (wisdom), the TRUTH must live WITHIN YOU.

In this world the scene of the crucifixion is an ever continuing scene, because TRUTH is forever being crucified between two "thieves," and these two thieves are called "Superstition" and "Skepticism." Now if we see only one of the thieves, we may mistake him for the TRUTH, for the forms of these two thieves are distorted. It is only when we are able to recognize the divine form of the "Savior" (TRUTH) between these two distorted "thieves" will we recognize the vast difference, and so find the "Redeemer."

Because curiosity is a quality inherent in man's nature, in all ages he has wanted to know intellectually that Supreme Architect whose presence he intuitively feels. So always there have been many men curious to know the nature of God, and so by intellect alone these men have tried to tear a hole in the veil which hides the sanctuary of the Supreme Presence, so that they might peep through it and satisfy their curiosity. It is from the vagaries of such speculators, visionaries, and false philosophers that the world has been flooded with pseudotheology, false mysticism, and entrenched superstitions.

DIVINE PRESENCE ETERNALLY HIDDEN FROM UNINITIATED:

The simple truth is, of course, that the Divine Presence is eternally hidden from the uninitiated, because it cannot be perceived by any external (outer) means. Neither can its existence be logically proved to those who are not capable of entering into this Presence. Because this is the Divine Over-Soul, it can therefore only be intellectually known to man when he enters into the Divine through the gateway of psychic ENLIGHTEN MENT.

Like the Divine Presence, the Ancient (Divine) Wisdom which has descended through the countless ages of the past to be treasured today in the Grand Arcanum. It is not of man's making, nor was it invented by him. Like the allegorical language of the Bible and of all the other great books of religion, our teachings are beyond comprehension if they are taken in the outer sense only and applied only from the material viewpoint. Your external reasoning far from helping you to understand, these teachings is instead an obstacle in your progress. But when you receive these teachings with the intuition which comes from the spirit, you perceive that they are the Divine, the Ancient Wisdom.

The Masters say—"The Initiate who receives and knows the DIVINE TRUTH has attained to the highest, and desires nothing more; for there is nothing higher than this attainment. Compared with this treasure, earthly possessions sink into insignificance; for he who knows REALITY cares nothing for ILLUSIONS."

THE TRUE HERMETIC BROTHERHOOD

So it must be understood that when we speak of our Fellowship, we mean something within, but yet greater and beyond our earthly and external organization, for we are today the one true Hermetic Brotherhood descended directly from the Ancient Mystery Schools. Thus when we speak of our Fellowship, we refer to a spiritual union, to a divine harmony of conspiritual and, nevertheless, individual power such as the "angels" are supposed to reflect.

It is of this spiritual association—this Hermetic Brotherhood—that we speak when we say:

Our Hermetic Fellowship has existed in varying forms and in the guise of many names since the first days of Creation, when God said "Let there be LIGHT," and it will continue to exist until the end of time.

"It is the Fellowship of the Children of Light, who live in the light forever. In this Mystery School we are instructed by the Masters in White, the "Heaven Born," in the Ancient (Divine) Wisdom, the "Heavenly Bride" whose will is above all, and who comes only to the Initiate whom she selects. The Mysteries imparted to our Initiates embrace everything that can possibly be known in regard to God, Eternal Law, Nature, and Man.

"We have among our members such as do not inhabit this earth; and our Initiates are everywhere throughout the land. Our invisible meeting-place is the King's Chamber, in the Temple of the Holy Spirit which pervades all Nature, Our Pyramid Temple is easily found by our Initiate but is forever hidden from the eyes of the outside world.

THE GREAT "ELIXIR OF LIFE"—DIVINE TRUTH

Again the Masters say of him who has tasted of the living waters of Divine Truth—the great "Elixir of Life":

"Blessed is he who is above want and poverty, above disease and death, who cannot be touched by that which give pain, and who is above all those wants for which (gross) mortals are craving."

As a student, in the light of the occult instruction which you have received, you will readily perceive that this refers to the "Inner Man," and not alone to his mortal, physical body. As you know this Inner Self is neither the physical frame with its external senses, nor is it the perishing material mind of man that can receive the Divine Truth.

As I have taught you, no man can attain this higher SPIRITUAL POWER until that invisible power becomes alive (is born) within him, and until he becomes identified with that divine energy. Our occult teaching is not entirely a matter of what one should KNOW, nor of what one should DO, but rather of what one must BE.

So if your Inner Self has become truly SPIRITUAL, not just in your imagination or in your wishes, but in your WILL, then the subtle power of your awakened spirit will shine forth even through your physical from, and will change your physical nature in the same way that darkness is transformed by light.

For GOD, according to Jacob Boehme, is the WILL of Divine Wisdom. Thus, if we rise up in self conceit we must fall, because we will be filled with delusion, false knowledge, and then even the Will of The Eternal can not awaken Divine Wisdom in us. Let us understand that true humility does not mean abject fear, but that it is the highest sense of dignity, and this can be felt only by him who realizes that God is IN and WITH him.

A true history of our Hermetic philosophy would reach far beyond even the storied Land of Atlantis (where our secret doctrines were taught) and would show our teachings descending through the oldest scrolls of an-cient Egypt, shining through the olden Vedas, and speaking in the words of Osiris, of Buddha, and of The Christ.

And today—even as always in every age—we teach that Spirit is AGELESS. Your Spirit, then is not of this world, it belongs to ETERNITY. There never was a time, even from the beginning of creation, when your Spirit was not; nor is its presence limited to this earthly planet. When you succeed in merging your consciousness with that of the divine Spirit which overshadows your physical personality—that Spirit which is actually your REAL SELF—then you can know your past forms of existence, and see far into the future. But the animal principles (elements) in man cannot partake of this higher state, for they die and so again enter into chaos—that vast storehouse from which all physical forms are produced.

THIS PLACE (?) THAT MEN CALL "HEAVEN'

Today we live in a highly developed industrial-machine age, or in other words an advanced scientific age.

And today Science accounts for the material existence of all "atoms" or particles which constitute our universe by the "atomic hypothese." This hypothesis sees the atom as an electric structure, and so our modern theory of cosmogony and our atomic theory of matter are based upon the fact that these particles (or atoms) are qualitative, or all exactly alike, but that it is their electric structure which differs.

Which is only another way of saying that the number of positive and negative charges of any substance or compound determines its physical properties, powers, or elements.

Today man has discovered that there is in reality no such thing as the annihilation of matter—only changes in electrical charge or content. As one example of the modern "miracles" which science is demonstrating almost daily—imagine a single electron and a single proton; now these two electrically charged atoms or particles coalesce or neutralize one another, when instantly their combined energy can be set free through the photon or light-charge of high radio activity.

All of which proves to us that in the slow but tremendous progress of mankind upward from the darkness of Ignorance, the scientist of today is ultimately leading us back to the vast mysteries of The Great COSMIC GEOMETER. And from these mysteries Science has wrested part of the gigantic secret of the inexhaustible atomic power which pulsates everywhere in the universe.

THE ALLEGORIES OF "HEAVEN" REFLECT DIFFERING

VALUES

It is indeed a far cry from the discoveries of modern science, and from this highly industrialized machine age, to the mythologies, the fables, and the allegories of the ages that have gone before. It seems pitiable that after these thousands of years of conjecture, of contention, and of battling to the death about a future state or sphere of everlasting life, mankind is afflicted with a thousand and one different preachments and different theories about this eternal realm where we may expect— WHAT?

Shall we investigate this subject of "Heaven," very well then—Where is it? When is it? Why is it? And what is it?

Granted, as we teach, this future life after "death," whose word of the "Two and seventy jarring sects" are we to believe as to WHERE and HOW we are going to spend this thrilling, this most interesting, this endless existence? For each of the "two and seventy" has claimed to be the one and only WAY, but unfortunately each of them seems to differ from the others in its pictures of "eternal reward" for virtue, "goodness," or "belief," and of its eternal "Hells" for the punishment of "sin."

Let us remember that we have evolved from the most animal-like and savage barbarism—from that primary status our racial heritage has passed on down through the ages of elementary communism, of tribal groups, of human slavery, of feudalism, of imperialism, to reach the centralizations of this present age of industrial development. Each of these passing epochs in the story of mankind upon earth has invented its own individual and different version of eternity, and of the realms beyond this earth-life.

These versions, conceptions, or allegories about man's endless future center for us around a place (?) or city (?) somewhat vaguely referred to as "Heaven." These allegorical pictures of "Heaven" range from the Golden City of the Christian belief to the shaded gardens ("Paradise" literally a park) of the Mohammedans, and to the "happy hunting grounds" of the Animists and the Early American Indians, to mention only three.

We can better understand the Mohammedan pictures of Heaven (or Paradise) when we remember that in the days of Mohammed brought to his people rare visions of a Paradise enriched with great rivers of flowing wine, and milk, and honey;

of forests luxuriant with all manner of delicious fruits; and of gardens where they (the men) should "enjoy the most beautiful "women" who would not cast an eye on any but themselves"— (see The Koran). To a sensual, voluptuous, and materialistic people would not this indeed be "Paradise?"

For religions, like every other human institution, change and modify their views, beliefs, and teachings about life and death and about worlds beyond this "vale of tears" in accordance with the greater social influences and the ruling factors and conditions of each passing age. Only THE TRUTH OF THE ETERNAL GOD-LAW, as taught throughout all the ages by the Masters in White, NEVER CHANGES.

For example, any Bible student can easily understand how, to the minds of those ancient scribes (writers) who compiled and assembled the sacred legends of Babylonian, Chaldean, Egyptian, Persian, and Assyrian mythology into our Holy Scriptures, to these ancient "ghost-writers" (scribes) the glory and the grandeur of jewelled monarchs and of golden thrones represented the acme of Godlike POWER and a MATERIAL "HEAVEN" beyond which their minds could not reach.

"A CITY OF PURE GOLD" (?)

So we find that the translators of the Hebrew Scriptures present to us a varicolored, if allegorical, picture of this object concept of a material "Heaven." With all due respect, one may see by looking through the gates with the eyes of Saint John, "a throne, and ONE sitting on the throne that is to look upon a jasper and a sardine stone; and round about the throne four and twenty elders, clothed in white raiment, and wearing crowns of gold"...all visioned as being within a "city of pure gold"; and the walls of this imaged city are garnished with all manner of precious stones. Twelve of these are listed, the first being jasper; the second sapphire; the third, a chalcedony; the fourth, an emerald; the fifth, sardonyx; the sixth, sardius; and so on to the twelfth, which is amethyst.

And the gates of this far city are pictured as of pearl, and the streets are paved with pure gold, transparent like glass. All of which, of course, are but symbols, and to us of this age these are but the symbols of material wealth and the pomp of a bygone age.

Today the Initiates and the Masters of The Higher Wisdom teach, instead of the crude idea of a literal brimstone Hell and a literal, bejeweled Elysium, that most beautiful TRUTH taught by Jesus, the Nazarite, THAT HEAVEN IS A CONDITION, a state of BEING best defined by the EMOTION' CALLED LOVE.

LOVE—THE SUPER VIBRATION, EMOTION DIVINE

As you have learned, your earthly, human ego (self) is one of three distinct divisions; the body, the mind, and the emotions you experience love or hate, friendship or animosity, happiness, or sorrow. It is this emotional self that the Masters teach is the Soul.

This is the central unconscious ego which, when developed to super-consciousness, enables us to attain to that state which is variously called Heaven, Godhood, A-u-m, Samadi, Kami, Allah, or Brahm.

The Divine Emotion is LOVE—the cosmic vibration of the universe-but as yet we are not attuned to dwell upon this highest plane of vibration, if we were we would be as the Gods.

It was Drummond who voiced our ancient teaching when he said, "Love is the greatest thing in the world." And he further voiced our truths when he said, "Where love is God is. He that dwelleth in love DWELLETH IN GOD. For God is love AND LOVE IS GOD." And it was Browning who said that "Love is the energy of Life."

Thus we see that the Soul, that emotional SELF of you which is the only REAL and eternal YOU, is eventually attaining to that everlasting state of Godhood (LOVE)—and so through the WAY of Love you have entered into the Kingdom of HEAVEN. Behold, yours is the Reception.

SERIES

FOUR

Lesson No. 1
THE HIGHWAY TO HEALTH, WEALTH AND HAPPINESS

Fourth Gateway of the Temple Invisible. Being The Secret Instruction Taught by The Masters in White, Whose Sublime Precepts are Now Exemplified In These Lessons.

The Degree of Illumination

CONCENTRATION—THE MAGIC GATEWAY

"Your Self—with its varied budles of habits, complexes and reactions which we term PERSONALITY—is somewhat like a modern automobile. Whether or not that personality be perfected, let us consider what road, and what kind of road, that Self is running over to reach the journey's end. Roads of every kind and running in every direction form an endless network about us; loways, highways, upgrade and down, bridle paths and byways, mountain ascents and sandy trails.

"You are the driver, and you alone choose the road over which you will travel, either to self attainment or to self abasement.

"These lessons are the sign-boards which will direct you upon this highway of self-attainment, from the valley of Indecision to the heights of Health, Wealth and Happiness. For even the most modern and highly perfected car cannot be driven with speed, efficiency and safety upon any road without a directing intelligence and that automatic skill which comes only with wisdom and experience." Creative Conception.

Deep within each of us there is hidden that Divine principle, the eternal God-Law. The highest purpose of our life on this earth is the complete union (harmony) of our souls—our inmost consciousness with this indwelling Divine Law. This union is established by concentration, and this conscious harmony with the God-Law is ILLUMINATION. When this Illumination is attained, we live naturally and without effort in perfect harmony with that Eternal Law which governs the world and the universe.

We are reborn—transformed—for then we no longer live in a self-made world of sickness, poverty and mental misery; we have left a world of shadows for one of Sunshine, of Health, of Prosperity and of Happiness.

CONCENTRATION IS ACTUAL CREATIVE FORCE

In former lessons you have been introduced to the more primary elements of concentration, and you were given certain elementary exercises sufficient to enable you to learn something of this tremendous Force, .for concentration is actual CREATIVE FORCE. But now we enter into the deeper phases of this secret pathway to a transforming Power, because concentration is exactly, that. And, this inner concentration, in its final forms in which we teach it to you also leads you to the heights of Spiritual unfoldment. And it is this higher Spiritual UNFOLDMENT which unfailingly, attracts Health, Wealth axed Happiness to you.

Concentration is not only a mental exercise, it is a creative process, and the highest form of self-unfoldment, This deeper concentration which we impart to you herein we teach you as WAY to Health and abounding strength and life, as the hidden WAY to true knowledge and to the conscious control of your inner psychic senses— the power that works "miracles." In its practical application in your life you will find more rapid results from concentration when you apply it to the attainment of a longed-for goal or ambition of yours, for after all true concentration is the most highly intensified and powerful suggestion (command) to your Subconscious-Mind-Self.

So, we are dealing here with an actual, a never-sleeping Creative Power which sends forth constant, invisible, illimitable vibrations which exactly correspond to that inner picture which you hold of that great goal or ambition of yours. Thus your entire mental attention is FOCUSED upon that goal or ambition, actually vibrating into complete reality and material existence that DESIRE-PICTURE You have outlined upon the screen of your conscious thinking.

Thus we teach you how to use concentration as the means by which you will weave, spin or project the clear-cut picture of your goal or ambition whether it be healing, abounding Health, objective Wealth or abiding Happiness—upon your subjective planes of mind, from which by silent vibration this creative force will surely reflect your "Heart's Desire" into your personal world.

Remember the guiding standard in your use of these eternal Divine Laws is very simple indeed. These Divine Laws must never be used for unworthy purposes, nor for desires which would harm your fellow-man, nor for anything which will not directly develop your own psychic powers or your physical welfare or the healing of yourself or others.

But you have signified that you are willing to put forth true effort in the ways that we shall direct, and that your sincere desire is to develop to the highest possible degree your creative powers your psychic faculties, so you may use these deeper, these closely guarded principles of concentration constantly, day after day, and you will find that the results will be marvelous—yes; almost unbelievable.

But, just here, in the beginning of this Degree of The Illumination, let us plainly warn you against certain mental barriers which can effectually hinder your progress—barriers of which you might even be unconscious. Especially let us warn you against two states of mind, or mental attitudes, which can utterly and absolutely bar you from further unfoldment, or the complete understand of yourself, or life, and of the eternal Divine Law.

One is that mental attitude which doubts, and which is skeptical of all lines of deeper thought, or occult or spiritual teachings or systems of belief which may belong to some other "school" or organization, other than that which you may have "inherited" to which you may lean.

The other particular barrier is the same as the one above, except that its expression is different, is that mental attitude wherein one feels that he has already discovered the last and final mysteries of life. It is true to a certain extent that after each new realization, anyone may have this feeling for a time. Yet if he then shuts his mental eyes and clings to this mistaken belief, he has closed to himself all the following pages of the book of life.

There are of course two main factors which may cause one thus to erect these barriers of skepticism and "all-knowledge" between self and further and higher unfoldment and Illumination. The first of these factors is conceit; conceit because one may have advanced beyond his lowly neighbor. And the second of these possible factors is that some persons whom you look up to has said that certain things

ONLY are true—and you accept that person as the final authority.

Of course, both of these factors are unreliable. For conceit bars us from all real advancement, and the person was never born who has given to anyone the COMPLETE KNOWLEDGE OF LIFE or of Eternal Divine Law.

YOUR PATHWAY OF UNFOLDMENT

You have now entered upon your pathway of unfoldment (recognition of your Soul-Self within) and faithfully followed this ever-developing unfoldment will give you the deepest understanding of Eternal Divine Law, of your self, of life and of the laws which govern Health, Prosperity and Happiness. This unfolding process is not one based upon either "education," (as in material schools) nor upon secular "science". This is a pathway which under our guidance, you must walk alone, for each unfoldment is a personal, and individual matter. For this higher development of the inner powers does not come in the same way, nor from the same direction, nor with the same degree with any two persons.

True unfoldment through concentration AND meditation simply stated means the crystallization in your consciousness, step by step, of deeper understanding of your own hidden powers and the HOW of using those occult powers to reach your most cherished goals in life. Thus, you are not required to acquire any "new" knowledge, for the path you will tread is a very ancient one indeed. For that development which may seem complete to you today will perhaps seem but elementary to you tomorrow. True unfoldment is entirely from WITHIN.

You will agree that the great mass of humanity is blindly seeking "money" and material possessions, fame or honor, some personal charm or qualities which will bring the adulation of others, and Physical health, strength and well-being. These three primary desires—for money and material possessions, for the love of adulation of others, and for physical well-being are inherent in the racial mind.

These great desires are natural to every one of us, because they seem to satisfy our inherent "need" for superiority among others. No individual of the human race lives who does not have some buried or perhaps unconscious feeling of inferiority.

These inferiority feelings are the driving forces which cause us all to seek that which gives to us a sense of superiority. Further, it is natural that we desire sensations of pleasure and to avoid sensations of pain. This is the intermediate stage of racial evolution. And the greatest of the Masters in White, together with every student, must have passed through this stage.

These things being eternally true our only road to real freedom lies in removing these false impressions, of inferiority, not by overcoming them but by proving that they are false, that they are illusions, merely shadows.

Now, since every man and every woman seeks health, wealth and happiness—the marks of "superiority"—even unknowingly often, we shall lead you on the pathway of unfoldment by appealing to these perfectly natural desire's of your heart, because when you have mastered these simple laws of unfoldment each. of these good things of life, may be yours for the taking. Remember, on this pathway to yet another and higher gateway, these are your rewards at the outer portals.

REVIEWING FIRST PRINCIPLES

In beginning these lessons on true unfoldment, let us now review the first principles of attainment, because each of these first principles underlies the possession of Health, of Wealth and of Happiness alike. First then we teach you that in order to reach your, rightful position of superiority (to the blind masses) either in success and possessions, or in friendship and service to mankind, to the people around you.

Of course knowledge of these teachings and of great psychological principles can be misused to secure wealth and many of the material possessions around us, without giving any thing of value in return, thus grasp-ing a purely selfish position of fancied "superiority." Even the misuse, of these teachings and principles can actually bring the desired results—yet, if nothing is given in return, only frustration and suffering will follow.

Before you can successfully travel this pathway of unfoldment, we teach you plainly that you must have chosen the goal towards which you will journey, the great desire or ambition which you have determined to attain. Unless you have a clearly formed mental picture of your Ideal, a definite objective towards which to direct your every effort, unless you yourself know exactly where you want to go, you will make no progress in this pathway. Because then you have no goal.

WHY do the great majority of the average men and women around fail? Because the average person divides his ambition in countless directions he or she wants to reach high positions in many lines of endeavor, and with little or no training. We must remember that this is an age of "specialists." Very rarely is it possible to be superior in more than one or two lines of work. So from your list of all possible activities or careers which appeal to you, by a process of elimination choose that which appeals to you most strongly. Choose carefully, and having chosen; LET THAT CHOICE BE FINAL.

In choosing, take the long look ahead. Choose a goal, or an objective, which is to be attained at some rather distant time, let us say in five or six more years. For time is one important element in this choice of yours »GIVE YOURSELF TIME. Because then you can cling to this pictured goal unwaveringly through all the ups and downs and the seeming reverses along the way. Also, before you have quite reached this goal yo can choose another and even more difficult objective beyond.

We teach you to be encouraged and inspired by the realization that .with proper development and unfoldment you can accomplish anything which is humanly possible—no goal of attainment is too high or too dis-tant—don't limit yourself. Along this pathway you will come to know that the faithful application of the simple laws and principles of your teachings can aid you in the highest, noblest form of specialized attainment, with its accompanying blessings of peace, plenty and harmony of Health, of Wealth and of Happiness.

We further teach you quite plainly and simply that to reach any worth-while goal, YOU MUST TRULY, ENTIRELY AND INTENSELY DESIRE THAT ONE GOAL ABOVE ALL ELSE. When this intense desire pulsates through your whole being, according to your earnest FAITH your results will be guaranteed. Because then you will realize for yourself that perfect and mathematically correct rule of THE Divine God-Law that even "according to our faith shall it be done."

In these lessons comprising the occult degree of The Illumination we teach you how to conquer the negative phases or moods of your own mental self, those covert enemies in your own household; within your own personality. Here we shall again impress upon you that your, own negative thoughts, your own fears, your doubts, your indecision are the real barriers to your rightful success. You will be taught simply and plainly exactly HOW to overcome these negative barriers by constantly building in positive confidence, in absolute assurance and in unwavering FAITH.

You will find here still deeper lessons in proven methods of continuously VISUALIZING (picturing) YOURSELF in just the position in life or which you long, and possessing the Health, the Wealth and the Happiness you so greatly desire, without any questioning or trying to see in advance just HOW all this shall come to pass.

Day by day, as your vision becomes REAL to you within, you will come to KNOW that your inner, mental picture is manifesting in your material world without. Because as you follow our teaching in weaving the pat-tern in the subjective mind, so likewise will its exact reflection mould the objective and external circumstances of your life.

MEDITATION—HOURS OF INNER SILENCE

In attaining to your great goal—on the pathway of unfoldment we would have you realize that the hours you spend in silent, subjective MEDITATION are just as helpful and just as important to your progress as the hours you will spend in the more intensive concentration.

Subjective meditation is just what the term implies—it is simply meditation, and meditation is reflection WITHOUT EFFORT. Very often, when it becomes profound, meditation induces a state of semi-subcon-scious trance, somewhat like a day-dream, and in this condition of subjectivity you are closer to the inner, the deeper planes of SELF than at any other time.

We want you to give your utmost attention to the immeasurable aid and benefit you .will find in simple, subjective meditation "in the silence." You will find its blessings and its strange powers in every stage of your unfoldment. To all alike from the elementary student to the Initiate and the Mystic Master, will, come the most powerful inspirations in the times of this strange silence we call meditation.

Meditation indeed simple in its requirements. First, YOU MUST BE ALONE. Next, just quietly disengage your, mind (10let loose") from any and all confusing and distracting surroundings, or conditions in your daily life. Now RELAX the body entirely, as you have been taught to do in your previous instructions. And then you just settle down comfortably for a half hour or an hour of silent reflection or meditation. Without effort reflect upon the good things you desire, and, quietly picture yourself as enjoying each one of your desired blessings.

You will find that you are now mentally freed from the confusion and the stress of your daily round in life. Your body is relaxed and at rest, your mind is at peace, and your perspective view of your life becomes uncolored, vivid and in true proportions.

Again in your subjective meditation, you are indeed very close to the infinite reservoir of all knowledge (world of the sub-conscious) and you may easily and simply workout every detail of your Vision (mental picture), not through strain and effort but by listening to the "still, small voice" of Intuition in, The Silence.

If you want to know whether you will succeed or find true happiness in some visioned future situation or in the attainment of the particular goal you have chosen, just turn to your hour of meditation in. The Silence and there picture to yourself the entire picture. See yourself, with the eye of imagination, actually living the life you desire or in reality being in the situation you have pictured, or vision yourself as possessing those material good things for which you have longed. Then observe carefully whether your inner reactions to these subjective pictures are uplifting, happy and joyous, or the opposite. The test is sure—it never fails.

Likewise, with those vexing, daily problems of your life, you will find your greatest help in solving them in your period of silent meditation. For there in clear perspective, and without effort, sooner or later perfect <u>answers to your problems will present themselves</u>.

BEACON LIGHTS ON THE WAY OF UNFOLDMENT

As you proceed upon your pathway of inner unfoldment, you will find in due time that you are walking in the white glow of those beacon lights which show the way amid the Silence and the shadows. For new thoughts and new realizations come to you now, and the meanings of each experience will clarify and crystallize within your mind as never before.

Please understand quite clearly that quiet meditation is NOT concentration—rather, it is an opposite process, or, we might liken these "two methods or states of consciousness to the tides of the sea—one the incoming tide, the other, the outgoing. For true meditation is base upon COMPLETE RELAXATION—and in this state you Are transported to the border-land between the HERE of this earth-life and the realm of the Infinite.

We want you to make a habit of this silent meditation, because habit is a laborless form of expression. And your greatest good from subjective meditation will come from this freedom from conscious effort. So form the habit of meditation by taking certain periods every day in which you will relax and meditate, if only for a few minutes at a time.

This habit of meditation is not easy to form and will call for persistence on your part. True meditation "in the Silence" is of course most effective in the quiet of your own room, and following the regular exercises which we have given you in your former lessons.

Once this habit is acquired, you will be able in your meditation periods to contact the Infinite Source of all Power the "giant within"—and even one little minute of this contact will flood your whole being with renewed, dynamic energy.

Cultivate this HABIT of meditation over the months and through the years, and before long you, too, will stand in awe and reverence before that WONDERFUL SELF WITHIN YOU.

For this wonderful SELF within you ever stands so close to you, waiting patiently for you to lay your so-lim-ited conscious mind aside for just a few minutes each day, so that HE may speak to you, and that you may learn to know him. Listen for his voice, and before long when you have hardened to him habitually in your daily periods in the silence of meditation you will come to know that no other being in this world is so important, so great, so mighty as THIS SELF WITHIN—and yet he is your humble servant. LISTEN TO HIM—IN THE SILENCE.

Lesson No. 2
THE HIGHWAY TO HEALTH, WEALTH AND HAPPINESS

Fourth Gateway of The Temple Invisible. Being The Secret Instruction Taught by The Masters in White, Whose Sublime Precepts Are Now Exemplified in These Lessons.

CREATING YOUR NEW WORLD BY FOCUSED ATTENTION

"To hold a candle before a mirror is to cause a reflection in the mirror; in like manner to hold a mental picture is to cause its reflection in the body. To change that picture every moment is to cause a change in the bodily reflection. To hold a picture continually in the mind is to keep its reflection constantly in the body. This Concentration does—it holds the candle of desire before the mirror of the flesh until the flesh reflects permanently that picture.

"Concentration carves in the marble of the material the model held by Imagination, the creator, who builds through thought. From this fact is reached the conclusion which I state in these Affirmations; "I am blind and deaf to all that is unpleasant; ill, painful, weak or that carries failure. I recognize only that which I wish to recognize. I pay attention only to chosen ideas. I see only that which I wish to see. I hear only that which I wish to hear."—Henry Harrison Brown in "Concentration: The Road to Success."

CONCENTRATION IS FOCUSED ATTENTION

Perhaps you have thought that the practice of concentration is some lost art, or some deep process shrouded in mystery, or something apart from everyday life. Nothing could be farther from the truth. Like every other human power, concentration is very close to you—it is here and now it is within you. And you concentrate every day—but usually unconsciously and wrongly. Most concentration is either useless or harmful, because it is either misdirected or aimless.

Have you ever had a blinding headache, or a piercing toothache? And if so, was not your attention FOCUSED upon that headache or toothache? Also, it is safe to assume that your focused attention sooner or later drove you to ACTION, and you sought relief, YOU DID SOMETHING ABOUT IT.

Dad you ever "fall in love?" Remember how you dreamed about that sweetheart by day and by night, and how you talked about that so wonderful person to just about everybody who would listen? Probably you made that sweetheart yours, because your attention was FOCUSED, and that was the one thing your heart desired above all others. And there was action—you did something about it, probably you married the girl (or boy)— that was concentration. And concentration GETS RESULTS.

Have you known people who worried from morning til night or others who were constantly angry, or still other misguided sows who lived in constant fear? Or have you known men or women who suffered a thousand deaths from imaginary ills, hypochondriacs who conjured up a new set of symptoms every day or two? Every one of these people was concentrating—but their attention was focused upon the NEGATIVE emotions, and soon their whole lives were negative. What a terrible price each of these paid, because concentration ALWAYS GETS RESULTS, but the results are not always GOOD. The result depends on WHAT you focus your attention upon.

THE SECRET OF REALIZING YOUR DESIRE

You have chosen the goal, the object of your one Great Desire for present realization. Very well, you have taken your first step toward possessing that great desire when you have thus mentally created that desire. And just now your part of The Great Work is to create that mental desire into reality in your actual, your material world.

The secret, then, of realizing your desire no matter what that desire may be—learn and to practice positive mental and physical concentration.

If perfect, vigorous, abounding HEALTH is your great desire, you must learn how to concentrate upon Health, for Health is first a mental creation.

If abundant prosperity—material wealth—is your great desire, you must learn how to concentrate upon wealth, for wealth, also, is first a mental creation.

And if joyous happiness is your great desire, you must learn how to concentrate upon HAPPINESS, for happiness, too, is first a mental creation.

The Key to all the good things of life is concentration, because by this focused attention we must first mentally create each of these good things within the mind—within the thought-world of our own consciousness.

Further, the Key to popularity, to friendship, and to love, to almost every worth-while position in this world is a strong, winning, charming personality—and this positive Personality, likewise, is the product of focused attention to Personality—again, a mental creation barn of concentrating upon a pictured image of that desired personality.

Directed concentration is the shortest road to success in attaining the Health, the Wealth and the Happiness for which you have longed.

So we shall teach you directed concentration very simply, very plainly and very certainly in these advanced lessons which lead to The Illumination.

And just what IS directed concentration?

It is nothing more or less than focusing (centering or fixing) every faculty of your body, mind and soul— your entire being—upon your goal, your desire, your great objective until it completely rules your whole life. In the words of the Masters in White, you thus become "ONE POINTED."

When you make your desire a GREAT DESIRE, not a whim or an idle wish or a passing fancy, when this Great Desire takes over the complete control of your mind, when this Great Desire fans the fires of Ambition within you, when you accept this Great Desire as TRUTH, and BELIEVE that it is already becoming REAL-ITY— when you focus all the thought-rays of your mind upon this Great Desire with intense attention, then your Great Desire WILL BEGIN TO MATERIALIZE BEFORE YOUR EYES AND IN YOUR LIFE.

EVEN NOW YOU DO CONCENTRATE EVERY DAY

To prove to you that there is nothing inherently mysterious about concentration, but that it is only misunderstood, let us point out to you that you yourself are concentrating all the time as you perform your daily work, no matter what that work may be whether it be the tasks of manual labor or those of mechanical or pro- fessional skills. The trouble is that we have gotten the idea that concentration, which after all is simply focused attention, is shrouded in mystery.

ENTHUSIASM—IT IS EASY TO DO THE THINGS YOU LIKE

For whatever we like to do becomes easy for us. Remember in your own life the times you have done the things you liked most to do—were you not happy and enthusiastic in doing those things? Of course you were. You concentrated upon those things because you were absorbed in them, and don't you remember how very EASY these things were for you to do? So, after all, now you can see that concentration is really easy, the secret is to choose the thing you like most to do, to choose the goal you most greatly desired and become absorbed in it.

Can you not still remember the games of your childhood and later of your youth, and how whole-hearted-ly you entered into those games, how real they were to you, and how ABSORBED you were in those games you liked best? That was concentration. Probably you did not know at the time that you were concentrating, but it was easy, wasn't it? Instead of being a condition of tenseness or of strain, of gritted teeth, or of closely knit eye-brows, or of a face distorted and wrinkled, true concentration works best through a calm mind which you direct with a fixed purpose. So, when you bring your mind under complete control, you can focus that mind and all its powers upon your goal in life with tremendous effect.

The very first step that we would teach you how to take toward positive concentration is to get the idea that it is either mysterious or difficult entirely out of your mind. Then you can master all of your energies and focus them upon your objective. There is a great Law of opposites which control almost all of life, like the ebb and flow of the tides of the sea, effort and relaxation, work and play, etc. Suppose you suspect that your mind scatters, or flits often aimlessly from one subject to another, which is more or less true of every one of us. Very well, yet the truth remains that when you gain control of that very same "flitting" mind, you will be able to concentrate your entire intellect upon the goal you have chosen IF YOU DESIRE THAT GOAL MORE THAN ANYTHING ELSE IN THE WORLD.

Let us show you how to change your work into PLAY—because if your life-work does not mean happiness to you, you will probably never find happiness.

So you think that your mind "scatters", do you? Of course, you are right, it does. So does every other human mind at times, Now, let's take advantage of that very quality of the mind which enables it to "Scatter," to flit instantly from one object to another. We shall do this by giving you a very simple and a very interesting exercise which you will find one of the most valuable exercises in the world in concentration—in focusing attention. This exercise will prove to you not only that you CAN CONCENTRATE but that you can concentrate on three things at one and the same time with a very little practice.

This is the exercise—here is what you do: turn your radio on, preferably tuning in to a musical program. Now listen to this program attentively for two or three minutes, then pick up a newspaper or a magazine, and read a story or an article. Take your time at first. Soon to your surprise you will find yourself listening to the music without missing a single note, and reading the article at the same time without missing a single word. So now you are doing both these things at one and the same time, and with a little practice, doing them well. Next, while the radio is playing, and while you are reading from a paper or a magazine, try talking to another person at the same time. Soon you will find yourself listening to the music and enjoying it, reading a story or an article with understanding, and talking to some one without missing a word of the conversation.

So you find that you can DO THREE THINGS AT THE SAME TIME, and do each one just as well as if you were doing that one thing only.

Contrary to your former ideas of concentration, this is true concentration. Now, when through practice of this simple exercise you have gained this mental ability to do three things at the same time, try fixing your atten-tion—focusing—upon some ONE object, and you will be amazed to find that you can concentrate as never before.

RELAX AND CONCENTRATE—"TAKE IT EASY!"

Now you have already taken a great step toward your goal—if you have mastered this simple three-fold exercise you have proved to yourself that your mind, which you had thought "scattered" hopelessly, is indeed very efficient when you take over its control in earnest. For you have directed that mind of yours to do these three things at once; (1) listen to the radio, (2) read a news or magazine article, and (3) talk with another person, and all with understanding. And afterward, when you directed your mind upon your goal you find you have increased your power to concentrate marvelously.

Our purpose in all of this is to convince you beyond all doubt that true concentration is not only possible but EASY for you when you learn HOW TO CONCENTRATE—HOW TO FOCUS YOUR MIND.

But perhaps you may have chosen some goal or some ambition before now, and then have found that you could not concentrate effectively upon this desire?

Most people fail when they try to concentrate because THEY TRY TOO HARD—they strain, they tense every muscle, they make great conscious efforts blindly, and all of course to no avail. As a result they give up in disgust, or quit trying because they are discouraged. If you have failed before, like these people, please know that you didn't fail in concentrating, because you were certainly NOT concentrating, you were only going through some useless outer motions which you thought were methods of concentration. Of course, they were not.

You have simply been lost in a mental wilderness because you have been given the wrong directions. Now, let us lead you upon the sure pathway of attainment. To awaken your dormant interest and to enlist the tremendous powers of the "giant within"—your indomitable Inner Self—it is necessary for you to choose a goal which comprises all the splendid things you like above all else—those finer, happier, greater things for which you have longed. Keep your goal one that is humanly possible, BUT DON'T LIMIT YOURSELF.

Once and for all break with the past, just boot every one of those dark and narrow and limiting and ugly things out of your mind, and wholeheartedly change your mental view from those dark shadows to the glowing happiness of your new goal. And almost before you know it you will be vibrating with a new-found joy and enthusiasm, and you will realize for yourself that real concentration is actually EASY, because you have become its master.

Simply RELAX and keep your mental eyes (your thoughts) fixed, centered, focused on your goal. In doing this, avoid all conscious effort and all strain—JUST "TAKE IT EASY." Just KNOW that hour by hour, day by day, and week by week your goal and all the good things you desire in that goal ARE MANIFESTING. Never allow yourself one little mental argument against your treasured desire. AND NEVER DISCUSS YOUR GOAL WITH ANYONE ELSE.

Laugh at your former fears and doubts—make a game of your exercises, and play at that game regularly. Don't let anything interfere with your daily exercises. You are in deadly earnest in developing those powers which will bring those good things you have decided to possess, and a very short time will prove to you the supreme value of these teachings and of your daily exercises. For now day by day you are developing that quiet enthusiasm and that one-pointed, focused mind-attitude which

WINS in spite of every obstacle.

PATHWAY TO MATERIAL MANIFESTATION

Of course, you know that when you are really and deeply interested in something which means a great deal to you, when you are absorbed in something WHICH APPEALS TO YOU GREATLY, hardly anything can distract your attention from that something. Then you can 'concentrate' on a speeding train, in a rattling street car, or in a boiler factory! So don't harbor that idea that you cannot concentrate any longer, because you can. The Secret is to fix your thoughts upon the GOOD THINGS OF THE GOAL WHICH YOU HAVE CHOSEN.

You are now traveling the pathway to material manifestation, so keep your eyes upon your goal, and keep your mind busy picturing that goal, that so-great objective. No matter what seeming diversions or unwelcome tasks Fate may force upon you along the way, no matter if you seem at times to be scattering your forces upon work that appears to be far removed from your objective, be very certain that if there is a strong undercurrent in your subconscious mind flowing toward your desired objective, none of these outer hindrances can prevent you from reaching your goal.

Just as long as you hold that goal in pictures before your mind's eye, that Great Desire is shaping itself in your consciousness, and will materialize in your outer, material world. For this IS concentration.

So, as you follow and obey these Cosmic Laws which we are teaching you in these lessons, you are linking yourself and your life to the universe of manifestation. Your health, your wealth and your happiness—your life, your personality and your destiny—all depend upon your application of this supreme God-Law. Thus this work of training your mind ye become a receptive channel for this Cosmic Illumination, and your study and application of Cosmic Law in your life becomes the greatest thing in the world to you.

Five hundred years before the birth of Christ, Heraclitus wrote, "Wisdom consists in one duty and only one to understand the Intelligence WHICH GOVERNS ALL THINGS."

From his earliest days Man has tried to pierce the secret of creative Nature by finding a single underlying principle as a "common building material" of which all things consist and from which all were created. From the Greek philosopher and mystic, Thales, of Miletus, who tried to reduce everything by mathematical precision to water as the common principle, to Anaximenes, who postulates air as the fundamental medium, we come to the modern scientific theory of an electro-magnetic-vibrating spacefield.

One of the greatest scientists of the age, the late Dr. Charles P. Steinmetz, stated his conclusions in these words:

"There extends through space an alternating (vibrating) electromagnetic field of force. Radio and light waves are properties of such a pulsating electro-magnetic space field."

SCIENCE APPLIES COSMIC LAWS

In order to know the supreme importance of science, let us realize that the story of science is the story of the great achievements of mankind in every age. It is philosophy which interprets and seeks to explain Cosmic Laws (the God-Law) but it is the mission of Science to enable you and every other Student, to apply these immutable Cosmic Laws to your material and intellectual needs by thus making possible the attainment of your goal in Health, in Prosperity and in lasting Happiness.

Our Philosophy is that great body of occult knowledge which offers to every member of our rulership over his or her environment.

Our Philosophy begins where Reason asserts itself, and where the "supernatural" (superstition) give place to proven facts and to man's ever advancing experience. As long ago as 1866 Liebig, the great chemist, addressing The Royal Academy of Science at Munich, said:

"The development of culture, I.e., the extending of man's spiritual domain, depends on the growth of the inventions which condition the progress of civilization, for through these NEW FACTS are obtained...

Future history will describe the victories of freedom which men achieved through investigation of the ground of things and of truth, victories won with bloodless weapons."

For countless ages our Masters in White and our 'Mystics' were almost alone in following their 'strange' studies of the immaterial and the invisible things of the universe, but today the orthodox scientist is carefully following a road, in his search for the HOW of things, which leads straight to the Pathway of old so long trodden by those Masters, Mystics and Initiates who alone understood in the earliest days of human history the DIVINE WHY—the underlying God-Law of every phenomena.

The breath-taking discoveries of our present unfolding age of Electronics are shaking the foundations of every "science" which is based upon the material alone. This now well known electron theory when carried to its logical conclusion leads us into invisible worlds of Divine Energy, reducing all MATTER to localized Cosmic, or electro-magnetic, energy, demonstrating as it does, polarity and spiral vibratory fields everywhere in space.'

Yet material science is still seeking an explanation of THE ORIGINATING CAUSE, and blindly seeks its answer in the solving of the mystery of the action of one electric charge upon another at a great distance, the like effect of polarity upon magnetic Apaes, bodies or the bending of light-rays by a magnetic field.

Yet, through thousands of years the Ancient Wisdom, as exemplified in our system of Science and Philosophy has held in trust for its followers the easily understood answer to this modern riddle of The Originating Cause, the answer which has given, our Adepts and Masters the power in every age to work "miracles."

In order to find your own true place in this vast, vibrating Cosmic Space-Field, a field as wide as the universe, you need only to realize that your DRAIN is a combination thought-wave transmitter and receiver. Your next lesson will expand this radio analogy, and teach you some of its marvelous applications.

Lesson No. 3
THE PATHWAY TO HEALTH, WEALTH AND HAPPINESS

Fourth Gateway of The Temple Invisible, Being The Secret Instruction Taught by The Masters in White, Whose Sublime Precepts are Now Exemplified in These Lessons.

ATTAINING HEALTH BY MENTAL FOCUSING OR CONCENTRATION

The late Professor James once said:

"I am sure that everybody who is able to concentrate thought and will, and to eliminate superfluous emotion, sooner or later becomes master of his body and can eliminate every kind of illness—our thoughts have a plastic power over our body."

And in "Our Unconscious Mind," Frederick Pierce says:

"In the presence of a strong enough wish we have no difficulty with concentration. The desire to escape, if the building is afire will be quite sufficient to keep the attention from wondering to last night's party or to one that is being planned for next week. The trouble is that achievement wishes are usually associated with the idea of work, and the word "work" has become, during childhood, loaded with unpleasant associations of effort, self-denial, confinement, etc.,—the negation of play and pleasure—until our actual wish, recognize it or not, is to be free from the irksome necessity course, the underlying, instinctive affect.

"Successful adjustment (mental focusing) requires the development and energizing of achievement (cultural) wishes to a point where they supersede and replace the instinctive one. Concentration upon the necessary effort-respons-es will rise steadily WITH THE STRENGTH OF THE WISHES. Throughout the entire program, Coue's law of reversed effort may well be kept in mind—'The harder I try to correct my faults, the harder I find it to do so.'..."

Understanding of this "law of reversed effort" will be priceless to you, as a student. The trouble is that in cases like the above the attention is generally most strongly focused upon the faults themselves, instead of upon their cure. This is entirely natural, because the method is wrong.

But let's reverse this incorrect method, and let us suppose that the "faults" are faults of the physical body, faults which we commonly call "sickness" or "disease". Now, instead of focusing upon the "faults"—the sick-ness—you focus your mind upon exactly opposite ideas or mental pictures, and so you focus your thoughts entirely upon HEALING, PERFECT HEALTH AND ABOUNDING

STRENGTH AND VIGOR.

Suppose that you persistently hold before your "mind's eye" this opposite picture of healing—of health— of strength and vitality, and that you turn your full powers of faith and of imagination upon THIS HEALTH PICTURE constantly, morning, noon and night, and day after day. Soon this picture will dominate your thoughts, and will merge into a Desire that will become almost an obsession with you.

This method insures that your concentration will grow with your desire, because the mental focusing which grows with your strong desire is almost without effort, because it is entirely natural. And this method of focusing the attention entirely upon the most vivid pictures of HEALTH (instead of sickness and disease) awakens the giant Healing Power within.

WITH THE MIND AT EASE IN THE SILENCE COMES HEALING

In the ancient Tagore we read:

"An austere silence is more adequate to the experience of God than elaborate descriptions." .

Inspiration, concentration and realization do not come from strain or effort, nor during times of conscious work, but these come often when you expect them least, when your mind is at ease, in a word, in THE SILENCE.

But first you must have a STRONG DESIRE. And that desire must be DEFINITE. That word 'desire' is a powerful, a dynamic word. Without desire you are lost. Perhaps you are where you are today because you have been afraid to desire the GOOD THINGS OF LIFE HARD ENOUGH, and NOT because of the will of God. It is never the will of God that you be unhappy, poverty stricken, suffering or afflicted by sickness. You will never achieve any worth-while goal in life without a driving desire.

And if your goal is a worthy one, as for instance Health, Abundance, Happiness and Soul- Illumination, the then DESIRE for that goal is not only just as holy as PRAYER, and in fact that desire IS prayer, because, as Montgomery once said, "Prayer is the Soul's sincere DESIRE uttered or unexpressed."

DESIRE IS PRAYER. What then is the true approach to prayer? First, then, the dictionary definition of prayer is too material in its meaning, which is given as

"Petition", "Entreaty, " "Devotion." Let US change this to "Attunement, concentration, communion in The Silence with Divine God-Mind."

Prayer then, is the meeting of the human conscious mind with the illimitable Divine Mind in the silence of the subconscious. In the time of true prayer your subjective mind quietly speaks to the God Within and expresses the deepest DESIRE of your heart and your soul. In that silent meeting your DEsire-Thoughts speak mind to mind with God-Mind, and Divine-Mind assures you that your desire IS granted.

Be careful not to confuse TRUE PRAYER with those orthodox prayers of mere words recited in form only, generally for public display, for these public prayers are simply "vain repetitious" and bring no replies. Countless numbers of good people go through life faithfully reciting words they have learned "by hear'" and yet without having prayed once in a whole lifetime.

Remember HOW Christ taught us to pray? He said: "Enter into thy closet (silence) and...pray to thy Father WHICH IS IN SECRET."

In reality, in our language He was actually saying:

"When ye pray, PRAY DE PROFUNDIS (out of the depths)—enter into thyself, into the silence of thy Soul, then in thine own inmost consciousness speak to the Divine Mind, which is THERE,"

The "Lord's Prayer" is the world's greatest example of HOW to pray. Note that the first half of this master prayer is reverence, recognition, harmony. And the second half of this model prayer is Desire and positive demand—"Give us—forgive us—lead us—deliver us—" each one a clear-cut, a definite request.

There is nothing positive, nothing attractive and nothing result-getting in self-abasing prayers—AVOID THEM, if you would avoid the curse of the negative. To parrot over and over "I am but a poor, weak work of the dust...I am unworthy and sinful,...I am just a poor humble failure in the vineyard of the Lord," is simply telling God that all His goodness has been wasted on you, while at the same time you are asking Him to waste more blessings upon you. Why should He?

DIRECT COMMUNION WITH THE DIVINE

True prayer—concentration upon desire—is direct communion with the Divine.

In establishing this direct communion with the Power that grants desire, it is not necessary that we pray—con-centrate—upon our knees, or that we bow our heads, or that we assume.any set specified physical posture. However, the condition most favorable to direct, personal communion with the Divine is one of perfect physical and mental relaxation. By this we mean the reaching of a quiet, passive attitude of mind and of body.

Now, having reached this favorable condition, direct your clear, positive, desire-thought to THE DIVINE WITHIN YOU—your inmost Soul-Self, because this is just another name for Omnipresent Spirit, Universal Consciousness, or the Divine God-Mind. This is definite, this is HERE, this is NOW—so do not waste your efforts by trying to send your Desire-Thought outwards and upward to some vague realm beyond the skies. Instead by this superb method you pierce through your own dense outer senses and you become intensely conscious of the Divine Self within.

You are seeking the state of Soul-Consciousness, and you can now understand why you can never attain to this mystical state of one-pointed concentration by praying in the usual, orthodox way amidst any assembly or crowd of "worshippers." The crowd merely confuses you, and the many, many "cross vibrations" will effectively neutralize your efforts. Also in such a case you must concentrate on what you are doing in a material sense, in order to follow the "form" and the "ceremony" with the crowd. You certainly cannot establish personal communion with Inner Divine Mind when falling out of step with the crowd.

Isn't it infinitely better to keep step with the Divine God-Mind WITHIN YOURSELF?

"Narrow is the way" that leads from Desire to Realization. You cannot give full sway to your inner and to your outer senses or faculties at the same time, for one or the other must be dominant. You must learn to exclude from your mind and thoughts the things you DO NOT DESIRE, so that this thing which you most greatly desire can have your focused, undivided ATTENTION.

The methods we are teaching you herein are simply designed to give your Inner Divine Power a chance to demonstrate itself, because that Inner Power is like electricity in that it is not made manifest to us until it leaps into action at our call— and until you do call it into action it does not exist FOR YOU.

Perhaps you have wondered why it is that so many ASK, but seemingly so few RECEIVE? Simply because the many know nothing about the science of true prayer—concentration, Their so-called "prayers" are merely idle words—just a form of "wishful thinking" out loud! And the things they ask are not in harmony with The Divine Plan.

Remember, answer to prayer is never direct, but comes to you through the Divine God-Law by way of natural law. In other words that answer comes to you through some perfectly natural means through which it can materialize in your personal world. You can be very sure that you will receive exactly as must as is due to you at any time, and no more.

"YE ASK AND RECEIVE NOT"—WHY?

And the answering phrase which follows this is simple—"because ye ask amiss (wrongly)."

To "ask amiss" (wrongly) simply means that we put material blessings first in our asking, and when you do this you are putting the cart before the horse'. In other words, you are concentrating first on the material instead of on the Divine, and it is from the Divine that all power to grant our requests must come.

Divine God-Mind is spiritual, and NOT material. You may naturally ask, how then can those material gifts which I have pictured in my great desire come from this entity which is spiritual only? The answer is that Divine God-Mind, once you have entered into harmony with it in The Silence GIVES OF ITSELF—inspira-tion, the higher understanding, spiritual consciousness, with divine wisdom and power. All of these are immaterial gifts, but remember it is the invisible, the immaterial which is transformed into the visible, the material HEALTH, RICHES AND HAPPINESS for which you long.

Divine God-Mind, once you commune with this supernal presence, gives to you the ethereal counterpart of that for which you long in the material world. And more, Divine God-Mind gives you the power to attract to yourself that material blessing which fulfills your great desire, and that power is increased in the same measure that you HELP YOURSELF. Thus is your answer to prayer (concentration) recognized and realized.

We want you to realize that what you greatly desire and what you WILL receive STARTS in this ethereal counterpart on the spiritual plane—this is its beginning. Its second phase is developed on the mental plane (in your mind) where in it is magnified by silent meditation and concentration and reaches the creative stage, and so it then reaches its third phase, completion and realization in your possession in the material world.

So, instead of saying that "thoughts are things, " shall we not say that THOUGHTS BECOME THINGS, when those thoughts are reflected INTO the material world from their ethereal counterparts? Every gift necessary to the realization of your great desire is supplied through the spiritual currents of Divine God-Mind, PLUS your own actual work toward accomplishment.

The Bible admonition that " Men ought always to pray and the faint not" does not mean that when you have prayed (desired in The Silence) you are to seek an easy chair and wait for your blessings to fall into your lap from the heavens without any particular work on your part. They won't.

Please understand that prayer (concentration) does not create anything which does not already exist, but that communion (and harmony) with God-Mind opens your pathway to the realization that the already existing good things of life ARE FOR YOU TOO.

THE DIVINE "NOUS" THOUGHT-VIBRATION CREATIVE

Centuries ago Anazagoras—of fame as one of-the Wise Masters—speaking of the marvelous, the unifying, the quickening power of the mystical "NOUS" over matter, said:

"But Nous has power over all things that are, and it is now where all the other things are, in the mass that surrounds the world, and in the things that have been separated off and that are being separated off..." Thus this ancient Master recognized so long ago that this tremendous God-Power is UNIVERSAL—that it is always, and everywhere.

For this Nous is creative thought-vibrations, and one familiar form of this mysterious Nous we find in the radiant, life giving energy which streams from the sun, of which William J. Luyten says;

"From time immemorial the sun has been worshiped as the ruler of the sky, as the source of light and heat, as the originator and preserver of life, the symbol of ultimate and immaculate purity...the sun has been shown by astronomy to be the central and dominating body of the planetary system, dominating not only by virtue of its great mass, which forces all other objects in its vicinity to obey its will, but, also because it is the only one that leads an independent existence, the one one shining by its own light."

According to Sir James H. Jeans, the Nous is the all-Powerful thought-vibration which permeates the entire Universe like one vast thought. It is the eternal FIAT (Command) which directs the stellar systems, AND ENDOWS EVERY ATOM HEREIN WITH LIFE AND MIND.

Said Thomas A. Edison: "Every atom of matter is intelligent, deriving energy from the primordial germ. The intelligence of man is, I take it, the sum of the intelligences of the atoms of which he is composed. Every atom has an intelligent power of selection, and is always striving to get into harmonious relation with other atoms. The human body is, I think, maintained in its integrity by the intelligent persistence of its atoms, or rather by an agreement between the atoms so to persist.

When the harmonious adjustment is destroyed the man dies, and the atoms seek other relations."

Such is the vast kingdom of intelligent atoms within your body over which YOU are the guiding ruler.

What a stupendous, what a fascinating study is the Nous—for in it we see the primordial Creative God-Energy which unties the solar and the stellar systems into a boundless Cosmic Whole for this is the ineffable luminous essence which vibrates with the currents of Divine Cosmic Mind—currents which will kindle YOUR intuition and fire your genius when you contact them in your prayer—silences of attunement and communion through meditative concentration.

So YOU, too, can contact the power-house of the Universe. And may we call your attention to Dr. J. E. Boodin's discovery that in addition to the action and reaction of matter upon matter, there are forty different recognized types.of radiant energy flowing from the Cosmos to this earth upon which we live!

These radiant energies composed of positive protons and negative electrons are the mystical NOUS in their very essence. And in the field of their manifestations we have pioneered in recognizing them not only as being material BUT ALSO AS SPIRITUAL IN THEIR NATURE. For we have found that atoms are BOTH physical and psychical.

It may seem strange, but the Ancient Wisdom contains the basic truths of modern science. The great advances of science today are not one step in advance OF the conceptions of the Masters in White throughout the ages. The only difference is that modern science differs in the KIND of foundations upon which these conceptions are built.

In proof of this we cite no less an authority than Dr. Robert A. Millikan, one of our greatest modern scientists, who writes that the principles of the philosophy of the ancient Democritus, only slightly modified and with a few omissions, almost entirely foreshadow the discoveries of modern science.

NOUS, FIAT, LOGOS (WORD)—INFINITE SOURCE

Dr. Millikan quotes the following principles from Democritus' philosophy in proof of his statement:

"From nothing comes nothing. Nothing that exists can be destroyed. All changes are due to the combination and separation of molecules."—

"Nothing happens by chance. Every occurrence has its cause which it follows by necessity."—The only existing things are atoms and empty space, all else are mere opinions. "The atoms are infinite in number and infinitely various in form: they strike together and the lateral motions and whirlings which thus arise are the beginnings of worlds."

"The varieties of all things depend upon the varieties of their atoms, size and aggregation."—"The Soul Atoms...are the most mobile of all. They interpenetrate the whole body and in their motions the phenomena of life arise." (Quoted by Dr. Millikan, from the writings of Democritus.)

Imperium in imperio—Vital life force and consciousness—the all embracing NOUS emanating everywhere throughout the universe as the thought-vibration, the Fiat (command), or the Logos (Word) from the absolute wisdom of Infinite God-Mind.

This is the INFINITE SOURCE, Eternal Universal Mind, from which, through your psychic self or intuitive mind, in your hours of Prayer, Meditation, YOU will draw to yourself the wisdom, the health, the riches and the happiness for which you have vainly sought in the past.

And the way is simple—in true prayer, desire concentrated, you commune directly with Divine God-Mind, and God-Mind is all creative, and YOU are a part of that Divine Mind! For your human mind is but the Luminous soul—atome Of Divine, Conscious Life imparted to you by the Nous-Vibrations from that Infinite Divine Mind. You are a differentiated yet an inseparable part of the Divine Mind. This divine flow of life and of consciousness which is yours today is the indwelling Soul that makes YOU the spiritual image and likeness of that Divine Supreme Mind.

Now that you are well upon the Way, you have discovered that the pathway from the valley of limitation to the heights of attainment is rough and rugged at times, as well as smooth. You have found that life leads through shadows as well as sunshine, through storms as well as through calm, through sorrows as well as happiness.

And great is the VALUE of adversity. We need the stimulation it gives us. Were the Pathway always smooth and the skies always sunny we would soon grow lazy and indifferent...and weak. Have you suffered reverses, calamities, "bad luck," and are you acquainted with poverty, ill health, ingratitude, or even betrayal? Well and good, these have been your friends in disguise, for it is their mission to awaken you, even if rudely.

Learn to welcome happiness as you would a bright and sunny day, and let sorrow be to you as the sadder rain—but know both as your friends and helpers, for the reflection of both are in your own mind.

For how can we appreciate any of our emotional experiences without contrasts?

LESSON No.4
THE PATHWAY TO HEALTH, WEALTH AND HAPPINESS

Fourth Gateway of The Temple Invisible, Being The Secret Instruction Taught by The Masters in White, Whose sublime Precepts Are Now Exemplified in These Lessons.

The Degree of Illumination

BE A MASTER—DEVELOPING YOUR DEEPER SELF

"The individual who does his work in an objective, forcing way, uses his body in its voluntary powers and exhausts far more than he creates or renews; one who lets go his Soul ('deeper self') to permit it to do the exercising of brain or body or all the being, puts the Master Chemist, the Master Electrician, the Master Engineer, the Great Physician, the Great Builder, the Supreme Creator, in charge, an Intelligence that knows the condition of every cell at all times and has command over every atom, therefore, when it has possession it keeps a balance between renewal and exhaustion, rather creating more energy than is used, so under the PASSIVE PRINCIPLE of expression one continues to construct in all the phases of his being, to unfold—to grow.

"In self-forgetfulness one is taken over by the Master that would do all things well, even would create each thing perfect. The Highest is always present, always easy of approach, and will always hear the prayer of the volition. The King is always in His Heaven and always responds to the child-like Prayer."—Dr. A. A. Lindsay.

Be a Master—that is why you are studying today, and to that end you are receiving these confidential lessons. For the Way to abounding Health is the Way of the Master, the Way to abundant Wealth is the Way of the Master, and the Way to lasting Happiness is the Way of the Master. And these are the Ways which you have chosen.

Very well then, let us determine just what kind of a person a Master is. What do you think of when you see that word 'Master'? Do you picture the sages, the magis, the prophets of long ago of Egypt, or Atlantis or of Lemuria? True, they were all masters, but these lessons though they are founded upon the Ancient Wisdom deal with life TODAY, and seek to lead YOU in the pathway of Master-ship here and now.

Let us first take a modern dictionary as our nearest approach to a common understanding, and turn to it for a definition of this word Master, and let us take this definition as the real starting point of our present lesson.

There we find this definition—"Master, a noun, one who rules or commands others, director, etc., also, an expert...(verb) transitive form, to subdue or overcome, intransitive form, TO EXCELS."

Under "Master" we find, "Dominion, preeminence, eminent skill."

Always the first step is to define that which you want to know, and to achieve to the position. of Master you must define and bend every effort to follow through on a definite, time-proven plan. Looking a second time at our definition, we see that within the limits of these meanings masters, may be many and of a great many kinds, for any superiority depends upon Mastery.

HISTORY OF SOUL—ASCENDING PLANES

"What is it that makes the history of a Soul? It is the stratification of its different stages of progress, the story its acquisitions, and of the general course of its destiny. Before, my history can teach anybody anything, or even interest myself, it, must be disentangled from its materials, distilled and simplified. These thousands of pages are but the pile of leaves and bark from which the essence has still to be extracted. A whole forest of cinchonas is worth but one cask of quinine. A whole Smyrna rose-garden goes to produce one vial of perfume."—Amiel.

There are masters in many fields, according to our definition. Perhaps your field of work is a profession, a business or a trade, or art, or music; whatever that life work of yours may be, in that field you are a master— perhaps not a finished master, or the greatest master in your field, but still a master. You understand your profession, or your business, or your trade, or your art, or music. You draw profits or a living from that business or that work, and you have mastered enough of its problems to pay you dividends.

Now, having become a master in anyone of these fields which affords you a living we want you to realize your power to achieve greater understanding and greater mastership, for our Pathway leads forever UPWARD AND ONWARD. Your expanding consciousness tells you of higher and still higher possibilities for your, because heretofore you have been self-limited, and now we want you to open your mental eyes to the greater view.

Mastery is an IDEAL held steadily within your own mind, centered (focused) deep within your inmost consciousness, ever evolving, never stationary. Each true student is ever traveling towards the heights upon a spiral of ascending planes.

The story of the Masters in White, whose teachings are now our heritage, runs throughout every age of man's history until it is obscured by the shadows of antiquity. These are the unseen Teachers who call to you in the voice of Intuition, saying, "Look Thou, and become a Master, even as I am a Master."

And they ask nothing impossible to you, for even in the physical world their teachings can bestow upon you a control and an understanding of your bodily processes far beyond the understanding of the uninitiated. This you should already have proven for yourself in your former degrees of instruction.

The first great requisite to becoming a Master—Master of Mind, of Self, and of Good Fortune—IS ABOUNDING PHYSICAL HEALTH. A sluggish liver, accumulated bile, kidney derangement, or almost any disorder of your vital organs will generate toxic poisons which will impair and slow down your thinking processes. This of course weakens and impairs your mind's objective function, by which we mean that part of your mind which contacts the material world of things around you.

You can hardly expect to develop the higher mind into keen intuition or vibrant psychic powers if your physical instrument, the body, is not even able to receive or to register the grosser vibrations of ill health, can you? When the brain is permeated by the poisons of physical disorders, the mind can only translate the higher impressions in distorted thoughts and in images that are badly "out of focus." Then the subconscious mind is diverted to seeking to correct our physical disorders.

A MASTER REQUIRES PHYSICAL AND MENTAL HEALTH

To live the ideal, the abundant life of a Master you will require both physical and mental health.

So in previous lessons we have taught you methods of making your physical "temple," the body, just as nearly perfect as possible. Thus, if you are afflicted with poor eyesight, is it not the part of wisdom to visit the oculist and the optician and have your vision corrected with proper glasses? If you are in danger of infection from deranged sinus tubes, follow the breathing exercises we have given you in a former lesson, and if these do not relieve your sinus trouble, as they usually will, see your physician.

We have given you thorough instructions as to the proper foods to eat. Following these simple directions will transform your body. We have taught you methods of breathing deeply and correctly which will fill your body with vibrant and ever renewed life. Follow the breathing exercises we have given you, and you will add a new and magnetic vitality to both body and brain. For you will find the "breath of life" properly directed your greatest stimulant, tonic and rebuilder of tired nerves.

Remember, the great trinity of life is formed from food, water and air—and these are the greatest medicines in the world. To achieve and to use the powers which you seek as a Master requires physical HEALTH. You must be vibrantly. ALIVE.

Then, with a healthy body that is trained to serve your needs as a Master, your next step is to become a deep and a thorough student of MIND—for it is the Mind that should govern the body, and by which you control "Fate." From our former lessons you have learned that your body has a dual (or double control, which functions through your physical brain and its mystic centers. Briefly we review some of the more salient points of your former studies of the mental, so that we can thus lay the ground work for still deeper studies that deal with the mysteries of even more and greater miracle-working powers of Mind and Soul-Self. After all, it is these greater, these miracle-working powers which, when developed, make you a Master.

In review, then, you will remember we 'explained quite fully those two great phases of Mind (or those two great Minds within), the objective (outer) Mind and the Subjective (or sub-conscious, inner or deeper) Mind.

First, you learned that the Objective Mind controls all the voluntary actions of the human body, that all your conscious commands and willed directions center in your Objective Mind. Also, you learned that these conscious commands and willed directions are at once carried to the Subconscious Mind, which then goes to work to put these laws (commands)of the Objective Mind into effect by clothing them with reality in your material world.

Further, the Subjective Mind, you remember, does no original thinking, no thinking of its own, but only seeks to carry the work forward from the point of command. We begin to realize the tremendous number of tasks which fall to the Subconscious Mind when we remember that all the involuntary actions and functions of our bodies are .under its control alone—the beating of the heart, every movement of the lungs in normal breathing, the parastalsis of the intestines, digestion and many, many other complicated processes.

In addition, all sense impressions are stored in the Subconscious Mind for future reference of use. This vast filing system we call Memory and before being finally referred to it for safe-keeping each and every incoming impression is received and catalogued by the Objective (or OUter)Mind, The power to command (recall) these filed impressions is entirely within the Objective Mind.

How soon these commands of your Objective Mind will be fulfilled by the Subconscious Mind, or whether they will ever even reach that deeper mind, or if heard by it will be obeyed, depends entirely upon the ATTUNEMENT of these two minds (or phases of Mind).

In that one word, Attunement, is the secret of the ages, the power behind miracles, the "philosopher's stone" that can make you a Master. When the physical (objective, outer) YOU can "tune in" to the Spiritual (subconscious, inner) YOU, as if by a mystical radio, THAT IS MASTERY.

GOD CONSCIOUSNESS MAKES YOU A MASTER

This mystical attunement (harmony-awareness) of the divine Inner Self by your objective (outer) mind we term God-Consciousness, and it is this awareness of the Supreme Intelligence within that will make of you a Master. In your lessons we have taught you some of the marvels of the spinal nervous system and of the sympathetic nervous system, because it is these which form your RECEIVING APPARATUS, both psychic and physical. Through development of this receiving apparatus alone can you attain to the higher degrees of the rank of Master.

In this ATTUNEMENT you will find powers unfailing and infallible for they are the vibrations of the God-Self within. We want you to realize that in soul and body, in mind and spirit, YOU are the embodiment, the incarnation of absolute and Eternal energy, because within you is the God-Power, the Source from which all things have sprung, just as light, heat, sound, color and even thought itself are but modes and rates of vibration of the same universal element.

We have classed the phenomena of human life in two (or dual) phases, to make the matter quite simple, the physical and the mental. Within this phenomena of life Spirit also claims its rulership. Our philosophy then recognizes that we live on three great planes, the physical, the mental and the spiritual. Now the relations between these three planes are so interwoven and their phenomena so complex that we cannot separate them entirely, nor deal with each alone, because they are Interdependent in their life.

Our physical senses recognize and record physical phenomena and deal with the material world, but our mental and spiritual selves demonstrate (are made known) only to our inner and mystical (Soul) senses.

We know that the mental Self is a superior to the physical Self, and that the Spiritual Self is supremely above the mental Self but yet the laws of these higher Selves (or Planes) do not displace or nullify the laws of the lower. No, because the secret of the absolute health of the body and of perfect happiness of mind lies in attaining complete harmony (attunement) of these three.

Generally, then, both mind and spirit must obey the laws of physical conditions in doing their work, for you cannot change the fundamental circumstances of your physical life through either mind or spirit. Remember, after all "That which is born of the flesh IS flesh," and is ruled by its own inexorable conditions of existence, and to disobey these laws leads to sickness, disease, physical suffering and unhappiness, no matter what the partial and incoordinate attitude of the mind.

POWER OF THE COSMIC OVER SOUL CAN BE YOURS

As you advance upon this mystic Pathway which leads you to the degree of Master, you will realize that there is a greater Self within which is indeed an integral part of The Cosmic Over-Soul, and that the Power of this invisible Over-Soul expresses in and through you.

And all along this Pathway there will be Guides to help you and to show you the Way. Never will you hold an earnest desire for help but what the Brother Masters know it and they will answer your prayer, spoken or unspoken. Who are these Masters? They are the unseen Brothers in White who have travelled this self-same Pathway—some perhaps yesterday, some perhaps ages and ages ago—for they have mastered all temporal and physical lust, and by virtue of Wisdom are freed from this earthly plane.

But before there is definite attunement between your own INMOST SELF and these unseen Brother Masters, you must train your inner consciousness to understand that although often you will be aided from without, your actual development of the estate of a Master must come from your conscious realization of that REAL YOU often described as Soul.

Now every man and woman in the world expresses life, activity, identity and various degrees of development, and this expression is in exact accordance with the plane upon which he or she is living, and in harmony with the directing force of their greatest desire. Many of us express life in widely different ways, and so each of us really and often unconsciously give individual evidence of our actual motives and aims, of our beliefs and our ambitions. So to those who can read we expose our innermost desires in our daily deeds and our mental attitudes.

As we have taught you consistently from your first lesson until now, all creating of new and better environment, conditions, circumstances and, possessions BEGINS and is really directed by Mind—all the good things of life, a worth-while home, a beautiful car, or a fat bank account, all are first created in the mental realm and we can only possess them through mental power as the attractive force.

Yet the greatest, the ONE creative force in the world is that force which is ABOVE the mental realm, the power of the Cosmic OverSoul. When you realize that your Soul-Self is your TRUE SELF (your true identity), and when you understand that You are a vital, yes, an individualized part of this Cosmic Creative Force, then by attunement of your Soul-Self with this supreme Creative Force you have established your right to possess all the good things of life.

Environment, education and heredity are but outer cloaks behind which shines this TRUE IDENTITY. When the higher Soul-Self directs, life becomes noble, happy and constructive; but when this Higher Soul-Force is suppressed or misdirected, life becomes drab, drear failure, lack, and discontent. The great difference in prople, and in their success or failure, can be traced to the fact that various people express MORE OR LESS of their Soul-Identity in their daily lives. For as we EXPRESS so shall we POSSESS.

Great are the rewards of spiritual understanding and attunement, so as students let us not grow weary nor discouraged in this WAY which the wise and faithful Masters of all the ages have so plainly blazed (marked) for us, because it not only leads us to Power and Peace profound, but to healing and happiness supreme.

ATTUNEMENT IS ATTAINED BY KNOWLEDGE AND EXPERIENCE

The key-note of Illumination for the Student is this one word ATTUNEMENT. And attunement is attained through our knowledge and our experience. Remember always, there is no such thing as second-hand experience, for such experience simply does not exist. We "learn to do by doing," equally we learn to live by living, and if we do not, we are not really living, we are merely existing. Neither of these things can be done for you by any other person in the world—the doing must be your own, and you must do your own living. For this is the one and only way by which knowledge can become yours—through experiencing.

So experience can become thrilling, happy and rich for you as the direct result of your personal USE and APPLICATION in your daily life here and now of the lessons and instruction which come to you in these courses and degrees.

Again, then, we repeat, attunement is composed of knowledge and experience, and this divine harmony comes to you by a process of listening IN THE SILENCE, through concentration, meditation and Soul-con-templation. For this reason, we have given you our time-tested methods and exercises which can most surely and most rapidly develop these three planes in your subconscious Mind.

Every possibility of health, of wealth and of happiness lies AHEAD OF YOU— the future is yours to direct as you choose.

So, if you have suffered and are tired of the combinations of fate and circumstances which you have unknowingly attracted in the past, know that you can change these today—these may have been part of your Cosmic Debt, but you need no longer chain yourself to any fancied Karmic retribution.

We want you to pause and carefully consider and try to justly analyze all of your past experiences, good and bad, happy and sad, for as you do this you will come more and more to realize that you are NOT bound by material shackles to surroundings, to negative people, or to damning circumstance. Change your OWN MENTAL ATTITUDE, and these untoward conditions will change almost overnight! For every slave to material evils is self bound.

We challenge you not to try to hold on to those negative conditions which only curse you with lack, limitation and unhappiness, but rather to register upon your consciousness, yes, upon your very Soul the lessons which these bitter experiences have brought to you—and then close the book of these darker experiences and KNOW that your Karmic debt is paid in that renunciation of it.

Our challenge now is to dedicate yourself to preparing yourself for The Illumination, to choose your environment and then understand that environment, to comprehend and to attune yourself to that tremendous power of the Cosmic Over-Soul which forever vibrates in creative force through-out even this earthly realm of changing material things, and through which you can possess any material blessing which you choose.

It is said that we are a part of everything and of everyone we have met—by attunement we are a part of— GOD.

Lesson No. 5
THE PATHWAY TO HEALTH, WEALTH AND HAPPINESS

Fourth Gateway of The Temple Invisible, Being the Secret Instruction Taught by The Masters in White, Whose Sublime Precepts Are Now Exemplified in These Lessons.

The Degree of Illumination

"TUNE IN" TO COSMIC RHYTHM FOR MASTER-POWER

"With every inch of stature, with every step to right or left, we see more and differently, and must needs correct previous impressions. Therefore we dare affirm positively only the truth of the center. All religions, all philosophies, sciences, doctrines, dogmas, are true at heart, but the, moment the seer attempts to too positively explain and define details he is a false prophet: for these limitations have no existence in nature, other than that they more or less truly represent the horizons of his outlook, the edges of his eye-scope.

"All emphasis about boundries makes a lie: all standing still at a preferred spot and insistence on that vista as final is stagnation and extinguishment. Buddha saw the truth, so did Moses, Socrates, Jesus, Mohammed, Mother Ann Lee, Swedenborg, Emerson, Whitman, and so do I. And you have, in yourself, a vision that no other may see for you nor exactly with you. But tomorrow comes one who sees more and farther: and next day a larger man than any, with stronger eyes and brain. There is no creed, no code, no definition, no limit, but for the moment: but all is LIFE and RHYTHM and flow of it."—J. William Lloyd.

The great but simple secret of the Master - Power—the creative power behind every 'miracle,' every healing, every trading of task for riches, every exchange of misery for happiness—is to ATTUNE ("Tune in") your body, your mind, and your soul to the eternal cosmic rhythm vibrating everywhere in the universe.

This is in reality simply a conscious recognition of your eternal oneness with the "Divine," in a word, "Godship!"

It is TO KNOW that eternal God-Mind has assumed human likeness in YOU.

And indeed among men the belief that Godship often assumes the robes of humanity is very old, again and again we find this belief reflected in the historical Scriptures.

For example, nearly twenty centuries ago when Paul performed what seemed a miracle in healing a hopeless cripple at Lystra, the people who saw this healing said: "The Gods are come down to us in the likeness of men."—Acts 14:11.

We are told that the Christ-Avatar "being in the form of God" took upon Himself (assumed) the likeness of men, and was "yet without sin.—Hebrews 4:15.

Let us remember here that in the metaphysics of REALITY "sin" is without existence. For as Omar Khayyam wrote many centuries ago:

"I sent my Soul through the invisible,

Some letter of that after-life to spell;

And by and by my Soul returned to me,

And answered I Myself am Heav'n and Hell. "

Calling upon us to realize the unthinkable power of Inner Mind-Self, hear once again the voice of Paul speaking to us from the ages:

"Let this (Psychic) Mind be in_you which was also in Christ Jesus, who, being in the form of God... was made in the likeness of men."—Phil. 2:5, etc.

Being with God before this world was created (and was you not there, also?), our Elder Brother in White, Christ was fully conscious that He had send Himself into this world, and also that he had assumed the likeness of men purposely because He had WILLED to do so. And if you yourself this moment are living a self-determined life, it is because you have WILLED to do this—you too had the power to take upon yourself "the likeness of men," because you manifest in that form today.

And yet from the day of His earthly incarnation, He was the misunderstood Christ. Was ever one more utterly misunderstood than the Nazarite Master? Misinterpretation and misunderstanding have shrouded His occult teachings for nearly two thousand years. Just as Ignorance has ever received the sublime tenents of all the Masters in White.

Only the Illumination of the student comprehends these hidden scrolls. For who of the ignorant has understood or can understand Osiris, or Krishna, or Buddha, or Christ, or... God? Who but the illumined can understand the Illumined Ones?

LAW OF TRIANGLE SOLVES MYSTERIES OF LIFE

Little can the outer world know of the true significance of the ancient symbol of the Triangle, Happy are, we who understand the mystical meaning of the Triangle, and who are able to rely upon the Law of the Triangle in solving the so-called mysteries of life, for everywhere we are confronted by enigmas that challenge us.

Let us consider the meaning of this most ancient of all symbols. For this symbol is our heritage from the ages, from the Mystery Schools of old. To us, then, the Triangle symbolizes (stands for) MAN in his complete physical and spiritual form of manifestation–body, mind and soul. You will note that the Triangle is three-pointed. The first point represents of symbolizes Soul, and this Soul-point uses BODY, the second point, to manifest intelligence and power through matter. The third point symbolizes Mind, born of the union of Body and Soul forces. On this earth (material) plane it is Mind that imparts identity, individuality, and personality to every man and woman.

It is at this third, or Mind, point that occult enigmas present themselves, and in the mind of the uninitiated they remain unsolved. For mysteries reside in the mind, and it is only by understanding the mind that we can hope to ever solve the constant occurring phenomena which confront us on every hand.

And it is terribly important that we should understand these riddles of life, because it is these very phenomena which stamp upon our consciousness the things in life which thus become actual mental, realities TO US. For among these myriad phenomena are the negative imprints of poverty, limitation, sickness, disease, failure, inferiority, and every unlovely and unhappy condition.

Actually these mental imprints are but reflected shadows at first, but by repetition and by receptivity these shadows soon become mental realities which assume actual form; in the physical life and body of their victim. And what an awful price the victim pays when these negative ghost-shadows grow into veritable demons, because 'the victim has clothed them with mental (and physical) reality! This dire result is the direct product of wrong thinking about the Self.

It is quite natural for you to pause here and ask, What, then, is the remedy for this sad mistake, how can I avoid bringing these negative conditions into my life? What is the cure for this 'wrong thinking?' The answer is simple—"Follow the (positive) vision of the Soul. Be true to your IDEALS..."

Christian D. Larson gives the answer in these words:

When you think of yourself do not think of that part of yourself that appears on the surface. That part is the smaller part, and the lesser should not be pictured in mind. Think of your larger self, the immense subconscious yourself that is limitless both in power and possibilities."

Believe in yourself, but not simply in a part of yourself..."

Give the bigger man (or woman) on the inside full right-of-way. Believe thoroughly in your greater interior self. Know that you have something within you that is greater than any obstacle, circumstance or difficulty that you can possibly meet. Then in full faith in this greater something (self) proceed with your work.

Follow the vision of the soul. Be true to your ideals no matter what may happen now. Then things will take a turn, and the very things you wanted to happen will happen."

The ideal has a positive drawing power toward the higher, the greater and the superior. Whoever gives his attention constantly to the ideal, therefore, will steadily rise in the scale.

Take things as they are today and proceed at once to make them better.

"Expect every change to lead you to something BETTER, and it will. As your faith is so shall it be."

HARMONIZING THIS "GREATER SELF" WITH TRUTH

Let us again repeat that all Healing, all Success, all Riches, all Happiness are 'miracles' (so-called) wrought through the power of this "Greater Self," the Subconscious Self, when focused upon the circumstances of the outer life and the material world. This "focusing" (centering) of the great Inner Self is the implicit obedience of the Subconscious Mind to the commands of the conscious, thinking Self

But first you must harmonize your "Greater Self," the Subconscious, with TRUTH, with things as they actually are, or you will waste your efforts upon distorted impressions, and upon mental mirages—illusions, because they are false. So you can only "tune in" to the master-power of Cosmic Rhythm through the harmony of Truth. Every false belief or impression is a discord.

Now let us consider the deeper phases of this "Greater Self" of ours, yours and mine, because the Subconscious is truly your Greater Self. As you know, you consciously receive many, many, impressions, and give your attention to ideas, ideals, desires, emotions and thoughts vibrating within ourself, and you purposely direct your expression of these ideas, desires and thoughts of yours in WORDS and in ACTION.

Please note that when you think of your Self, it is almost if not always of your conscious self, and this "I" of which you think seems to you to be centered in that part within your head where these pictures, ideas and thoughts vibrate upon the screen of your conscious attention.

Yet invisible to us in that deeper, greater Mind (or phase of Mind) which invisibly, silently, inevitably guides and influences our conscious thinking and action, as well as our fortunes good or bad, but always in direct obedience to the commands which WE have (generally unknowingly) impressed upon that deeper, hidden Mind.

Throughout the ages the Masters in White have approached these seeming mysteries of the "Greater Self" in varying ways, but each of these ways have agreed with the others. Some of the Illumined Ones have taught that it is an occult, individual personality center which as received and fixed impressions about everything contacted in the personal life, and that upon these impressions depends the destiny of that life.

Other ancient Masters in turn have taught that this mighty, hidden Self is like a city filled with countless individual dwellers, that within this City of Ideation dwells a multitude of "little people," imbued with every kind of impression and idea, and all seeking expression in the outer life or world. Each of our teachings of the past and of the present is equally correct, as seen in the different planes or levels of UNFOLDMENT.

But now our purpose is to give you a picture of the Subconscious Self or Mind so simple, so plain and clear that you can always recognize your own Greater Self, because only thus can you most easily and surely utilize, its mighty power in making your dreams come true.

In order to clothe this concept of the Subconscious with reality in your own mind, and so visualize this "other self" of yours as tangible—an actually existing self which you can know and direct, here is our simple method.

Being relaxed and alone, just mentally picture this inner, Subconscious Self as your individual and very real OTHER SELF. Now locate or place this pictured Deeper Self at some exact place within you, either in what you regard as your "thinking center," or picture it as in the base of your brain, or in the solar plexus—any-where you choose, but just be sure to select a tangible point of location.

The next step is to realize that this Subconscious Self is not only the center of your greatest Power, but that it is also your unfailing FRIEND—a friend ruled by three basic impulses of devotion to YOU; to protect you, to express you and to obey you, the "you" in each case meaning the CONSCIOUS you.

BY REASON YOU ALONE CAN DIRECT YOUR SUBCONSCIOUS

Now, delving still deeper into this mysterious Self, we want you to realize that your Subconscious Self, which is the great and powerful Divine Force in your life, exercises no reasoning power or judgment of its own. You alone, although unconsciously until you learn differently, direct and command that Subconscious Mind through the commands and the impressions which you send to it. And remember that whatever commands or impressions you have (even unknowingly) transmitted to your Subconscious Self have been and are accepted by it as truth. Its mission is to react to impressions and to obey your commands and to materialize them in your material world—not to reason or to question.

Further, let us warn you that this means that any statement, impression, or command which you repeat often to this Sleepless Giant within you, no matter if it be utterly false, negative or destructive of your own health, prosperity or happiness, will be accepted by it as absolute truth, and that it will work in exact conformity to each such repeated impression or statement. For it accepts each of these as a command.

Now you can begin to see how the Subconscious Self moulds circumstances—and often in an adverse pattern. WHY? Because throughout your life up until now your Subconscious Mind has doubtless received many, many false, negative and harmful impressions from the misguided thinking of your conscious mind, due to your struggles, defeats and misunderstanding. For your life has not escaped its share of bitter experiences, has it?

From your teachings you will now understand that your Subconscious Mind attracts and materializes every phase and every condition of your outer life, and so you will realize the limiting and the destructive effect false, negative and adverse impressions and suggestions if constantly repeated can have upon your life.

Remember, every impression, every statement and every affirmation or denial which you permit to reach your Subconscious Mind unquestioned is accepted therein as being absolute fact. So if you would change negative impressions and false or distorted images and beliefs in the Subconscious, you can do so by purposely sending to it constantly and regularly strong and unwavering affirmations of Healing, Prosperity, Success and Happiness. For that is the one pathway that leads straight to attainment.

We are teaching you to view your Subconscious Mind as being your Inner or True Self, or your deeper personality, and from this viewpoint you can easily realize that this inner Self of yours has already accumulated a multitude of impressions, of ideas and of thought-images about everything which you have contacted; about the outer world, about other prople, and about YOURSELF.

As we have pointed out before, these impressions, ideas and thought-images NEED NOT BE TRUE AT ALL but true or false, they make or mar your life accordingly. Because while these impressions, true OR false, exist in our

Subconscious Self, they are TRUE AND REAL to you.

OBJECTIVE IMPRESSIONS IMPERSONAL—SUBJECTIVE EMOTIONAL

Pursuing our studies together still deeper into this subject, which is of the utmost importance in your life, let us divide these impressions, ideas and convictions into two. main classes.

In this first broad class then we group all your impressions, memories, knowledge and general ideas concerning the outer or objective world, the world of nature and of this material world. This group includes your knowledge, your general ideas and your impressions of objective nature, its general appearance to you, the difference between colors, flavors, odors, sounds, shapes, climates, etc. All of these impressions make up your interpretation of physical life and of the material world, yet you will note that all these physical impressions might be termed impersonal—their effect is seldom emotional, because they do not GUIDE your emotions.

The second of these broad classes of impressions held in the Sub-conscious storehouse of mind comprises those ideas, images, and feelings (Negative or positive) which concern the SELF. Here we find the ideas, the reflected beliefs, and the mind-images that make up the individual's likes and dislikes, his loves and his hatreds, his reactions to what he wants and to what he wants to escape, his fears and his pet superstitions, and his real standards of right and of wrong.

We have noted that our first class, which contains our objective or, worldly ideas and impressions, does not directly effect the emotional self, either with pleasure or pain, because they are impersonal, and concern the outer world. But the second class directly concerns the Self, and contains all those things that are closely linked to one's Self, and so interprets all of the person's experiences in life in terms of pleasure or pain, in happiness or misery, and forces us to struggle to possess the things which we most greatly desire. You will note that all of these reactions are emotional.

Whether these impressions, ideas and images hidden in our Sub-conscious Selves are true or not, the EFFECT upon our lives is exactly the same as if ALL WERE TRUE. For the Subconscious cannot judge between truth and falsehood. Its one mission is to obey—to recreate impressions into reality, hence it knows neither good or bad.

For example, let us turn to the HOW of the well-known "inferiority complex." Suppose a man has repeatedly sent into his Subconscious Mind the idea, the fear, or the belief that in some way he is INFERIOR to his fellowmen. In time this becomes an impression that is entirely buried in the Sub-conscious realm. This may be absolutely false; this man may be equal to or even superior to others, yet because he has stamped this impression upon his deeper Subconscious Self, he will suffer the same penalties as if he were actually inferior.

Now this is equally true of every other false, mistaken or untrue idea or impression. For the outer circumstances of every person's life directly reflect in every effort in life the accumulated ideas, reactions and impressions in his or her Subconscious Self. Perhaps this great truth may seem difficult to you—it may be hard to see or understand just HOW ideas, impressions, desires and fears which we carry buried in the Subconscious can attract outer, material circumstances in their own exact likeness. But they DO!

In former lessons we have sought to explain, tho' briefly, some of the means and mechanisms underlying such attractions. Within the great GOD-LAW we have pointed out two of these mechanisms, one of which is the Law of Attraction, and the other the Law of Vibration. The Law of Attraction—LIKE ATTRACTS LIKE.

The Law of Vibration is rather more involved, however, let us start with the fact that ALL THINGS, both in objective matter and in personal circumstances, become manifest through Vibration. Everything that we see or know in the Universe is the reflection of the Divine Creative IDEA. Upon every plane and everywhere this Divine IDEA OR PLAN manifests (exists) to its most minute detail solely through Vibration.

Once you realize that you are but a re-creation (or a re-incarnation) of this original Divine IDEA, you will see that you in turn as a creator of your own environment and circumstances, will vibrate into outer manifestation in your outer world the exact reflection of the composite of the impressions, ideas, hopes and fears which hold sway, probably unknown to you, in the depths of your Inner world of the Subconscious.

LESSON NO. 6
THE PATHWAY TO HEALTH, WEALTH AND HAPPINESS

Fourth Gateway of The Temple Invisible, Being The Secret Instruction Taught by The Masters in White, Whose Sublime Precepts Are Now Exemplified in These Lessons.

The Degree of Illumination

HEALING, RICHES AND JOY THROUGH MIND MAGIC

An unknown author thus explains concentration as fixed attention:

"To a chemist a concentrate means an essence, a saturated solution which contains the exact amount of substance a solvent will hold of dissolve. When people use their minds as solvents of doubt, worry and fear, or of envy, hatred or jealousy, is it any wonder that they obtain solutions of inharmony, DISEASE AND POVERTY? They tell me they can't concentrate, that it is impossible to keep their minds for more than ten seconds at a time from wondering; yet there are those who lie awake all night worrying about obligations or debts. Good concentrators, certainly, but not concentrators of good. Concentration is keeping the attention FIXED UPON ONE SUBJECT, the forces turned in one direction."—Author unknown.

"The mind is a magnet. At the core of the soul lies our attracting power. We get what we expect. We see what we look for. Every thought we think images itself in the mind, and every image that is persistently held in mind is bound to materialize. This is the law. I cannot tell why it is so, any more than I can tell why from a few seeds sown in fertile soil we reap an abundant crop. I only know that the law of thought—externalization is as definite and as sure in results as are the laws of seed-time and harvest."—T Jean Porter Rudd.

From that time so long ago that it is lost in the shadows of the ages when man first began to dimly think, he has forever been searching for the secrets of youth, healing, riches and happiness. In former ages man sought these secrets in alchemy, in magic, in dark rites and incantation, and in chanting superstitious spells.

Yet we know through our unbroken heritage that even in the supposedly "lost" or forgotten civilizations of thousands of years ago, the Masters in White handed-down from age to age the secret instruction (called today the "Ancient Wisdom") that recognized and taught a marvelous power WITHIN MAN which, when subject to his mental command, could attract and materialize these good things of life for which he longed so deeply. Even some philosophers and thinkers who were outside, who were no students, had some vague conception of this mighty, pulsating power, but never understood it clearly enough to teach any exact methods or rules for its practical use.

Today, we teach you plainly and clearly that Healing, Riches and Joy can be yours through "Magic"—yes, Mind Magic.

Further, we give you a complete understanding of the pulsating power of Mind which works every "miracle," and we give you the simple rules and methods through which your mental command will bring to you a golden flow of Healing, of Prosperity an of Happiness from the Cosmic Bank of Life.

We want you first to, realize that this Inner Shrine of God within you, which call "MIND," is the most sensitive, the most marvelously organized and the most mystically high-powered "machine" in the world.

THOUGHT IS DIVINE INTELLIGENCE VIBRATING IN YOU

This marvelous mental machine of yours, your mind, constantly radiates THOUGHT, and thought is Divine Intelligence (or Universal Cosmic Mind) vibrating within and through you.

No mechanical instrument ever invented by man can weight, measure photograph, reflect, remember and transform the things of this world as can the human mind—that mind which we blindly take for granted. We want you to realize the tremendous importance of your entire being as God's most perfect machine.

Thought, the ultimate product of your mind, in its invisible impulses and vibrations goes forth to reach and meet the Infinite Cosmic Mind, and returns to you in material manifestation. May we not compare this with the wireless s short "wave currents of communication which today girdle the earth with human voices?

Probably you have in your home or in your room a radio, and yet wonderful as it is that radio receives DOES NOT CREATE SOUND. No, for that is not its work, the work of that radio is to collect the uncountable sound vibrations that are everywhere pulsating in the "ether" and by focusing these sounds to make them one more audible to your ears as words, music, etc.

Perhaps you have seen a mighty dynamo in action transforming electricity into power and transmitting that power with almost human intelligence? But the assembled zinc, and copper, and iron, and steel of that dynamo do not CREATE electricity. But combined into the form of this dynamo they collect electricity which is everywhere and focus its currents to a point where they manifest as power, light and heat.

Just so the human Mind gathers the psychic currents that pulsate everywhere in the universe, and focuses these mystic forces into the ego (self) that is YOU, and you can send them forth as streams of power to do your bidding, when you learn how to control them. These are the forces which focused in you at birth to cause you to become YOU.

Now this Inner You dwells in a physical, material house (or "dynamo",), which we know is made up of sixteen chemical elements, and—each one of these elements is vibrating at its own individual rate, a ratio set by the interplay of Divine Cosmic Mind through its psychic influence. Now when these sixteen chemical elements are all co-ordinated into ratios of pre-determined harmony we have that excellent condition which we refer to as "perfect health." This condition of harmony, of perfect health, is maintained by human mind-power governing, maintaining and continuing it by attunement (often unconscious) with the Eternal God-Law.

The Eternal God-Law (Universal Divine Mind) is made manifest in you, and in every human being, through

(a) your own conscious, voluntary, or thinking mind. This is the mind which consciously controls and directs your will, your reason, your thinking and your purposeful, self-determined actions, words, deeds and movements. When you abuse or misuse this conscious mind, as for instance, by evil or negative thinking, you hinder or obstruct the perfect coordination (harmony) of the various elements of your body, and this registers in your body as sickness or disease. For as a man thinketh so is he!"

STOREHOUSE OF MEMORY—SUBSTATION OF POWER

(b) Next we have Universal Mind manifesting through your Subconscious Mind—Your storehouse of memory—your substation of power. This vast storehouse of memory in exact and detailed recollection of all the individual experiences of your entire life, and also all unknown to you influences your life by the reflected experiences of your ancestors. These reflected ancestral experiences influence your life through your hereditary traits, from which come many of your "intuitions," "instincts", and those strange premonitions which we sometimes call "hunches."

And then there is that deepest phase of Mind, which we shall term the "unconscious" or subliminal, which we know as the Cosmic Mind, that phase of your mind which is attuned to the Cosmic Realm, and thus knows everything and is endowed with those mystic powers which underlie every "miracle."

The outer-world knows little about this Cosmic Mind, for it has only been revealed to the students through telepathy, clairvoyance and advanced states of hyposis is know as deep trance. Later in these lessons we shall reveal to you startling truths about this Cosmic Mind, perhaps unused but present in every normal man and woman. However, just now it is sufficient to point out that the Cosmic Mind is the coordinator of the physical, the mental and the soul "Bodies," or phases of the, Self.

In passing, let us also say that the GREAT WORK of the entire system is to teach our students HOW to attune (harmonize or "tune in") the conscious, thinking mind and the subconscious, memory-materializing mind to the Cosmic Mind and to subject them to it's perfect control.

This perfect control of your conscious mind by that higher, or Soul—Mind, which we have termed the Cosmic Mind, enable you to live in the most complete security, happiness and safety by protecting your conscious mind and through it your physical body from the dangers and the ravages of FEAR, DISEASE AND NEGATIVE EMOTIONS.

For your conscious mind, 'which permeates your brain and your nerves, is your physical (bodily) "response mechanism" to your environment or surroundings, and to the things you meet in that environment.

As you already know, when fear, danger or negative vibrations impinge upon (strike) your brain and nerves, then your conscious mind, if uncontrolled, sends messages throughout your entire organism—messages which cause intense and injurious reactions in your body.

For instance, suppose your very life is threatened by a madman with a gun in his hand. Instantly your conscious mind senses your peril and flashes its messages of alarm through your entire body over its brain-and-nerve telegraph system. Every cell in your body responds at once, and the normal workings of every organ in your body is completely upset, and you are "unnerved."

In the face of such danger the whole chemistry of your body is changed. In that very minute powerful poisons are sent into your blood by the glands, these are stimulants to help your body to deal with this outside enemy our digestion stops, your heart and brain and nerves expend energy at a terrific rate.

No wonder the body is exhausted and poisoned after such an experience, for there is' a terrible emotional response_ to_r.,ank stark FEAR OF DEATH, FEAR is a destructive process, which works through physical poison and disorganization, and so it is our business to protect the body from the many and various dangers which so often threaten its health and welfare.

So it becomes clear that in this business of protecting the physical body and insuring its health and well-being, the control of the conscious mind is of the utmost importance, and also through it the control of the subconscious mind is equally important, so that it may not materialize harmful conditions. And here we can trust the complete control of the bodily processes, as well as the conscious and subconscious minds to COSMIC MIND, for this is the one unfailing guardian of body, mind and soul.

COSMIC MIND ENDOWED WITH MIRACULOUS POWERS

You have learned from our previous instruction that your Subconscious Mind is the storehouse of memory, and that this Subconscious memory can be developed by earnestly following our secret methods to an astonishing degree. Further, through your training, everything filed in this deeper storehouse can be recalled to your consciousness at will, given due time and effort, because no mental picture or impression is ever really lost.

But now we want you to consider with us that most stupendous phase of Mind known to man—the Cosmic Mind, known to some simply as the Great Unconscious (Self). Going backward into the dim ages of the past our records inform us that from time immemorial our Masters in White have taught of the mysteries of the Cosmic Mind under various names and symbols in the Ancient Wisdom.

As far as we are permitted to commit to writing or to the printed word, we shall now lead you in some of these mysteries. Remember, in this we are transmitting to you here an interpretation of these ancient wisdom teachings, hence be not too surprised or startled at revelations of the seemingly impossible.

First, then, the Masters taught that the Cosmic Mind is endowed with miraculous powers, and also they taught how WE may use these miracle-working powers and so prove the truth of their teachings for our-selves. Soon you will realize that all of your previous lessons have been leading you step by step toward this supreme height of Soul-Mind—development:

The ancient Masters taught that not only the powers but the field of the Cosmic Mind is infinite. The Cosmic Mind draws whatever it desires or needs not only from the individual mental "storehouse," but also draws to itself whatever is necessary from any other personal or individual consciousness silently and in secret.

Again, the Masters in White teach that your Cosmic Mind has the strange power of overcoming time and space, and is able to transcend gravity and like material laws, and to transform its own physical (bodily) home. These ancient Masters tell us that this Cosmic Mind can (and does) at times project itself in astral (substance) spiritual form into an independent and often visible materialism.

The deeper teaching still further instructs us that in this strange occult guise the Cosmic Self may enter the portals of the astral or spiritual realm (or world), there to view either the buried past or the unborn future, and to commune with other entities; during these astral journeys, they tell us, the human or physical body is left in a state of lethargy or "deep trance" (suspended animation) almost simulating (like) death.

In due time, in accordance with the command of a set time this Astral-Cosmic-Self returns in obedience to the conscious WILL, and the body returns from deep trance (simulated death) to normal life.

But we must understand that this borderland, called the astral realm, CANNOT be entered by a non student, and it is a rugged and difficult Pathway known as Self-MASTERY which leads to it's gates. A guardian who never sleep or relaxes keeps endless watch at the entrance. Those who enter, must qualify. First your volitional or conscious mind must be able to command the opening and the closing of the portals (doors) of the Subconscious. Entrance to the first Gateway of the Temple Invisible can be gained ONLY through perfect Concentration, focused Meditation and clear Introspection—and each of these IN THE SILENCE.

This mental work, which faithfully performed will endow you with a magnetic personality, with miracle-working healing powers, with abundance and prosperity, and true happiness is threefold—meditation, introspection) and concentration. Because you can now realize the tremendous importance of their goal, you can now see why we have so strongly stressed these three mental planes, and have in former lessons given you methods and exercises in each.

At, this point we would strongly advise that you go back and review each of these exercises, and resume there if you have neglected to continue them, as you should have done.

Let us again make clear to you the meaning and the supreme value to you of each of these mental state or planes of development.

First, then, let us briefly consider meditation, and let us again repeat that each of these mental state is to be sought only when you are alone and can enter The Silence. Meditation is induced by relaxing in the silence and by freeing your mind of doubt, confusion, worry and conflicting thoughts in other words, JUST LET GO. Stop struggling. Be still. Open your mind to the flow of directing guidance which is only waiting to enter your mind from your Intuitional or Subconscious Self.

If you have followed our methods a.nd exercises, you will find that your body AND mind are completely relaxed, that you have reached a state midway between, sleep and wakefulness—almost a dream state. Your one desire now is to receive guidance upon your life's course in accordance with the Divine Light, which you pray may illuminate your Pathway. Express this prayer not in words, but in the SILENT DESIRE OF YOUR SOUL.

And your prayer will be answered by inspirational guidance which will later amaze you.

Introspection is a companion state to meditation, the difference being that introspection is devoted to quiet self-analysis—and in this self-examination we can see our own imperfections and our mistakes, and in facing these and becoming quite fully aware of them, and perceiving that they are but ugly, negative shadows, we are freed from them. And so step by step we can approach that perfect Illumination.

We walk in the Pathway of Illumination, hand in hand spiritually with our ancient Masters. For now the Divine Wisdom of our Cosmic Mind guides our destiny.

Perhaps you have wondered why throughout all of these lessons we have placed so much emphasis upon concentration. It is because concentration is the Key which unlocks the gate of the Inner Shrine—and that is the Shrine where full understanding rewards the faithful. Indeed it is concentration which unlocks both the material and the spiritual worlds. When you have acquired the secret of concentration, and its secret is really simple, then the veil is lifted and you behold the Grandeur of the Soul Illumined.

In fact, this ability to concentrate is the yard-stick of humanity, as you can readily see. Those who have developed concentration to an advanced degree are the recognized geniuses of the world; those who have developed just a moderate ability to concentrate made up the great class of medium or every-day intelligence; those who entirely lack this ability are the morons, the brutish and unawakened who comprise the overwhelming majority of earth's teeming millions.

Now you can understand why we stress concentration as being so absolutely necessary to your progress, for it is the fountain of Illumination.

REMEMBER—CONCENTRATION IS FOCUSED ATTENTION

Only through concentration—focused attention—can you be raised above the hum-drum surroundings of

gross materialism to those higher realms where you are attuned to the Divine. And it is only in those astral realms that the Infinite speaks to the finite, to man.

Now to come to the practical application of these-developed mental powers, which ere now should have become yours in some marked degree through our instruction. Every conscious human enterprise, every endeavor of yours to fulfill your cherished desires HAS ITS BEGINNING IN YOUR THOUGHT-WORLD. Whatever your sincerest desires may be, whether for material possessions, a comfortable home, a modern car, a fat bank account, or for business prosperity, promotion, or influential friends—each is first a mental picture, a desire-picture.

Concentration creates your desire-picture into Reality. But remember, there is a vast difference between A MERE DESIRE and the creating of that desire into material form. That difference can only be bridged by THE POWER OF ACTION 'which you put into your desire-thinking.

The result, if there is to be any, BEGINS WITH YOU. A wish in itself has no mysterious power, the wish may be your goal, your objective, your desire—but if it remains only a wish, it will never be realized.

But let us suppose that you have created a mental picture in your mind of that which you most greatly desire, and that this picture is complete and suits you perfectly. Then your next problem is to materialize your picture, isn't it? There is no magic word or secret formula which will transmute your picture into REALITY without action on your part.

Your mental picture must also be linked with the present. There must be something about your mental picture which you can start doing now.

By analogy, let's compare your DESIRE-VISION to a ladder, no one rung of your ladder will enable you to climb very high, but your ladder must have many rungs combined to make your upward progress possible. Just so, make your mental picture as high as you wish, as great as you wish, but don't leave out that FIRST RUNG— your own present capabilities, and capacity, and powers.

LESSON No. 7
THE PATHWAY TO HEALTH, WEALTH AND HAPPINESS

Fourth Gateway of The Temple Invisible, Being The Secret Instruction Taught by The Masters in White, Whose Sublime Precepts Are Now Exemplified in There Lessons.

The Degree of Illumination

POWER OF ACTION MATERIALIZES MIND-PICTURES

"Too long have we looked upon practicing of concentration as a lost art or else shrouded in mystery and occultism. Concentration, like every other great thing, is not far away, but here; it is not hard but easy. A great deal depends upon...the start you get. Have FAITH in your purpose. Have faith in YOURSELF to consummate your purpose. Have -faith in the great God-Power residing within and without. The Intelligence which rules the universe works in all things for your good. For faith, belief in the attainment of a desired end, is as essential to success scientifically sought as sought in any other way because, as you have seen, it has set in motion ACTUAL FORCES"—David B. Bush.

And here we wish to continue and to expand the concepts and the suggestive thinking with which we closed our last lesson (Number 6) in this series of instructions in the Degree of Illumination.

You will remember that in that last lesson we left you with the Truth, as we stated it, that while concentration creates your mind-picture into reality the result, if there is to be any, must begin with you, and that this result is materialized by the power of action which you put into making your dream come true. We pointed out to you the vast difference between a mere desire and the creation of that desire into a reality, a material form in your actual possession.

But now, having a mental picture in your own mind of that thing, that possession, or that attainment you most greatly desire, be very sure right now that this picture is complete and suits you perfectly. Because now your next step is to begin to materialize that picture, to really possess your desire, to reach your goal, to attain your objective.

Of course you have long ago realized that in all the world there is no magic word or secret formula that can transform your mind-picture into reality without action on your part. So, your desire-picture must be linked to the present, and that means that you must find something which you can start DOING RIGHT NOW to help make your dream come true.

Therefore; right now, in this eternal present, and here in this lesson we are going to help you to find those practical, down-to-earth ways you can focus both ACTION and DESIRE upon—ways that will lead to success and the fulfillment of your

"Heart's Desire."

First, then, in beginning, let us quote the last few lines of your last lesson, (Number 6):

"By analogy, let's compare your DESIRE-VISION to a ladder, no one rung of your ladder will enable you to climb very high, but your ladder must have many rungs combined to make your upward progress possible. Just so, make your mental picture as high as you wish, but don't leave out that FIRST RUNG—your own present capabilities, capacity and powers."

CONSIDERING YOUR BUILDING MATERIALS

For your own present capabilities, and capacity, and powers are the basic materials from which you will build, whether your proposed building be that of a house, renewed health, the healing of others, the gathering of abundance financially, or the creation of a joyously HAPPY LIFE.

The first step, then, in any building is to compute the cost and to measure the cashable assets with which you will meet that cost, is it not?

"For which of you," asked the Master in White, "intending to build a tower (house), sitteth not down first and counteth the cost whether he have sufficient to finish it? Lest haply, after he hath laid the foundation, and is not able to finish it, all that behold it begin to mock him, Saying, This man began to build, and was not able to finish."—Luke 14: 28-29

As we have pointed out to you, then, no building of your dream into reality is possible until you link your mind-picture with the present with something which you can AND DO start doing NOW. Very well, let us suppose that your Great Desire is a home of your own, a house well located and as spacious and modern as will suit your needs.

Let us say that in your own mind you have created a mental picture of this desired home which seems quite complete and which suits you, and which will meet your needs quite acceptable. Your next problem then is to materialize your house, for to make your dream come true it must be translated into a visible structure of stone and brick and mortar and wood, and every other material which enters into the construction of a modern house. And to properly construct this house from its many materials will require the effort of many and varied skilled workmen.

As we have warned you, there is no kind of mental magic nor secret formula by means of which you can transmute this dream-house of yours into an actual building WITHOUT THE POWER OF ACTION ON YOUR PART.

So your first step then is to follow the example indicated in Christ's allegorical question, that is, sit down first and count the cost. This however be assured does not imply merely a counting of dollars and cents, or just now even of your present cash reserves. Instead, let us understand that it is you have planned, two courses of action are open to you. In taking the first course you must simplify your mental picture, which requires that you plan a cheaper, more modest home. Scale downs your pictured house and make it one which you can pay for more easily, and then later you can build another house from a more elaborate, a more expensive plan.

The second or alternative course is to draw a substitute picture in your mind for the present—this substitute picture to vision yourself achieving a rapid and worthwhile advancement in your position, your work or your profession, an advancement which will provide the greater income which you need to materialize your desired home.

In creating this substitute picture in your mind, your very first step is to determine for yourself exactly WHAT is needed, what you must do, to insure your advancement and your greater income. Does this first step call for more limes or for more earnest effort in your position, your work, or your career? Then put in more time, redouble your efforts, apply action to create this substitute picture into a FINANCIAL REALITY.

looking into your affairs more closely, you will find that in addition to putting in more time or more earnest effort in your position, your profession, or your business, you can greatly increase your income by developing new values in your position or profession, or by expanding your business, or some practical way of reducing costs or expenses.

You can readily see that if you succeed in thus increasing your income you are materializing your substitute picture, and that by succeeding in your business or professional affairs, as evidenced by more abundant finances, you are bringing into existence (creating) the first and most necessary power (money in your possession) to REALIZE YOUR FIRST AND GREATER PICTURE—the HOUSE you most desire.

So we learn that concentration, in order to succeed in bringing us the power to acquire the things we most greatly desire, must be linked by some element to the present. We have used the example of a house or home as your great desire simply as an illustration, for the laws and principles which we have pointed out in this example rule all realization, all possession, all materializing of desires. As we have told you again and again every creation by men and women in this world is first a mental creation, and begins in what we call imagination, a mental picture imaged ("Imagined") inside the human mind. Whether this creation be that of a beautiful home, healing of bodily sickness, abundant finances or a fine social position, or romance, or love, or hap-piness—each is first mirrored as a picture upon the screen of "imagination" within the mind before it is reflected as a reality in the material world.

But whatever the picture you are holding upon the screen of imagery in your mind AS YOUR GREAT DESIRE, you must seize upon some element in that mind-picture and start WORK upon that element right NOW, no matter an "intuition,," or a "flash," And no matter how impatient you may have been, when this answer comes to point out THE WAY to you, it will come at the opportune times, at just the "psychological moment" when all things will work together to help you to begin realizing your dream. Looking-back, afterward, you will see how true this is.

For you see, by thus releasing your stimulating mind-Picture into the subjective realm of your mind—your answer—your guidance—really comes to you (to your conscious thoughts) from the Infinite Intelligence WITHIN—from the inner shrine of Spirit.

In reality you learn from WITHIN how you can create or possess in the material world the good things in life which you picture in your mind. Again we repeat, creating mentally involves no mystical process or magical mummery whereby your mental desire-picture without any directed activity or physical effort on your part, will ever be materialized.

Yes, the Masters do teach that all creative work in the mental world means that A HIGHER POWER is attracted or drawn to the person accomplishing creative works that are worth while, and this is true—but still the God-Law requires that the individual himself must exert the ACTION back of the creating. "The 'Higher

Power" takes the form of revealed personal energy, or inspired action, of an intuitive wisdom which guides in this "Great Work" of transforming dreams into reality. You must look within.

It is your Soul-impulses (vibrations) which enable you to create objective realities. While there are many roads that lead to the heights, to the mountain top, one road is destined for you and you can never reach the heights by traveling a little ways on each of many roads. Instead you must concentrate on the ONE WAY to reach your goal.

AFFIRMATION ("SUGGESTIONS") AWAKENS CREATIVE POWER

Validivar says, "No matter what else, we can be daily grateful we have been put in touch with knowledge, for its SOURCE is inexhaustible."

And of course it is MIND which is that inexhaustible source of all knowledge, and knowledge is Power. So, for the source of the power that will enable you to create your dream, your great desire, into reality, again we say, LOOK WITHIN.

According to the sublime teachings of the Masters in White as interpreted for you in your lessons, the SOUL is fixed—enduring, one in all things, eternal. Your physical body has form, but is limited in strength, in growth and in its life-span. But your MIND is almost limitless in scope and in power of achievement, if you give it freedom. But if that mind is enslaved by forms, by superstitions and by lack of development, it is limited, narrow and ineffective.

It is through your mind that you contact God, and it is in your mind the third point in our sacred triangle that occult miracles have their source.

Now there are many, many avenues or roads to your mind, ranging from the five objective senses to the thousands of nerve terminals and the many plexuses. One of the shortest and surest of these avenues to your first of all necessary for you to carefully analyze your mind-picture of this house you desire, in order that you may find what materials, or element: or parts of your house already exist as realities—and how you are going to obtain them.

First, the location, the ground, the plot, upon which this house of yours is to be erected—that already exists, but where? This location you must choose. A multitude of materials of different kinds already exist in this country from which your house may be constructed. So, which materials will you choose?

One of the first steps in helping to materialize your dream house is to select the architectural PLAN which suits you perfectly—and there are many, many plans, all of them good, from which you can choose. Choose your plan carefully, and once having made your choice, let that choice be permanent—only under very exceptional circumstances should you ever change this plan which you have chosen so carefully.

YOUR OWN DIRECTED ACTION LINKS DREAM TO PRESENT

As. you look again and again upon your mental picture of this house which you desire just now more than anything else and as you examine the plan and the blueprints of the same, you become "More pleased with its design every day, and every day you find that your desire of ownership deepens. Of course, you realize as you study its design that all the materials for the construction of your dream house already exist—stone, brick, lumber, mortar, plumbing and electrical fixtures, all are here in the world and perhaps within easy reach of the location which you have mentally chosen.

And very likely you know just where all of these necessary building materials can be obtained. Just what is it, then, that is lacking to bring your pictured house into actual existence? Only the power of certain, effective, DIRECTED ACTION on your part to build your dream house into material form.

Now, since you probably do not own any of the necessary materials for the building of your pictured house and because you cannot do all the labor of building this house yourself, the power of your own skill, or service, or action must be transformed into MONEY. For thus. your power of action is exerted through the power of money to buy the needed plot of ground, and all the materials for your house, and to pay the workmen for their skills and services in its construction.

So your first link of your dream to) the present (of which we spoke previously) in creating your pictured house into material form is the acquiring of money.

The next question to ask yourself is—just HOW shall I obtain this necessary reserve cash (money) to build the house I have planned? Is immediate future, or eventually, and if eventually, when?

In answering these questions, analyze your capabilities, your earning power and your financial resources fairly and quite impartially. If, after you have taken, a true Inventory of your source of financial supply, you find that it will require too long for you to acquire sufficient funds to build the house how small that element may be, just so it is an actual element of your picture, you must bring it into reality.

Concentrate upon some one thing in your mental picture which already exists in your material world and which you know it is possible for you to acquire. No matter how small a part of your mental picture this one thing may seem to be, ACQUIRE THAT THING and your subconscious mind will then project that small success into the FUTURE and will multiply and enlarge that small success into greater and ever greater success, if you will but persevere with entire faith (belief) that your dream IS COMING TRUE.

Creating mind-pictures into reality by concentrating and by work, effort and directed activity is a mystical process, and is called THE GREAT WORK by the Masters, but that does not mean that you cannot understand it, because you can. All that is necessary is that you understand and follow the simple instructions we are giving you in our lessons.

The one great mistake which we want to warn you against above all others is the idea that some Unseen Power will wave some kind of magician's wand because you merely WISH it, and make your dreams come true with no more work on your part than just picturing what you think you want in your mind.

LET INFINITE INTELLIGENCE WITHIN GUIDE YOU

But here is a difficulty which may happen in your case, as it has in many others. This particular difficulty springs from a somewhat natural impatience—we want to see our dreams come true NOW, and especially we are impatient to begin work on the first element which links our great desire to the present. Just here it may happen that your mental picture is complete, down to the last detail, but for the life of you it seems that you cannot find the primary factor which should be your point of beginning.

In other words you cannot discern just what is the very first thing you should DO to begin your "Great Work" of materializing your desire. You realize that you are the moving factor in this work of realization, and you know that the result depends upon you and your own directed activity, and that you must BEGIN—but where?

The answer is simple, and has been taught to you in our previous lessons—JUST RELEASE YOUR MENTAL PICTURE INTO YOUR SUBCONSCIOUS MIND. Actually there is nothing involved or mysterious about this, except as some "teachers" have made it seem mystical. You release your mental desire-picture into the subconscious mind by dismissing the whole picture from your conscious thinking with the silent command that the Sub-conscious in its own good time inspire your conscious mind with the answer to your problem. Relax in THE Silence, and calmly, quietly, and in perfect faith, commit your picture into the keeping of the Subconscious Self, and stop struggling with this question yourself.

The direct answer as to exactly where and when and How to begin work upon your project will come to you consciously in a flash, it may come to you tomorrow, or next week, or even next month, but you can be very sure that it WILL COME.

This answer will come to you in what people usually call a "hunch," Subjective Mind (Subconscious Self) is by way of affirmations, or suggestion to your Inner Self, often called Auto-Suggestion. In earlier lessons we have given you some primary instructions and forms of affirmations to use in this work, and we should like you to review those lessons this week in connection with this lesson.

Now that you have reached an advanced stage in your work, we may tell you that it is not always necessary to establish a binding routine for your self-suggestive work. Yet, your results will be greater if you denote a certain time every day to this work. Of course, you may continue your affirmations as you walk along the street, or when riding, especially when you are alone.

In framing your autosuggestions (affirmations) be sure that you know exactly what you wish to become, and have a clear-cut mental picture of what you want to be made manifest in your life.

Then short, direct statements (affirmations) of what you most greatly desire are to be made in the present tense direct, unqualified assertions that these things ALREADY EXIST FOR YOU AND ARE YOURS TODAY.

For example: "I am well and healthy" "Money wants me," "I can meet every test," "I will move into my NEW HOUSE soon," or "I have plenty of money!"

And right here we are going to reveal to you the real inside secret of the marvelous power of affirmation—IN THE BEGINNING YOU DO NOT, YOU NEED NOT BELIEVE THE STATEMENTS YOU ARE MAKING! In your own heart you may know that you don't even have the necessities of life, that you feel half-sick and weak, that money has always run away from you, and that your "new house" is but a dream.

What of it? Just keep on endlessly repeating your statements, being detached from your surroundings and fixing your attention upon your affirmations, and your Subconscious Mind will accept, and believe, and REFLECT YOUR DREAMS INTO REALITY.

LESSON NO. 8
SERIES 4
THE PATHWAY TO HEALTH, WEALTH AND HAPPINESS

Fourth Gateway of The Temple Invisible, Being The Secret Instruction Taught by The Masters in White, Whose Sublime Precepts Are Now Exemplified in These Lessons.

The Degree of Illumination

DIRECT SUGGESTION AND FOCUSED THOUGHT WORK "MIRACLES!"

"We cannot only gain information and get proper directions in this way (visualization), but we can develop working and thinking powers. We can absolutely know, DO and HAVE nearly anything we desire if we will only see what we want at all times, and hold to the thought continuously. Not that we need to have the one thought in our minds every minute of the time, night and day, but whenever we have leisure from our regular duties we should let our mind rest upon the same ideal, never vacillating, wanting and working for one thing today and running after another tomorrow. GO STRAIGHT AHEAD.

"Apparent failures should never discourage us. The fault is never in the principle (of The God-Law), for this is absolutely correct. It should be remembered that in the pursuance of the practice of suggestion we have the hereditary tendencies and race-beliefs of all mankind to contend with..."But if we do not realize our expectations at ALL times, we should remember that the world was not evolved in a single day. When single effort does not give us what we want, we repeat them with renewed energies and zeal. We never judge the future by failures that are passed. We are living in the eternal NOW. He who carefully studies the principles of suggestion, and live and earnestly applies them must and will succeed. We acknowledge no such thing as failure. All we ask is a chance, an opportunity to demonstrate our work, and we can and we will succeed.

"All things are ready if our minds be so."—Dr. George Pitzer.

ONLY THAT IS YOURS WHICH IS A REALITY IN YOUR MIND

Just what is this "principle" (this God-Law) of which Dr. Pitzer writes in our quotation, and what has this principle to do with reality—and just what is it that gives reality to our existence, and to these good things of life which we so sincerely crave?

If we can imagine a time before the beginning—before the worlds of material form were created then in that time we must agree that if only realities existed, and their only existence was as they were conceived and pictured in Eternal Divine Mind.

Only by being thus conceived and realized first in Ultimate Mind could this world of form and substance, as we know it, with all its stupendous and wonderful harmony, have been created into material existence.

From this we deduce. THE DIVINE EQUATION the only equation that can explain life, form existence and reality.

So Eternal Divine Mind, being the source of everything, gave without measure and of Itself, created every-thing, and thus becomes the One Great Fundamental PRINCIPLE, ruling the entire creation in harmony with those divine laws, which taken together form the GOD-LAW, our heritage from the Masters in White.

Divine Creative Mind is the great Prime Mover of the universe, and from this Over-Soul life and consciousness flow into all living things, to whom they owe their growth and their existence. For each was first a reality conceived and created in the all—pervading Mind of the Infinite.

So it follows that you are an individual part of this creation of reality (or into reality), your body of course is a part of the material world of form, shape and substance, but your mind and soul are personalized expressions of Divine Creative Mind, one with and unseparated from the Supreme Intellect. Thus in mind and soul you partake of your heritage of the same attributes and the same powers as the Supreme, limited only by your physical plane.

Your body, then, was a conception first, before it became a physical form in reality. That body of yours was first conceived and realized in Divine Mind, the same Mind which vibrates in your every thought. When this Mind of the Divine All-Intelligence lives and functions in your body as it was intended to do, you live in harmony, in perfect health, in prosperity and in happiness. And it is the mission of our lessons to teach you how to attain this goodly life, which is your rightful heritage.

But everywhere around us men and women are living in confusion rather than harmony, in sickness instead of health, in poverty instead of prosperity and in misery instead of happiness—and well you may ask, WHY.

Because men and women are reversing the Divine Equation—far from following the Divine Plan, they are putting the physical, the mundane, the material things first, and the REALITY of MIND second in their mistaken scheme of life. These millions of the mistaken either do not know or they have overlooked the eternal fact that man cannot become conscious of physical actualities, such as health, wealth, love and happiness much less possess them, until each of them has become a REALITY IN HIS OWN MIND. We must realize that in fact and in reality nothing can affect or influence our harmony, or attract to us love, healing, peace and happiness, until that thing becomes a REALITY in our thinking. This simply means that no GOOD (or EVIL) thing exists FOR YOU until it exists in your own consciousness, whether you are aware of it or not.

MAN HAS ACQUIRED ILLUSIONS FROM THE MATERIAL

From the material world man has acquired grievous and terribly costly illusions. Everywhere in the world today this tremendous force of illusion is at work, creating war, famine, disease, destruction and sorrow. Whatever readjustments in erroneous thinking and in human conduct the optimist may see it these disasters eventually, the cost is certainly terrible.

Thus we see that the accepted values of the world are based upon illusion—and this illusion man has acquired from the material world, of which he is a part only physically. According to this illusion we are led to conceive of the material world and its supposed actualities as being the most important things in this present life of ours. This is the great illusion which now deludes and directs the thinking of most of the human race.

So we would warn each student that in the material world and all its creations are only EFFECTS, and we must not mistake them for the CAUSE, or else illusion will assume the cloak of reality for us also. Knowing as we do that everything in this material world is but a result produced by Eternal Mind, operating through the Immutable God-Law, let us look to this same POWER for the good things of life, rather than to its illusive shadow in the darker pools of the material world.

The higher vibrations within you—which you master and become aware of through our WAY—these are the expression and the manifestation of the life and mind of GOD—the One Source of all things for which you long and strive. The truly sinful man is he who sins most against himself by trying to suppress and to deny this Divine Mind (Soul) within in his greedy grasping for only the material things of life. Beware that you do not commit this terrible sin against your own Divine Self.

For it is our own thinking which is the cause of all our woes, and most of our misfortune. For if our thinking is negative, selfish, grasping or filled with fear, we create into reality those misfortunes which sooner or later take actual form in our lives. Most of the "evils" which rise to plague and torment us are self-created.

And yet the happy truth remains that also in our THINKING when that thinking is joyous, positive and radiant with FAITH the tremendous power vibrates which can and will completely reverse our every unhappy condition of today. Simply stated, when we attune our thinking to harmonize with the Divine Pattern our reward is a life filled with peace, plenty and success.

Mankind as a race has substituted the human equation for the DIVINE. He has reversed the Divine Pattern, and seeks to put the worship of SELF first. So man blindly attracts to himself the demons of war, of hatred, of fear and of doubt, and it is these demons who threaten and again and again destroy everything he cherishes and values most. For destruction is their business.

Let us then return in penitence and in humility to the Divine Equation, if we have strayed from it, and let us understand in the Supreme Mind alone are realities conceived and created as unchanging Causes, and that we are part of that Supreme Mind, and that in our outer, material world the counterpart of these causes are the happy effects, the actualities of health, abundance and the joyous life that is awaiting us in the kingdom of right thinking. Behind the mirror of your own mind, behold! the "Kingdom of Heaven'" is very near to you.

Your thinking then, is a very real power either for good or for evil. Your every normal physical act or deed first existed as a thought in your mind, and everything you have builded or accomplished was the result of your thinking. Not only that, not only does your thinking shape your own destiny, but through your words and by the subtle radiation of your thoughts you are affecting, you are influencing, or you are shaping the lives of others. "For no man liveth to himself."

UNITED IN 'ILLUMINATION'—COSMIC "LIGHT"

What then is the GREAT WORK? What is the eternal mission?

It is not Religion, nor is it Hermeticism, nor Metaphysics, nor the Ancient Wisdom, nor Mysticism—FOR IT IS ALL OF THESE! In this Great Work, we are not limited to some one branch of knowledge, but each true student is a true philosopher in the sense that he or she is seeking wisdom in the unity of ALL knowledge. Our great mission is to discover the abiding inter-relationship between the God-Soul of the universe and our eternal Soul-Selves.

Gross and material thoughts have distorted the reflection of that which men call "the world of today," Men stand today before the wavy, warped and narrow mirrors of their brute-like minds in hatred amid the shadows of approaching war, in FEAR, in despair, in poverty, in sickness and in suffering. Our mission is to turn the pained eyes of those who are called to us from these false reflections of Illusion—beyond appearance to the joy, the healing and the beauty of Cosmic-God-Reality.

Amazing as it may seem to us at first thought, yet it is actually true that this objective world which you see everywhere around you is only a reflection. Have you ever laughed at the antics of a puppy when he seems himself for the first time in a looking glass? Perhaps the glass was upon the floor, leaning against a wall. How surprised the puppy seems when, approaching closer and closer to that "other" puppy in the mirror, his nose finally bumps into the glass! Curiously he looks around behind the mirror to find nothing—there is no other small dog there.

We smile at the surprise of the puppy before the mirror, and yet perhaps we often make a similar mistake, but we do not smile then for it is no laughing matter to us. True, when you stand or sit before a mirror in your room and see the image of yourself mirrored against the background of that familiar room, you know that your image is only a reflection.

But have you ever really realized that your MIND is the most marvelous mirror in the world? This mirror of the mind we call "consciousness". It is in this mirror that Divine MIND seeks to reflect to us the beauty, the glory and the happiness that can be ours, if we will just mentally LIVE in worlds above—dwelling in thought upon that higher astral plane for according to the Divine Plan, "As above, so below."

But this reflection, though it be a reflection of the divinely PERFECT MIND, depends like all reflections upon the condition, the degree of perfection, of the reflector, the glass, the medium, in this case, the mind and its degree of consciousness. So, if the mirror is wavy, curved, or imperfect, how can we hope to see a perfect reflection? Now if our friend, the puppy stands in front of an imperfect mirror which distorts every image, he is looking at a very ogle, misshapen little monster—but with due investigation he will learn in time that there is no monster there...only himself. The reflection is simply distorted—it is "out of focus."

Then let us accept the deeper truth, that what we see as our outer, physical bodies, as well as everything objective in the material world, may not, DO NOT exist in REALITY as we see them, for we are perceiving reflections in the mirrors of our minds—and may mirrors not sometimes be clouded, or reflect distorted images?

From the earliest times the Masters have taught in the Ancient Wisdom, and modern science has now discovered, that all the matter which composes everything objective in this world, consists of one thing and one thing only, and that one "substance" is ENERGY forever vibrating. We have told you something about vibration in your former lessons, but here is your deeper instruction about this tremendous energy-"substance,"

As we have told you previously, there are numberless rates of vibration, all different. As these different rates of vibration reflect through our physical senses their different images upon the mirror of our minds, we recognize one and say, "This is a rose," or "That is a man," or "There is a rainbow in the sky," but in reality every image that is reflected to us is Spirit Energy made manifest to us through Divine God-Law.

So we build up from reflections in our minds pictures of the outer (objective) world, as it exists for us.

THERE CAN BE NO EVIL IN ABSOLUTE REALITY

We become so absorbed in these reflections that we forget that they are only reflections and that their validity depends upon the mirror which reflects, the MIND. In these reflections we often rivit our attention too intently upon the seeming evil in the objective world about us, and thus we may forget that in Truth, which is absolute reality, there can be no evil, because Truth must be perfect, and Truth alone is realm.

Probably you have at some time seen the unreal and grotesque figures reflected by the different curved mirrors in some "Fun House", in the "Hall of Mirrors," ? You know that these images are not real, so you can enjoy laughing at them. Just so, Life is a Hall of Mirrors through which we pass. The God-Law is composed of the many separate laws which are set to control this vast realm of Spirit-Energy that we call the universe,

and these laws act to form patterns which reflect the perfect beauty of the World Above.

But because they are LAWS, they are inexorable, unchanging.

Man in his ignorance does not heed these laws, or else in his blindness knows nothing about them, or thinks that he is above law. So by wrong (negative or evil) thinking, and by wrong acts, man himself sets in motion reactions in the world of law which create those very things which he calls "evil." And the more man looks upon the "evil" in his mind-reflections (pictures), the more he becomes obsessed with the false idea that this "evil" is reality the more warped, distorted and unnatural his mind-mirror becomes.

So, gazing constantly into these so-imperfect mental mirrors mankind has imputed REALITY to the distorted images which reflect seemingly ghastly images—images that reflect sick, diseased and crippled bodies and minds, the horrors of war and of hatred, poverty and even famine, failure and despair, to name just a few. And shall WE then believe that these mind-mirrors picture EVIL AS TRUTH OR REALITY and sit down to concentrate upon these illusions, and bewail the fate we have ourselves invoked, and not realize that these reflections are distorted?

No—clear the mirror of your mind, and the reflection of the PERFECT will shine forth with a Light that will Illumine your Way. For in Truth—in Reality—there is only perfection. Let it be your goal to vision that perfection in your own BODY, MIND AND SOUL. Begin with your body—no matter what image the mirror of your objective (outer) mind may show now, clear the mental glass and look deeper, seek truth in your Subconscious mirror.

The Image of you in the Mind of God is of a Perfect You. For only the perfect dwells in Truth. Learn to know this for yourself, and dwell (meditate) upon this grand thought in The Silence. For it is the eternal Truth. No matter what may be the image that the outer world may see of your body—no matter what may be the reflection of your body in your own mind-mirror—remember that the God-Idea of your perfect body can never be other or less than perfect.

To be specific, then, the God-Idea or Divine Image of your heart, your lungs, your stomach, the glands, and every other organ of your body, creates them to be perfect, and Nature sees them as perfect, no matter how imperfect their reflection may be upon your mirror of finite mind. Remember always that no matter how imperfect the image of your physical body seen by the world may seem, the God-Idea of your physical body is of a perfect body. Has it never occurred to you that reflections of the imperfect are in reality illusions?

And if you clear your mirror, finite mind, of error, fog, false belief and distortion, then the reflection of the PERFECT will shine forth.

But through ignorance, and often all unknown to us, our objective minds reflect to us and to the world imperfect images of ourselves—distorted reflections of our negative fear-thinking. But when we realize that our bodies are individual centers of the same vibrant Spirit—Energy which forms the substance of the universe, and animated by the one Eternal Life-Force, then it becomes our Great Work to reflect that perfect Self which is imaged in the Divine Creative Mind of God.

MIND-MIRRORS CANNOT REFLECT BOTH PERFECT AND IMPERFECT

Let us be very certain, however, that these mind-mirrors of ours cannot reflect two opposite images of Self at the same time the one perfect, the other imperfect. And so by purposely changing the image we shall reflect from the imperfect to the perfect ideal, we transform the outer physical body into the picture of health, of success and of happiness. For it is entirely within our own power to choose WHAT you will reflect.

The lesson is, then, that you must synchronize (attune) your inner Ideal (image) to reflect that Perfect You which the Supreme Creator holds of you in Eternal Divine Mind, and in due time you will behond your reflection changing splendidly in the outer, objective world. And change it MUST, because this is the fiat of the omnipotent God-Law.

Behold the perfect God-Idea of YOU in the mirror of your mind—and you can reflect little else.

In this supreme degree of The Illumination, we teach that the greatest, the highest degree of development is that each student learn to Look Within, and so discover Truth, Reality, Soul-awareness deep within himself or herself.

This philosophy teaches One Life, One Divine Power, One Destiny and ONE PATH. You will find plain symbols of our system of ancient wisdom in the vision of Isaiah, in the law-codes of Moses, in the Egyptian Book of the Dead, in Plato's Dialogues, in Shelley's Prometheus Unbound, even in Wadsworth, Browning and Tennyson—in all these we discover truths from our fellowship.

But the final goal of the student is to need no guide, no highway markers, no instruction, when he rises to consciously contact and talk with the Divine MIND OF THE OVER-SOUL.

Says Magre, in "Alchemists and Adepts;"—"The emotional substance of the soul strives through the filter of the senses, to transform itself into spirit and to return to unity with the divine. The movements of Nature are governed by a single law (The God-Law), which is diverse in its manifestations but uniform in its essence. It was the discovery of this law that the alchemists sought. If there were many of them who discovered the mineral agent, fewer were able to find its application to the human body, and only a very few adepts knew of the essential agent, the sublime heat of the soul, which fuses the emotions, consumes the prison of form AND ALLOWS ENTRY INTO THE HIGHER WORLD."

LESSON No. 9

THE PATHWAY TO HEALTH, WEALTH AND HAPPINESS

Fourth Gateway of The Temple Invisible, Being The Secret Instruction Taught by The Masters in White, Whose Sublime Precepts are Now Exemplified in These Lessons.

The Degree of Illumination

THE INNER SECRETS OF PSYCHIC HEALING
"Thought in the mind hath made us, What we are by thou it was wrought and built. If a man's mind hath evil (negative) thoughts, pain comes on him as comes the wheel on Ox behind. All that we are is what we have thought and willed; Our thoughts shape us and frame..."—Sir Edwin Arnold.

In 1908 a medical Practitioner, Dr. Sheldon Leavitt wrote these significant words about mental therapeutics (psychic healing)—

"The problem of health, then, rests primarily on the regulation of mental action. Illness is always a sign of weakness, and, primarily, mental weakness, I have no wish to deny that unconscious action may be modified for good by the toxical (poisonous) action of drugs...

"The irritant drug communicates a suggestion of augmented energy in certain areas, and organs, and nerve tracts,which effect desired results That drug treatment does often effect cures in this manner cannot be denied. But drugs are uncertain in action and cannot be relied upon in a series of cases without at the same time, by virtue of collateral irritation, doing possible harm. The great defect of the drug system is found in its unreliability. Uniform effects cannot be obtained.

"The advantage of mental treatment lies in the fact that it can be directed with precision, while its effects are not scattering and collaterally harmful. It can also be made to reinforce drug action and thus render it efficient. Moreover (and this truth should sink deeply into the memory), while using drugs as a means of modifying functional activities we are teaching reliance on artificial stimulation. In mental therapeutics the mind learns to acquire permanent control in its own realm. "(The italics are ours).

DESIRE AND FAITH—KEYS TO HEALTH, HARMONY AND JOY

First, then, there are two simple keys to the cosmic storehouse of Health, Harmony and Happiness, and these two keys are Desire and Faith.Desire is NOT wishful thinking, and Faith is not a daydream of mere hope.

In these lessons we are confronted with the very great task of simplifying just as much as possible the teachings of the Masters of the Occult WAY. We should like you to understand that in their original forms these advanced teachings of The Illumined Masters are so profound and often so abstract that the Initiate can only approach the study of their instruction by rising into a degree of harmony with the consciousness of the Masters. That is why we have provided the Pathway of Initiation, a Pathway marked by mystic Degrees, because these tremendous truths can never be imparted to the unthinking and the unprepared.

In other words only students trained in Intuition and in Spiritual Perception (inspiration) can hope to understand the deeper, inner meanings of our ancient Masters.

Simply stated, the Masters teach that the miracles of Psychic Healing is the result of the reflection of the Perfect, Radiant, Ever-Healing SELF shining forth through the mental, the spiritual, and the physical body.

The first elements of all success in Healing combine the vibrations of Desire and Faith, and these two in turn activate and focus WILD, which is the true psychic factor in all recovery of sick or diseased human bodies.Just as the Christ taught so long ago, we would have you understand that by Faith you can KNOW that the Healing which you Desire and Will is already a definite, concrete, tangible REALITY. The resultant cure, to be made manifest "according to your Faith," is embodied in your Desire—when you realize this, the real work is done.

To find ("know") himself is the real, the Spiritual destiny of man. In this curative work, let us say that your Desire and your Faith are the little knobs on your psychic dial that tune you in to the illimitable Powers of healing. Men and women by the millions pay a terrible price for focusing their minds upon disease, poverty and unhappiness, for thus these negative,these evil things become realities in our human awareness.

isn't it simple, then, to understand that to focus our thoughts upon abounding health, upon prosperity and abundance, and upon love and happiness, is the first step towards attaining them? "Whatsoever things ye desire, when ye pray BELIEVE THAT YE HAVE THEM,"—not whatsoever things you say with your tongue or idly wish with your mind, while you actually desire something else.

"Whatsoever things ye DE,SIRE..." said the Nazarite Master—because when you hold fast to your Desire that Self within that KNOWS and Forever IS, is vibrating its unseen power into your visible world, and you can SEE that the outer symbol of your inner picture is taking to itself material form.

Desire to DESIRE. And know that when you desire health, prosperity and happiness for yourself, or for another, you are simply desiring the true; the positive, the God-ordained condition of human destiny, consciousness and expression. Results are measured by the intensity, the reality of your Desire. But you may say, "I fear that I lack Faith." The answer is that your Desire for Faith when it becomes intense and real, will bring FAITH.

Surely, you cannot expect to receive anything which you do not desire, nor can you get anything worthwhile which you do not believe you can ever have.

WEAK OR FEEBLE EMOTIONS DO NOT AROUSE YOUR INNER POWERS

Desire must be intense, and Faith must be actually strong, or they will never arouse your Subconscious Self, because that Inner Self will not respond to weak or feeble emotions. Remember, in that Subconscious Mind of yours is the buried wisdom of the ages, and you cannot deceive it with spurious commands—you must be in dead earnest. True Desire, to be effective, must be the real yearning of your Soul reaching out for that which you crave. For instance, without such a strong, irresistible yearning for healing and,for health, the sick will continue to suffer sickness.

Now let us turn to that vexing subject of Faith, vexing indeed to the multitudes who cannot seem to understand so simple a thing as BELIEF. The multitudes shout, "Show us the results, and we will believe." Of course, that is not Faith, because it is quite easy to believe a thing which has been proven to our senses—Such "belief" is cheap, so cheap that it brings no reward.

But indeed it is a far different matter, and often a matter of some difficulty, to actually and honestly believe something which has no present proof in our senses, although that something is declared to exist by the voice of Intuition, or by the dictates of Reason. But today more and more even the "man in the street" the (common man) is advancing in the belief that" he DOES have a conscious power over his physical body, and its health and well-being, and also he is coming to realize that he CAN rule his own environment; or choose his surroundings.

And the realization of these powers over self and over surroundings, even though that realization be imperfect as yet, helps to give to modern man and woman a degree of self-confidence, and it is this faith-in-self which makes human self-expression dynamic. Without self-confidence education, intellect, and even great natural talents are useless, because they will remain unused.

But please understand we are not talking about blind faith, because blind faith is a poor gamble. Simple trust in some unknown divinity, or a blind faith in luck, when all the chances are against success MAY win—once in a thousand times. But such a gamble is against odds that are overwhelming; how infinitely better is thorough preparation for the battle, securing every possible advantage, and then an intelligent, informed faith which rests upon self-confidence.

True, every power of your Subconscious Mind is yours to use, when you know how to use this invisible mental energy, but don't depend upon such power ALONE to work miracles for your—it works miracles only when it is aroused by life, action and determination.

In certain former lessons of yours, we have stressed the tremendous importance of mental attitudes. FAITH is probably the most powerful, positive and magnetic mental attitude in the world. Faith focuses your mind until it truly becomes "one-pointed"—and obstacles, enemies and frustrations are powerless against you when you meet them with a burning zeal, a towering faith.

When the Devil (fear) whispers, "Look out! There are wild lions in your way," then the Spirit of Faith answers, "All right, but when I get there they will be chained." When Fear whimpers, "I hope so," Faith shouts back, "I KNOW it is so!"

Fear pleads, "Just stay in bed, Success is not coming to your door," but Faith arouses you at 7 A.M. to go right out and meet Success!

Fear listens to every discouraging tale, and exclaims in dismay, "Just what I expected!" But your Faith replies—"Those stories don't mean me, because I can and I WILL!"

Fear doubts—Faith believes.

Yes, Desire and Faith are the first essentials—but while these two are the first psychic elements necessary to success in healing, or in prosperity, or in happiness, or any other form of success, yet there are several other important factors concerned in every attainment. So, if you would succeed—and YOU CAN—you must understand these other factors, and learn to use them all.

Next, then, let us consider the tremendous part that your WILL, your Determination, must play in your every success. It is the dynamic power of your Will which brings Desire and Faith into life and action in your Great Work. But—exactly what is Will?

Even those who compile our dictionaries seem to have failed to define WILL satisfactorily. Yet every conscious move we make is the result of will, and will is behind all of our thinking. Suppose you take a step forward, isn't that action directed by your thought? Very well, then, what is the mental action that translates that thought into your physical step in walking? Let us agree that it is your attention focused upon your purpose to express this directed act of taking each step. You do not doubt your ability to walk, if you are normal physically, so your focused attention directs your step with sureness, without doubt, with faith.

CONSCIOUS WILL (PURPOSE) DIRECTS ACTION

Focused attention, then, stimulates conscious will, and in turn conscious will directs all physical action in your life, whether you are aware of it or not. And yet we must remember that in reality it is the great Sub conscious Mind which carries out every demand of the conscious will, once we have focused attention and a determined purpose. Your conscious will gives the orders; your Subconscious Mind sees that they are carried out in your physical world.

We have pointed out that weak or feeble emotions do not arouse your inner powers. Your degree of power and effectiveness in any physical action depends upon the power of the emotion behind that action. We have started this discussion by stating that Desire and Faith are the first two great elements of all success. Both of these elements spring from the emotions, but there is still a greater emotion which stimulates Desire and Faith into directed, effective ACTION, and that greater_.emotion is your aroused, dynamic WILL—your determined purpose.

In other words, Desire and Faith are potential elements, dormant until they are transformed into vital electric energies by the dynamic power of your WILL. Suppose, for instance that you honestly Desire the healing of a disease or sickness, and you have the Faith to earnestly believe that you shall receive that "gift of healing"—perhaps you even almost believe that you already have it. Fine! There you have the first two great elements of success, in healing—but now these emotional forces of Desire and Faith must combine to demonstrate that healing through WILL (the determined purpose), which reaches into The Infinite and CLAIMS (possesses) that healing.

But without that active, dynamic, vibrant WILL, you can Desire that healing, and you can believe (dormant Faith) that healing to be possible for a whole lifetime without any effect at all. But when Desire and Faith unite and find their center in a determined WILL, Desire is transformed into dominant energy and Faith becomes a flaming vibration, and, behold! A miracle—a miracle of healing.

This, then, is the WAY OF ATTAINMENT—But make no mistake, and don't be misled into searching for "short cuts." You will find no short cuts and no easy paths when you travel this WAY, because the Way leads ever upward, the climb is often steep, and the rocks of experience are sometimes rough and jagged. Attainment takes time, in healing work, just as in every other form of success. But you are building a Temple for Eternity, and you can afford to take time.

Just as we must teach the little child to walk by easy lessons, at every turn giving the child a helping hand, and words of loving encouragement, and kindly instruction, just so you, as well as every other student, must be taught the WAY of Healing Power (by little,) by degrees, one step at a time, That is why we are devoting our lives to teaching you how to acquire this Psychic Power whereby you, too, can command 'miracles'.

use in combatting serious diseases. He fairly exudes "faith" in his supposed "remedies", and here and there he does meet with fair success in his first small struggles with disease. Forgetting that Nature is always working on the side of recovery, the medical student prides himself upon the skill which he has shown in utilizing drugs.

But it is significant that after some years of experience this same medical enthusiast tempers his use of drugs with extreme caution, and if intelligent,the doctor of mature experience realizes that he is practically helpless when confronted with dangerous diseases. For he has learned full well that his best medical skill, with all the drugs known to man at his command, can do little more than offer minor aid in lesser sicknesses, and can only offer slight changes in the course of momentous diseases.

Few mature doctors will contend that any drug in itself has curative powers. Remembering that the sympathetic nervous system is under the immediate control of the Subconscious Mind, we can understand that any drug can only cause such curative effects as may follow by the subtle and powerful suggestion that accompanies its administration by the doctor. So we can trace any curative effects of a drug not to the drug itself, but to suggestion—for it is suggestion alone which arouses the dormant psychic healing power of MIND AND SOUL.

Uncertainty and discouragement due to constant failures are the "dry rot" which is destroying confidence in "medicine"(drugs) both on the part of the public and of doctors themselves.

In all kindness, when the average doctor is referred to as a "scientific man", meaning by that term one who KNOWS ALL THE NECESSARY FACTS AND TRUTHS which relate to his professions, we fear the term is far from true. So vast is the field of scientific research, even in its relation to medicine and surgery, that the doctor who is busy from morning til night trying to minister to a host of sufferers simply does not have time to gain scientific knowledge of the ever-changing essentials of his own profession. After all, let us remember that the doctor is only human—HE, too suffers from all "the ills that flesh is heir to!" And his day has only 24 hours.

And after all science seems to be contented with only what can be proven to the five physical senses.

This course of study teaches the ageless axion of The Ancient Masters—that matter, while it remains matter, is the unfailing medium through which infinite Divine Mind expresses its inexhaustible energy in a world of phenomena. And further we teach the Oneness (the Unity) of all phenomena.

Spencer realized this truth when he wrote: "The Power that manifests throughout the universe is the same power which in ourselves wells up under the form of consciousness."

Emerson uses these thrilling words in describing this universal power from the cosmic:

"It is a secret which every intellectual man quickly learns, that beyond the energy of his conscious and possessed intellect he is capable of a new energy by abandonment to the nature of things; that besides his privacy of power as an individual man, there is a great public (cosmic) power on which he can draw, by unlocking, at all hazards, his lawman (mental) doors and suffering (permitting) the ethereal tides to roll (vibrate) and circulate through him; then he is caught up into the life of the universe."

MODERN DOCTORS AGREE THAT DISEASE ORIGINATES IN THE MIND

Modern doctors agree that the origin of disease is in the mind. Describing this origin, Prof. Elmer Gates, wrote in the Monist—"Introspective (mental) states affect metabolism, circulation, respiration, digestion, assimilation, excretion, secretion, growth, sleep, wakefulness, strength, health, seeing, hearing, tasting, smelling, temperature, the pressure senses, dreams movements, complexion, voice, gesture and environment."

Every medical man today admits the injurious effects of negative, fearful or pernicious thoughts upon the human body. We are teaching and our students are proving that the healing, curative effects of positive, psychic FAITH-DESIRE-WILL-TO-HEALTH are just as certain in their action for GOOD upon the physical body.

So, if the origin of disease (discord) is within, it must logically follow that the process of rebuilding HEALTH, as well as prosperity and happiness, must start from within yourself, or within the mind of the sufferer. Again we would remind you that to you, you are the center of the entire universe. And what you hold in your consciousness, whatever picture is focused in your mind, that you are.

You will remember that we have taught you that every cell in your body is imbued with mind, in reality, each of these cells IS mind. Now when you know an recognize the fact that the control of all mind within you is in your hands, then by that same power you can remedy any inharmony in your health, or in the other material affairs of your life.

In using "you" as an example, we have taken it for granted that you will develop this power within and for yourself. Yet we realize that for every one who will develop this power to heal self there are thousands and thousands of good, earnest people who lack the confidence or ability to do this for themselves. So, it is necessary to train and develop many others who can do this for them, and this is the reason for the many trained practitioners who are doing a remarkable healing work throughout the land today.

And the use of this unseen power within is not new. Down through the ages in every country "divine healing," or healing by that marvelous inner psychic power, has been practiced under different names, by various religions, societies and sects. Their many "miraculous" cures cannot be denied.

Various cults and occult "teachers" claim that what the world needs to know is that disease can be conquered by the psychic power of MIND. However we do not ask our students to be satisfied with that, for we know that you must become aware of the tremendous fact that YOU ARE THAT POWER—it is within YOU.

LESSON No. 10

THE PATHWAY TO HEALTH, WEALTH AND HAPPINESS

Fourth Gateway of The Temple Invisible, Being The Secret Instruction Taught by The Masters in White, Whose Sublime Precepts Are Now Exemplified in These Lessons.

The Degree of Illumination

LIMITLESS HEALING POWER OF THE SUBCONSCIOUS

Speaking of drugless healing, George F. Butler, M.D., writes;

"This universal truth is what makes possible the fact that mental (psychic) healing has been known and very extensively practiced ever since the dawn of history...Yes, it was the first method of healing practiced by mankind. In comparison with its age, the art of physical medicine (drugs) is a new-born babe."

And Prof. Elmer Gates, in "Mind Building," thus illustrates our limitless subconscious powers;

"At least ninety-eight per cent of our mental life is subconscious. If you will analyze your mental operations you will find that consciousness—conscious thinking is never a continuous line of consciousness, but a series of conscious date with great intervals of subconscious. We sit and try to solve a problem and fail. We rise and walk around, try again and fail. Suddenly an idea dawns that leads to the solution of the problem. The subconscious processes were at work.

We do not volitionally create our own thinking. It takes place in (within) us. We are more or less passive recipients. We cannot change the nature of a thought or of a truth, but we can, as it were, guide the ship by the moving of the helm. Our mentation (mental action) is largely the result of the Cosmic Whole upon us. Annihilate the Cosmos and our thinking would instantly cease.

In this particular lesson we are entering still further into the psychic realm of healing—and among all the miracles of phenomena of all time, none is more striking nor of such tremendous interest to us than the eternal truth that the healing power of our Subconscious Mind is limitless!

In our studies in psychic healing, we cannot ignore the proven phenomena of those countless cures which have been called "miracles," nor the fact that cures that seem miraculous result from psychic power today even as in the ages past. We shall not lessen our inquiry or our belief just because the ignorant and the unscientific have advanced wild theories about such cures, nor because charlatans and pretenders have built fantastic pseu-do-religious organizations around them.

The world has not yet rid itself of slavery. Countless men and women are living life-times of pitiful servitude millions all about us are just as truly living from day to day under the dominion of FEAR, as were the galley slaves under the lash of the masters. Wherever they go these multitudes are the slaves of fear—that most terrible of all fears, fear of sickness, of disease, of suffering. Everywhere fear drives these slaves to doctors, but doctors can do little to aid them, indeed, sometimes heartless physicians intensify these fears, either consciously or unconsciously.

For no matter where they go, and no matter what bitter dosage they may take from bottles, these fear-slaves cannot escape self. What these people sorely need is freedom from their slavery to the FEAR of sickness, and liberation from imagined ailments.

THE REALM OF MIND IS THE REALM OF CAUSE

"It is not a question of the correctness or incorrectness of a physician's diagnosis; in his treatments, the healer must look deeper; never losing sight of the truth, that the realm of mind is the realm of cause, and the realm of matter the realm of effect; that he must deal with the causes and thus change effects."

Today undertones of sickness and suffering fill the world. Fear stalks the land, and the cry of man goes up in the words of the Bible, "Who shall deliver me from the body of this death?" We in these modern days have done much in preventing the epidemics and plagues which were the horrors of the past by cleanliness and san-itation. In the words of Christ we have made "clean the outside of the platter," and for even this our outer reward has been very great indeed.

But that inner fountain, from which springs health, abundant prosperity and happiness—that inner fountain which we call the mind is too often choked and muddy with the disease-dealing germs of fear, of worry, of imagined disease, of impure and negative thoughts.

How does your mind affect your body? Read these significant words from the pen of Professor Elmer Gates:

"The mind of a human being can, by effort of WILL, properly directed produce measurable changes in the chemistry of the secretions and excretions in the vasor motor blood supply to areas and organs, and in the temperature of selected areas, and so on. All of this goes to prove that the mind has a direct effect upon the functioning of the cells that compose an organ, and that if we can properly train the mind, we can produce definite effects upon any physiological function."

Everywhere men and women are seeking HEALTH, or healing, or financial success, or that elusive joy called "happiness," but alas! always they seem to seek to acquire these goodly things through some magic or some power outside themselves. Under the great God—Law, each of these priceless possessions is the result of thought—so the magic or the power which you may have sought so long in the outer world is already within you.

What you think upon intensely TODAY you become TOMORROW, if you hold that thought focused in your mind. What you picture in your mind with Desire and Faith TODAY will be yours, if you WILL it dominantly, TOMORROW. Whether that "tomorrow" is to mean the day following the day of your thought or of your mental image, or whether it will only materialize after many days, after many "tomorrows," depends upon the degree and the quality of the though-power which you concentrate upon your goal.

Idle or wishful thinking has little power to heal, or to. bring you success, or to light your pathway with hap-piness—for thought only acquires the good things of life when you bring it to a focus.

So we want you above all else to concentrate your attention upon what you DO and DO NOT want—but most intensely upon those things you DO most greatly want. In doing this you will form the perfect mental pattern or image which you will project upon the astral screen of manifestation.

FAILURE OF "MEDICINE" NATURE HEALS BY INVISIBLE PSYCHIC POWER

As we have pointed out, sanitation of our material surroundings and in the handling of our foods have triumphed over the epidemics and the plagues of yesteryears, but now mankind needs inner sanitation—the cleansing of mind and of thought. And this inner cleansing—this mental purification which eradicates fear, doubt, worry, apprehension, jealousy, anger, hatred, etc.,—is the greatest preventive of disease in the world.

And it is certain that it is far easier to prevent sickness than to remedy it. And doctors agree even those diseases which are almost always fatal can almost always to prevented—and that the greatest preventive is healthy, trained, fearless thought.

How shall we attain such protective thinking? First, by purposely casting out all conscious fear from our minds and then developing an absolute FAITH that the immutable God-Law protects us as if by a wall of fire, together with an unswerving obedience to the common-sense laws of healthful living.

Psychic healing rests upon the changeless truth that the organic functions of your body can be consciously regulated by your conscious, objective MIND, because the magic powers of your Subjective Self obey your conscious commands.

In spite of all the boasted advances of medical practice ("medicine") in the last fifty years, if we leave out contagious diseases, which have been greatly lessened by sanitation, the sum total of sickness and disease in this country certainly has not shown a reduction, but rather a steady increase.

While it is true that medical men have made very great progress in the matter of diagnosis, yet they have made no similar advance in cure. It is true that during the last one hundred years the average span of life has steadily grown longer, this increase in the general life span is due largely to better and better sanitary conditions, to decreased consumption of "medicines," and to more generally available trained nursing. Of course, every day sees an increase in "remedies," and "medicines" without number stock the druggists' shelves, but doctors themselves will tell you that few of these have any established or determined curative value. Each vaunted "remedy has its little day, and is forgotten.

Healing throughout the ages proves beyond the shadow of a doubt that the cure of disease depends upon the PSYCHIC EFFECT of that mind and soul power which forever works "miracles," And it is very certain that this miracle-working power cannot be found in bottles at the corner drug store.

When this psychic power is at work in your physical body it is the DIVINE within working through subtler matter to unfold the tremendous emotional power that heals. Let us emphasize this more strongly than any other thing just now—when you rebuild health; you BUILD FROM WITHIN. Shape a mental matrix (mould) for perfect health from your positive, happy, joyous emotions—desire, faith, hope, expectancy, smiles, laughter, happiness.

Above all, if treating yourself, learn to expect what you desire, or if treating another, teach that person to expect what he or she desires. Probably you have already observed that the man who succeeds, the happy man, yes, and always the HEALTHY MAN is the man who has the cheerful, joyous mental attitude of expecting health, he expects success, he expects happiness. And this, absolute, unswerving, undoubting expectancy of GOOD is nothing less than the realization of the God-Law in harmony, health, happiness, success.and abundance. It is as simple as that.

HEALING ENERGY DIRECTED BY RULING EMOTIONS

Health, healing and happiness are simply forms of emotional energy which attune our bodies, our minds and our souls to the Cosmic Rhythm of the universe.

Taking a lesson from medical practice, a doctor with a radiant, magnetic personality has a very great healing essence in his presence alone, for he sends forth vibrations of health and of happy confidence (faith). It is not his "medicine" or the drugs which he prescribes that are curative, but rather the magic of his remedies lies in the suggestions with which they are given and his radiation of healthful reassurance.

Let the students beware of the fatal weakness of the hurried and superficial methods which rob many doctors of the tremendous healing effect of any personal magnetism which they may possess. This weakness arises from the fact that the doctor in general practice tried to minister to many, many patients each day, so being forced to limit the time of each patient to but a few minutes. In such a hurried practice, how can the doctor give deep, serious, personal attention to any particular patient, no matter how grave the malady may be? In such practice the physician has only time to consider a few of the leading symptoms, and hastily prescribes some drug that is supposed to remedy some one or two of these symptoms. Often then Nature is left to not only struggle against a disease, but also to wage an added battle against some depressant drug.

Our words upon this phase of medicine are not to be construed as in any sense an attack upon honest, efficient, or conscientious physicians, for we are merely pointing out these inherent weaknesses in medical methods. Of course, we realize that the basic drive behind the busy doctor is financial, and we realize full well that often the physician is underpaid for his ministrations. Baldly stated, usually the doctor cannot afford to lessen the number of his patients, so as to give to each one his most efficient and undivided attention.

In effective HEALING the intense, riveted attention of the patient must first be secured, and then the mental doors of the sufferer are open to the inflowing, concentrated psychic force of the healer, and this together with his powers of suggestion work the curative "miracle." And it is self-evident that these conditions of perfect rapport cannot be secured in a few hurried minutes.

The doctor, the medical man, is trained to see life from the point of the physiologist, and that is entirely a materialistic view-point, From this training the materialist explains the functioning of the human body in chemical and physical terms—to him life, human life especially, is but a series or a sequence of chemical and physical changes,

On this same material basis, then, he would explain. the seemingly simple process of eating a meal as only a chemical, only a physical process.

But does not the physiologist, and often the medical man, ignore the very evident fact that in human beings the mental and the psychic factors dominate, rule and control every function of life, and even life itself ?

But suppose you should try to eat when you are in the midst of a great sorrow, or when you are very excited, or perhaps when you are very angry, or greatly frightened. You would very soon be made to realize that all of your chemical and physical processes are vitally changed, and you could indeed become very sick from self-poisoning! Probably you have encountered more than one instance of the power of emotions and of -mental states to cause harm to the digestion, and often to the circulation.

Doubtless you have often noticed how human faces flush (turn red) in anger or in embarrassment, or how blanched (white) the face is in a case of sudden fright? Thus, the mental affects the circulation visibly.

HEALING—ONE GREAT PRODUCT OF MENTAL SCIENCE

In order to thrive animals must be physically adjusted to their surroundings; but in order to possess health, prosperity, and happiness man must be mentally and spiritually adjusted to his environment, as well as physically. As we ascend the scale of life into the human domain, we find that MIND becomes the guiding, the directing, the dominant factor. Always both the human body and the human mind must obey the great God-Law, or they are self-destroyed, because in every realm Nature demands harmony with her laws of order.

How wonderful is that process which we call life! From outside raw materials, food, water, air, etc., are taken into the human body, and by the constructive activities of the many living organs of the body these raw materials are transformed into new and changing forms of energy—life—sensation-consciousness. It is in the building and the use of these complicated, ever-changing, ever-renewed and ever-cumulative energies within that the physical body and the mind of man that human nature is creative, existent, and filled with healing power.

So we see that this mystic life-energy is the basic, the fundamental ESSENCE of the universe. This is the essence which is made manifest in BEING, in conscious, thinking life. The law of change decrees that energy can never remain stationary, The impetus of energy is irresistibly directed into expression.

The natural course of human life-energy is to express the normal conditions of health, of abundance, and of happiness, and it will follow this normal course by attracting these better things of life UNLESS IT IS IMPEDED. If this life-energy is impeded or obstructed so that it cannot express its normal course, it will seek the line of least resistance, just as an electric current will do, for both must manifest:

An electric current, when its natural flow or course is impeded or retarded by either a "short" or a loose connection manifests in intense heat, a heat that can be very destructive, as you know. Likewise, this life-energy, this mind-energy, if retarded or obstructed by negative emotions, such as doubt, fear, malice, envy, hatred, etc., will turn its power INWARD upon the inner, the mental self, dwarfing and perverting all normal thoughts, promoting every sort of mental disorder, and sooner or later these mental monstrosities are reflected in the body in some crippling disease, or some serious sickness.

For the old theories concerning all matter have faded in the light of modern science. Probably you can remember quite well when atoms were supposed to be the smallest particles into which matter could be divided. In those days we were taught that matter was in itself an entity, a solid entity.

But modern scientists tell us that atoms, which compose matter, are in reality vortex: rings of ether, and that atoms themselves are divisible into infinitely smaller units. For instance, radium contains 150,000 of these infinitely smaller units to the atom, with each unit or "ion" rotating at terrific speed.

No wonder that Prof. Crooks wrote "that not only are the atoms apparently going to pieces, but the masses of molecules probably dissolve themselves into the ether waves which fill the universe or into electrical energy.

"Thus we stand on the border line where matter and force Pass into each other,"

So we see that this merging of the material and the spiritual scientifically proves the truth of the teaching of the ages—the oneness or unity of all things and the oneness of all POWER. The power that gives you consciousness this very minute is the same power that developed your present physical body from the first protoplasmic cell that was you. The tremendous power of the cyclone is the same power that sends forth the perfume of the rose!

The mental science of our WAY seeks to teach you to focus this same power, harnessed and directed by thought, into the merciful channels of HEALING.

DISEASE ORIGINATES IN THE SUBCONSCIOUS

Emerson sensed the truth taught for ages past in the 'Mystery Schools'—that the causes of man's fortunes, either good or bad, are born in the metaphysical realm, for Emerson says: "The soul contains in itself the event which shall presently befall it, for the event is only the actualizing of its thoughts."

Let us here and now make this one tremendous FACT startlingly clear to each and every student—disease and healing, poverty and riches, sorrow and happiness, EACH of these exists in the MIND OF MAN KIND, not in his drug stores or doctors, not in his markets or banks, and not in his churches or temples.

The amazing wisdom of the ancient Masters in White long, long ago traced the causes of diseases to the subtle and negative effect of invisible forces, misdirected forces, acting upon the Subconscious Self (or Mind). Today the greatest medical authorities, and the great scientists and philosophers, agree with our Masters of old.

The actual cure, then, or the effective healing of sickness and disease will hardly be found in drugs or in "medicines" that depend upon mechanical action, but rather in the psychic powers that flame forth to heel when Divine Universal Mind is contacted and connected (tuned in) to the divine Mind in Man.

To attain this divine cycle in Healing, it is of course, necessary for the practitioner to attune himself or herself mentally to the Universal Cosmic Mind, so that he or she can become a channel for the expression of this curative power which works "miracles" today just as it did two thousand years ago in far-off Galilee.

These striking words written long ago mirror the HOW of this truth:

"There is one mind common to all individual men. Every man is an islet to the same and to all of the same. What Plato thought, he may think; what a saint has felt, he may feel; who hath access to The Universal Mind is a party to all that is or can be done, for this is the only sovereign agent."—Emerson.

LESSON NO. 11
THE PATHWAY TO HEALTH, WEALTH AND HAPPINESS

Fourth Gateway of The Temple Invisible, Being The Secret Instruction Taught by The Masters in White, Whose Sublime Precepts are Now Exemplified in These Lessons.

The Degree of Illumination

ALL PHENOMENA OF LIFE AND HEALING ARE PSYCHIC

"We know as a matter of fact that a vast number of impressions are constantly being made, upon us, of which we take no heed; they do not interest us, or they are not strong enough to arouse consciousness. But the impressions are there. They leave a mark upon us, though we are not aware of it, and they may float to the surface, or be evoked at some future time. One of the most certain and striking results of the investigations made by our society is that the content of our subconscious life (mind) is far greater than that of our conscious life.

"Our minds are like a photographic plate, sensitive to all sorts of impressions—but our Ego (self) develops only a few of these impressions—these are our conscious impressions—the rest are latent, awaiting development, which may come in sleep, hypnosis (suggestion), or trance..."—Prof. W. F. Barrett, President. Society for Psychical Research (London).

But while it is absolutely true that all phenomena of life and heeling are psychic, we must warn you not to make the mistake of deciding that these phenomena ("miracles") of healing, of success or of happiness are showered upon us by a benign Providence without any effort upon our part. Putting this warning into plain and simple words, we quote this significant paragraph from "Paths to The Heights"—

"Mere thinking must not be expected to do the whole work. Such an attitude will no more bring results in Health and success than a similar attitude will bring food and raiment. The lily of the field is clothed and fed by the Father's hand, it is true; but the lily has a part to perform. The elements of nutrition are at hand, but the rootlets have to look for them. They go out on their labors day after day, seeking with avidity and finding abundantly. The stalks climbs up into the sunlight and air at the expense of a strenuous effort, and extracts from these sources the supplies that it needs.

Let us agree, for example, that your Heart's Desire—the one great NEED in your life—is Healing, healing power for your own ills or the power to heal others, Perfect Health, then, is your goal, for granted abundant health you can secure the added blessings of success, prosperity and happiness in the enjoyment of the good things of life.

Perhaps you have been giving the most of your attention to the obstacles you see in the way of attaining to this goal of yours, (this is generally the first mistake we make, no matter what our goal may be). Perhaps you have felt that your environment, your surroundings, hinder your progress towards your goal. You may find yourself upon the treadmill of everyday work in order to provide a living for yourself and your dependents. The horizon of your hopes seems to be limited at times, doesn't it, and you see many clouds on that horizon, don't you?

Yet we have taught you, even as the Christ before us did, that your heartfelt, burning desire is a promise of its fulfillment.

CREATING THE AURA THAT ATTRACTS FULFILLMENT

Right here you may very reasonably ask, just what must I DO to insure the fulfillment of my burning desire for healing, for health, or to develop that magic power which will make me a healer of others?

Your first step, then, is to create the aura that attracts the fulfillment of your Heart's Desire. By aura we simply mean the atmosphere which surrounds you, or the vibrations which your own personality sends forth to surround you. You must make a bargain with yourself, with your inner Ego, that you will purposely and consciously devote every energy of your being to this work of attainment, with every bit of faith which you can summon today. And in this matter of faith, start with what faith you have right now, be it little or great.

You are beginning a journey to the mountain-top of realization, of possession, your goal is at the top, your goal is to actually grasp the "substance" of this thing you hope for, so start from where you are today.

But you say, "I cannot see very far along the WAY." Of course not, but like one who carries a lantern at night, with each step you take the light shows the way that much farther. In the silence, and even in the busy thorough-fares of life, always hold the picture of your Heart's Desire, your goal, your longed-for success, before your "mind's eye," affirming and reaffirming over and over THAT THIS SHALL COME TO PASS.

No matter how unfriendly or how hopeless your surroundings seem to you when you start, all in good time as you persevere the WAY will open and lead you right through this hostile environment to the promised land of your fulfilled desire. But you must do the traveling yourself, and don't expect blessings to fall into your lap from "Heaven" without any effort on your part, because the ravens are probably too busy to fee you, and bread (manna) has not fallen from the skies for some time.

First you must prove your worth by being faithful in your directed activity and then you can be made ruler over the many good things of life that wait only upon your concentrated effort, your faith, your determination (YOUR WILL). When you DO these simple things you are creating an aura about yourself that attracts the vibrations of success, of healing, of perfect health, of fulfillment.

Already you must sense the truth of this great statement from the Upanishads.

"Each man is. required to pass through the Asramos (states of unfoldment) before he is admitted to spiritual freedom. As on a ladder no step is to be skipped." And "spiritual freedom" is fulfillment. And "unfoldment" is from within.

As to your surroundings, let us advise that you should maintain a positive mental attitude to all except Universal Divine Mind. By that word "positive" we here mean on guard mentally. Only in The Silence, and when alone, should you open your mind to the invisible, astral guidance from higher MIND. For that is the time of your unfoldment, and that is the time you should listen to the whispering of intuition.

Eternal Wisdom—the ancient lore of the God-Law—is hidden deep in your Subconscious Mind, heed its voice and KEEP MOVING ONWARD TOWARD YOUR GOAL.

And with every step, the skies of your life brighten.

CELLS—THE BASIS OF THE MYSTERY CALLED LIFE

Because you must understand as far as possible the phenomena of Life in order to direct its invisible energies into the healing of disease, or into the attraction of material blessings, we here start with the medically proven fact that cells are the basic containers of this mysterious energy which we call "Life."

Everywhere around you there is life, and life is pulsating within you at this very minute. Upon the side of your higher or spiritual awareness through thought you can contact("tune in") Infinite Cosmic Mind, from which flow all the tremendous currents of life-energy in this world; again, upon the other side of conscious thought you are aware of Self—YOURSELF—and through this awareness you can see the material things you have attracted to yourself by your thinking and your directed activity:

Yes, you can see the results of your thinking, which proves that you have within you a conscious Mind, and with all its mystic and little known processes, with powers which sometimes fill us with silent awe. But, also you have sensory proof that you now possess a physical body, and that the life-process within that body of yours prove that this human machine is directed and controlled by an Infinite Intelligence. But it is idle for us to seek to know or to understand this Primal or Absolute Intelligence with minds that are after all still earth-bound, finite human.

Life in this world of ours exists bound up in infinite-small, tiny round (Spherical) cells, each, cell filled with a half-fluid, translucent matter, called by doctors and scientists "protoplasm." Protoplasm consists of a combination of oxygen, hydrogen, nitrogen, carbon, etc. the same chemicals which enter into everyday matter. Yet no scientist on earth can tell us where this living matter, called protoplasm, came from or how it originated. Certainly the, living cell did not create itself, and is not governed by the laws which control other forms of matter.

As to size, these tiny spheres called cells range from three-thousandths to one two hundredths of an inch in diameter. These are the needle-points of life, and distributed throughout the organic body of man they make non-living substance vibrate with living energy by their very presence.

Alone, or in company with only a few cells, the cell cannot exist for any length of time. But, remember cells too are intelligent, and they seem to realize that if they would long exist they must join with great numbers of other cells. So myriad of cells unite to animate a living body, and so combining their intelligences they work under one control, and vibrate through a single, individual BODY AND BRAIN, in every living being.

For instance, let us consider this union of individual cells in that marvelous mechanism, the human brain. Staggering indeed is the fact, as stated by scientists, that your brain is composed of SIXTY MILLION CELLS which contact and unite to enable your mind to think and to carry on the countless complex processes of your body. And these harmonious bodily processes must not cease for a single minute, for while your conscious mind sleeps, or perhaps wonders away, the Subconscious Mind must carry on this vast and intricate work without stopping FROM THE CRADLE TO THE GRAVE.

THE MANY WORLDS OF CONSCIOUSNESS, AND MEMORY

Memory is the golden chain which links us to consciousness. .Without memory there could be no individual awareness of a continuity of passing events. But memory holds impressions of our many and varied experiences, impressions, which may be indelible.

These impressions received upon the sensitized consciousness and there recorded can be recalled, re-enacted, and received by the magic wand of memory. True, experiences and events occur which relate to us while we are asleep, or otherwise unconscious, and these impressions seem beyond recall by our waking minds, yet our records of mind-phenomena convince us that the Subconscious Self overlooks nothing in our experiences, and never forgets. Mark that statement well, because it will explain many very puzzling things in the mental life of mankind.

Just because you cannot recall or remember at will many past experiences or events which have taken place in your life, that does not prove that these impressions are not recorded in your archives of the mind.Be advised that your Subconscious memory does not make itself known inordinary ways, but that these impressions are locked safely away in separate tiers of files, as it were, and only the proper key of similar thought can unlock each separate file, according to its index in its own separate tier of consciousness.

Of the "many worlds of consciousness" within each of us, Prof. William James says:"

"The whole drift of my education goes to persuade me that the world of my present consciousness is only one out of many worlds of consciousness that exist, and that those other worlds must contain certain experiences which have a meaning for our life also; and that although in the main their experiences and those of this world keep discrete (separate), yet the two become continuous at certain points, and higher energies filter in.

"You came into this life the child of 'racial heritage,' that is, endowed with impressions within your Subconscious Mind bequeathed to you from a tremendously long line of ancestors, added to the heritage of your Subconscious Self of perhaps many, many antecedent lives (incarnations) of your own. You, then, as an infant was, as you are today, the product of countless lives that have gone before, but whose echoes forever reverberate in the depths of your Unconscious "world."

In that infant stage of your existence, then, you really had no distinctive personality (no matter what fond parents may have fondly imagined) no developed self-hood. You merely bore deep within you the heritage of the generations that have gone before. You were a bundle of inheritated tendencies, of racial impressions. But as you slowly emerged into a consciousness of the material world about you, and as you were gradually or quickly (as the case may have been) thrust into the grim struggle of life, and as you had to engage in battle after battle in both the conscious and the subconscious realms, you began to demonstrate your inheritance, and to develop a distinct Selfhood, that Selfhood that we have named "Personality."

Unfortunately, there are literally millions of people who glide through life like gray shadows sliding into a mist—they are neutral, colorless, because they develop little or no Personality, content to remain vague shadows of racial impressions that have grown dim and faint. As we have pointed out in previous lessons, such people grow, but they only grow physically. And the terrible price they pay is the price of bondage, for they remain the helpless slaves of circumstances and of surroundings, helpless because they will not even try to HELP THEMSELVES, nor will they allow anyone else to help-them.

Personality masters Life—but the neutral is Life's slave.

THROUGH MIND YOU CAN GOVERN OBJECTIVE ENVIRONMENT

Throughout these lessons we have devoted a great deal of attention to your objective (outer or material) existence, for this objective life, is the only life lived in the realms of the Conscious Self. And in this present life your objective environment is of a very real importance to you. For either you will rule in the material world, or you will find yourself the slave of circumstance. Yes, the great lesson is that you can govern your objective environment, but only through Mind.

When you yield your life of the senses to the inner spirit of the Subconscious Mind, imagination pictures to you something of the meaning and the power of your own individual personality in the world you have build-ed around yourself. But let us warn you that you must keep your imagination under due control, lest it mislead you.

Previously we have taught you that you are a marvelously complex being, and we have again and again stressed that the countless activities of your body and the phenomena of your life are subject to the control of MIND, and that we recognize two distinct phases of mind—the outer, objective, conscious mind, and the inner, mysterious, all—powerful sub-conscious' mind. Each of these phases of your—mind is inter-related to. the other, and each rules in its own realm, but is responsive to the calls of the other, thus preserving harmony in the intricate business of directing and preserving your life.

The human being—man or woman—is a composite being, and HARMONY is the balance of life, perfect harmony among all the organs of this body means abounding life and health and consequently harmony also mean happiness.

But loss of harmony within the body, which is but a reflection of discord in the mind, leads to that physical disturbance which we term sickness or disease. Just as long as the organs and processes of the body function in harmony, you do not sense them, but let the activities within your body become perverted or discordant, and there goes up from your body a cry for help, and this cry we call PAIN. We believe and teach that pain is simply a call for help from the Conscious Mind, and that the SUB-Conscious Mind has abundant power to heed that call and to give that help, when developed and trained to do so.

We have taught you in previous lessons that you can impress your beliefs, your demands and your commands upon your deeper, inner, Subconscious Self by the proper use of your conscious mind. Thus we see pain and suffering caused AND eradicated, emotions or sorrow erased by emotions of joy, intuitions and impulses leading on to success and prosperity from former failure—all at the magic behest of mental suggestion, faith, affirmation, and directed activity.

Yes, we often behold with amazement the phenomenal powers of mind to heal disease, those same powers which directed into other channels bring success and prosperity, and from the ashes of sorrow rebuild many a lost happiness. But at the same time we must realize that these marvelous mental and spiritual powers can only be developed and applied in accordance with certain ordained LAWS in these realms.

Because we teach and hold that MIND IS SUPREME, it.does not follow that we are so foolish as to assume for one moment that Mind must not, or need not conform to those certain eternal laws which the Infinite God-Law has ordained to govern it.

CONSCIOUSNESS—MIND—SUBJECT TO LAW

Mind, operating through consciousness, rules our physical bodies, attracts us to our particular environments, moulds our fortunes, and makes or mars our happiness, but in all of these Mind, mighty marvel that it is, still is subject to the laws that govern any sphere or realm in which it is directed. So, in ruling our human bodies Mind must and will comply strictly with the laws of the physical body. True, man does not yet understand all these laws, but to obey those that he does know means health and material well-being.

The ancient Masters understood this truth very well, for they taught that a healthy mind dwells in a healthy body. Thus, Mind and body must live in harmony, and only through law is harmony possible. To break the mental or the spiritual laws is no greater "sin than it is to break the laws of your physical body. For if you starve your body or if you subject it to evil influences or to poisons, no power of your Mind will keep that body of yours from paying the penalty, and under such conditions all of your thinking can avail little to maintain its health.

These human bodies of ours are tremendously important to Nature—if you prefer, you are at liberty to call this great protector of your physical body GOD, but we regard this intelligent, manifested, protective power the Subliminal Self, the Inner Spirit, the "Subconscious Mind." This Inner-Divine-Self, then, is the kindly, all-knowing Spirit that is always seeking to protect our bodies from the rigors of climate and from the fierce, if invisible, danger that lurk in our artificial "civilization."

Life lasts in comfort and in health only so long as we are in physical harmony with the laws which govern our surroundings and our bodily, health, and to maintain this harmony so necessary to our physical welfare we live in a constant state of flux—of continuing physical and mental changes that keep us adjusted to our material environment.

And pause a moment and think, and you will realize that nearly all of this constant process of mental and bodily adjustment is carried on without your even being aware of it consciously!

Suppose that your, comparatively limited conscious mind had to plan and carry on this constant adjustment within your body, suppose, for instance that your objective, conscious mind had to provide those intricate adjustments of your body to heat and to cold, to varying temperatures, to changes of climate, to different altitudes and pressures, to changes in food, water and clothes, not to mention adjustment to the ever changing moods, emotions customs, habits and thoughts of your objective mind (all of which affects your body), would not all of this stagger your conscious mind with its impossibility? Of course it would.

The above is only a brief glimpse of the vast and complex work of adjustment being carried on minute by minute, hour by hour, day and night, within your physical body by the Divine Mind—(the essence of universal, intelligent energy) by the Subconscious Self which never sleeps. (confused terms).

This is the mystery of mysteries, this dual (double) consciousness. For all human consciousness is simply the awareness of life, the sensing or recognition of SELF as a living individual. Only by accepting the omnipresence (the all-presence) of the INFINITE OVER-SOUL in the oneness of each human life, only thus can we begin to understand something of this mystery.

LESSON No. 12
THE PATHWAY TO HEALTH, WEALTH AND HAPPINESS

Fourth Gateway of The Temple Invisible, Being The Secret Instruction Taught by The Masters in White, Whose Sublime Precepts Are Now Exemplified in These Lessons.

The Degree of Illumination

ALL PROBLEMS OF DISEASE AND HEALING ARE PSYCHIC

"Each sphere (plane) of being tends toward a higher sphere and has already revelations and presentiments of it. The Ideal under all its forms is the anticipation and the prophetic vision of that existence, higher than his own, toward which every being perpetually aspires. And this higher and more dignified existence is more inward in character, that is to say, more spiritual.

"Just as volcanoes reveal to us the secrets of the interior of the globe, so enthusiasm and ecstacy are the passing explosions of this inner world of the soul; and human life. The degrees of INITIATION are innumerable. Watch then, disciple of life (Initiate'), watch and labor toward the development of the angel (The Divine Self) within thee.—Amiel's Journal in Time.

Of the projection (sending forth) of the psychic self (which is the basis of healing), Schofield writes:

"Our unconscious influence is the projection of our unconscious (Subconscious) mind and personality unconsciously over others. This acts unconsciously on their unconscious (Subconscious) centers, producing effects ,in character and conduct, recognized in consciousness. For instance, the entrance of a good man into a room where foul language is used will unconsciously modify and purify the tone of the whole room. Our minds cast shadows of which we are as unconscious as those cast by our bodies, but which affect for good or evil all who pass unconsciously within their range. This is a matter of daily experience, and is common to all, though more noticeable with strong personalities.

Always, from the most ancient times, the philosophy has taught the unchanging truth of the Hermetic statement, "There is but One God-Law, and He that worketh is One."

This great teaching took its place among the other proven truths of the inductive, the positive and the exact sciences, as they emerged into absolute monism and perceived the oneness of all existence. For when Lavoisier in 1789 stated the chemical law of the "persistence" or "indestructibility of Matter" he established anew the oneness of spirit and mind, as taught in our olden Mystery Schools under the concept of the oneness of energy and matter. It remained for Mayer, in 1842 to demonstrate in this one treat law his, "law of substance"—and "the persistence of matter and force."

Developed manhood and womanhood are the first steps toward Godhood. For then the doors are opened along this mystic WAY to the attainment of God-Power over the physical body, and thus over sickness and disease, and to the possession of the keys of destiny. So the WAY is opened before us that we may claim our Lordship. And then we can realize that "immortality" is here and now, and by this we can know that we have already entered into that higher realm of consciousness where the LAW OF CHOICE for us transcends the lower laws of Retribution and of compensation.

But to voice such tremendous truths to the outer world is but to offend the sleeping, dormant or sluggish minds of the ignorant, for these uninitiated have not yet awakened to a consciousness of their own Divinity. And fear, bred of this woeful ignorance, makes these who have forgotten or never knew their own Divinity or the Eternal Plan of Existence, bitterly oppose and condemn all that is beyond their dull understanding.

So let every student "keep the faith," WITH SEALED LIPS! Wisely did our Elder Brother advise, "Cast not your pearls before swine."

For as Starr King has said, "The chief difference between a wise man (Initiate) and of an ignorant one is, not that the first is not acquainted with regions invisible to the second, away from common sight and interest, but that he understands the common things which the second only sees."

UNDERSTANDING COSMIC GOD-LAW WORKS 'MIRACLES'

To the degree to which we advance in understanding the mighty God-Laws (Cosmic Laws) which govern everything in this world, to that degree we ourselves are linked with the vast, invisible energies of the Universe. The all important need of this understanding of the Cosmic God-Law was voiced 500 years before Christ was born by Heraclitus, when he said:

"Wisdom consists in one duty and only one—TO UNDERSTAND THE INTELLIGENCE WHICH GOVERNS ALL THINGS."

Looking into the world of material achievement, we see everywhere around us proofs that we are entering the age of Electronics, based upon the discovery by modern Science that all matter can be reduced, to focalized Cosmic or electro-magnetic energy.

In the so-called "material" world, the wonders of radio, television and facsimile (or picture) transmission are due simply to the modern application of many Cosmic (God) Laws that were formerly unknown. In bringing these electronic MIRACLES to pass electrical waves of energy are sent forth to travel in all directions and these, obeying. another Cosmic Law called "induction," produce a flow of electrons into the antenna of the receiving set, and thus received these delicate electric carrying currents are then converted into audible sounds or into visible pictures.

"Miracles?" We live in an age of 'miracles'. Today, and even as you read these lines, intelligence, messages, and living pictures are being flashed across thousands of miles of space without wires or any other visible connection because man has learned more of the Cosmic Law.

In order that you may realize something about your own destiny in this Cosmic rules "space-field" which we call the Universe, and that you may understand something of your own undreamed powers, let us apply this electronic analogy to your own being. So mark this statement well—your own brain is the most marvelous combined thought-wave transmitter and receiver in the world!

Just as in the marvels of radio and television, thought-waves carrying messages, communications, and subtle influences—are received and translated in your brain cells, your glands and your nerve-plexuses, and travel upon your nerve currents.

Herein you have the rational explanation of telepathy and clairvoyance, both of which are examples of these same Cosmic laws applied to the mental realm. These same Cosmic. laws are the changeless principles behind the phenomena taught in our higher degrees. All around us today you can see the breaking down of the former barriers between the discoveries of modern science and the more ancient teachings of the 'Mystery Schools' whose mission has been entrusted to our Fellowship.

In, material and mechanical fields modern scientists and inventors, who so far have only touched the hem of the garment of Cosmic Laws, are now performing "miracles" every day which would have heralded them as "Gods" if done in the olden days of less advanced "civilizations."

Yes, the world of today is materially a world of wonders, a world transformed by the harnessing of energy through the application of the God (Cosmic) Law in the field of "electricity" alone, which we use as just one example. Think of it—by juggling atoms and directing the electrons of matter modern science can reach around the world seven and one-half times in one second, or blow a huge city into nothingness in the twinkling of an eye! And today man uses the light of stars that are unthinkable distances away in outer space to do his bidding on earth, and from the humblest material he "creates" new chemical compounds and new materials a hundred times more useful than the natural products which they replace.

FAITH—THE CONSCIOUSNESS OF YOUR OWN POWER

And even greater "miracles" await us when we enter into the realm of the psychic world, the world of the mind, spirit and soul. But, just as working wonders in the material world the scientist must work through and with Cosmic Law, just so in bringing to pass the wonders of healing, of abounding success and of joyous happiness to the sick, to the poverty-stricken, or to the sorrowing, we, too, must work through and with the immutable God-Law.

Happily, however, the Cosmic (God) Law which governs these mental, physical and spiritual 'miracles' is not so intricate, not so technical, not so complex as are the material Cosmic Laws of the scientist. Indeed the WAY of these miracles is so plain that the Christ pointed out that "the way-faring man, though a fool, NEED NOT ERR THEREIN."

You will remember that in our last lesson we pointed out how our Subconscious Self cares for your physical body during each minute of your life on earth with masterly skill. In carrying, on these innumerable tasks this Subconscious Self of yours shows at every turn the highest intelligence, and the deepest protective, interest in your welfare physically.

Seeing these proofs of its almost limitless power and of its super-human insight, isn't it logical that you should have unwavering. FAITH in this matchless.Subconscious Self within, for after all, this "Faith" is simply the consciousness of your own powers. It is very certain that you can safely trust this psychic Inner Self in any emergency, in any hour of need or, of danger, for it is the essence of Universal Mind, it is the God-Law made manifest in you.

Remember, this is in no sense a religious or a theological lecture, for now we turn to some of the extremely practical and simple laws by which you can communicate with this Inner Self, and by which you can consciously direct its powers, which are supreme in conducting all the functions of physical life, into the channels of Healing, of Success, and of Happiness in life through the fulfillment of your heritage of the finer things of life.

As we have told you, the cure of disease through mental, psychic, or spiritual methods has been demonstrated throughout the ages since the dawn of history. And the teaching proves that these various forms of drugless or psychic healing have been the result in every age of the use (consciously or unconsciously) of ONE AND, THE SAME POWER.

Further, it is this self-same power, properly directed, that heals ailing pocket-books by attracting fat bank accounts, that bind up the broken-hearted by leading them into the flowering fields of love and romance, and that with its magic wand points the WAY, to happiness through the unfoldment .of that inner joyousness which One of old said "passeth all understanding."

Many theories and many claims have been put forth to explain these seemingly "miraculous" cures by the various exponents of the different methods of healing, many of these theories being entirely religious, ascribing this healing power to God, or to the gods, or to certain shrines or "holy" places, to sacred "relics," while others have described this mystic curative energy as mental, emanating from the MIND in mysterious waves. The one great truth common to all is this; each of these methods, or theories, seems to effect just as many and often just as wonderful cures as the other, in proportion to the numbers of persons treated.

We mention these theories and claims in passing in order to bring out that last truth very clearly for you, for it explains many very puzzling and often seemingly contradictory effects in the field of drugless healing. All of which may suggest to you that it is not the theory, the claim, or even any set method which governs this mysterious healing power, but rather that it is a manifestation of the God-Law subject only to the same laws and the same mental attitudes which rule all other psychic phenomena.

Let us understand quite clearly that all psychic phenomena ("miracles") are simply outer manifestations of the immutable God-Law, and are "miracles" only to those who cannot understand that these seeming. mysteries are but the logical and unvarying results of supplying the conditions and applying the laws which rule in the realm of this unseen energy of the infinite. Strangely enough, these laws are very simple indeed. So simple that we may even overlook them because of their very simplicity. But remember, these simple laws WORK WONDERS!

To prove this truth—the great, the basic, the divinely SIMPLE law governing ALL PSYCHIC PHENOMENA, ALL HEALING, AND EVERY. OTHER MIRACLE OF GOOD FORTUNE comes to us in the direct words, of our Master in White, Christ, when He said to one he healed, "Daughter...thy FAITH hath made the whole (well)."

Significantly, Matthew tells us: "And the woman was made whole (well) from that hour."—Matt: 9:22.

TWO GREATEST FACTORS IN HEALING: SUGGESTION-BELIEF

Suggestion and belief (faith) are the two first and the two greatest factors or elements in all psychic healing, and very true it is that every cure of disease is psychic, simply the restoration of psychic harmony of vibration in the human body.

When the suggestion comes from outside the patient, we may call it "hetero-suggestion," or simply suggestion, but when the suggestion comes from within and is administered by the patient's own mind, that is called "auto-suggestion." But be assured of one unchanging fact the curative power, the efficacy, the wonder-working results of suggestion in any form depend upon FAITH.

Your attainment of the health, the prosperity and the happiness you desire depends entirely upon whether or not your conscious mind shall use its power to command, by power of your self-directed WILL, these transformed conditions. Always remember that any sickness, any failure, or any lack or limitation which you may dread actually have NO OTHER REALITY in your life than you give them by accepting NEGATIVE SUGGESTIONS suggestions which picture the things you fear—as your OWN MENTAL ATTITUDE. SUGGESTION is the invisible power that is forever shaping your life for good or ill, either consciously or without your knowing it. Suggestion moulds our lives every passing hour.

Let us review our former definition of suggestion, so,that we may be very certain that we understand the deep truths which follow in this and later advanced lessons this higher degree of The Illumination.

Reviewing then, you will remember that in your degree we told you that

"Suggestion is the power behind the throne of your destiny." And we gave you this definition, "Suggestion is the introduction into the human mind of any idea, impression or mental picture by the use of any direct or, indirect methods, means or words. Please note carefully that word 'indirect' in this definition. The most powerful forms of suggestion are usually indirect."

Because of its very great importance, let us consider indirect suggestion, for especially in healing (wherein we may encounter doubt) skilful curative suggestion avoids argument and conceals its subtle power to heal, as well as to transform life and action, by this very indirectness. Suggestion in its indirect form works through the association of ideas, in hints, intimations, and through the use of various impressions of a hidden or covert nature. Of course, you understand that suggestion does not depend upon spoken words alone, nor upon gestures, nor indeed upon human contacts always. Often the strongest suggestion is expressed by inanimate objects and by our surroundings—always our environment though silent is eloquent beyond all words in its effect upon our ever receptive minds.

And there is the secret of this subtle yet tremendous power. Because we human beings are so receptive to the numberless suggestions which always and everywhere surround us, this is the great power that silently shapes life for us. Every circumstance,.every event and every experience of your life, together with, each person you meet during your entire life, each is, a: potent suggestion, either good or .bad for you, either upbuilding or destructive, either positive or negative.

We speak of "life's journey"—yes, life IS a journey, and a journey, too, over highways (or low-ways) where: all traffic is directed by suggestion. And you will either travel blindly, or with seeing eyes—and you have chosen to travel with seeing eyes. That is why you are a student. Let us then realize fully that all we shall become, all that we shall possess, all our health, all our success and all our happiness, all of these good things we will attract when we learn to USE the power of suggestion.

We are teaching you how to use this universal power not only that you may gain healing for yourself, or that you may be the bearer of healing to others in this suffering world but so that you may build wisely in the realm of the soul, AND LIVE RICHLY. For you live in a world ruled by suggestion.

MIND AND BODY REALIZE REALITY IN MAGNIFIED THOUGHT

Your mind and your body reach or realize, ultimate reality in this world in magnified thought, but whether that reality shall be the reality of GOOD for you, or the false reality of EVIL in your life, depends entirely upon which thoughts you magnify, the positive or the negative.

This thought has been strikingly expressed in these words by a modern philosopher:

"Both mind and body have their roots piercing back into the ultimate reality—call that reality what you will. Religion calls it God, philosophy calls it the Absolute, science calls it Nature, physics calls it Force, psychology calls it Mind—all names for one and the same entity."

Any thought which you hold in your mind, either positive or negative, is magnified by your acceptance, belief, and by your constant repetition, and is transformed into material existence made into reality.——by the effort, the action, and the work you put forth in obedience to that thought. Thus, the magnified thought has undreamed power and almost unbelievable possibilities in your life.

Are you sick? or failing in business, profession or in domestic affairs? or uncertain, discouraged and unhappy? or. are you -living in an environment or lack and limitation? If so, look within—search your mind. Fear-thoughts, doubt-thoughts, disease-thoughts and inferiority-thoughts—all negative—these are your enemies, these are the disastrous influences which can utterly ruin your life. So, stop talking about "bad luck" or "chance" because these are only meaningless words invented by fools to hide their futility and their ignorance.

In that mighty God-Law which rules all life there are no mistakes, and there are no accidents that can be called "luck." Writes Paul, in The Misunderstood Book, "Be not deceived, for whatsoever a man soweth, that. shall he also reap."

In the garden of your mind the flowers (health, Happiness, prosperity) can grow magnificently, and by your thoughts you can magnify their beauty, a thousand fold, but remember that the weeds (thoughts) of negative suggestion can also grow to giant size and kill every flower of attainment. The richness of your mental garden depends only upon careful selection and constant cultivation, for you alone must reap the harvest, the results.

"It is the mind which makes the body rich, " wrote Shakespeare. We have defined the law of thought attraction for you elsewhere in three words, and we repeat them here: LIKE ATTRACTS LIKE.

Informer lessons you have learned that thought can be directed, thought can be felt, and thought can be measured. So, now we want you to realize in dead earnest that your thought attracts to itself, and to you, those things in the outer, the material world, which are like itself.

Think HEALING (positive) THOUGHTS for.yourself or for one, whom you would bless, then magnify those thoughts by belief (faith) and constant repetition, and you attract to yourself or to your patient the mighty forces of health, of well being and of physical recovery.

For your multiplied healing THOUGHT is the magnet which draws to itself its own likeness, and this is the tremendous, invisible, power which manifests that "miracle" of healing in the physical body. Magnify positive (GOOD) thoughts, and you will bring renewed life, love, laughter and success into your life.

LESSON-No. 13
THE PATHWAY TO HEALTH, WEALTH AND HAPPINESS

Fourth Gateway of The Temple Invisible, Being The Secret Instruction Taught by The Masters in White, Whose Sublime Precepts Are Now Exemplified in These lessons.

The Degree of Illumination

THE SELF YOU LIVE WITH—MASTER HEALER

"Whether we will or no, there is an esoteric doctrine, there is a relative revelation; each man enters into God (the God.-Law) as much as God enters into him, or as Angelus, I think, said, "The eye by which I see God is the same, eye by which He sees me.

"Let mystery have its place in you; do not always be turning up your whole soil with the plow-share of self-exam-ination, but leave a little fallow corner in your heart ready for any seed the winds may bring, and reserve a nook of shadow for the passing birds, keep a place in your heart for the unexpected guests, an altar for the unknown God.

"Then if a bird sing among your branches, do not be too eager to tame it. If you are conscious of something new—thought or feeling, wakening in the depths of your being—do not be in a hurry to let in light upon it, to look at it; let the springing (growing) germ have the protection of being forgotten, hedge it round with quiet, and do not break in upon its darkness; let it take shape and grow, and not a word of your happiness to anyone! Sacred work of Nature as it is, all conception should be enwrapped by the triple veil of modesty. SILENCE and night."—Amiel.

Let us remember that health is but the positive mental attitude of well-being reflected in the physical body. For we have shown you that modern medicine and modern psychology agree that sickness and disease originate in the negative emotions of the individual mental world. In other words, in the beginning these complexes are simply the symptomatic FEARS of sickness and disease, which are given form and seeming reality by the FEAR-EMOTIONS of the mind. If given rulership long enough, however, this seeming reality becomes an actual physical condition.

Actually, it is the emotions that are sick first. We call the victim of fear symptoms or complexes a "hypochondriac," because as long as these symptoms result from complexes this misguided victim is suffering from sickness or disease that exist outside his (or her) body, in the realm of mind.

Often given the most capable doctors do not realize that in such cases they are diagnosing complexes, and so they honestly READ INTO such fears the disease of tuberculosis, angina pectoris, cancer ulcers of the stomach, diseases of the liver, tapeworm, or even appendicitis. For fear is the greatest imitator in the world in the field of symptoms. Actually such fears often actually indicate the emotion-disease of hate, revenge, regret, shame, discouragement, frustration or failure—and often reflect a home life that is a hell on earth, a bankrupt business, or ingrown "inferiority" complexes.

In many cases such negative emotions of fear and failure are more or less cleverly disguised in the martyr's robes of (assumed) sickness or disease, and so the victim tries to claim the "center of the stage." So, disease—complexes may mask the pitiful bid of negative personality for the attention it can never merit!

THE (INNER) SELF YOU LIVE WITH ATTUNED TO COSMIC ENERGY

When you consciously attune the Self you live with in the invisible realm of mind to cosmic energy, then you can manifest that Master Power of Healing that is able to perform "miracles", Your psychic Self is formed from the union of countless millions of cells, and this process blends into one Soul (your Soul) the many, many psychic elements which are materialized in the Personality which is YOU—a personality endowed with present power at this very moment, and with unlimited possibilities. If you will be realize it, your existence is unlimited except for the limitations of your own thinking.

Let us tell you frankly that the Source of this psychic power of the self you live with is beyond our scrutiny, for that Source is THE INFINITE. Simply we say that this is Cosmic Energy—all-pervading and all-wise. For when the wisest of our modern scientists come face to face with this. Unknown Force that lies behind all phenomena they are confronted with the fiat, "Thus far shalt thou go, and no farther."

So material science is halted this side of the psychic world, from thence only the soundless voice of Intuition as taught by the Masters leads the chosen Initiates farther upon THE WAY.

We teach that this Universal Energy manifests according to LAW—and that Cosmic Law we term THE GOD-LAW. For example let us turn again to the phenomena of what we call "electricity." Now what electricity actually IS no man knows, or ever has known. But what electrical workers DO know is what to do and how to do it in order to harness this unknown energy to the purposes of our present civilization.

Even:in the ancient days of our Masters in White who understood and taught many of the wonders of universal Cosmic Energy, they knew that the rays of the sun carried much of this universal and mysterious energy to this earth through the medium of the ether and this caused vibration, radiation, heat, and when certain of its rays acted upon the eye we perceived light. These manifestations of energy which culminate in life, in chemical changes , in marvels and miracles of radiation from the sun have existed on this earth-for millions of years, so the scientists tell us.

As one says in Paths to The Heights: "Exactly as the universal store of Nature from which we draw physical energy does not dictate to us in what form, or in what quantities, or for what purpose we shall use it, so in like manner the Universal Principle (Cosmic Energy) does not dictate the specific conditions under which it is to be employed, but will manifest itself under any condition that we may provide for it by our own mental attitude; and therefore the only limitations to be laid upon our use of it are those arising from THE LAW of love..."

Religion and medicine have seemed to be always rather bound together, which need not seem strange when we remember that "medicine" (the medical profession) grew out of the mental and psychic healing which is interwoven in the history of every great or root religion. So it is that even today there are countless superstitious people who either openly or furtively believe that disease and death are sent upon human beings as punishments for "sin."

Such superstitious souls seem to see no contradiction in picturing a kind and loving "Heavenly Father" as sending the most horrible suffering upon His earthly "children" in order to draw us closer to Him in the bonds of affection! But today only the person of low intelligence is superstitious enough to believe that sickness, suffering and physical ailments are the work of a personal devil, permitted, if not sent, by God so that Satan can prove our frailty.

You, as an advanced Initiate, can now realize fully that no student ever can become a true Psychic Healer of the sick until he, or she, has attained to a working concept of Cosmic Power behind, within and OF his or her own healing thought.

HEALING, LIKE ALCHEMY, TRANSMUTES VIBRATION

Healing, like the ancient art of alchemy, is the process of changing (altering or transmuting) vibrations through Natural (God) Law.

Among The learned men and the advanced thinkers of the fifteenth and sixteenth centuries the teachings of the Ancient Wisdom of The Masters were hidden under the name of ALCHEMY. In those two centuries especially alchemy came to its height as the symbolism of that which is now our Philosophy. As we have pointed out in a previous lesson, in those days the world was ruled by the iron hand of superstition, and the material religions of State and Church chained the minds of the common people in a long, long night of bondage.

Then all scientific knowledge was in its infancy, and to be suspected of such knowledge was to court death at the hands of a "Church" drunk with power. And yet alchemy fortunately flourished, and under a symbolism impossible for the uninitiated to understand, perpetuated the OCCULT SCIENCES OF THE MASTERS. In reality the alchemists were secret Teachers and Masters of the Ancient Truth, they were sages and philosophers who not only never made a single grain of gold, but never even tried such an experiment. They simply pretended to be smelting and distilling secret elixirs in the seclusion of their laboratories, while in reality they were developing their students and initiates in the Great Work of the occult realm—the realm of mind and soul, of psychic phenomena and of physical healing.

Their writings appeared senseless purposely, and were worthless without the secret keys. For no matter what we may think about these Alchemists of the Renaissance, our twentieth century owes more to alchemy than we realize. Modern science inherits such words as crucible, distillation, quintessence, and affinity, among a host of others, to alchemy. Again, these olden alchemists made many discoveries in the material world, thus, modern science owes the discovery of corrosive sublimate, the red oxide of mercury, nitric acid, and nitrate of silver, to Gebir; for the modern telescope, the magic lantern, etc., to Roger Bacon; for the properties of gas to Van Helmont; for laudanum and the idea of the medical. clinic to Paracelsus, etc., etc.

Long, yes, very long before such phenomena as psychic healing, the subconscious powers, hypnotism, magnetism, suggestion and telepathy had a name, these "alchemist"—Masters were teaching them to their students. Such phrases as "the philosopher's stone," the "elixir of youth," or the "transmutation of base metals into gold"—all were just symbols of a deeper Spiritual meaning. The alchemists guarded their knowledge zealously, even as the deeper knowledge is guarded from the outer world today.

We have defined alchemy as being the art or science of transmutation, which is simply the altering of vibrations in accordance with the Laws of Nature, which comprises the majestic God-Law which controls the universe.

Let us ask then, is it man, the Initiate, The Master, or the Avatar, who actually performs this work of changing the rates of vibration? Of course, the answer is No, because man, even tho' he be the Master-Alchemist only uses his superior understanding to reproduce the conditions utilized by Nature to transmure vibration from one visible form to another, and then he depends upon the invisible powers of Nature's laws to work this seeming miracle.

For example, consider the farmer who creates as far as he is able the conditions of soil, seed, and timely planting which Nature requires for the generation of the seed— yet we could hardly say that the farmer produced or grew the crop, he harvests, for it was Nature that really performed this miracle of multiplied growth.

TRAINING STUDENTS TO BE TRUE ALCHEMISTS

Our entire system of lessons and of training is devoted to the one great central purpose of developing our students into the true, modern Alchemists—Alchemists of the Twentieth Century. For the four great purposes behind the study and the practice of the science of the ancient alchemy are the same four great purposes we hold for our Initiates. What were these four great purposes or reasons?

The first great purpose or mission of ancient alchemy was TO PREVENT DISEASE; the second was the HEALING OF DISEASE; the third was TO PROLONG THE HUMAN LIFE (by delaying decay as with the prophets of old); and the fourth purpose was the attainment of material (financial) success, which was symbolized by their cryptic phrase "turning base metals into gold."

And their inner teaching was that all of these purposes were the work of ONE COSMIC POWER— and to confuse their enemies these alchemists of other days gave this power a thousand names, each of which was an enigma, a puzzle without meaning to outsiders. Indeed these ancient alchemists were simply Initiates and Masters in the same Mystic Philosophy of the ages which our modern lessons teach you today as a member of this Fellowship. In proof that this mystic philosophy was a symbolism shadowing forth the truths we are teaching today, we quote this passage from the book, "Alchemists and Adepts," by Magre:

"History records many men who were able to make gold. But this was only the first stage of the secret. The second gave the means of healing physical illnesses through the same agent which produced transmutation. To reach this state, a higher intelligence and a more complete disinterestedness were necessary. The third state was accessible only to a very few

"Just as the molecules of metals are transformed under great increase of temperature, so the emotional elements in human nature undergo AN INCREASED INTENSITY OF VIBRATIONS which transform them and make them spiritual. In this third stage the secret of 'the philosopher's stone' enabled a man's soul to attain unity with the divine spirit. The laws of Nature are alike for that which is above and for that which is below. Nature changes according to an ideal.

"Gold is the perfection of terrestrial substances, and it is to produce gold that minerals evolve. The human body is the model of the animal kingdom...The emotional substance of the soul strives, through the filter of the senses, to transform itself into spirit and to return to unity with the DIVINE."

The greatest proof that these ancient alchemists were mystic philosophers who perpetuated the Ancient Wisdom in their day, we find in the ancient archives which record that their occult science combined every department of life, of healing, of mind-development, and of material success. From the understanding which we have gained of their symbolism, we learn that the alchemical teachings of mysticism, philosophy, science, religion, healing, literature, music and art—that in all. of these the alchemist told the story of the high destiny of the Soul, and THE WAY to attain to that divine destiny,

SPIRITUAL GOD-LAW FOUNDATION OF THE WORLD

The symbolic teachings of the alchemists is the same Divine Truth that we are teaching in the eternal now— and that is that the Spiritual God Law (Cosmic Mind—Energy) is the foundation of the world.

So the medieval alchemists were teaching that after having passed through the "crucible of fire" or human suffering, that soul which emerged was the refined and purified "gold"—a divinely previous treasure. The following alchemical aphorisms we quote from the little-known occult archives—compare them with our precepts:

"The greatest of all facts is the fact of consciousness. Apart from consciousness there is chaos...Experience becomes clearer in relation to how we reason about it and classify it.."

"Mind-consciousness is man's greatest power for good or evil... Evil is of the mind. Having mind we do not need to depend upon the instincts in choosing."

"...Of the beginning and the end no one knows anything, but this we know of the NOW: that if we be patient in the study of things present, we shall in time know things eternal. If you ask about Creation, the answer is NOW, but at this moment (of consciousness) the world comes into being; and if you ask about the last day, it is NOW...As the sun rises in one land, it sets in another."

"Life is Change, for Change is this: that the present moment is both beginning and end, and that the world is ever becoming new, just as it is ever growing old... for past and future are but an expansion of the present, while the present is the moving image of the Eternal."

"The wonder of life is this: that in every moment is the whole of Time, and a perpetual recreation of the World."

"From this we see that if we go forward, holding fast to nothing, nothing shall then hold us back from attainment."

"Our present existence (life) is of the greatest importances. If we could remember a previous incarnation, it would be of a different person in different circumstance."

"Suffering is neither a curse or a blessing save as a particular organism (being) reacts to it."

So, now you can readily realize that this great Fellowship of which we are Members and Initiates, is not Alchemy, it is not psychic healing, nor Philosophy, nor Science, nor Hermeticism, nor Metaphysics—no, this universal Fellowship is not any ONE of these—IT IS ALL OF THEM!

Hermes himself was the first Alchemical Master recorded in the outer history of the ages, and it was Hermes who first gave us that golden precept: As above, so below."

THE VOICE OF INFINITE DIVINE MIND

Some wise man once said, "Man has an apparently incurable determination to attempt solutions of problems without knowledge." How true it is that the amount of knowledge or the degree of wisdom a man possesses makes all the difference in the world, not only in solving problems but also IN LIVING THE LIFE TRIUMPHANT.

And one further thing is very certain—granted the knowledge of the Initiate, then the errors, the mistakes and the failures in life will almost entirely vanish before the light of our knowledge of, and our reliance upon, INTUITION—for while it comes to us as that "still small voice" within, sometimes sensed as an inner urge, still it is the voice of Infinite Divine Mind. And this is the Mind universal that knows all things.

But men and women, sometimes even after they have become Initiates, often fail to heed that divine inner voice, and you may well ask, WHY? Because human beings are often stubborn, willful, and often have not developed sufficiently to recognize the voice of true Intuition. Men and women are very often too hasty, too impulsive, and so base their decisions upon outer or objective "reasoning." They mistake their emotions and their attempts to rationalize (to justify Self) for that divine Inner Urge. Such people make the mistake of thinking that they can do what they will to do without consulting the Subconscious Mind—that Mind which attunes to the wisdom of the Infinite.

The great mission of our teachings is to reunite each student with the divine purpose which the Infinite Mind holds for that individual student when he or she shall have advanced to the sublime degree of Master.

For each sincere student is a brother or a sister in THE DIVINE WAY along which we journey together to ever higher and greater cycles of life. And every true student comes to have an awareness, a conscious knowledge of the higher destiny which awaits him or her—this higher, this secret goal.

So we are striving to teach you to know that, within human reservations, the only limitations, draw-backs or frustrations which seem to hold you back are those which YOU impose upon yourself! Right now we want you to stop looking upon yourself as an inferior, handicapped or limited person, because when the REALITY within shines forth your life can be glorious and radiant.

Over and over, and time and again, you have heard those words of the ancient Greek philosopher parrot-ted—"KNOW THYSELF." And a more sublime admonition never fell from human lips. BUT to "know thyself" does NOT mean that you are to merely learn about the outer, the physical, the material self.

For instance, which do you think is true—IS man a body with a SOUL, or do you realize that MAN IS A <u>SOUL with a body</u>?

Of course, those who think that man is a BODY with a soul hold the materialists' view point, and all things to them are both physical, limited, mortal.

We believe and teach, in agreement with the Scriptural concept, that man is forever and eternally a "living Soul," and that this human body is but the (temporary) "temple of the Soul." We believe and teach further that man is ONE (attuned to) INFINITE CREATIVE MIND, and as such is the heir of creative power, creative truth and creative Mind.

So would it not be foolish indeed for you to be forever seeking outside of yourself for the very things which you can find only WITHIN yourself ? Remember how vain and hopeless this search was for you in the days of the past. Now those truths which were then shrouded from you by mystery have become simple and clear to you.

Simply stated, then, before we can impart health to others, we must within; ourselves BE the spirit of Healing; before we can find love, we must first BE love; before we can find wealth, we must first BE the consciousness of riches; before we can demonstrate power, and harmony, and happiness, we must first BE the living, breathing manifestation of power; and harmony, and of happiness.

Of course, when any man thinks of himself, as so many do, as being but a poor, human being (a weak worm of the dust"), doomed to be the victim of "circumstances," constantly hounded by "fate" or "bad luck", that man is dead to the Voice within, and forever blind to the healing, the renewing, and the glorifying powers within himself.

Yes, YOU are a living Soul—Spirit—and everything around you is subject to the Spiritual Power of the ineffable God-Law, and that is why you can change the vibrations of all so-called "matter" in your own personal world BY THE POWER OF YOUR MIND, when that power is developed and focused.

This means that you—the Divine YOU—are the Creator in your own personal world, and you as the directing and controlling Master-Mind scan so change the vibrations within your own body as to attract "whatsoever things ye desire."

THE PATHWAY TO HEALTH, WEALTH AND HAPPINESS

Fourth Gateway of The Temple Invisible, Being The Secret Instruction Taught by The Masters in White, Whose Sublime Precepts Are Now Exemplified in these lessons.

The Degree of Illumination

"I TOUCH, BUT GOD HEALETH!"—MIRACLE-POWER

The most beautiful poem there is, is life—life which discerns its own story in the making, in which inspiration and self-consciousness go together and help each other, life which knows itself to be the world in little, a repetition in miniature of the divine universal poem. Yes, be man; that is to say, be Nature, be Spirits, be the image of God, be what is greatest, most beautiful, most lofty in all the spheres of being, be infinite Will and Idea, a reproduction of the Great Whole...

"Be humble, devout, SILENT, that so thou mayest hear within the depths of thyself the subtle and profound Voice; be spiritual and pure, that so thou mayest have communion with Pure Spirit. Withdraw thyself often into the sanctuary of thy inmost consciousness...that so thou mayest free thyself from space, time, matter."—Amiel.

The ether fairly teems with the vibrating thoughts of by-gone ages, and all that is necessary to become possessed of this store of universal knowledge is to become sensitive to ether vibrations and learn how to translate them into ordinary language.

"The conscious mind is the balance wheel; it is the regulator which determines the rapidity and character of vital action.

"The Subconscious is able to do many marvelous things and does them even when the conscious mind is poorly calculated to give wise direction; but its action is not uniform and balanced and persistent." - Leavitt.

Let us explain the latter words of this quotation by saying that any lack of uniformity, or of balance, or of persistence in the action of the Subconscious mind is due to the fact that these same qualities or powers have not been developed in the Conscious Mind.

Our ancient teaching that man is a three-fold being is in agreement with the more recent Christian faith of our present 'civilization' in this country. It was St. Paul who expressed this concept in the words, "body, soul, and spirit." But it was the poet Browning who more beautifully pictured the same belief in these eloquent word.

"WHAT DOES, WHAT KNOWS, WHAT IS, THREE SOULS (ENTITIES) ONE MAN"

Our mission is to demonstrate (to manifest) rather than to merely believe in the reality of the presence in every normal man and woman of the Divine, the Infinite, whether you call that divine indwelling the Spirit, the Soul, or the Inner or the Higher Self. This tremendous realization is not something to be imposed upon the modern thinker by any outer priestly authority, nor by the old-time "revival" methods of religious frenzy, but instead by the actual development of an inner miracle-power.

It is self-evident that even the more or less purely FIFTH RACE peoples who inhabit those parts of the earth controlled by the Western civilization have not yet reached the zenith of either human or racial evolution. As you probably know the evolution of the root races of humanity on this earth has progressed in great cycles of time, many of these cycles measuring thousands of years. In the distant time of beginnings the Lemurian Age according to the divine plan was devoted to the development and the perfecting of the material physical body as the habitation of the human life-vibrations, and to the evolving of consciousness.

When they had served their purpose, Lemurian forms and culture disappeared, but the human-life-wave vibrations were incarnated anew during the Atlantean Cycle, wherein new developments were born of new experiences. Apparently the good during the Atlantean Cycle was to complete the emotional side of mans nature, through emotional reactions developing still higher states of consciousness.

This great Fifth Race, which composes our Western civilization, has achieved a marvelous degree of achievement along mechanical and material lines, and great powers of concentration and a marvelous healing power over the functions of the human body. For in this undisputed heir to the ancient Mystery Schools, the Spiritual Realities are uniformly taught and held, and our mental and spiritual powers are directed to concentration and to meditation, and to deep philosophical and metaphysical studies. And all this with the same great objective as in ancient times— that we may train and develop HEALERS, LEADERS AND MASTERS, who in turn will help to guide the blind and suffering masses in the WAY of health, the WAY of success and the WAY of happiness.

"I TOUCH, BUT GOD HEALETH"

Certain very old archives witness that Aesculapius (the "father of medicine") himself really performed his cures of disease principally by working through the FAITH of his patients. So we have in like manner the story of "the royal touch" in Britain, where for many hundreds of years the English people actually believed that their ruler or sovereign possessed the mystic power to cure disease, especially scrofula ("King's evil" or Syphilis) just by the touch of his royal hand.

Edward, The Confessor, was the first to practice this peculiar but simple form of healing in England, according to William of Malmsbury. There is abundant proof that this healing practice was in use in Britain in the thirteenth century. And in the fifteenth century, during the reign of Edward IV, a learned English legal writer, Sir John Fortescue by name, wrote of the gift of healing as possessed by the kings of England "from time immemorial." Sir John ascribes this royal gift of healing to the unction imparted to the kingly or queenly hands during the ceremony of coronation!

But the striking thing is the widespread and the implicit FAITH in this gift of royal healing held by the English people—actually, so deep was this belief that there was a regular ritual in the Book of Common Prayer (Episcopalian) for the proper performance of this ceremonial healing. According to the historical accounts of those times in England, all those victims of disease or sickness who sought this royal healing were introduced by a bishop or other church official, suitable prayers were intoned, and suggestion was freely used to arouse a firm FAITH that the curative power of God was to be made manifest in the touch of the royal hand. As he laid his hand lightly upon each sufferer the king repeated these words—"I touch, but God healeth."

English history further records that Queen Elizabeth often made personal appearances before her believing subjects in this role of royal healer, and that the ruling Stuarts were firm believers in their mysterious royal powers of healing, and that they often put these powers on public exhibition.

And it was Edward I, of England, you will remember, whom Shakespeare flattered in "Macbeth, " by those lines which record not only how he healed the sick by his royal touch, but that King Edward has also bequeathed "the healing benediction" to all who should succeed him upon the throne.

This practice of royal ceremonial healing was carried on regularly by both Charles I and Charles II, of England, and history tells us that this practice reached the height of its popularity during the reign of Charles II, and this Charles, known as the "Merry Monarchs," extended his healing touch to some 92,107 sick or diseased people during his rule, according to Macaulay. He tells us that the largest number so treated was in the year 1684.

In order to get the picture clearly, let us remember that in those days "theology" (organized religion) and "medicine" were as always closely united, but judged in the light of today both were rather crude, and not too far removed from the "medicine man", from witchcraft, nor from priest-craft! In those days kings ruled by "divine right," and the people were taught to believe themselves to be simply helpless pawns in the hands of an often irascible and angry God! To the dim minds of the multitude it was perfectly plausible that sickness, suffering; disease and death were either visited upon them directly by this fearsome God, or were permitted by Him so that the Devil, as with Job, could test their endurance.

PSYCHIC HEALING CONDITIONED BY OUR CONCEPT OF GOD

From the most ancient days the "miracles" of psychic, spiritual, mental and occult healing, as well as the marvelous "religious" cures that history records, all have been based upon and conditioned by the concept of the ruling deity, no matter by what name that deity (god) was called. That explains why healing and religion have always been inseparable companions. And also, by the way, that is why "theology" and "medicine" are in such a hopeless tangle today - and we do mean hopeless.

Psychic healing—by whatever name it is known—is measured and conditioned in its effectiveness absolutely by our concept of God. Just what does that statement mean? It simply means this, that in order to develop the true "gift" of psychic healing one must first of all clearly conceive the mystic power that vibrates within him, through him and from him. The Healer must perceive that Power is being invisible, unknowable, all-pres-ent, inexhaustible and limitless when directed by focused WILL and unwavering FAITH.

That omnipotent Presence, that Supreme Power, WE call GOD. An intelligent study of psychic healing, as we teach it, takes the Initiate into the field of cosmic phenomena, and in this field of tremendous truths we must rise far above the narrow, outworn conceptions of the cruel, changeable, all-too-human tribal god pictured by the ancient Jewish mind under various names that are now all translated into the one title of "GOD."

Let us rather conceive God—the true Supreme Being—as Power-Law personified—unthinkable Energy-Intelligence—Power-Law unchanging, eternal, and vibrating in every manifestation of life upon earth, or throughout the universe. This concept of the Supreme Being we often refer to as the immutable God-LAW. This Supreme Intelligence this God-Power-Law not only is with you always, but you yourself are a living, breathing, vibrating expression of this Divinity. But for you to be able to draw upon this inexhaustible Power, to work with this Divine Self, and to direct its incomparable energy to the healing of disease, or to attracting wealth, or to attaining happiness, to do this you must first be conscious of your essential UNITY WITH THE INFINITE.

Once you clearly conceive yourself to be ONE WITH GOD—.yourself an expression of THE DIVINE— then your old, false, and fear-filled notions about sickness and disease, and your ideas about their origin and their cure give way to truth.

Have you vaguely pictured God as a huge, mysterious, fearsome tyrant, like unto some greatly magnified human form, sitting amid a blaze of unearthly light upon a great white throne, stern, angry, austere—in fact, as being at times unutterably cruel?

Is this the picture that orthodox "religion" or churches steeped in superstition have imprinted upon your mind, perhaps in the helpless days of childhood?

In the cold light of reason, tell us, are not such horrible notions of an anthropomorphic God, an avenging Deity chasing hapless souls into a "hell" of eternal torture, are not these the fear-filled nightmares of the infancy of the human race?

GOD is none of these—for God is the Great Absolute, the Abiding Over-Soul, the Love and the LAW that inspire Universal Energy. He is the Divine Mind that inspires YOU.

GOD speaks in the silent intuitions of YOUR Soul.

All is Life, Spirit dwells in Life—"God is Spirit."

PSYCHIC HEALER A "DOCTOR OF MINDS"

Each true psychic healer is first, last and at all times truly a "doctor of minds." For sickness and disease originate in the mind.

And yet we shall perhaps shock the tender sensibilities of many unthinking people when we speak of ministering to the sick minds and to misdirected emotions first, and so eliminate the cause of the ailment from its center, and depending upon Nature then to adjust the body to the restored mental rhythm of health.

For, sad to say, we find that all too few medical "doctors" have advanced mentally far beyond the "bewhiskered" pretensions of the 1880's,. or even much beyond the medical pose of the "gay 90's!" Then doctors were in.reality little more than "medicine men," whose business it was to dose sick bodies with drugs.

If you think that we have advanced very far along the pathway to new horizons in treating sickness and disease, go back with us to those "good old days" of just a few years ago when the doctor was little more than a prescriber of pills, an injector of "serums." (today we call them "shots"), or a dealer in symptoms.

Frankly, is not the medical procedure up to today pretty much the same as in those yesteryears? If your symptoms appear to indicate that there is something seriously wrong within your body, doesn't the medical man of today confine you to bed, advising that you "need rest and quiet, NO excitement, NO intoxicants, and NO heavy meals!" Of course, unless you are an utter fool, you certainly should know, that Nature is demanding these simple conditions for her own remedial work.

But even as in the days of old, your doctor even now must needs provide suitable "atmosphere" (showmanship) in order to satisfy your mental demand that something be done—and quick. So the good doctor leaves some colored or sugar-coated pills or tablets, or some vari-colored capsules, or he injects some strange serum into you which is gravely claimed to annihilate certain germs, microbes, or bacteria, inside your body, and then writes a prescription in scholarly Latin (which, is "Greek" to you), and departs.

Now is this first "treatment" fails, another is administered, and another and another, and on and on until either your money runs out, or until out of a thousand drugs at his disposal, the doctor may find one which is mild enough to permit Nature to heal your sickness. Whereupon the good doctor is credited with another "cure."

But suppose the good doctor guesses wrongly, and some drug is administered which thwarts Nature's strenuous efforts to restore life's rhythm within your body, and she gives up in despair. Is the good doctor ever credited with a death? Think that question over with care.

While many doctors have never risen to,the heights of mystical understanding where they are entitled to that prouder title of physician, yet many others are advancing into the sphere of the mystical science of healing where they are beginning to sense the tremendous importance of adjusting (healing) the MIND of the patient first, and trusting the mighty power of Nature to harmonize the body to the vibrant rhythm of a mind restored to abounding health. For should the bodily symptoms of disease be suppressed by some pain-paralyzing drug, with any healing of the mental self that is sick, dangerous complications would follow later.

TODAY'S ADVANCED PHYSICIANS AND MENTAL THERAPY

The simple truth is that today's advanced physicians are depending more and more upon mental therapy, and are abandoning the doubtful dependence upon copious drafts of drugs which were the stock in trade of the outdated "doctors" of yesteryears. Leaving our own doctrines concerning health for a few minutes, we find that in 1943 Dr. Bela Mittlemann and Dr. Harold G. Wolff reported that they conducted certain experiments which prove beyond question that peptic ulcers are caused by negative emotions of the mind.

Further, the report of these eminent medical authorities claims that there is an amazing connection between the states of the mind and the gastric. juices. These experiments confirm our teachings that fear, anger, worry, jealousy, anxiety, etc., (the negative emotions or mental attitudes), that all of these directly affect the digestive processes harmfully, increasing the gastric secretions and causing excessive acidity.

Turning to an article by another medical authority in the magazine "Fortune," we find these significant words:

"Medical and surgical treatment is generally only incidental to the mental therapy (mental healing) more and more widely applied today. Until the underlying PSYCHIC CAUSES of the trouble are remedied there can be little hope in the chronic cases of doing much more. than easing the discomfort temporarily."

And Dr. Walter C. Alvarez, of the Mayo Clinic, says—"If the patient is worrisome (worried) and temperamental, operation is probably useless."

Healthy men and women are happy men and women. Harmony and health of MIND provides the most necessary condition for the higher understanding of the deeper psychic and spiritual phases of life, as we teach them.

Psychic Healing (mental therapy) has always been a most important and practical part of the great doctrine, even as it was in our parent bodies, the Mystery Schools of the days of the Nazarite Master in White, Christ.Throughout the ages the "miracles" of The Masters have proven beyond the shadow of a doubt the tremendous healing importance of mental adjustment. Nor do we confine the effective healing effects of the mind to the stomach or to the cure of ulcers.

Your MIND not only has power to affect your stomach and your digestion, but when you have developed the power of focusing your mind by the direction of your WILL, then at your command your mind can and will affect all and every part of your body. Would you like to prove this? Then all you need to do is to center your thoughts for two or three minutes on any particular part of your body, and if your thoughts are positive (happy) very soon you will become fully aware of reactions that are comforting, stimulating and healthful. Try it.

So now it becomes very easy for us to understand how negative or sick emotions, such as hatred, fears and worries, can and do call down upon us a host of diseases, physical inharmony, high or low blood pressure, and countless nervous ailments. Barring contagious diseases, virus poisons, and a few other outer diseases, no man or woman becomes sick without first either consciously or unconsciously becoming the victim of negative mental attitudes, or in other words, negative thought-habits.

NATURE PLAYS NO FAVORITES

Let us clearly understand right here, and now that Nature plays no favorites. She does not say to one child at birth: "Now you are doomed to a life of misery, to be filled with fear, and to, fail in all that you undertake, and you are fated to be a weak and sickly "nervous wreck;" or to another child: "Now I have chosen you to be strong, and healthy, and happy, and to be showered with the world's choicest gifts, and I bless you with success in every effort you make!"

So, never say to yourself, "I wish I had been born with a different temperament, or that I had a personality like so-and-so!"

Instead of such vain and wishful thinking, strive to use the powers you have, study to gain the understanding of your own personality, and how to develop that personality which is YOU intelligently, and it is entirely possible for you to reach to heights of health, of success and of happiness that this person whom you now envy could never reach.

Life will be what YOU make it. Mastering your own "destiny" is simply a matter of learning and understand-ing,.just what to do with the unconscious powers you now have, and DOING...being willing to pay the price in study, in deed and in ACTION.

THOUGHT, then, is THE ONE GREAT POWER for either good or evil, for either sickness or healing, for either success or failure, for either discontent or happiness in YOUR LIFE. Every physical act of yours is preceded by thought. Everything you build in this life, must be fashioned by your thinking. And your thoughts radiate into other lives. Master thought—AND YOU ARE MASTER!

LESSON No. 15
THE PATHWAY TO HEALTH, WEALTH AND HAPPINESS

Fourth Gateway of The Temple Invisible, Being The Secret Instruction Taught by The Masters in White, Whose Sublime Precepts Are Now Exemplified in these lessons.

The Degree of Illumination

FAITH HEALS DISEASE—THOUGHT RULES YOUR WORLD

Thought rules your own personal world, just as it rules the world of everybody else, and faith (belief imaged in thought) heals disease. Illustrating this great truth we quote the following from, a work on Psychology by a Yale professor, from the book "As Ye Will:"

"Warts have been charmed away by medicine which could have had only a mental effect. 'Dr. Tuke gives many cases of patients cured of rheumatism by rubbing them with a certain substance declared to possess magic power. The material in some cases was metal; in others, wood; in still others, wax. He also recites the case of a very intelligent officer who had vainly taken powerful remedies to cure cramps in the stomach. Then he was told that on the next attack, he would be put under a medicine which was generally believed to be most effective, but which was rarely used." When the cramps came on again, a powder containing four grains of round biscuit was administered every seven minutes, and while the greatest anxiety was expressed (within the hearing of the patient) lest too much be given. Half drachm doses of bismuth had never produced the same relief in less than three hours. For four successive times did the same kind of attack occur, and four times it was met by the same remedy, and with like success.'

A house surgeon in a French hospital experimented with one hundred patients, giving them sugared water. Then, with a great show of fear, he pretended that he had made a mistake, and had given them an emetic, instead of the proper medicine. Dr.

Tuke says: "The result may be easily anticipated by those who can estimate the influence of the imagination (imaged faith). No fewer than 80, four-fifths, were unmistakably sick."

We have a well authenticated case of a butcher, who, while trying to hang up a heavy piece of meat, slipped and was himself caught by the arm upon the hook. When he was taken to a surgeon the butcher said he was suffering so much that he could not endure the removal of his coat; the sleeve must be cut off. When this was done it was found that the hook had passed through his clothing close to the skin, but had not even <u>scratched it</u>."

Here we have three or four examples of the vivid effect of strong suggestions. There is a well-known saying or axiom among scientific students of mental phenomena: "Refuse to express a passion (an emotion, a fear, or a mental evil), and it dies." And this gives us a master Key to our own control over a host of the ailments which afflict the unwary and the unwise. So it is just as true that if we refuse to live an affirmation, a suggestion, or a fear, each will in time vanish. Only by living, and so proving our faith (belief) in them, do we give reality to any mental attitude.

You will agree, I am sure, that happy moods help to restore physical health. So, this being true, is it not simple common sense for every one of us to cultivate glad and happy feelings?

ENERGY TRANSFORMS MATTER—THOUGHT-ESSENCE HEALS

Have you tried the methods and the directions of self-appointed "teachers" of "the occult" and found them useless and uncertain? Have you followed faithfully the dictates of some man-made church in vain, and have you listened for the voice of some Elijah-like prophet, and it came not? And did you not once feel, after these vain experiences, like one who stood alone upon a desert island, and saw only darkness all around you?

If so, each such experience was but a prelude to your preparation for The Illumination. And the proof that you are in truth an Initiate ready for that Illumination is the sound in your thought-world of a Voice which seems to say "Now, Call upon me, for I am that Celestial Self, the Voice of our Soul, I am our Thought-Energy, I transform the world, and I HEAL DISEASE.

So that Celestial Self—the Master of Energy—stands before you as your servant, and with bowed head and folded wings, awaiting only your COMMAND to go forth upon missions which prove that you are the Master of your personal world, once you have learned to direct the Energy that transforms matter, and how to focus the thought-essence which heals "all manner of disease."

In the field of natural phenomena, the ancient Masters who have handed down to us the hidden teachings of our Order devoted great time and study to matter and its physical composition, and to the laws which govern it. Many of their. discoveries of thousands of years ago have been re-discovered by modern scientists.

One of the most vital discoveries of these ancient Masters was that all matters, whether animate or inanimate, is alive and vibrating with pulsating ENERGY, and that this energy is the CAUSE behind all matter. This universal energy, which we describe as electrical in its nature, is in eternal vibration, and the rate of that vibration is governed by the form in which matter manifests.

For instance, if you combine two hydrogen atoms, with one oxygen atom you create or form water, which has an entirely different rate of vibration than either hydrogen or oxygen.

Because this universal energy which composes matter and vibrates in all matter is electrical, there is an "electrical field" surrounding every form of matter. The strength of this magnetic "field" depends upon the vibra-tion-rate of the form of the matter which it surrounds. So these magnetic "fields" '(or fields of influence) differ greatly. Various sensitive instruments can now detect and measure these various magnetic fields.

Some of these modern instruments can detect both earth rays and cosmic rays. For example, if you should bring a vial of radium active salts into its area of influence, such an instrument will visibly record the radio-like waves given off or sent forth by the radium salts. Radium, of course, has the highest atomic count of all the elements known to man and so it has the strongest electrical field..

In, passing we might add that the vibration rate of matter is so high that it is in the same scale as radio waves, but it is tremendously higher in frequency than any man-made radio waves. (STATIC)

For many years men of science have been deeply interested in these electrical properties of matter, and the only, thing that is "new" about the discoveries of science as to the "mysteries" of the atom is simply the method of harnessing its unthinkable power.

COSMIC ENERGY MANIFESTS IN MATTER

Scientists now agree that the basic and universal essence is energy. Being that is, LIFE—is but one expression of energy, because Being emnages from the flow of energy. Movement we recognize as a primary factor of energy—all motion is simply energy becoming manifest. Disease, sickness, and suffering are the direct results of misdirected energy, and again this same energy focused and guided by intelligence and will is the one great healing force in this material world.

And it is equally true that poverty, limitations, failure and negative or repellent personalities are likewise the products of energy, misguided energy.

Energy, then, gives rise to the law of change, because this basic movement (constant motion) which manifests energy is a constant variant, and this consists of cycles which mark the flow of force (energy) away from and back to a central point. So each human being forms one of these central points from which depart and return these currents of energy. This flow of energy we perceive, according to the Secret Wisdom of our Masters in White, as occurring in alternate cycles—cycles of attraction and of repulsion.

The "cycle of attraction" denotes this current of energy (or power) flowing irresistibly back to the unit-point, or person, and bringing with it all things which thought directs it to bring, while the "cycle of repulsion" is this same powerful current flowing forth, outward, and away from its unit-point. This unit-point, in the case of human beings, is of course the Inner Self—the Mind—or Soul-Self.

So, according to the ancient God-Law, the conscious development and the purposeful direction of these cycles of energy so greatly increases their power, and at the same time adds to the length (the reaching-out influence) of each cycle. Thus cosmic energy manifests in matter—and that energy is so tremendous that the human mind cannot measure it.

So now we understand that all of life, all of creation, and all of existence falls into cycles, either short or long, either small or great. For example, an atom may be formed in a single instant, while the growth, the development and the life" span of a human body may require a cycle many years in length. Thus. the cycle of a human body is limited to the length of the cycle during which consciousness makes that body its "temple." While the life-cycle of any certain human body is today limited, let us remember that the cycle of the Mind-Soul-Spirit (what we call consciousness) is illimitable, endless, eternal—each incarnation is but an incident in its progression or in its retrogression, as the case may be.

We spoke of the different length of cycles. Picture the cycle of the explosion of a grain of gunpowder, or the terrific explosion of an atomic blast, and you are picturing a cycle which can last but a tiny fraction .of a second. Now picture the growth of a rose bush, the slow developing bud,. and finally the full-blown rose, and you are picturing a cycle which takes many weeks. Now in your mind's eye see the picture of the growth of a star, its development into a planet, its slow deterioration, and its final disintegration, and you have mentally reviewed a cycle lasting perhaps a thousand million years!

Basically universal energy is unrestricted, and if not directed and controlled it is highly dangerous and unstable, so we must provide definite channels for its expression through us and in our lives, or in seeking expression this cosmic energy will run wild, and will drag us backward swiftly down the spiral of retrogression into the primitive nether-worlds. Compare the indwelling spirit and mind of a Buddha with those of Nero, or compare the indwelling Spirit and Mind of a Christ with those of a Hitler!

Crile, Otto Glasser and Daniel P. Quiring, working in collaboration, had discovered that all of the human body is electrically negative, but that the brain and nervous system are electrically positive. According to their report the negatively charged red corpuscles, of which there are some three trillions, as they travel through the 62,000 miles of capillaries transfer a part of this negative current of electricity to the tissues of the body. At the same time the brain and nervous systems of the body are drawing their positive electrical charge constantly from the oxygen. Thus again we see modern medical research proving the ageless truth taught by our ancient Masters about the positive and negative currents of Spirit Energy infusing the material elements of the physical body with Life.

This Cosmic-Spirit-Energy vibrating invisibly in the very air we breath imparts vital life force and consciousness to the blood cells as they course through the tissue-like membranes of the lungs. So this ever-renewing supply of Spirit-Life-Energy charges them with the electrical positive polarity required to.carry on the processes of metabolism in the human body.

Thus the electronic: currents (electrical nerve energy) which these eminent doctors found to be positive in the brain and nervous systems and negative in the further or peripheral parts of the body is in reality the force generated by the chemical action of these currents upon the foods assimilated in the corpuscles of the blood stream.

Now we. see how this 'human battery system is supplied with its positive and negative electronic energy, and it is upon this invisible force that all impressions to and from the psychic centers, every reaction of the nervous systems, and every movement or activity of the body depends.

Hidden within these electronic energies of the brain and the nervous system of every man and of every woman, there vibrates the Psycho-Spiritual Self, and it is through the recognition and the development of this Greater Self that the Initiates, the Masters, the Illumined Ones, attune themselves with the tremendous Cosmic powers of the, universal ether. And it is this harmony with these occult forces which rewards the faithful with healing, with success and prosperity, and with happiness.

Some rather recent startling applications of the electrical forces of the erstwhile rather neglected "atom" to the mass destruction of human life have called the attention of mankind to the tremendous "aliveness," of the 'electrical properties of matter. Present-day scientists now recognize that every particle of matter is surrounded by its own electrical field, which they now refer to as its "magnetic aura."

"EVERY BIT OF MATTER EMITS RADIO WAVES"

As we have pointed out before, is recent years our modern scientists are RE-discovering parts of the Ancient Wisdom. As a further illustration of this fact, we quote the following significant dispatch by the Associated Press which appeared in various newspapers throughout the nation in 1939, we believe, under different headings, as follows:

"ATOM MAY GIVE "OOMPH." "SECRET OF PERSONAL ATTRACTION IS BELIEVED FOUND." "TELEPATHY AND THE 'FEELING' OF PRESENCE OF OTHERS,"..."POSSIBLY SOLVED BY PROOF THAT ALL

MATTER EMITS WAVES."

"Columbus, Ohio, December 30.—The American Association for The Advancement of Science today awarded its highest commendation and a prize of $1,000.00 to Dr. I.I. Rabi, of Columbia University, for his report on the radio frequencies of atoms and molecules.

"Dr Rabi proved for the first time(?) that every, bit of matter emits radio waves. This finding, which is at present only of theoretical interest may, prove to be one of the most fundamental discoveries of science, ranking with the finding of X-Rays by Wilherlm Conrad Roentgen, or the discovery of radium by the Curies.

"Dr. Rabi and his colleagues, Dr. P. Kusch and Dr. S. Millman, proved for the first time (?) that every particle of matter emits radio waves in the same way that radium emits particles of matter (energy) useful in the treatment of cancer and other diseases.

Scientists who have studied Dr. Rabi's report said it furnishes for the first time (?) an explanation of such things as telepathy, heretofore a quasi-scientific phenomena, and the 'feeling' that someone else is approaching in a dark room. It also may prove the source of attraction or repulsion between individuals, since all the atoms of the body are continually broadcasting weak but detectable radio waves.

"Dr. Rabi's work has opened a way of measuring such subtle properties of atoms and molecules as the magnetism of their component parts a hundred times more accurately than was possible by any instrument available up to the present time, the committee declared.

"Of even greater significance to the scientists, the committee added, is the fact that the Columbia scientist's work proves that the nucleus of the atom is a magnet and that "there are no forces between the nucleus and the electrons because of the spinning of the electrons around the nucleus."

Remember, it was only five years after this report was published widely in our newspapers that American scientists had learned how to harness and how to unleash a part of the terrific energy of the atoms of matter in the death-dealing "atomic bomb!"

Outside the followers"of our teachings, where are the Masters, the Healers or the Leaders who are demonstrating and harnessing that more Sublime Power behind atomic force, and who outside our fold are focusing this greater power to cure the ills of mankind?

Echo answers, Where? and echo answers, Who?

For we alone are teaching and demonstrating plainly and clearly that cosmic consciousness is the vital essence of God, and that this GOD-ESSENCE (consciousness of God) is the Divine Over-Soul vibrating through the entire universe, and that your Soul, and the Soul of every other human being, are forever linked by eternal life-forces TO THE INFINITE, because each Soul is (consciously or unconsciously) one with—a part of— the Divine Over-Soul.

As we begin to perceive something of the unthinkable force imprisoned in each atom of matter, can we not also even faintly conceive that this Cosmic Universe is simply a tremendous. unity conceived and created in the Divine Intelligence of the Infinite Over-Soul in which each one of us exists as an integral part?

Everything in this world, yes, in the universe itself, is in a state of flux, the flux of evolution. For as our arcane science teaches—"The only thing that is permanent is change," and indeed the words of the Masters are being proven anew every day by science—"Everything is becoming some-thing else!"

GOD GAVE YOU THE POWER TO BECOME A MASTER

Recorded in Genesis we find these significant words: "And God formed man out of the dust of the earth." Here are pictured man and the universe. Man, the dot, and the universe; the unmeasured circle. And yet man is endowed with the power to master the earth by mastering himself.

But, you say, where is this power that will make me Master? Where? "the dust of the earth"—the DUST: composed of atoms and particles of tremendous, vibrant wave-energy. Atoms and particles of matter that vibrate in harmony with the eternal God-Law.

Do you wonder, or perhaps even smile, at the idea that so infinitely tiny particles of matter as an atom contains unbelievable energy? Remembering that all metals, like man, are primarily formed "out of the dust of the earth," consider a few of these startling discoveries of today's men of science picture a bit of pure metal the size of a pinhead, and realize that this bit of metal is made up of millions and millions of infinitely little universes which we call "atoms," Further, every one of these atoms, or "universes" contains a positive "sun and several negative "planets."

Hidden inside the atom science has re-discovered the ultimate, the smallest particles of matter called "electrons." And the whole universe is built of these ultimate particles of matter inclosed within the atom. Now, just how small do you suppose the electrons are? Science tells us that they are so minute that fifty billions of these electrons in line would only extend across the period at the end of this sentence.

Electrons and protons are the same size, electrons are composed of negative electricity, and protons of positive electricity. Each atom contains both of these elements, but in varying numbers, Let's peek into a few atoms with the eye of imagery. For these atoms contain the secret of the ages.

Remember every electron is exactly like every other electron, and every proton is exactly like every other proton. Inside an atom of hydrogen we would find one of each of these, the negative electron spinning on its own axis, and revolving with terrific speed around the nucleus (center) of the atom formed by the positive proton. Oxygen atoms each have 16 electrons and 16 protons, and the heavier atoms have still more—the heaviest atom, that of uranium, contains 96 of each.

Each atom is a miniature solar system, and the speed of the revolving electrons and protons as they revolve inside the atom reaches a velocity of many thousands of miles per second!

And just tomorrow these invisible atoms may light the world. From the Chicago Daily News, of April 26, 1946, we quote:

"ATOMS GIVE VAPOR LIGHT"

"Jostling atoms, squeezed out of shape by heat and pressure, blazed our today to open the International Lighting Exposition in Spectacular fashion.

"Harnessed to commerce instead of war, they powered the brilliant vapor lamp which featured the address of Samuel G. Hibben, Westinghouse director of applied lighting, in launching the week's technical conference and display in the Stevens Hotel.

"To get this illumination," he explained, we squeeze or bump atoms out of shape, and sometimes break off chips of them. It's atomic commotion, rather than atomic disintegration, as in the case of the atom bomb.

"This vapor lamp alone produced about 60,000 lumens about 150 times more light than the filament lamp with which George Westinghouse lighted the Columbian Exposition in Chicago 53 years ago next Wednesday."

And these same atoms, electrons, and protons are the very same elements which compose every star and planet in the heavens as well as our own earth.

Sir Francis E. Younghusband writes concerning the atomic universe—"But, incredibly numerous as are the stars, we have not to note that they are all built of the same ultimate materials & and that these materials are not hard solid bits of some inert stuff, but excessively minute units of very active electricity. "These thousands of millions of stars, are, every one of them, composed of the same elements as the sun, this earth, and our own bodies are made of,..."

Untold POWER—"out of the dust of the earth."

Lesson No. 16
THE PATHWAY TO HEALTH, WEALTH AND HAPPINESS

Fourth Gateway of The Temple Invisible, Being The Secret instruction Taught by The Masters in White, Whose Sublime Precepts Are Now Exemplified in these lessons."

The Degree of Illumination

YOUR CREATIVE FORMULA FOR HEALING AND SUCCESS

You—the Real You—are a personalized expression of God—your life is of endless duration., you exist in a boundless space, and you are endowed with unfathomed psychic powers. Because this is true, your present Lesson is devoted to translating for your "mind's eye" your creative formula for healing and success.

So long, long ago Amiel wrote in his "Journal In time:"

"There is but one thing needful—to possess God. All our senses, all our powers of mind and soul, all our external resources, are so many ways of approaching

Divinity...We must learn to detach ourselves from all that is capable of being lost, to bind ourselves absolutely to what is absolute (Power) and eternal, and to enjoy the rest as a loan."

Writing about the Divine God-Law Plan, (upon which our philosophy is founded), that plan in which Unity is made manifest in Duality, the author, J. William Lloyd, in his "Dawn Thought," in these striking words expresses much of the sublime simplicity of that Plan in these thoughts:

"...everything is convertible (the 'philosopher's stone' not such a chimera after all) and in the 'last analysis all are one and the same. Matter is but congealed spirit, and spirit but sublimated matter, and each transformable into the other. Granite is no more substantial than hope, and thought is as real a substance as marble or diamond. The One (God) must be life, and everything must be alive, metal and sand, lightning-flash and rainbow, imagination, laughter and pain...

"For Life is, One...And when the Center throws off a germ to form an individual, as we say, the first thing to be emphasized is the apparent separation, the feeling of distinct individuality and self-importance. Therefore, all souls primitive, young on the PATH, and intensely egoist, even to selfishness. But as the return accelerates, separation grows less certain and distinct, unity is more and more felt and accepted, and altruism ("Fellowship") manifests itself more and more in active gentleness and love."

And in another passage in the same book Lloyd states another great truth which may explain why your own revelations may sometimes seem unfinished:

"All revelations are but partial and imperfect, there is no one (human) and nothing infallible, yet every man, every nation, yes, every beast, flower, crystal, has the light. Every independent thinker stains his words through and through with the pigment of his thought, and they are not as other men's words are."

Again, Lloyd points out that your revelation can never be understood by anyone who does not stand upon the same plane of consciousness as you yourself do: "You may spend all your days in explaining your views, but those below you on the ladder will never see it as you see it till they also stand where you stand. I sneak to my own, and my own will understand."

THOUGHT ENERGY DECREES YOUR IDEAL INTO REALITY

Scientists agree that the highest evolved energy is the most powerful force in the world, and it is this power which is manifested in those higher phases of your Thought, and the very highest phase of your thinking is that which pictures an IDEAL. And what do we mean by that word "I deal?"

According to the Secret Wisdom of the Masters an IDEAL in your mind is the perfect, pictured result in your mind of the reaction upon each other of two currents of conscious energy. One of these currents or phases is that by which you understand quite clearly THAT WHICH ALREADY IS, and the other phase is that by which you comprehend and picture THAT WHICH YOU MOST GREATLY DESIRE. So, in the field of the good things of life, your own IDEAL may be the mentally pictured goal of healing, of perfect health, or of joyous romance, or of abundant finances, or of success in a career, each of which will bring you the highest happiness in achievement.

Your IDEAL is projected upon the screen of your conscious thought by Imagination, outlined and brought to the earthly plane by Reason, and evolved into material Reality by every related energy with which you give it life. For you must remember that your Thought directs and controls every other evolved energy of your being.

Hence, your IDEAL—born of Imagination and powered by a great irresistible Desire—vibrates with almost unbelievable energy. Or in the words of the Arcane Mysteries—"The mere fact that consciousness (your thought) perceives that it (your Ideal) would be desirable to be DECREES THAT IT SHALL BE."

The first steps towards realizing your IDEAL, then, begin its first cycle of attraction of everything necessary to fulfilling your Dream, are the steps of your mounting Desire. The first stage of manifesting your Ideal has already been attained in your Desire that it shall materialize, Now if your Desire is deep, determined and unchanging, then the emotional energy vibrating in that desire compels your conscious and your subconscious to focus their mighty energies that you may realize that ultimate goal.

And here, in the process of realizing your desired Ideal, another of the immutable rules of the mighty God-Law comes into play. As you pass through each phase of experience in realizing your IDEAL (your Great Desire), your own Thought is raised that much higher, but with each upward change in your thinking, your Ideal will also change, and be transformed into ever greater concepts in your own mind. This is due to the universal God-Law of Change, your Ideal is evolving, so that you may be led to perceive still greater and nobler Desires.

Your Great Desire must vibrate with emotional intensity. No half-hearted efforts, and no "wishful thinking" will realize any worthwhile Ideal. Ideals are manifested as realities only through the directed inherent energies of strong emotions. Let us bear in mind that the emotions have their mainsprings in the natural instincts, and our emotions are basic energies which can be made to impart their power to any Ideals, positive or negative, good or "evil," creative or destructive alike.

So we should not blame the emotions for misfortune, for frustration, or for failure, but rather let us understand that WE have perverted, we have misdirected these powerful energies.

THE WORLD IS ONE,
BUT MAN SEES IT THROUGH VARI-COLORED LENSES

art. As our mission is to magnify our consciousness, and to enlarge not only our knowledge of this world but of the universe. So we need a Master Key to the symbolism that everywhere about us tells the story of this world, and of the Infinite Mind from which the world was made manifest.

Material science has devised space and time as symbols by which we are to define everything we are to know of life and of this world in terms of sense-perception. But our inner philosophy teaches that space and time are simply two forms of our own perceptivity—they are two mental windows through which we see and measure the world of Life. Space is simply the imaginary backdrop against which represent FORM, and time is but the artificial symbol by which we measure MOTION.

Actually, of course, the world 's one, and the universe one, any apparent division simply exists in our own minds as symbols. Remember that each 'miracle,' each 'phenomenon' in our material world is only the expression of the Infinite Mind—

limited by the limits of our five physical senses. Only through developed and illu-minated cosmic consciousness can we know anything of the Infinite and this Illumination is the Master Key of symbolism.

This development of Cosmic Consciousness is the growth or expanding of the intellect in harmony with a like growth or development of the higher emotions—that is, the emotions of love, of faith, or fellowship, of healing thought and of mystical inspiration.

For we are able to comprehend many hidden things not only by means of our thinking minds, but also through our emotions we of the Initiate's Way learn many things which cannot be understood by the logical mind alone. To the Initiate the emotions are currents of knowledge, and not merely the vibrations of "feeling."

Rightly understood, to the Initiate the emotions are the beauteous stained-glass windows of his or her Soul. The Soul gazes through these many-colored lenses at the panorama which we call the world. Each of these different colored lenses helps us to find its own or like colors in every scene (experience) and so we each need many of these emotion-lenses because every experience in life is of many hues. So the man or the woman who is limited to one or two emotion-lenses (a "one-sided" nature) cannot attain to any developed emotional understanding.

Each emotion has its own particular phase in either developing or retarding our knowledge of and our attunement to the Infinite Mind plane of existence. So we must realize that certain emotions (the negative) are harmful, devastating, and destructive.

When we can free our emotions from the purely selfish, the earthy, small, personal "I", and sublimate those emotions on the higher psychic planes, we may know that we are approaching the heights. Selfishly per-sonal,emotions are always negative, harmful and hateful, because they oppose every noble, unselfish, constructive emotion and the more personal and selfish any emotion is the greater are its delusions, illusions and evil effects.

SUPERSTITION—GIANT FEAR-EMOTION THAT BLIGHTS

It is of course the FEAR-emotions, the NEGATIVE emotions which blight the lives of mankind, wherever they rule. All negative emotions are sensuous, materialistic and create narrow, little and mean personalities. Among these negative emotions, FEAR-OF-THE-UNKNOWN (superstition) leads all the rest in this destructive procession, then hatred, envy, egotism, pride, jealousy, cruelty, beastiality, and every other diseased and selfish emotional element.

Every religion and all religious teachings are based upon an appeal to the emotions of mankind. In this country alone today there are hundreds of religious sects, denominations and cults, all founded in greater or less degree upon the "revelations" handed down from the darker ages in the traditions, the religious myths, prophecies and legends of man-made, dogmatic, institutions which now survive in "churchly" forms.

The magnificence of our modern temples and cathedrals, the imposing rituals of worship, the costly vestments of priests and clergy, the solemn religious music, endless 'sacred' processions, ceremonies of 'sacrifice,' etc.,—all these are deep psychological appeals...to what?

To the EMOTIONAL NATURE of man.

And what, then, is the real, the underlying, the absolute purpose of this powerful appeal to the emotions, and just wherein is its tremendous power?

Priests, prelates, clergy, ministers and rabbis all agree in the claim that these religious, appeals to the emotions are designed to lead mankind to enlightenment and to knowledge—in other words, to give to man a true understanding of God and of the Universe.

Please understand that we have the deepest belief in TRUE religion—the religion which unfolds the supreme God-Law, and which practices the Fellowship of all mankind,. which simply teaches that "ye love one another," that follows the divinely human GOODNESS taught by the Masters, Jesus, . the Christ, Gautama, the Buddha, Osiris and Zoroeaster; that goodness which vibrates in the words:

"...Become as little children...and

Blessed are the pure in heart."

So, while our Fellowship is not "a religion," per se, we hold the divine intuition that TRUE Religion seeks and sees God, Love, and Beauty in every person (potentially) and in everything in this world—and it is this reasoning intuition that opens the mystic doors of the higher realms (the Cosmic World) to the Initiates who holds this magic key.

True religion vanishes the moment that it ceases to seek for God and Love and Beauty and Fellowship, thinking that it has already found them in their mere counterfeits, their "lip-service" imitations. For then "religion" becomes merely a man-made sham that thrives only upon the fear-emotions of its blind and ignorant votaries.

And this false "religion," this man-made sham—what, we ask, is its REAL name? And we answer, Superstition. And in turn, what is Superstition?

Superstition is terror of the unknown, FEAR of the mysterious. And has man-made, church-organized "religion" humanized American 'civilization'! Any daily newspaper of current date will answer that question, Going back a short twenty years, we find a bird's eye summary, which quite accurate today, increased a hundred-fold BY A SHORT SCORE OF YEARS.

SUPERSTITION AND PROGRESS—MORTAL ENEMIES

We quote the following passage from the address of Franklin Henry Giddings, Chancellor of Union University, given at Schenectady, N.Y., in June, 1926:

"Wealth per capita increases, but so also, we fear, do envy and bitterness. The growing splendour of our cities increases and amazes, but the perils and discomforts of our thoroughfares multiply. We communicate instantaneously with near and far; we travel over longer distances at accelerating velocities.., but our nerves are worn, and insanity so incroaches upon sanity that alienists are asking if the whole race of man is destined to madness.

"Scientific medicine, availing itself of chemistry and biology, has demonstrated the possibility of ridding the world of epidemic diseases and of many others, but we scorn its teachings to follow after ignoramuses and quacks. We have churches and schools, home and, foreign missions, your men's and young Women's Christian Association, colleges and universities; but we remain superstitious, afraid of knowledge, bigoted and intolerant, truculent, gun-totin and murderous."

From this picture of yesteryear, just as in the American scene today, we perceive again a startling proof that superstition and progress are mortal enemies, because they represent two irreconcilble concepts. Superstition is the child of tradition, or darkness, the unholy spawn of FEAR OF THE UNKNOWN, and seeks always to clothe itself in sanctimonious robes; but progress is the child of intellectual development, and welcomes all mysterdispelling knowledge, and finds itself opposed at every turn by the priests of "magic," the sacrosanct heirs of the "medicine man" of the jungles.

In this eternal conflict between superstition, with its cohorts of darkness and fear, and the mystery-erasing knowledge of The Masters, every enlightened Initiate stands as the champion of intellectual liberty.

Superstition most often hides its hideous features behind the mast of (so-called) "religion," and is arrogant and despotic, and is the bitter enemy of the Wisdom of The Masters, for it hates all scientific knowledge with an every-lasting hatred, because such knowledge exposes and discredits fear-worship.

History exposes superstition as nothing else but the obsession of the "Mob," the multitude, by MYSTERYFEAR. Such terrible dread as this finds its outlet in mass-crimes of uncontrollable fear, as witness the unthinkable cruelties and the countless murders of "witch-craft" persecutions in the not too distant past in America, in England and in France.

Collective (mob) superstition in those days tried accused men and women by "ordeal," and proclaimed duelling as sanctioned by divine judgement. This same mad psychology of the mob proclaimed in the name of "religion" that human slavery was a divinc institution because Canaan, mythical ancestor of the negro race, had been cursed by "God!"

From this same shrewdly cultivated fear-obsession of peoples was hatched the "divine right of kings," a pseudo-right firmly supported by every state "religion" through many, many ages, until finally the dumb multitudes found leaders among the unrecognized Masters in their midst, and over-threw this "divine right" of tyrrany. Then, by an adroit about-fact, superstition donned the mast of political expediency and shouted from the house tops that "the voice of the people is the voice of God."

Today these same prophets of the great god, Mumbo-Jumbo, are busily preaching the mystical sanctity and the divine origin of the Laws of the State—but behind the scenes these same false priests of fear dictate every "tablet" of the statute law.

THE NIGHT OF A THOUSAND YEARS

The rise of the ancient Greek civilization was marked by the appearance on earth of certain Masters— Initiates into the Secret Wisdom who opposed the rule of the sorcerers, the "medicine Men," and the priests of "magic" over the superstitious mob by proclaiming certain truths which marked the glimmer of the approaching dawn of scientific inquiry. The names of many of these Masters have been lost under the dust of the ages, and most of their priceless works were destroyed.

But there yet remain the stories of Anaxagoras, who explained the material world by natural laws and as a reward was banished, after narrowly escaping death; also Democritus, who discovered that all matter is formed of atoms; and Aristotle, the father of comparative anatomy; and Archimedes, the first great Physicist of those days. Their works endured, even in the fragments of their writings which have escaped the fires of the ignorant and the superstitious.

The first 100 years, A.D., Lucretius left as his monument his "De Rerum Natura," which blazed the first trail among the Greeks of what we now know as "evolution," But a little afterward the Physician, Galen, finally gave anatomy its basis as an indisputable science.

Then the darkness of a night that lasted a thousand years fell upon mankind, and superstition once more reigned almost supreme.

Meanwhile, amid this darkness, this mental night, we can discern the progress of the then new religion called Christianity as it was carried from Galilee to Rome, and then spread from Rome throughout a superstitious and a "heathen" Europe. But along the many pathways upon which it journeyed Christianity encountered many strange legends, myths; traditions and ceremonies of older religions and worships which were the inborn heritage of different races; tribes and peoples who came into the Christian fold, bringing these older beliefs and traditions with them, and now sanctified by time; others were quietly rejected.

Many of these "barbarian" beliefs and ceremonies were accepted and made a sacred part of Christianity, where they remain revered to this day. The former pagan festivals which marked the seasons and the changes in Nature are now sacred Saint's days, or appear as Chrismas("Christ Mass")—Easter, etc., To the student of the primitive, Christianity is abundantly diluted with demonism, witch-fear, spiritualism, magic, and "mana," (in Latin, Virtus, a spirit-power of magic-remember Jesus is reported to have exclaimed, "I perceive that virtue has gone out of me.") and many other vestiges of paganism and its ghost-worship.

Have you ever read Kipling's story of "Mowgli?" Read it, and you will find it drawn from hundreds of myths (many of them sacred, and it will find quite a clear picture of the story and the theory of superstition. Only different because they are more ancient than are the "sacred" allegories of the beginnings of the world and of mankind.

Lacking every other proof, these allegories depend upon the word of unknown writers that they are divinely "revealed,"—to impart their real meanings, to interpret them as allegories to be read with mystery-dispelling knowledge is to court the brand of "heretic."

As a passing example, consider with us for a few moments the "jungle-story" of Eve—for this IS a story of the jungle—an allegory filled with hidden meanings.

These larger, hidden meanings can never be understood by theologians, priests or preachers who can see in this only a divine account of the birth of "sin" on earth, and of the "fall of man."

Read that story in Genesis once again, and see if you do not catch the revealing significance of the words as reported which prove that Eve knew the language of the jungle, else how could she converse with the "serpent and understand his words?

Note that when, Eve told the serpent that she and Adam had been warned that to eat of the fruit of the Tree of Knowledge meant death, the serpent ridiculed this as untrue—and Eve believing the serpent, experimented. Eve did not die, and she persuaded Adam also to investigate, which he did, lamb-like.

Now, neither Eve nor Adam died that day, or the next, nor for many years to follow. The Elohim ("the gods") were amazed and confused, because, as they said, this pair of "sinners" have "become as one of us." Yes, the disobedience was punished—but not with death, you will notice.

Thus, experimental science was born.

And the false priests of Mumbo-Jumbo, the "medicine men," kings, monarchs and religious tyrants have striven ever since that fateful day to keep the sons and daughters of Adam and Eve away from that mystery dispelling Tree of Knowledge. But the glorious minority of advanced thinkers have risen above the jungle law to the heights of the God-Law.

Illumined—they walk with God.

LESSON NO. 17
THE PATHWAY TO HEALTH, WEALTH AND HAPPINESS

Fourth Gateway of The Temple Invisible, Being The Secret Instruction Taught by The Masters in White, Whose Sublime Precepts Are Now Exemplified in These Lessons.

The Degree of Illumination

SUCCESS AND HAPPINESS VIBRATE FROM MIND AND SOUL DEVELOPMENT

Probably you have been impressed when you have read the stories of the lives of the great Masters (Holy Men) of the world of the ancient East by the phenomenal powers which they possessed—powers which seem hidden in the occult realms beyond our reach today. To believe that psychic powers are veiled in impenetrable mystery is a misconception.

It is true that these Masters about whom you have read did manifest unusual and seemingly mysterious powers, but it is also equally true that these same seemingly mystic powers exist as latent forces within you, just as they are dormant in every normal man or woman. When properly developed and trained, and in due time these powers can manifest in your life. But just now we would not have you seek these occult powers as your chief goal, but rather we would have you develop those powers of your mind and soul from which vibrate success <u>and happiness</u>.

Of course, in developing these "occult" powers of your mind and your soul so that they will vibrate success and happiness into your life you will encounter opposition, misunderstanding, and obstacles, but we would point out, in the words of J. William Lloyd, in "Dawn Thought," that—

"Evil is Only Another Name For Opposition..."

From this same book, we quote the striking passage in which this phrase occurs:

"Nothing that lifts fails to experience resistance (opposition) and its value is accurately measured by that resistance...The stone is heavy so that the seed it weighs upon has to struggle to escape and grow off sideways to get to the light, but at last it has, for that reason, all the longer root, and the stone on its root becomes its anchor.

"Evil is always potentially opportunity, but at first the opportunity is disguised and the compulsion emphasized. We have seen that in order to have action there must be an actor, and a thing acted upon, and opposition therefore is the first vital necessity...

"Evil is only another name for opposition, and opposition becomes the fulcrum of leverage, the foundation of building, the dam of fountain heads, And this evil makes itself more and more intolerable, until its opposing good becomes inevitable as the only exit of escapes...in proportion to the deadness of the weight will be the stability and force of the uplift.

"Whenever the battle of life has lifted a man high enough to have ideals of peace, unselfishness, cooperation and liberty, he has evolved enough to no longer need the unmitigated pressure of evil as a driver...

"Be sure when some trial, or sorrow, or fear, or perplexity, or straining demand upon your virtue returns to you again and again, that here is a weak spot in your soul which the friendly Adversary has found and to which he has fitted an appropriate battle as a gymnastic, and it is for you to accept the lesson,and go through, the discipline until it is easy and joyous for you, you fear no fear, your weakness is transformed into a new and higher strength."

In this lesson we should like above all else for you to grasp the simple reality of the truth that, just as Lloyd points out, this "battle" of life (as we call it) is not something evil but a blessing, often disguised as "Evil." To use a homely metaphor of curs, 'live fish swim upstream—the dead ones are all going the other way!'

Viewed in the light of this truth, then, we can see that each and every opposition, obstacle, every steep and laborious hill, injury, mistake, fault, "sin." calamity, or danger, was in reality an Opportunity for mind and soul development and strengthening, the stepping-stones to success and happiness for those are rewards which must be WON, not merely longed for.

We have too often looked upon each of these as an enemy—actually, we should value them as the champion athlete prizes his trainer, the football team their coach, or as an understanding student values his teacher.

True, what we call "evil" is a paradox—a seeming contradiction.

Most occult students when they encounter a paradox in the Cosmic Plan seem content to shut their eyes and affirm, "All is unity—there is only UNITY." All of which becomes a glib but a meaningless affirmation, unless the student learns to understand and to combine the opposing factors of that UNITY.

For, as Lloyd says elsewhere, Nature herself affirms opposites—the tremendous powers of the universe itself are generated in the meeting of opposing forces.

CONSIDERING THIS PROBLEM OF "EVIL"

Undoubtedly, if you were like the average student of the "occult" before you became an Initiate, you have read or perhaps studied much about unity and duality, "Karma" and reincarnation, compensation and retribution, tradition, and religion, and perhaps you have "accepted"! some or many of the truths thus taught.

But now we want you to realize and accept the fact that each one of the laws contained in the great God-Law has a direct counterpart or counter-law which opposes it. Yes, for every law of Life you will find an opposing law—and each is equally important in the Divine Plan—thus; good and evil, rest and action, victory and defeat, happiness and sorrow, unity and separation, health and sickness, wealth and poverty, passivity and resistance, day and night, ILLUMINATION and darkness. Opposites. All are seeming paradoxes, because fundamentally there is only unity—oneness.

To understand, therefore, that "evil" (so-called) is simply a paradox, and to separate this word "evil" from its dark cloak of guilt or badness with which religion has invested the word is to free you from yet another lingering shadow of fear. For after all, only the priests of superstition and the heartless masters of tyranny thrive upon FEAR.

From the earliest days of man's thinking, "evil", has been a philosophical problem. But as a heritage of the dark (Medieval) ages of Europe, "evil has loomed large as a religious concept, and, true to the standards of the ruling religion of these dark ages, this warped concept has pointed its features as horrible.

Yet before we cower in fear before this shadowy image of Moloch, let us together examine somewhat critically this crude, narrow, revolting concept. Let us look behind this distorted image set up in the market place by sanctimonious schemers to scare the infantile mind of the mob. Mayhap we shall find that "evil is only the opposing half of the God-Law of Compensation—of GOOD!"

First, then, let us free our minds of those arbitrary and narrow standards set up by man-made "religion," and see for ourselves just the part this opposing force which men call "evil" plays in the cosmic plan of human affairs. The true, the broader interpretation of evil, as taught in the archives of the Masters, commends itself to reason, to logic, and to the enlightened mind of the Initiate.

So we are quite sure that you, too, will agree with that interpretation, because it very simply teaches that evil means any obstacle, any opposing force or circumstance, which interferes with our desire, our attainment, or our possession of any longed-for condition, circumstance or material thing as for instance, health, romance, fame, fortune, career, properties or money. Without regard to any moral or religious meaning attached to it, evil, then, means any force or influence or circumstance which we encounter in life which destroys that which we have toiled to possess, or opposes our reaching desired goals. From OUR viewpoint that opposing force or influence is definitely deemed to be evil.

But why attach blame, personal animus, or guilt of a force which is just as utterly impersonal as the force that flashes through the electric wire, or the invisible force of a mighty rushing wind? Is not -all force, all energy, all power IMPERSONAL?

UNAVOIDABLE EVILS EXIST–MISDIRECTED POWER IS EVIL

Remembering that we have agreed to define evil as opposition, resistance, or any obstacle which thwarts our desires or plans, evil then also comprises anything; or condition which retards or hinders, our full development of Mind and Soul, for all success and happiness vibrate from developed personalities.

Our welfare, our success, and our happiness depend almost entirely upon the way we meet, deal with, or control as far as possible the many evils (obstacles and adverse conditions) we encounter. Dire or disastrous consequences, which we so often call "evil," are not inherent in the evils (obstacles) we meet, but are the direct result of our reactions bring destructive results; hatred, strife, envy, failure, crime, poverty and almost all human suffering have their origin in our own wrong or mistaken methods in our encounters with evil (opposing forces).

Hence, each Initiate must be thoroughly armed by a complete understanding of these adverse forces we call "evil," because knowledge is the only safeguard against wrong or negative reactions—for it is from these reactions that we suffer.

In order to simplify this important subject, let us divide these opposing forces, influences or conditions into two very broad classes—in the first class we list all the results of certain uncontrollable energies of Nature, as for example, the destructive force of lightening, earthquakes, tidal waves, floods, droughts, etc. Of course, these outbursts, of Nature's power are entirely beyond our control—we can only seek to develop control over our reactions to their results. So, mankind constantly rebuilds what Nature destroys. For Nature is both the Great Mother and the "destroying angel."

We classify in our second division all evils or opposing forces and conditions which we have the power to control, if we only realize that power and use it. In this second class of evils we place every result of wrong or mistaken negative reactions to the obstacles, the oppositions or the frustrations that we meet upon life's pathway, such as sickness, disease, poverty, fear, failure, and futile, useless living.

One basic truth will help to clear up our understanding of this problem of evil is the simple fact that the meaning of this word "evil" depends largely upon each man's personal viewpoint. Evil (that which opposes your desire or plan) also is given as something which is governed not only by your individual viewpoint but also by place and time.

Suppose you have worked very hard to accomplish a certain plan or purpose, or to attain success in some career. But perhaps you have a neighbor, Sam Jones, who does not even understand your work, or has no interest in your plan, and no sympathy for your disappointment, then that evil which overthrew your plans and desires does not exist for Sam Jones, does it?

So, that which looms large in your life as evil, 'may not even exist for your next-door neighbor! And the opposing forces he meets may have no meaning to you.

Then, as to time—it may seem strange to you, but at one time in history even kings and queens looked down upon every learned or educated man, and spurned those of literary talents as being of "the lower classes!"

In time of war, the cry is "kill-kill-kill"—death to every enemy, man, woman, child,—aced, sick, crippled—KILL.

Then, paradoxically enough, in modern days in time of peace, we, of the United States, turn (outwardly) to the doctrine of Christ, "Love thy neighbor...," and feed and clothe our former enemies, even at the expense of hundreds of thousands of our own poorly fed and illy clothed citizens.

Another striking anamoly we find in the historical fact that robbery and enslavement, torture and mass murder have been sanctioned by 'religion,' and committed freely in the name of "God" all through the ages. Only a hundred and fifty years ago men and women were tortured and killed as "witches" by the prevailing 'religion' in this country. And this terrible persecution was GOOD in the eyes of "God," according to the zealous religionists of that rather recent age in America.

Actually this problem of evil has never been fully solved, because man has been unable to define clearly what this word means, for it seems to mean so many different things to so many different men. We have illustrated this by pointing out that what is evil to you may not be at all evil to your neighbor.

From the most ancient times, as religious concepts have taken form and developed, as represented by different man-made organized groups commonly called "churches," these religious groups have each stamped different deeds, activities or habits, or careers of men, as either good or evil, approved or disapproved, "holy" or "unholy". And we can but observe with amazement the bewildering changes in these religious definitions of "good" and of "evil" from time to time. That which was stamped as "good" by churchly approval yesteryear becomes "evil" today, and vice versa. And according to each churchly group their particular "God" will disperse "heavenly" rewards or mete out eternal torture based entirely upon whether or not the person, in question had followed the narrow concept of "good" and "evil" as taught in the doctrine of that particular group of religionists.

So we see that 'religion' as represented by either ignorant or scheming "leaders" resorts to the most absurd teachings in order to best serve the ends and ambitions of its "holy" men!

THE AGE-OLD QUESTION ASKED BY EPICURUS

Long, long ago Epicurus, the philosopher, asked a deep and searching question—a question we should like to help you, as a student to answer satisfactorily to your own judgment, for it is indeed a momentous question. Epicurus asked whether God COULD NOT or WOULD NOT keep evil out of this world.

Epicurus decided that in view of the fact that God is represented to be an all-loving Creator, and since evil actually does exist in this world, we must conclude that God is not Infinite but that His power is limited.

Epicurus reasoned that if God's power was unlimited, He would never allow evil to exist as a power opposed to His own purpose and nature.

Undoubtedly some men have been satisfied by the reasoning; and the conclusion of Epicurus but could you honestly and whole-heartedly worship and rely upon a God whose powers, like your own, are limited? No, because the God whom, as an enlightened, an illumined Initiate, you would rely upon for power and to whom you would turn in adoration must have your implicit belief, your unwavering faith as ALL-powerful, ALL-good, ALL-creative—in a word He must be the immutable, the eternal. GOD-LAW personified, and not merely a glorified reflection of human frailty.

Let us beware the worship of a man-made, distorted IMAGE!

We seek only reality, only TRUTH, so we cannot accept mere unsupported tradition as proven truth, nor can we bow before the blood-stained altars of superstition. In seeking the truth in answering the question of Epicurus, instead of agreeing to limit the changeless and illimitable power of The Great Creator let us delve beneath the surface of the specious religious sophistry which has shrouded this question in false conclusions based upon false and narrow premises. Evil, then, is just a human word by which I-man reflects his own finite, narrow and limited conception of the tremendous creative design of the universe.

To illustrate our meaning in the above statement, let us suppose that you are a person who knows nothing at all about art, especially the art of painting pictures. Yet, understanding little or nothing about technique, color shading, perspective, or the intent of the artist, you are inspecting a master piece of some great painter.

Now the closer you are to the canvas, the more things you will see in the painting that seem to you to be faults, mistakes, or imperfections. Being so close you are examining the picture from a narrowed viewpoint, you are examining details separately. Thus, you lose all sense of perspective, and you miss the true intent of the picture as a whole.

But step away from the painting and look at it from a suitable distance. Then every detail falls into proper perspective, and every scorning imperfection blends into a perfect whole, and from the proper distance that which appeared to you from too limited a viewpoint merely sought daubs of color or course outlines now merge into a truly perfect, a beautiful scene.

This simple illustration brings us to a deeper., an eternally TRUE understanding of the solution of the problem proposed by Epicurus. Just as with the painting, we are all too close to the world in which we live, and too close to our own lives, and every circumstance of our environment is too close to us for any of us to perceive the world, or life, or environment as blended into a complete, a perfect DESIGN`

Just as a too-close view of the painting brings into our vision many details which seem imperfect to us, so it is in our imperfect view of life, of the world and of the universe. If we could only view this entire earthly scene from the distance of a detached viewpoint, we could see how beautifully each detail, each "imperfection," fits into the divine design as a whole, as a complete picture. As it is, we must live in our environment, and this brings us so intimately close to each integral part or detail that we are surrounded by apparent (seeming) imperfections. Each of the integral phases or circumstances that WE see as imperfect, we call "evil."

And why do we call them evil? Because we see only the separate, the disassociated details, and many of these details or (to us) "imperfect" phases of life or circumstance seem to oppose our plans, our efforts, our desires.

You will remember that it was St. Augustine who taught that what man believes to be evil is only his own misunderstanding (his wrong viewpoint) of THE WHOLE. And further the good St. Augustine believed that the great purpose of life was that man should learn to understand the intent (the design) of God—and that then we would perceived that those "imperfections" which we call evil are actually errors in our own vision and understanding.

SEEING EVIL AS REALITY BARS SUCCESS AND HAPPINESS

The lesson we seek to impress upon you is that evil in itself has no REALITY except that which you give to it in your own mind, because evil is simply a name which man gives to any obstacle, influence or circumstance which opposes his quest for success and happiness. Remembering then that success and happiness are the results of the magnetic vibrations of developed minds and souls our Great Work is to attain that Illumination by which we can attract to ourselves these godly gifts.

True, our lessons lead you into realms of unexplored thought, that it, into realms unknown to the material masses, to the unitiated. As you walk with us mentally toward your dream of limitless Spiritual Power and attainment, and as you look back upon the seeming trivial and futile experiences of your former every-day life, you will begin to ask yourself, "What is Real, what is actual substance, what IS the answer to My life, and what is its goal?

And these are exactly the questions that these secret doctrines answer.

You will doubtless realize that as you have followed our teachings, you have felt that your former perhaps confused conception of "material" and of "spiritual" things has been undergoing a surprising change. In the past your contradictory thoughts have painted your world of consciousness with the colors of doubt and of uncertainty.

No wonder you were struggling for years, perhaps, with the confusion induced in your mind by the empty traditions, the superstitions, and the obviously false and self-seeking claims of the many man-made "religions" which surrounded you on every hand.

According to the wisdom, you now realize the quite simple truth that there are TWO separate and distinct realms or phases of manifestation—two different worlds—one, the solid, material, earthy world, this world being visible and limited; and, two, the invisible, spiritual, infinite world. In the earth-world all is limited by time and space; in the God (Spirit) World neither time nor space exists.

One great fundamental truth reconciles these two worlds in our mental concepts of them—and-that universal truth is the UNITY (the oneness) of the universe. The second great and basic truth is that YOU are one with that universe.

It is the infinite God-Law made manifest everywhere that binds the universe into this unity, this oneness.

And it is that same infinite God-Law which will , as you work: with and through it, manifest in your Healing, your Success and your Happiness.

Now you can begin to see that those apparent contradictions, those seeming separations of things into GOOD and EVIL were simply your own mistaken ideas, your misconceptions, which resulted only from lack of understanding of this eternal UNITY.

Separation and limitation are misconceptions, mistakes, which exist only in our own minds—all limitation is within, ourselves.

WE create limitation, frustration, unhappiness and failure by THE WAY WE THINK, and our thoughts are of course in direct proportion to our knowledge and our understanding of the Infinite, the Creative, the Ever-Present Over-Soul, of which we are every one a son or a daughter...heirs to power illimitable!

LESSON NO. 18
THE PATHWAY TO HEALTH, WEALTH AND HAPPINESS

Fourth Gateway of The Temple Invisible, Being The Secret Instruction Taught by The Masters in White, Whose Sublime Precepts Are Now Exemplified in these lessons.

The Degree of Illumination

ONTOLOGY OF YOUR MAGNIFIED SELF

"Understand this, Reksa, and get it clearly into your mind: it is plainly not the intention of the (Divine) Plan that Messiahs could come to us, or Bibles be written for us, to tell us all things, once for all. We are to find out things for ourselves, and to GROW through the struggle of finding out. How could we grow (develop) if everything were told us and everything done for us?

"...there is in the Cosmos a Divine Order, Power, and Safety, a real Consciousness that all is well. Again there are all degrees of Cosmic Conscious Vision, apparently.

Some only barely touch it, some more, some much more. This difference must always be remembered

"What then, O Eneres, does the Cosmic Conscious (Illumined) man get'?

"He gets profound conviction, like the consciousness of his own existence, that there is a Meaning in the universe, and that that Meaning means well for him; that he is safe and will be taken care of. With that, of course, goes the conviction of an Order, System, and Government that can hardly be described other than Divine. Almost, if not quite invariably, follows the conviction of Unity, of Oneness in the universe...

"In all forms comes the conviction that evil is not as EVIL as it seems; that it is either not evil, but good, or else that it will finally be transmuted (changed) into good, or fully compensated for.

"GOD IS and WE ARE. But before the mind has time to grasp all this comes a sublime and wonderful joy, which is never forgotten while life lasts." From "Eneres," by Lloyd.

In this lesson we shall devote ourselves to discussing with you the power which is yours to MAGNIFY YOURSELF, and give to you certain rather simple, but great, secrets of how to focus this power into a transforming magic. Let not the title of this lesson dismay you, for there is nothing in the ontology (scientific knowledge) of your magnified self which will prove too hard for you to understand or to apply to your everyday living.

Within certain quite fair limitations, we have each one been given the ability to choose our own course of action, to even choose our own individual personality, whether we realize this or not, and each choice we make is the result of our own decision. Now, as life goes on, and as we come face to face with the realization that realities make up the sum total of our existence, and as we are made conscious of the effect upon others of our decision, we will be wise to wake up to the fact that these decisions of ours are important to us beyond measure.

If you will reflect seriously upon this matter, you will realize that most of your decisions, once you have made them, are irrevocable, they must stand as you made them. And the consequences of your decisions are a part of your lot in life—they seem to "come home to roost" sooner or later.

Of course, as you learn to magnify yourself—as you develop into a greater

SELF—your power of decision is magnified, and each choice you make becomes better, wiser, greater. Little selves either make little decisions, or, defeated, let some one else decide for them. It is rather a sorry business to go through life trying to rectify the self-imposed evils of wrong decisions, for the law of compensation has ordained that we reap what we sow and no man or woman can break that law and escape its penalty.

DEVELOPING PERSONALITY TO REFLECT THE GOD-SELF

Every lesson you have received from us is one farther or advance step upon your Pathway, and each of these steps is skillfully designed to teach you how to reflect your greater, your divine, your God-Self, which is within. Remember, our Elder Initiate, Christ, said: "The Kingdom of God is within you." And that greater, that magnified Self is materially expressed in your developed personality. That development is a most important part of the Great Work of our Fellowship.

Turning for a moment to the faraway East, we quote these words from a Hindu philosopher:

"While we recognize God, it is really only the Self, from which we have separated ourselves and worship outside of us: but it is our true Self all the time, the one and only God."

And the eminent medical authority wrote:

"MIND never fails to impress itself upon matter. For every mental process, there never fails to follow some physical response. Every thought of mind, every process of consciousness., is unfailingly translated into some sort of material movement."

Ever since his advent upon earth, man has ceaselessly tried to contact the Unknown. Crumbling amid the dust of the echoless past we find the ruins and fragments of temples, altars, and shrines, each of these, together with every cathedral, church or temple of TODAY, each is a mute monument built by man to try to bridge the chasm between that which he understands and all that he deems to be hidden in mystery.

To each of us, our environment is limited by our understanding. The endless struggle of mankind has been to broaden the limits of his understanding, to make the unknown known. In this quest, you will observe that man has always visualized, realized and often he has IDOL-ized, a Supreme Mind, a Divine Intellect, which infinitely transcends his own (slowly) developed mind.

Everywhere and always man has builded material temples in which to "worship," and the symbolism back of each of these temples is to represent the sacred place where "GOD" (The Supreme Mind) resides. But the Great-Over-Soul whom men call God resides in all things, and vibrates in every beat of your heart and in every magnetic thought-wave in your mind.

Yes, you yourself are a physical expression of God, and the individual God-Soul within you, which IS "YOU," is ageless. Let us quote these words of Christ from the Aquarian Gospel:

"Our God is Spirit, and in Him all wisdom, love and strength abide...In every man these sacred attributes (of the God-Spirit) are budding forth, and in due time they will unfold ("The Unfoldment); the demonstration completed be, and man will comprehend the fact of unity."

Leaving then these man-made "temples of God," wherein men but, glorify themselves, where then are the TRUE temples of God?

The true temples of God are everywhere that human beings live, for as the Bible tells us, our human bodies are the temples within which dwells the God-Soul, created in the image of Gods and vibrating with creative power.

Within each human body, each of these physical "temples," there are none principal shrines—the endocrine glands about which we have instructed you in previous lessons—and each of these gland-shrines may be likened to a temple altar, upon which glows a vari-colored light of personality.

Vibrating through and around each of these shrines of the human body, which we call "glands," are the currents of hormone secretion, which manifests in energy, according to its work in the temple. So, let us be conscious of these shrines in our bodily temples of God, because these attendant secretions carry in their mysterious living cells inner knowledge that contacts the God-Knowledge of the universe, and this inner knowledge is made manifests in our minds through INTUITION, or "inspiration."

Only in The Silence, in Meditation and Concentration, can we truly hear the voice of intuition, or feel the divine urge of inspiration—for these are the wonders brought to us by the silent priests that guard our inner shrines. So when you feel an impelling urge to be alone, to be in The Silence, to meditate—never suppress that inspiring impulse. Follow that urge—and enter WITHIN that perfect "temple not made with hands," and worship before its shrines IN SILENCE.

YOU DO NOT WALK ALONE—BROTHERHOOD IS UNIVERSAL

Always remember, true brotherhood is universal, so never think that you walk alone in this world.

All things that endure in this universe, work together perfectly under the eternal God-Law, for anything or any being which does not abide by that Law perishes. Famine, pestilence, discord and disintegration results from disregard of this Law.

"Bringing this question to its narrowest, most personal sense, then, when you recognize and accept the brotherhood of man as a living fact, and more especially that brotherhood as expressed in our fellowship of the students, this active realization is for your own greatest benefit.

Let us forget the various religions, churches, fraternal orders and secret societies which TALK much and loudly about "brotherhood" but fail to practice it, and rather set an example of brotherhood IN DEEDS. Every great civilization of the past, and there have been many, has fallen because brother-hood was overshadowed and forgotten in the race for selfish power. And that is usually just as true of each individual life that fails.

So, here is the simple truth, if you would live healthfully, if you would enjoy success and prosperity, and, above all, if you would be HAPPY, first realize that you do not walk alone, know that all men and women are your brothers and your sisters, and that by seeking to serve (help) others you are sending forth magnetic vibrations which will return to you carrying those finer things of life which you desire.

Throw all of your God-Developed powers and abilities into some form of service to others, if you would gain MORE for yourself. For always you walk with your fellow men. Then, and then only, you will RECEIVE bountifully, because you are obeying the immutable mandates of the God-Law.

That is the Law of the God who said: "Let there be LIGHT." And do not think that God is Confined within the stone walls that men call "temples", "cathedrals, " or "Churches", for as ancient Sebe said:

"God has not been confined in stone walls with only stained windows for light and alter candles for heat. Ah, truly, God must be the light of a thousand candles."

YOUR ENVIRONMENT CHANGES—AND YOUR PROBLEMS VANISH

You will remember the story of the oriental king whose wise men prepared for him a four-word aphorism so laden with far reaching prophesy that it was carved above the entrance to the greatest temple in his land, and these are the four words: "THIS TOO WILL PASS."

Here is a silent reminder that all material things, all man-made things, all man-made problems will pass, will one day be no more. Only the creative God-Soul, who vibrates in the elusive realm of man's developed Inner-Mind-Soul, the universal Over-Soul "without beginning and without end," exists eternally. And only through this stupendous truth can man attain to ageless continuity of existence.

ENDOWING YOUR IDEAL PERSONALITY-IMAGE WITH LIFE

Very few people enjoy being criticized, and probably fewer yet welcome any experience which leaves them dissatisfied with themselves. And still we would advise you to welcome criticism, and to value that feeling of being dissatisfied with yourself—for both these usually unwelcome visitors can be made priceless to you in attaining a magnetic, attractive and outstanding personality which you have never even dreamed possible. Why? Because criticism is proof that your vision of a perfected personality is a noble vision, one with a perfection you have not yet attained—and also criticism from without shows that others EXPECT you to LIVE in accord with your own vision. Again, your own dissatisfaction with yourself is born from the source of all advancement, Imagination. In other words, in Imagination you have dreamed a waking dream of a highly developed personality.

In this waking dream you have caught a glimpse of a higher realm. In this higher thought-realm you have created for yourself an ideal personality-image, a loftier vision of yourself than is yet manifest.

So, you were dissatisfied? And you have dared to dream a FINE dream? Stop right here then, and realize that your fine dream CAN become you. Because that winning, charming, powerfully magnetic personality of which you have dreamed as THE REAL YOU is honestly, actually nearer your grasp than you have thought possible. Your Great Work in life is to become the REAL YOU of which you have dreamed.

With the colors of Imagination picture yourself NOW. as really being that IDEAL SELF of your waking dream. So you have a vivid mental image of yourself at this very minute as in the state of BECOMING the SELF you want most to be.

Now, the secret is to HOLD THAT IMAGE. Remember, that mental image is the working model of yourself AS YOU WILL BE SOON.

In creating your mental-ideal-image be absolutely literal and in dead earnest. Adorn this working model of the Self you WILL (determine) to be with the clothes for which you may have longed, and endow this self-to-be with just the gifts and the graceful carriage that belongs to the developed personality.

Be definite in forming that image—imagine yourself to be like a sculptor who fashions a mental image in stone, and so you must be exact in your mental work. Thought and Imagination are your chilled steel chisels, whose cutting edges are so sharp that, driven by the hammers of Desire and Will, they cleave the rocks of Opposition and Resistance easily.

Let this image reflect yourself, but yourself Illumined. Let this working model reflect your body, your own characteristics, your particular features and expression, but idealized. Make this image so life-like that you will know that it is YOU when you look at it, yet picture your new Self without limitations. For most of your frustrations have come to you because you limited yourself!

Keep your image above and beyond your usual line of vision, so that you will be forced to look upward and ahead when you want to see it. Further, enrich your mental image of the Self you are going to be, beginning today, with every good quality and with each magnetic attribute that you have often perhaps wished you were "born with."

Of course, as a matter of fact, you WERE born with each of these good qualities, and with the magnetic powers for which you have longed, but through circumstances or environment you have let them lie dormant and unrecognized.

Now, how will you transform your image of the Ideal YOU into vibrant, magnetic, triumphant life? Very simple. For your dream IS you , your image IS you, this is your NEW Self.

Always carry this mental image of your NEW Self with you wherever you go, and a new and a great joy will come to you as you walk the highways and the byways of life, the joy of attaining. For you are walking in the reflected light of your new, your recreated, your glorified Self. No longer are your mind's eyes (your attention) fastened upon the drab and dreary life you used to lead, but upward and beyond, upon the heights where your IDEAL SELF beckons to you to follow.

For you have passed through a personality-Illumination, and truly you "walk in newness of life." Your New Self heals and vitalizes your body with renewed health and with electric energy. Day by day, this image of the Ideal You, if you hold it firmly before your "mind's eye," will inspire you to leadership, because you will do outstanding work in your career, and because your mental image embodies every quality which will make people admire and -respect this "NEW" (Real) Self that is becoming YOU.

This IDEAL YOU is pictured in your waking dream as always perfectly groomed, and always well dressed— so just as fast as possible, you must begin to reflect these qualities in your personal self TODAY. Your new self will be socially conscious and well-poised, because you must acquire these refinements in order to reflect the IDEAL YOU of your vision.

You will sculpture this figure of the New Self, the model of your renewed life, with the utmost attention to detail. So in getting down to details you must give some thought to analyzing your former (or present) self and environment with an eye to basic causes and to practical remedies for any ills in the situation, or in the imperfect self of other days.

First, then, just what was the reason you became dissatisfied with yourself ? Here you can afford to be really honest with yourself, because you have everything to gain.

ANALYZE YOURSELF CAREFULLY—LEARN FROM YOUR CRITICS

None of us relishes criticism. Yet from your critics you can learn more truths that will be useful to you in fashioning your Ideal-Personality-Image than you can ever learn from your friends. For critics, especially those who dislike you, are brutally frank. So, is it not the part of wisdom to weigh each criticism well, no matter how unpleasant it may seem to our natural vanity? And if the criticism does point out a real fault or an imperfection in your present personality, you can profit immensely by perfecting that fault or weakness, instead of blindly seeking to justify your self-love by angry resentment.

So, people have criticized you, have they? Then here's how you profit by every criticism—suppose someone has said of you, "Yes, he (or she) has many fine qualities but Oh! what a temper!" Instead of flying into a rage just calmly, impersonally analyze yourself, examine yourself impartially as to temper. For it might just be that this critic is telling you the truth. Very well, then, you can remedy that.

You will imbue your mental personality Image with self-control, with balance, with smiling GOOD TEMPER. Thus, as you transmute your mental ideal-you into your every day living your critic will not only be con-founded, but you have gained a new perfection, or you are attaining a NEW ideal in emotional control. Your critic has unconsciously helped you beyond measure to cultivate, to value, and to possess a ten-fold, yes, an hundred fold more attractive personality.

And so with every criticism—make of each one a stepping stone toward the heights of superiority.

Again, suppose someone has said of you, "Yes, I could like Smith (or Mrs. Smith) very much, but he (or she) is TOO EMOTIONAL (or 'too timid' or 'lacks self-confidence,' or 'too boastful,' or 'too egotistical.' etc.)"

Then each of these criticisms, which are given here mere as samples, is an unmistakable sign-board advising you to analyze your own emotional stability, and your mentally Imaged Self can be perfected and strengthened in each of these points.

Following this kindly guidance, you are creating the Ideal image of the Self you have longed to be day by day. This IDEAL Self is now your goal, your objective. Now, and we do mean right now, begin to live this ideal, let it be your guide in your work, in your play, let this NEW personality inspire you to greater ambitions, to nobler attempts, to higher achievements.

Because this Imaged You is a mental image, a picture in your mind, do not dismiss it as a shadow, because this image is NOT merely a shadow, it has reality, it is a subtle substance, for it is of the essence of the God-Within.

This "new" personality'-presence has been waiting to become you since the beginning of time—and before! It is simply the REAL YOU which has been silently waiting your arrival clothed in the shadowy film of the false materiality which you have so long thought of as "ME." While your mind has been slowly awakening in this fleshly clothing of the physical this REAL YOU has waited; ageless, eternal, unknown.

Dressed in Light and adorned by the Illumination of the Divine, the unrecognized memories of this REAL YOU spans the thousands and the tens of thousands of years as though they were but yesterdays. In The Silence his ageless YOU is always waiting.

And as you follow faithfully your regular periods of concentration and meditation someday and perhaps soon, as you gaze in rapt attention upon this silent Image ever-present in The Silence...it will speak to you in the hushed voice of intuition. No one else will hear this soundless voice, only you, but if you listen intently it will be your unfailing guide upon the WAY. This voice will tell you of the things you have left undone that separate you from your personality-goal.

So as you accomplish each of these tasks, as they are pointed out to you by your Inner Voice, you will find that you are being lifted day by day nearer and nearer to this splendid vision of the illumined YOU. For as you thus fulfill the immutable God-Law you are bridging the gulf between you and the higher realms where you will commune with the Masters.

You will not work in vain, for you are working with the tremendous powers of desire, ambition, and inspiration. You have endowed your own present personality, in the reflected glory of your perfected mental Image, with a NEW life, a vibrant vitality, and TRUE NOBILITY—and these are the grandest achievements of any life upon this earth.

For, if you have faithfully followed the guidance of this lesson, you have created in your mind a vision of perfection, and just as surely as you hold that vision, just so surely will its glory illuminate your material personality. Now you can appreciate His mystic meaning when the Master, Christ, said to His Initiates, "Ye are the LIGHT of the world."

Remembering that The Cosmic—the unseen universe of God—is

IMPERSONAL, our philosophy teaches each Initiate to be the same. Because when you are impersonal, you no longer waste your strength or scatter your emotions in envy of another's progress in the WAY, unless it is to help him or her to higher attainment. And should you perceive that someone else has passed you upon the Pathway, remember that advancement has been earned.

FOCUS YOUR INNER DESIRES INTO CLEAR-CUT CONCEPTS

To seek something which you cannot define to your own satisfaction is indeed a vain quest. That is why we are helping you to focus your inner desire for a strong, developed, attractive personality upon the creation of a clear-cut image (concept) of that longed-for personality—that real, that perfected YOU. And don't be dismayed when you meet seeming paradoxes and contradictions all along the WAY. You have already studied something about the laws of Nature, and the laws of electrical polarity, and you have learned that these laws represent both the positive and the negative currents of vibration. So you should not be surprised to find both positive and negative influences at work in every experience in your life, just as you find these opposing forces in every manifestation of life and power in the world around you.

As you have long ago learned the supreme purpose of the Great Work of these teachings is to help guide your Soul, and that of every Initiate, to its utmost evolution and to its very highest development. Thus, in gaining Illumination yourself, you are in turn equipped to guide the elementary students, in their strenuous climb toward the heights which you have attained.

In order to reach your own goal, in order to attain the heights yourself, you have been required to master they technique, and the changeless laws and principles of our psychic and cosmic science—all of which have been carefully hidden from the eyes of the unprepared multitudes in our arcane of the Ancient Wisdom.

Let us be perfectly frank and realize that those who are not prepared to receive our advanced teachings actually shrink from the thought of becoming Masters—because they are unwilling to really work to attain the powers that go with Master-ship (or Mastery), The masses are content to play aimlessly, to be idly amused, to waste life in wishful thinking, or vapit dreaming. And because of this you will see on every hand crowds thronging into theatres, amusement parks, saloons, and (in lesser numbers) into churches, shrines and cathe-drals—and in each of these places the multitude seeks just one thing—ESCAPE...FROM REALITY.

Of course, these masses of misled humanity in their blind rush for escape are like stampeding cattle, they actually do not SEE what they are running away from they need a new perspective of reality. This new per-spective—reality as it is—we give to each Initiate in this sacred Fellowship.

But perhaps we should not judge this countless horde of men and women who are seeking escape from reality too harshly—because they have been taught falsehood and misconception about Life, about Love and about God. They have been taught that Life is a drab, dreary prison, that Love is just a forbidden sex-hunger, and that God is some terrible, cruel, vengeful Being up in the sky somewhere beyond the clouds. And that gracious living, good clothes, fine or desirable homes, a good bank account, a luxurious car, abounding health, laughter and fun, and happiness are mortal sins in the baleful eyes of this "...jealous God!"

No wonder the world seeks escape,

But, like the stampeding herd, blind flight from false reality may plunge the herd over the precipice into UNREALITY.

Lesson No. 19
PATHWAY TO HEALTH, WEALTH AND HAPPINESS

Fourth Gateway of The Temple Invisible, Being The Secret Instruction Taught by The Masters in White, Whose Sublime Precepts Are Now Exemplified in These Lessons.

The Degree of Illumination

RADIANT DESIRE-ACTION ILLUMINATES LIFE

We live today .in a world torn by dissension, by strife, by "wars and rumors of wars," by distrust, by hatred and by misunderstanding. Social, economic and political systems are being tested, and many of these are falling to pieces before our eyes. And these often ugly and destructive conditions in the world at large are being reflected in neurotic, unstable and unhealthful conditions in the individual lives of the people around us.

Of course these diseased conditions both in the body politic and in the physical bodies around us are being forced upon our attention every day, and everywhere "Evil" (the negative) is clamoring for still more attention. In simple psychological self-protection, then, let us DETACH ourselves (our attention) from these destructive currents of thought, and look at those problems to a great extent impersonally, for unless we do, mayhap, we, too, venturing too far from our sure foundation, shall likewise be lost in the depths of the quick-sands around our Pathway.

For each student is heir to a "vocation, " a mission, and in that mission only will we find Illumination. This truth is strikingly expressed in these words:

"Every being has a definite vocation (mission), and his vocation is the light which illuminates his life. The man who disregards his vocation is a lamp unlit.

"He who with sincerity seeks his real purpose in life is himself sought by that purpose. As he concentrates on that purpose a light begins to clear his confusion— call it revelation, call it inspiration, call it what you will.

"It is mistrust (doubt) that misleads. Sincerity leads straight to the goal.

"Every soul is born with a certain purpose, and the light of that purpose is kindled in his soul."—Herald of Light (India).

The so-called "mystery" life is nothing else than the lack of understanding—the lack of knowledge. Men walk in darkness because they are walking in their own shadows. And yet today man persists in blindfolding his eyes against the Light within, the mystic brilliance which radiates from the Soul, the "Heavenly Man." Witness these words from the ancient wisdom of The Zohar:

"Believe not that man consists solely of flesh, skin, bones and veins. "The real part of man is his Soul, and the things just mentioned, flesh, skin, bones, veins, are only the outward covering, a veil, but are not the man.

"When man departs (Dies) he divests himself of all the veils which cover him.

"And all these different parts of the body correspond to the secret of the divine wisdom.

"The skin typifies the heavens, which extends everywhere and cover everything like a garment.

"The flesh puts us in mind of the evil side of the universe.

"The bones and the veins (and the nerves and glands) symbolize the divine chariots, which are the servants of God.

But they are all the outer coverings. For, inside man there is the secret of the 'Heavenly man.'

"Everything below takes place in the same manner as everything above...'God created man in His own image.'

TEACHINGS FOUNDED UPON BROTHERHOOD

The great and basic truth underlying our teachings is that they are founded upon the brotherhood of man, and within the great general brotherhood of all men and women, ours is a closely knit Order of our students. These are mutually bound by their common knowledge of the ancient wisdom of The Masters, as revealed to them in ever advancing degrees—a knowledge unknown to the masses of mankind and worthless to them until they have attained at least a primary degree of understanding of the occult.

Upon every hand today we hear much about the "brotherhood of man," and writers constantly re-iterate these fine sounding words, but as you investigate you will discover that this is generally a very empty phrase— meaningless because little or no brotherly spirit or action backs up the words. Among nations the phrase "brotherhood of man" cloaks territorial grabs, aggressions, persecution, and WAR; among individuals the same glib words usually reek of the oil of hypocrisy dripping from the lips of deceit. For without brotherly spirit, help and understanding proven in deeds these words are just a cruel mockery.

But to those advanced in knowledge of the Infinite God-Law and the secret wisdom imparted in our arcane instruction, the brotherhood of man is a reality, because he knows full well that all men are interdependent— depending upon one another, and this in turn necessitates the inter-relationship of mankind. Each is related to all and all are related to each.

In the outer universe we behold that the suns, stars and planets of every system bear exact relationships to each other, and that all are held rigidly in their relative positions by the unvarying God-Law, and in the same way and under the same changeless Law all human being journey in their appointed, relative courses in life.

Fundamentally, a number of the root-religions, including Christianity, were founded upon this elementary idea of "the brotherhood of man," but in each of these religions this noble sounding idea has been debased by limiting "brotherhood" to mean only those of the same religious faith.

But in our system of philosophy, we interpret fellowship to mean some-thing infinitely greater than merely the idea of a universal life-energy which animates every human body, a bond far more divine than the mere fact that all men are created from the same material substances, which is about all that is implied by that outworn word "brotherhood" today.

In other words this "brotherhood of man" is something which almost everybody talks about, but usually their words mean nothing because they aren't DOING anything to prove its reality.

"First, you will agree that as you learn how best to meet and to understand and to use your environment (surroundings) just so you will prosper and gain happiness, and enjoy health in mind and in body. Again, unless you are living on a desert island (and few of us do), you are going to find quite a few other people included in your environment. So, in just about everything you do, in everything you want, and in everything you possess, you must consider these other human beings, for they are part of your picture, and no matter what you think, these people are related to your own life at every point.

Because each one of us in our environment is related to every other person within our personal worlds, in turn in this gregarious human family every other person is related to us either directly or indirectly, "For no man liveth to himself " These human relationships bring various forms of pressure to bear upon every one of us. And just as others must consider you in their lives, even so you must consider them, for you are a part of their world, too. This remains forever true, whether you literally believe that all men are the "children of God" or not.

We live in a World of change—before our eyes shifts this endless panorama of passing conditions, nations, races, continents and civilizations, including our own. Indeed, each student must echo with realization these words of old, "For I am a stranger and a pilgrim here." Detach yourself from your part in each problem of this world, and you too will exclaim—"This too will pass."

Why not stop living as if you were going to live forever on this earth or even in your present environment; because your surroundings and the circumstances of your present life can (and often do) change overnight. Today you are faced with problems that spring from your own particular environment, so your problems are different from the problems of your neighbor. But change that environment, or change your perception of that environment, and you solve your problem, for they change and pass and are no more.

These material things, or these material conditions which cause your problems are changeable and transient, even as you yourself, are, and in this way you are growing, advancing and developing far beyond the limitations of your problems.

You can outgrow problems, just as the child can outgrow childish toys. And when we point out to you the transitory existence of all earthly things, conditions and circumstances, it is not because we are fatalists and view the scene as hopeless, but rather because we realize that eternal change means eternal growth, eternal development, eternal progress.

By CHANGE life has grown, developed and progressed from the tiny one-celled amoeba to the vibrant physical body of man, "fearfully and wonderfully made."

Because you are endowed.with individual Soul—indeed an integral personality vibrating within the eternally existing Over-Soul of the universe—know then, that your power to change every problem and every adversity into a victory or a success is, like "the kingdom of God," within you.

In the world around you change is everywhere. Each `birthday of yours marks change. Yet 'tis but a sorry part you play if you just take a back seat and bemoan the fact that those things or even those persons upon which or upon whom you have pinned your hopes and desires can no longer serve you because they have changed. Or, mayhap, they, too, have 'passed' away from your environment.

Rather, is it not the wiser, the nobler part to realize that`you are destined to live in a changing world, and that you, too, in the light of this knowledge must change and adapt yourself to the changes which remake your environment almost daily?

For change is the first lesson in this mystery school of the Creator—this school that we call "life."

Someone has well said that we are a part of everything we have met. In other words, you have absorbed something from everything which you have contacted. No, you do not take with you the material, objective thing or element which you have contacted, but you do take with you the Impression, the experience, or th knowledge which you have gained by perceiving this object by your physical senses. Everything of material form that you find in your environment was ordained by Supreme Intelligence to be placed amid your surroundings so that you may gain knowledge, experience and understanding through contacting or using this material substance. When we no longer have physical contact with any material thing that thing no longer exists for us, except as impression or experience. We live in a mental world of remembered impressions and of remembered experiences. Even remembered dreams.

SELF-ADJUSTMENT—THE MASTER KEY TO HARMONY

Without imagination there is no freedom., without harmony there is no happiness, and the adjustment of self to conditions and to environment is the Master Key to harmony. And here is where so many people fail in life, suffer lack and limitation, and succumb to their problems because they lack the imagination (the vision) to adapt or adjust themselves to new and unexpected circumstances.

And again many people create new conditions and entirely different environment by entering upon a new career, business, partnership, or making other definite and radical changes in their lives—and each such change of course calls for our satisfactory adjustment of ourselves to harmonize with the new circumstances and with our changed surroundings.

In order to attract success and to attain happiness we must develop the ability to harmonize (adjust) to the everchanging conditions of our present environment, or in any new surroundings which we ourselves seek, for upon harmony depends your ultimate satisfaction in life, as well as your success and your happiness.

For you have within you the potential power to adapt yourself and to live in harmony with the world about you, and as you cultivate your power of adaptation you will be surprised to see how.your material problems work out their own solutions almost automatically. Without this ability to readjust yourself and so gain harmony with your environment, circumstances, and with the people in your personal world, you are simply courting life-long sorrow and failure.

Remember, this power of adapting yourself to your surroundings and to other people is a MENTAL Power, so don't let your mind dwell on those fancied "good old days," (after all, they were really not so good, you know), but instead concentrate upon harmony in the living present, in the "eternal NOW. " Hob-nobbing with the ghosts of the past is just a short cut to failure and to discord in the present.

Would you escape from the gnawing memories of your yesterdays? Then adjust yourself to the wonderful changes of today, and live in mental harmony with the glowing promise of tomorrow. For the great and irresistible law of change is touching the life of everybody in the world, either directly or indirectly. None can escape, and every one of us must either work WITH this law of change, adjust ourselves to harmonize with the new and unexpected conditions, and live in vibrant attunement with the new order, or like the dodo-bird, we shall be eliminated because we WOULD NOT Harmonize our pulsations with the heart-beat of this changing, evolving, developing world in which we live.

One of The Masters has said:"The final perfection ('the-Illumination') of the human self is absorption in the Infinite," In other words, the final stages of Initiation ('the final perfection') lead us to such harmony with The Infinite that we are one with the Creator, and our whole initiation has awakened us to cosmic consciousness.

This constantly changing, gigantic panorama which we call the universe is Thought-inspired and Thought-directed—and these universal thought-forces are similar to our own, but infinitely magnified in the Divine Mind, emanations of the Supreme Intelligence. We are everywhere surrounding by the vibratory currents from three worlds or realms—the material (physical), the mental and the spiritual.

These vibrations are currents of energy or power that are silent, invisible; but they abound with the unthinkable force that can change a life, (or a nation or a world) over-night. You can "tune-in" to these magnetic, attractive, rebuilding forces at any minute of your life, but whatever gifts you receive from each will depend upon the degree of your own receptivity (FAITH).

And here you are in the-midst of these three worlds, you, the microcosm, endowed with a MIND which you can train to respond in perfect harmony with the vibrations from each of these three: realms, and day by day you are evolving your personality by your harmony with these unseen forces through your conscious thought, Or if through ignorance or neglect, you ignore these finer forces and seek the coarser influences from negative planes, then your personality retrotrades to the purely animal realm.

MASTERSHIP—TRANSCENDING THE HUMAN SELF

In your own life today, as you study these words, you may be very much nearer to becoming a Master than you suspect—Perhaps you have not valued highly enough the things you have already mastered—just pause and realize how many things you have that other persons around you lack. Never complain about those things you think you ought to have, but instead give thanks for what you have attained, and reach for, those other things even if one of them is a star. Yes, even reach for a star, but while you are reaching don't lose any gems you now have in the dust beneath your feet.

Let us illustrate just what we mean. Have you ever decided that you .were a failure in life, have you been discouraged and ready to give up, just because your idea of your personal success was based upon the ambitions which you had not yet realized? And yet probably just at that time you had many things in your life which were real gems—things which others would give the world to possess, such as perhaps abounding health, strength, education, mastery of a trade or a profession, a happy home life, or happy, intelligent children, and/or the admiration of true friends.

Any or all of these, plus a host of illuminating experiences and a broadened understanding of life. Maybe you have overlooked these blessings because they were not of your immediate ambition—so don't forget to appreciate these priceless things that ARE yours, and keep right on reaching for the star of success.

Many of your lessons have really been journeys in the esoteric, because this course of study is the modern prototype of the ancient, 'Mystery Schools' and our inner teachings are descended from the ageless wisdom of The Masters in White. And our mission is not to hide this knowledge or to make it a secret to those who are drawn to us as members and students. But instead our mission is to reveal much of the unknown and to unveil the mysteries of life to those who qualify.

From your first lesson, on that day when you became our, student, our work has been to help you to mentally change the centering of your conscious attention upon the very small area which was then your personal world, and to enable you to unfold your powers of mental vision so that you might a draw away from this smaller world and view this world and this universe from a proper perspective.

This we have done so that you might be able to see the WHOLE FOREST rather than the close trees and leaves which hemmed you in.

Through constant practice of your exercises and your faithful following of the thought of each lesson your field of awareness has gradually expanded to approach cosmic consciousness.

And yet nowhere have we found any proof of "Divine Punishment," no vengeful or malicious retribution." Nowhere have we found a horrible or cruel "God" who measures our "punishment" for mistakes, errors or "sins". Instead everywhere we find the beauty of harmony and the rhythm of the God-Law protecting us upon the WAY.

For we would have each aspiring student realize that but one great thing is required of us upon this Pathway—that we evolve. Each must become conscious of the desire to evolve, and then develop the WILL TO EVOLVE, and then we shall be rewarded with our own rich heritage of the finest things in life.

LESSON NO. 20
PATHWAY TO HEALTH, WEALTH AND HAPPINESS

Fourth Gateway of The temple Invisible, Being the Secret Instruction Taught by The Masters in White, Whose Sublime Precepts Are Now Exemplified In These Lessons.

The Degree of Illumination

"UP FROM COMPULSION" COMES YOUR MASTERY

"Up from muscle and Compulsion, through brain and discussion to sympathy and persuasion and, lastly, agreement, equality, liberty, the progression is inevitable, the series persistent. After the man of brawn has beaten his way, the man of brains argued his way, the man of kindness coaxed his way, comes the serene, superior man (The Master), liberating, loving, with nothing to hate and nothing to fear, setting all free and being set free, demanding nothing and receiving all, wise, loving and beloved.

"And so, after all fetishisms, idolatries, superstitions, incantations, sacrifices, rites, polytheisms, theisms, comes a serene, participating enlarging including Godhood; without temples, ceremonies, prayers, obeisances, creeds or dogmas reverencing all, believing all, accepting all, loving all, equal with all, blessing, uniting with all.

(Liberty and Necessity).

Our liberty might be compared to that of a passenger on a long railway train, He goes right and left, here and there, up and down, and by starting at the forward end of the train may really seem to go a long way back toward the place from which he came. But all this liberty to go back and reverse his journey is trivial and practically deceptive, for all the time the mighty train is hurling him forward in one direction like a projectile. Even while walking backward he is going forward.

"So it is with all of us, We turn here and there and boast of our liberty, which seems real enough, and believe we have power to go back to any extent, but all the time the universe is carrying us forward in its mighty purpose with resistless speed and absolute inclusion. We may neither stop this train, retard its motion, nor jump off."—from "Dawn Thought," by Lloyd.

Compulsion, or necessity, which men call evil, makes its presence first known (manifests) as a giant lever, working against man's resistance, but to the Illumined Initiate this "evil" called compulsion is transformed into Opportunity. And Mastery sees opportunity as the servant of the Master-Will.

Let us simply state two great truths concerning that advanced thought-realm known to The Masters as "Illumination"—which is in reality attunement to the God-Law (the Infinite) through cosmic consciousness, or universal awareness. This higher consciousness may dawn upon you suddenly, or its light may filter into your mind gradually. As Bucke says of one: "There was a clearly marked moment when the light began to break through, but Illumination came gradually," and he further points out "it must be remembered that Illumination that comes gradually may be as complete as that which comes instantly."

We trust that still you continue your regular periods of aloneness in The Silence, sitting before your altar, lighted by candles only, amid the invisible odor of your devotional incense, in rapt MEDITATION. Simply relax and without strain or effort ponder upon this mystery called Life, calmly seeking to visualize the invisible, reaching forth in thought to touch the intangible.

Now that you are treading the Pathway of Illumination, through the gateway of silence, ascending slowly the mystic stairway of Meditation you approach the conscious meeting of that part of Self that is deathless, Soul, and sooner or later through that mysterious link that we call intuition you may contact the all-present Over-Soul. And then in that presence you will feel and know the vibrations of the creative God—Within infinite in love, in wisdom and in power.

For in your hour in The Silence, in rapt meditation, only then can you cast aside your earthly worries and your personality problems, and lift your consciousness to oneness with God. Thus you contact ("tune-in") the Divine—the inner Soul within your own "heart" (mind). Only through communing with your Soul-Self can you learn the mysteries of life, only through Soul-Consciousness can you become truly an Illumined One—a Master.

> Hundreds of years before Christ was
> born, these words were written in the
> Bhagavad Gita (the "song Celestial"):
> "Death am I, and immortal Life I am.
> Arjuna. Sat and Asat—visible Life
> And Life invisible. I am alike for all! I
> know not hate, I know not favour.
> What is made is Mine. But them that
> worship Me with love, I love; They are
> in Me, and I in them."

ILLUMINATION—AWARENESS OF THE DIVINE GOD-SELF

I think you will agree that anything of which you are not aware of does not exist for you. Very simply stated Illumination is in its final definition your AWARENESS (recognition) of _your own God-Self, and the knowledge that it is one with the Infinity of God—in other words, your conscious unity with the Divine Flame ("Light") which vibrates within you. This is the final step of the Adept. This attainment Christ referred to when he said "Ye must be born again." This was the crowning mystery contained within His teachings. But a as probably you yourself know how this divine mystery has been debased, made common and vulger in the doctrines of our modern "Christian" churches!

Truly, the "pearls" have been "cast before swine", and how could the animal minds of the "Swine" comprehend the divine mysteries of Illumination when Hidden beneath the word "pearls?" Christ plainly told His Disciples that His teachings were clothed in mystery so that the unitiated could not understand them.

It was Emerson who said, "The purpose of Life seems to be to acquaint man with himself ".

So, begin to realize that your every-day experiences are but stepping stones to ever greater experiences, and that every forward step of yours is a link in an endless chain of steps leading to a greater destiny for you. As you journey upon the WAY to Illumination, your consciousness is expanded in ever greater circles.

Perhaps now you begin to perceive that this material world around you is not what you have thought it to be at all—you yourself have limited this physical world by your own thinking. Your own thoughts have been limiting in direct proportion to your former limited understanding of the infinitely creative God-Law.

TRYING TO MEASURE THE INFINITE WITH LITTLE YARD-STICKS

Mankind imagines the universe to be a limited, a finite creation, because the concept of Infinity staggers the human mind, until that mind is Illumined. So man has evolved two little, artificial yard-sticks by which he seeks to measure that boundless infinity which surrounds him. These two inadequate yard-sticks we call time and space, and both are artificial because neither of them exists outside of human consciousness—each is just a product of the groping human, "mortal" mind.

The idea of time depends upon change, or relative movement. You cannot conceive of time without at the same time relating it to change, or movement, and it is almost impossible to conceive of the surrounding universe as infinite, boundless, measureless and without beginning or end. The idea of time alone, unrelated to anything else, is meaningless.

This boundless ocean of vibrant, creative God-Mind-Energy which surrounds us must have always existed as eternal Movement, Force-In-Action, everlasting, circular MOTION. Motion is only dimly perceived by Consciousness. We seek to measure changes around us, changes born of motion, by trying to hold our tiny stop-watches in weak mortal hands to time the vibrations of Nature. Thus we would time the heart-beats of God.

The Cosmic World is the infinite cradle of our tiny material world. It is the mighty hand of God that gently sways that cosmic cradle of the universe.

The multitude lacks knowledge, and the faculties of the masses of humanity are limited to animal sensa-tion—else why did our elder Master, Christ, weep over the sleeping multitudes of Jerusalem? So this second little yard-stick which we calls space can only exist to the multitudes of the non-Initiates as picturing a separating "time-lag", (separateness), between objects or material things. Of course, in REALITY this is but a mistaken interpretation, a consciousness of an assumed separation. For in the infinite sequence of creative God-Energy there can be no breaks, no actual "space" between the links in this endless chain of the continuity of vibration.

Our mortal (physical) eyes are sadly out of focus, we look upon unrealized motion and cannot see its unbroken transmutation from one movement to another, but we must divide its eternal ONENESS (unity) into spaces, and we even behold the rainbow as a broken arc because we see only its upper portion.

Following this all too brief analysis we draw very near to the astounding truth that what you have mentally conceived as being separate worlds or realms, as for instance, the material and the spiritual, are simply different aspects, view-points or manifestations of the ONE great, vibrant God-Power. These worlds each man sees through the colorings and the degrees of his own consciousness.

As our ancient Masters taught in the long, long ago, numberless other and higher, "worlds" (realms) are just now waiting only an arm's length away from you, waiting to be revealed to you through your awakened, developed, Illuminated consciousness. You have from now until the end(?) of eternity to explore these now unknown "worlds".

We would have you realize that between every manifestation of the universal God-

Law there is an unbroken relativity, every phenomena is related to every other phenomena in an unbreakable chain. You cannot measure the Cosmic with a 3-foot yard stick.

"THE WORLD IS TOO MUCH WITH US"—RISING ABOVE IT.

Cries the poet, "The World is too Much with us," a truth which should become very clear to you in your hours of weariness, of monotony, or of disappointment in people who have failed you. Yet it is within your power to withdraw from the turmoil, the constant strife, and the aimless rush of the world about you simply by banishing this lower, earth-world from your thoughts and entering the higher world of meditation through the door of Silence. Withdraw your attention from this lower world around you and instantly your mind can soar to higher realms at your command, as we have so plainly taught you in former lessons.

For God's realms (worlds) above this are countless. Yet upon the foot-steps of thought you can walk unafraid through these many mansions of your "Father's" universe.

You, too, can catch the cadence (vibrations) of "the music of the spheres," just as the wonders of the azure skies above you on a clear night, when and where all is silent, may unite your Soul with the wordless song of the universe, You, too, can attune your mind and heart with thought-vibrations from The Masters—thoughts which illumined their minds thousands of years ago. Thoughts never die, you know, and these mental vibrations forever flowing onward can reach your mind with magnified momentum and power across the ages if your mind is but receptive.

Some such wave of vibration and inspiration from a more distant past must have entered the consciousness of the Psalmist, as he, gazing into the Palestinian skies, murmured:

"The heavens (skies) declare the glory of God, and the firmament showeth His handiwork."—(Psalms 19:1)

From perhaps some even then long-lost Atlantis an even mightier message was mystically wafted to the Psalmist, God's ONENESS WITH MAN, as reflected in these majestic words:

"When I consider the heavens, the work of Thy fingers, the moon and the stars, which Thou hast ordained; what is man that Thou art mindful of him? and the son of man, that Thou visitest him?—Psalms 8:3-4.

Thus also from the starry skies fell gently upon Job in his hours of MEDITATION the echoing grandeur of the wisdom of the Holy Masters who were long gone in his time, because his words yet live, though..spo-ken into the awful immensity of the dome above his earthly couch of affliction—listen to his words:

"Canst thou bind the sweet influence of the Pleiades, or-loose the bands of Orion? Canst thou bring forth Mazzaroth in his season? or canst thou guide Arcturus with his sons?"—Job 38:3;-32.

Through these words we trace Job's recognition of the stupendous fact that the immutable God-Law had sustained the gigantic universe in perfect harmony from the beginning, and that likewise the Creator would forever maintain ceaseless vigil over His unnumbered incarnations in human form.

The mantles of the great Masters of antiquity await our claim today—you, too, can receive the power and the vision of splendor that comes in meditation to The Illumined Ones. Just as the Psalmist of old looked upward into the heavens with a receptive mind, so you in turn by developing receptivity can contact the divine harmonies of those higher and nobler vibrations.

The wise Masters of old often referred to the star-studded universe as "God's living garment." Even as you yourself are related to the farthest star, even so each star reflects God. Hark to these words of the Psalmist:

"...O Lord my God...Who coverest Thyself with LIGHT as with a garment; who stretchest out the heavens like a curtain." (Psalms 104:1-2)

Meditation upon the wonders of the universe has always lifted the minds of men to new realms of power, to new perspectives of glory; to new heights of attainment. For our own lives, our own minds and our own futures are interwoven into the very fabric of the cosmic universe. No wonder that the prophets of old and still more ancient Masters did obesience to the sun, the moon, the stars and the phenomena of the skies. They knew, just as we know today, that all life that exists in this world of ours results from and is sustained by electromagnetic vibration-currents from the sun, and that the moon and stars combine their vibrations with those of the sun. From these combined vibrations we perceive earthly electricity, extremes of weather, perhaps even tidal waves, earthquakes and the gradual rising and sinking of entire continents.

MEDITATE UPON SOULS THAT WALK WITH THE STARS

The higher, the nobler, the more spiritual your subject for meditation, the higher, the nobler, the more spiritual your own life becomes.

We grow like that upon which we focus our minds, Thought transform. Each revolving planet and each vibrant atom obeys the God-Law-Source of:all power and of all life. You will remember that we have taught you that the. suns, planets and stars are giant power-houses, each sending forth into the cosmos vast streams of energy which feed power into other parts of this inconceivable mechanism which we call the universe. Let us not forget that all of this unthinkable power originates in the Supreme Intelligence.

And it is that same Supreme Intelligence vibrating in your Illumined Soul that will enable you to walk with the stars, yes, and more...to walk with God. Let us say with Paul, "Think on these things."

May we not understand with Thomas Carlyle that "the universe is not dead and demoniacal, a charnel-house with spectres; but godlike, and my Father's."

Now this Supreme Intelligence—which some of our Masters have named The Cosmic Mind—evolves in your mind, and every Illumined Human Mind, through developed consciousness, because each such mind is an emanation of the Cosmic Mind. So we would have you realize that your mind is capable of almost unlimited heights of development, power and expression.

First, then, know that nothing in your life today is so great that it cannot become greater, and no good in your life is SO good that it cannot become better.

Your life is NOT stationary, but is itself a process of evolving, of developing. In your life day by day Spirit is descending through your mind into the material circumstances of your environment, and has power to transform your surroundings. Such is the meaning of the circle enclosing the triangle among our secret symbols.

Let us ask you frankly, have you made meditation a HABIT of your life? Remember, habit is an effortless method of expression. For this reason we have striven in your earlier lessons to impress upon you the necessity of persistent and constant practice, until both concentration and meditation should become a sort of "second nature" to you. If you have followed the exercises we have given you, you will realize how easily it is to acquire this priceless habit of mental control.

After the first few weeks or the first few months of relaxation and .meditation, which you have made a habit of following at regular periods set aside for this purpose, you will wonder at the ease with which you are able to enter at will into these higher realms of psychic awareness. Also, early in your mental exercises you will be surprised to perceive parts of your dream coming true. And no matter how small these first results may be, yet they are actual, and are the proof that greater manifestations are on the way.

When you have followed this psychic method of attainment beyond the first few months and on for a year or two years, you will become amazed at the miracle-working powers of the wonderful Self within. You will come to know that this hitherto unrecognized Self is in reality a giant of accomplishment, with a power and an intuitive wisdom of which you had never dreamed.

When in meditation you focus your "mind's eye" (your concentrated attention) upon this inmost Self, you are attuned to the divine center of love, of understanding and of abundance. Never sleeping, always alert, and ever obedient to your commands, this giant genie within waits day and night to serve you—waits for you to contact him in The Silence, where you can submerge your confused, warring, worried conscious mind into the peaceful depths of the psychic sea of meditation.

Then, "lost to the (material) world" listen to the soundless voice of this boundless Inner Self first—sound-less because this is the voice called "Intuition" Some call this voice mental impression. Again we tell you, listen to this voice everyday and before long you, too, will prove that this SELF WITHIN, even though your humble servant is seeming, is the mightiest friend you can ever have in the whole world.

SECRET OF TUNING IN TO YOUR PSYCHIC SELF

Again, and in other words and with deeper meaning, we give you the secret of "tuning in" to your psychic self. That secret is first of all found in the habit we trust you have already formed, the habit of physical and mental RELAXATION at will, and almost instantly. If you have not formed this habit, by all means go back over your lessons until you come to our exercises in relaxation, meditation and concentration, and begin to acquire that habit today.

When through practice you have acquired this habit of contacting your Inner Self at a .certain period each day or night, then at any time and anywhere no matter what your surroundings, you can make this mental contact within a very few moments, and your guidance will come to you quite clearly through the voice of intuition (impression), or sometimes the flash of a mental picture so plain that you may almost feel like exclaiming, "I must be seeing things!"—as indeed you are. But be very certain that you heed the voice, and seek the meaning of the picture...and let that meaning guide your action in any matter that is at issue.

The priceless advantage which this habit of the inner contact with the psychic world gives you is this, suppose that circumstances suddenly seem to go all wrong, there is a crisis in your life, and you are facing an unexpected emergency. Instead of "going to pieces," wringing your hands helplessly, or giving up in despair and losing all, you simply, trustingly, and calmly withdraw into the Silence within a few seconds, turn to that giant Self within, and unerring guidance comes to you almost within the minute. Once you train your smaller conscious mind to become the servant of that greater psychic Mind-Self within, life may not become even then a bed of roses, but you will develop the unseen powers to triumph far beyond your fondest expectations.

Each student, before he can claim the crown of Illumination, must make the habit of inner meditation his "second nature."

The Divine Plan of Life does not concern itself primarily with physical, material, animal life as its GREAT OBJECTIVE, but uses the lower physical, bodily life simply as a means to an end, and that great end or purpose is THE MYSTICAL LIFE or SOUL, SPIRIT or PSYCHIC LIFE. That is the tremendous teaching of The Masters in White, and to carry forth their wisdom and doctrines is the divine mission of these lessons.

We all know that if we would have normal, healthy, vigorous physical bodies we must give those bodies intelligent care, we must learn something of the rules of good health, we must give due thought and consideration to our physical bodies.

But, as we have said, the physical life is not the GREAT REASON for existence here upon earth, that great reason is the mystical life of the God-Soul within.

When we desire to see our physical selves, we look into a mirror. But this Inner-Self—this Psychic Self—in what mirror can we behold that mystical Self ?

Briefly, the name of this great mirror is MEDITATION, for in meditation we turn consciousness back upon itself, we introvert thought, so to speak. This understanding of the understanding we call meditation—the attunement between the two consciousnesses, the eyes of inward-turning thought which behold the fact of... GOD.

LESSON NO. 21
PATHWAY TO HEALTH, WEALTH AND HAPPINESS

Fourth Gateway of The Temple Invisible, Being The Secret Instruction Taught by The Masters in White, Whose Sublime Precepts Are Now Exemplified in these Lessons.

The Degree of Illumination

"I HAVE SAID: YE ARE GODS,"—(CHRIST)

Abdul Baha says—

"To life the life is

To be no cause of grief to anyone.

"To be silent concerning the faults of others—to pray for them—and to help them, through kindness, to correct their faults."

To be a cause of healing for every sick one, a comforter for every sorrowful one, (like) a pleasant water for every thirsty one, a heavenly table for every hungry one, a star to every horizon, a light for every lamp, a herald to everyone who yearns for the Kingdom of God.

Consider the candle how it weeps its life away drop by drop that it may shed its light.

And note these words from Amiel's "Journal"—

"To the materialist philosopher the beautiful is a mere accident, and therefore rare.

To the spiritual philosopher the beautiful is the rule, the, law, the universal foundation of things, to which every form returns as soon)as the force of accident is withdrawn...Heroism, ecstacy, prayer, love, enthusiasm weave a halo round the brow, for they are a setting free of the soul, which through them gains force to make its envelope transparent and shine through upon all around it. Beauty is then a phenomenon belonging to the spiritualization of matter. It is momentary transfiguration...a token fallen from heaven to earth in order to remind us of the ideal world.

"As a powerful electric current can render metals luminous, and reveal their essence by the color of their flame, so INTENSE LIFE AND SUPREME JOY can make the most simple mortal dazzlingly beautiful. Man therefore, is never more truly man than in these divine states."

Teaching that "the most simple mortal" can actually rise to the beauty of the divine estate, when Illumined, Christ when on earth quoted these words, "I have said: ye are Gods," from the Mosaic Scriptures to His Initiates, For the truth is that the Avatar, Christ, was the Master of a secret Mystery School, and those whom we call His "disciples" were in reality the Initiates of that far—away age. In these cryptic words their Teacher was simply reminding them of the Illumination, the Great Awareness, into which He had led them upon THE WAY.

This Great Awareness—this Illumination—was later actually demonstrated before the Physical eyes of His Initiates by the Christ-Master in the Transfiguration, as you will remember.

It is inspiration which transforms, which illumines, and which transfigures. When you are inspired you are transformed—you are transfigured—you are no longer your old, dull, listless self at all. You are joyously ALIVE, you are ENTHUSIASTIC, you are VIBRANT with inner power.

And inspiration is NOT limited to the realm of "genius."

THE FIRST STEP–HARMONY WITH UNIVERSAL MIND

No, inspiration is not limited to the realm of "genius" only, for this spiritual energy, this rebuking force, is everywhere about us, and is within the reach of every one who will qualify for its reception. And this force of inspiration can and will work wonders for you in your every-day life, because it is a transforming power.

But, like every other worth while "gift", if we would receive these higher vibrations of inspirational thought, we must qualify ourselves for their reception. Before you can attract any incoming wave of inspiration there are certain steps which you must take, and the first of these steps is to establish harmony with Universal Mind. Someone has well defined this first step as being "in tune with the Infinite."

This state of harmony simply means that every faculty, every thought, and every purpose of your whole being must be attuned to oneness with the Divine, the Supreme, the Universal Mind—that Mind which you call God.

The next step is awareness—in other words, you must be always alert, watchful and expectant, so that you can recognize the answer to your plea, prayer or your great desire the moment that answer is manifest in your personal world. You must be not only vigilant so that you can recognize the answer to your answer from the Unseen Realm will come in the form of mental guidance toward your goal, and you must be able to translate or interpret these mental guidance-impressions into a workable plan.

Let us explain this seeming paradox this way. Blessings do not fall into your lap from some mystical tree in a vague and far-away Heaven without effort or action on your part, but your training does show you how to draw upon Universal Mind for the guiding, "impressions" which will effectively direct your own energy and action to the possession of those blessings which are your goal.

But of course first you must master the technique of expressing (translating into action) these impressions (guiding impulses) which are sent to you from Divine Mind. Here, for instance, is an advanced musician who is composing beautiful melodies. In other words, he is expressing, or translating, certain musical impressions which he has received mentally, because perhaps a lifetime of musical awareness has rendered him sensitive (receptive) to these impressions.

But before he can express (or interpret) these musical impressions, no matter how beautiful they may be, the musician must master the entire technique of music, from the primary rudiments of music to the most intricate tonal combinations. Music does not "just happen," music is inspiration PLUS, mastery.

Just so, the artist is expressing upon the canvas the artistic impressions which his mind has received because that mind was sensitive to this unseen guidance. But first that artist must spend time and effort in acquiring the technique of drawing, of form, of color and the skill to blend all these into a perfect harmony. without this training he remains a "dauber."

Only through training, practice and faithful devotion to mastering detail and technique, only thus can the musician or the artist acquire those skills which proclaims the Initiate a Master are never haphazard or accidental.

When you have consciously sent forth a prayer, an affirmation, or an appeal for some coveted good fortune, and that good fortune comes to you as a direct result, it is easy for you to understand this as being the result of a known cause and a recognized result. But what is the explanation when, for example, you have not knowingly sent forth a prayer, an appeal or an affirmation, and yet unexpectedly "out of the blue" seemingly you receive some golden idea, some distinct impression, or some effective inspiration which leads you straight to your desired goal?

We have told you that in the realm of the God-Law, that realm which includes all of life and the entire universe, nothing is haphazard or accidental. In this world, as in the universe, all is ordered by Divine Plan, and nothing "just happens," "without a cause." "Whatsoever a man soweth, that shall he also reap" is eternally TRUE.

In such a case as we have stated above, the fact is that you have not connected cause and effect because you are not now conscious of the cause. In such cases you have established a "rhythm" (harmony) of thought with Universal Mind, you have developed attunement and receptivity with the unseen forces, so that your unconscious prayer, petition or affirmation has brought its sure and certain result. Perhaps your appeal has gone forth to the Mighty Universal Mind while you were in a semi-trance, or "lost to the world" in concentration, or in the twilight of meditation, or even while you slept, because, remember, only the conscious mind, while that deeper mind never slumbers but keeps a vigil that is constant.

But, you may ask, what becomes of this divine guidance, this inspired response to .my prayer or my affirmation if I fail to receive it, or, having received it, I do not follow it, or because of obstinacy I reject it altogeth-er—is the response then lost? Not at all, because then the guidance simply enters another and more receptive and sensitive mind, still retaining its identity for manifestation in that other life which also has the same need as yours. Nothing is lost in the Divine Plan—it is just lost to you,.

We would have you realize that you can follow this inspired, intuitive, divine guidance only so far as your own understanding and sensitivity are developed. That is why you have become a student and that is why you receive these incomparable lessons—to help you to develop these faculties.

In other words, the higher your development of these occult faculties, the more perfect will be your reception of these "soundless voices," and the greater your reward. Since we have assumed the tremendous duty, as inspired by The Masters, of helping you to perfect your reception of these cosmic guiding impressions we seek to impart a three-fold preparation; the physical, the mental and the spiritual. These are the three points symbolized by our mystic triangle.

As we have taught you from the beginning, what you FOCUS your thought upon today, you will become (or attract) tomorrow.

Someone has said that "tomorrow never comes," but it DOES.

And that "tomorrow" when you will see your dream come true can be the day after today, or it may be deferred to more distant days—just when that "tomorrow" of your realization arrives depends upon the quality, the intensity and the power of your thought-processes. And further, to a great extent your thought-power will be magnified by the perfect focusing of your attention upon your goal, and upon these lessons which point the WAY you must travel, to attain your objective.

YOUR GREAT WORK IS TO EXPRESS NOT TO ACQUIRE

Remember the old saying about putting "the cart before the horse?"Of course you do. So many misguided people in this world fail because they insist upon reversing the God-Law of Attainment. These people reverse the steps toward attainment by trying first, last and all the time to acquire, instead of seeking to express the health, the riches and the happiness which are potentially already WITHIN themselves.

Expression, not acquisition, is the watch word. The power to attain, to possess, to attract is within you, always available to you, always waiting to manifest itself in material form, if you will only recognize, direct and express that power. The raw materials of your fortune are always within your reach, and these lessons plainly point out to you the tools which you possess with which you can fashion that raw material in exact likeness to your mental pattern.

For whether we know it or not through our physical instruments (our bodies) our inner "model" or in what we call character, or personality, in other words, these picture our real selves to the world.

Because this is unalterably true, we have stressed in all of our instruction to you the great importance to you of concentrating your attention upon what you do and do not want to either express or to acquire. Because whatever mental pattern you fashion within your own consciousness by that very act you will impress this mental image-pattern upon your silent astral vibrations, and this will be made manifest through your physical activities, deeds and attitudes, whether refined, attractive and magnetic or gross, repulsive and negative.

According to our occult Masters, the Real Self within dwells in what they call the "casual body." When we manifest or give form to an inner pattern through the use of the mental, emotional and physical bodies, we set in motion certain similar vibrations in this casual body. These vibrations are the creative forces which fashion the inner pattern into material form in the outer, material world.

Only the student who is master of his emotions, his thoughts and his physical impulses can be Master of his own life.

Steadfast moods, harnessed emotions and controlled, focused thought—these spell Illumination.

From this CASUAL BODY within which flows that vibrant energy which creates for you and through you those things which are both good and everlasting, this is the force of the unfolding divine nature within you. The life you live within is eternal. So, cease grasping at the unstable baubles of the crass material, outer world as if they were of the utmost importance. In reality, they are secondary. Stop fighting the outside forces which seem to oppose you, for that is just a waste of time and energy—your only real enemies are those unrealities within which would destroy you.

However, if you have made the common mistake in the past of putting material things first in your life, if you have waged a fruitless battle for possessions without suitable inner development, and if you have found your struggle to overcome outer forces first, from all such failure you have learned the great lesson that there IS another way. For these failure-experiences have led you to seek and to find the TRUE WAY, the hidden WAY, of attainment.

In building for yourself a new or a transformed environment, and in creating a new personal world for yourself and in attracting into your renewed personal world those finer things for which you have longed, you are using the image-making powers of your mind. Thus you are following the God-Law, and Nature herself always helps you in creative effort. - To obey that creative Law is to launch your bark upon the irresistible tide of universal tendency, which is forever creative.

Only definite, one-pointed, focused endeavor succeeds. The gigantic power of the cosmos is behind such creative effort, and nothing opposes you except illusions—and illusions are less than shadows, illusions are nothing unless you endow them with reality in your own thought-world.

Stop giving illusions reality—stop being frightened by shadows. "Evil" is an illusion, and the so-called "bad" influences around you and the negative qualities which you may think are yours—all are shadows, you alone give them existence or life or power. These "evil" influences, circumstances, or qualities you view from the outside, and actually they only exist in the seeming.

Of course, while we are yet incarnated in these mortal bodies and while Mind must manifest through physical brain-matter, we cannot fully comprehend the vastness of the God-Law, nor can we yet understand completely the absolute perfection of the Divine Cosmic Plan. But through your studies of the hidden wisdom of the Masters and through the lessons gained from our own experiences we can acquire sufficient knowledge of the Divine Plan to realize that when we express in our lives and thoughts the positive powers of love, of faith, of fellowship, of health, of abundance, and of happiness, then the ETERNAL GOOD (GOD) behind all things vibrates through each one of us.

BUILD A MENTAL MATRIX MOULD FOR YOUR EMOTIONS

Let us realize the inherent impermanence of all so-called "evil" or negative emotions—they are not really lasting, for they are self-limited, either we conquer negative emotions or they destroy us. Negative emotions, such as anger, hate, sensuality, greed, envy, cruelty, selfishness, etc., are simply the lower, animal forces running riot through undeveloped and imperfect personalities.

But as a student yours is a developing and a perfecting personality, and the positive, constructive, healthful emotions which you are cultivating are LASTING EMOTIONS. So you are creating a mental mould for your lasting emotions.

Of course, in this work you build from within. The great power which you use in building this matrix or mental pattern is your unfolding power of imagination. This mystic power of mind-picturing (image-making) you will use to reflect the images of those ideal personalities whom you most admire and whom you would be like. You will use these ideals to picture the superior qualities of these outstanding "pattern" personalities whom you admire—qualities which you wish to manifest in your own personality.

Or, you may picture the faces and forms of the Masters in White, those great Avatars of the past who have made their lives vibrant examples of love and sacrifice for humanity, as the patterns of those higher qualities which you desire to reflect in your own life.

Remember the unseen influences (vibrations) of these holy Avatars is as near to you as your own heart throbs, and in making them your pictured patterns you are making yourself receptive to their presence, and so draining them near to your conscious mind you enable them to impart to you some of their power and wisdom. You become like what you think them, "for as a man thinketh in his heart (mind), so is he," proclaims the Scriptures. How true!

In your "chamber of imagery," your imagination, picture yourself clearly as the living embodiment of these superior virtues and qualities you most want to express. In meditation see yourself creating the deeds, words, thoughts, and the emotions which express the Master within, and picture suitable situations, circumstances and surroundings, in all of which you play the part of Master. As we have taught you before, pay particular attention to that word "emotion", because from emotion thoughts are born, thoughts are incased in words, and thoughts and words manifest in deeds, action, life.

Make affirmation and meditation your twin acts of devotion and you are building the Master-Personality; through concentration upon this higher personality you will reflect this objective of your focused thought.

Just mentally draw the image of the Master you would become until it is changed into a living picture touched by the highlights of Illumination. It is very important that you endow your mental picture with life, for when these pictures become living images they are like guiding angels to you.

THE PAST IS YESTERDAY, THE FUTURE IS IN TODAY

Be wise and know that your past is all in your yesterdays, and your yesterdays are buried, why try to dig them up? Your future is in TODAY—LIVE! As a student advancing to the Master's Degree of Illumination let the objective thought of self-reliance be your watch word, for only by self-reliance can you advance toward your goal.

Whatever your need is today, take that need with you into The Silence. "In that Silence command yourself to know your true needs of today, and never reverse your requests—don't ask that the thing you asked to be done today be undone tomorrow. Your hour is NOW, weary not, go forth in faith and master "fate" (circumstances). Build on the mistakes of yesterday, and then ignore those mistakes—let past experience be your guide, but keep your face toward the future.

Growth is the great revelator of life—suppose there are dark places in your life, sorrow, failure, mistakes, then why not set a light in each of those dark places, so that other travellers need not stumble in that darkness.

In this lesson we have dwelt somewhat at length upon mental patterns as aids in reaching our higher objectives or our desired Divine goals. Each of these ennobling mental patterns is then in reality an Ideal. We have explained that an Ideal is the perfected result of the comprehension of both THAT WHICH IS and THAT WHICH IS DESIRED TO BE, projected upon your thought-screen by Imagination, tempered by meditation, and evolved into material form by Faith.

Your Ideal, then, when it becomes to your mind's eye a living picture, has behind it the most powerful energy of the universe. When it is REAL, your desire has behind it the emotional energy which will impel your mind, yes, your whole being, to gather all of your powers and all of your resources to bring to pass the ultimate realization of that desire.

As we have repeated in lesson after lesson the most powerful energy in the world is found in the higher phases of thought. For by its power, focused nth thought can direct and control every other energy known to man, Have you been worrying about obstacles? The energy of evolved consciousness, which we call "thought" acknowledges no obstacles but in fact USES impediments and obstacles which seem to threaten its purpose as simply another means to its further success and attainment of Ideals.

The power of thought within you, evolved and developed, can you meet every obstacle, and defy every challenge of "Fate".

Lesson No. 22
PATHWAY TO HEALTH, WEALTH AND HAPPINESS

Fourth Gateway of The Temple Invisible, Being The Secret Instruction Taught by The Masters in White, Whose Sublime Precepts Are Now Exemplified in these lessons.

The Degree of Illumination

JOY, HEALING AND SUCCESS IN SELF-CONQUEST

"Each bud flowers but once and each flower has but its minute of perfect beauty: so, in the garden of the soul each feeling (emotion) has, as it were, its flowering instant, its one and only moment of expansive grace and radiant kingship.

"Each star passes but once in the night through the meridian over our heads and shines there but an instant; so, in the heaven of the mind each thought touches its zenith but once, and in that moment all its brilliancy and all its greatness culminate. Artist, poet or thinker, if you want to fix or immortalize your ideas or your feelings (emotions), seize them at this precise and fleeting moment, for it is their highest point. Before it, you have but vague outlines or dim presentiments of them. After it you will have only weakened reminiscence or powerless regret; that moment is the moment of your IDEAL." Amiel.

And, speaking of the joy and the rewards of self-conquest, here are some inspired words from the teachings of Buddha, as recorded in The Vedanta:

"The illusion of self originates and manifests itself for the enjoyment of self, but entangles us with the net of sorrow.

He who conquers self will be free...he no longer craves, and the flame of (sensual) desire finds no material to feed upon. Thus it will be extinguished."

He who is wise will enter The PATH and make an end of sorrow.

"Most men move in a sphere of worldly interests, and find their delight in worldly desires. The worlding will not understand the doctrine (teaching), for to him there is happiness in selfhood only. He will call resignation what to The Enlightened One is the purest joy. He will see annihilation where the perfected one finds immortality. He will reward as death what the conqueror of self knows to be life everlasting.

"The TRUTH remains hidden from him who is in the bondage of hate and desire. Nirvana (the divine world) remains incomprehensible and mysterious to the vulgar mind that worldly interests surround as with clouds.

"The outward form does not constitute religion. Thus the body of a shramana (priest) may wear an ascetic garb.while his mind is immersed in worldliness.

"All worry about the self, is vain; the edge (outer self) is like a mirage and all the tribulations that touch it, 'will pass away. They will vanish like a nightmare when the sleeper awakes. He who has. AWAKENED is free from FEAR: he has become Buddha; he knows the vanity of al his cares, his (worldly) ambitions, also his pains.

"This is the state of mind of one who has recognized that there is no (earthly) self; that the cause of all his troubles, cares and vanities is a mirage, a shadow, a dream.

"Happy is he who has found the Truth."

JOY, HEALING AND SUCCESS ATTAINED BY INSPIRATION

Only through Inspiration do we attain the fulness of joy, healing and success. And only through self-con-quest do we become receptive to Inspiration. True Inspiration is the intuitive voice of the Cosmic Soul which, if we but follow its call, offers each receptive Initiate unerring guidance.

The Greek Masters in White knew this truth full well, for they were the unsung authors of Greek Mythology, and this mythology, like the allegories of the Hebrew Bible, taught our great occult truths in story form. Mythology and Allegory simply make from the vulgar, the undeveloped, the eternal truths of the -ancient "mysteries".

Probably you will remember the story in Greek mythology of the slaying of the Gorgon Medusa by Pegasus, who, after cutting its head off, was given wings for his homeward flight by Mercury. According to this Greek story, now more than twenty centuries old, Pegasus carried this fearful dragon's head with him as a trophy, and on his flight blood constantly dripped into the ocean from the monster's head.

Of course, each part of this story is fraught with a symbol, if we but read between the lines, or in other words, if we can interpret its symbolism.

The monster's head is the symbol of imagination, and it was this blood, which again is a symbol representing imagination as being vitalized, given life, by emotion—and from this was transformed Pegasus, a lightning-swift steed (horse), whose true name is Inspiration.

In astrology these Greek Masters represented what is called the "travel-decanate" of Aquarius, in which the sun is located from January 30th to February 19th of each year his flying horse, Pegasus.

Pegasus, so this ancient story goes, struck the rocky ground with his hoofs while he was flying over Mount Helicon, and the sparkling, Clear waters of the spring known as Hippocrene at once poured fourth. By this the Greek Masters taught that all Initiates who would become illumined (raised to mental and spiritual heights) must first drink of this fountain which gushed forth when struck by the hoofs of Pegasus, the steed that represented Inspiration.

You will note that in this mythological story Inspiration flows forth when the earth is struck, Inspiration springs then from. earthly contact. Interpreted this simply means that the higher objects which exist in (inspire) the subconscious mind be connected with some more earthly thing already in the objective (outer) mind before we can materialize it upon our earthly plane, or in the world of physical things.

In these ancient astrological allegories, you will remember that Neptune is the planet assigned to the rulership of the theater, the drama and showmanship in all its forms. The old Greek story then goes on to tell how Neptune tamed Pegasus, the flying horse, and then later presented him to Bellerophone, son of the king of Ephre, to help him to conquer the Chimaera.

Now this Chimaera, from which we derive our word (chimera) was a curious sort of sea monster, was made up of many different and unrelated parts, none of which fitted the other, and so is the symbol of wild, foolish or fantastic imagination.

So, if Neptune was to succeed in producing believable works of drama, the theatre, etc., these vain; fantastic imaginings must first be conquered, and it was Pegasus, the symbol of Inspiration, who is represented as overcoming these discordant wraiths of the imagination.

MILLIONS OF YEARS TO DEVELOP INTELLIGENT MIND

Of course, you realize that drama, melodrama (such as modern moving pictures), and all works of the theater appear to the emotions, and to primitive "emotional thinking", and little or no true intellect is used either by those who compose or produce drama, nor by the audiences who support them. Dramatic "art" flourishes upon "feeling," rather than thought—and so is a survival of the infancy of the human race, refined somewhat now, of course, but still a survival.

The use of intellect, concepts, ideas, reason, and yes, even words is a comparatively recent biological development of man, and may well mark his last and highest unfolding upon this earth. For only through intellect can man become God-like, because only through developed intelligence can man master and direct his emotional Inspiration—only thus can he conquer self.

Words, objects, and ceremonial forms we use as symbols whereby we can compare, reason and examine in our own minds the outer world about us, as well as the hidden, personal world within us.

In the matter of tracing LIFE in this material world of ours, the scientist give us almost unbelievable figures, because they calmly claim that life has existed upon this earth for hundreds of millions of years. And to prove this they will point out to you the footprints of this multi-million-aged life in the sea, .within mighty rock-beds, and a hundred other places that, bear silent testimony to life in bygone millenniums.

The great battle of every form of life upon the face of the earth, whether in the valleys, upon the mountain tops or in the.depths of the oceans, has been to adapt itself and its forms to survival. amid its surroundings, And during every age each environment was constantly changing, so forcing life to change and to adapt, or to perish. This adaptation resulted. in development for each surviving form of life and this development scientists call evolution.

Going back, then, mentally, along the corridors of the millions of years of earth-life the scientists tell us we shall find the beginnings of life in this World in the form of the single protoplasmic cell—there alone in a world of darkness and of silence (without hearing or sight) this protoplasmic cell contacted food and found a hiding place, and these spelled survival—so the first dim feeling of what we might now call (happiness) was experienced in this one-celled protoplasm, because more survival is primitive happiness.

But when this tiny, tiny one-celled life met enemies, or lack of food, or any other condition which might hurt, cripple or destroy it, then and there primitive suffering ("pain") was born, and with it the twin of pain, <u>fear</u>.

Thus, in elementary life between which life and ours stretches a vastness of time that no man can understand, we find the origin of those common enemies which man himself has found it impossible to conquer until he has first conquered (mastered) himself.

Just as it is even today in that highest manifestation of physical life upon the earth, mankind, so it was with the protoplasmic cells of that ageless long ago, anything which brought hunger, pain or fear, or anything which brought food, happiness and safety to the amoeba brought a primitive response in the form of more or less suitable ACTION. Although primitive life was a system of "trial and error," yet even then instinct was there to guide the amoeba towards the "good" things of its life, and to make it recoil as much as possible from hunger, pain or danger.

FEELING CONDITIONS REACTIONS OF LIVING ORGANISMS

So we see that feeling conditions (controls) the reactions of every living organism from the lowest or elemental one-celled protoplasmic amoeba to the present complex and highly developed organism called Man. In human beings these controlling feelings are known as "emotions", and our emotions (feelings) of either happiness or pain stimulate us to ACTION, just as they do in the blind instincts of the lower organisms, and further, just as with the lower forms of life, these "feelings" tend to set up a habit of reaction when like circumstances again arouse these same emotions or feelings.

From the most ancient wisdom of the past, as well as from the most recent biological discoveries, we are led to believe that the Soul-Mind, which now lives in and functions through our human bodies of today has in its dim and distant past motivated other organisms and functioned side by side with every other and more elemental form of life.

The story is that this Soul-Mind, which is now individualized within you and within us, has developed its rulership over and through every other elementary organism, advancing by evolution through countless ages from the simplest to the most complex forms of life. Degree by degree, progressively developing through unknown aeons of time, this Soul-Mind has slowly transformed the original elemental human mentality through hard gained experience into our more complex, capable, knowing, reasoning mental powers of today.

Today the results of every racial experience, together with all the knowledge, all the wisdom and all the potential powers acquired during this million year climb up the spiral of progression is hidden away in that vast and mystical storehouse, your Subconscious Mind, or what our Masters term your "astral self."

We must realize that language, which is a series of spoken or written symbols crudely representing thoughts and "feelings" is rather a new thing to this "Astral Self " or Subconscious Mind, for language, concepts, ideas and reasoning, as we know them, ALL OF THESE HAVE ONLY BEEN ITS MODE OF MANIFESTING SINCE IT ENTERED INTO RATHER MODERN HUMAN LIFE.

You are limited to but a comparatively few short years in which to communicate with this Astral Self through these intellectual processes—just the fleeting years of you present earth-life. Thus you must strive to impress upon your INNER SELF the desires, the needs and the commands of your objective (outer) mind in a language of symbols which are both new to your subconscious mind and perhaps imperfectly by you.

And yet, if you would contact Healing (Health), you would attract abundance wealth to yourself, and if you would draw happiness into your life, you MUST establish a clear and sure communication with you "God-Self," your Soul-Mind, your Astral Self, in a word, with your Subconscious Mind. Because it is from this vast storehouse that healing, riches and happiness proceed.

Speaking again of language as a means of communication with the Sub-conscious (Astral) Self, there is another language besides that which depends upon spoken or written symbols for the transmission of messages to the Subliminal Self, and that is the language of emotion, or to put it more simply, the language of feeling. Universal among all living things, conveying messages everywhere either blindly or knowingly understood, and older by countless ages than any other, we have the language of feeling.

When the first elementary life-form appeared upon this earth, then was born the language of feeling. And when the first human being was developed on the earth, this was the first wordless language communicated through the sympathetic nervous system.

UNLESS CHARGED BY FEELING, WORDS ARE LIFELESS

As we have told you, the words either spoken or written of our language of today are symbols, and unless these symbols are charged by feeling, vibrant with emotion, they are lifeless, and are devoid of power. Thus, affirmations, no matter how beautiful they may be, and no matter how often you repeat them, avail nothing unless they vibrate with feeling, such as emotional (faith)expectancy.

In former lessons we have pictured to you how the Subconscious Mind controls the functions of the human body, controls the ductless glands and supervises the manifold work of your physical body, whether you are awake or asleep, guided not by your objective mind, not by your intellect, and not by your brain, but guided entirely by the unspoken language of feeling. For since the dim and distant days of man's beginnings on earth, the Subconscious Self has silently performed its everyday miracles obedient to other and far more potent symbols than words—the symbols of feeling—emotional symbols.

Through unnumbered ages the Subconscious has communicated, and been communicated with, through this language of feeling. It knows no words—it understands only and it obeys only the emotional currents upon which your words are carried. If emotion is absent you cannot communicate with your Astral (inner) self.

We have instructed you that all the health (and healing) all the abundance and all the happiness you can possibly desire are stored in the reservoir of your Subconscious Mind—and here is the ageless secret of lossing the flow of the good things you long for from that boundless reservoir.

Just stop centering your attention upon your intellectual processes, and instead concentrate upon these instructions which we have given you in discovering, in developing, in directing, and in understanding this language of feeling—your emotional expression, rather than upon mere mental gymnastics.

For example, the artist, the musician and the orator who succeed in reaching and arousing the deeper feelings of the world does not make his direct appeal to the intellect, but to the feelings of people—always it is the emotional appeal which arouses and which stirs human beings to suitable reaction. You can only speak to the Subconscious in the language of feeling.

Master this language and you will conquer yourself, and you will find that others will proclaim you their leader.

Suppose you pick a beautiful rose to pieces, petal by petal, analyze by your intellect a master painting, critically read an orator's address in cold print—have you not destroyed them? And Why? Because these finer things appeal to the Subconscious, and only emotional symbolism arouses the Soul to perceive their beauty, and you have applied to them the dull symbols of your material ("mortal") mind.

The beauty of the rose, the melody of exquisite music and the invisible power of the life of mastery, of abundance, and of Illumination all of these are borne to us upon the wings of feeling (emotional response), because through the ages that has been the language of the Subconscious realm.

LEARNING THE EMOTIONAL LANGUAGE OF FEELING

You desire to explore the invisible world of your Subconscious? Then do not limit that unseen realm to the mere words which your intellect (mind) has learned and uses as symbols, because those words alone are meaningless to your deeper (Subconscious) mind, which can interpret only the language of emotion (feeling). This deeper mind, remember, understands and is only receptive to the emotional vibrations which give your words power., Not the mere words themselves reach the depths of being, but the feeling which vibrates within those words—if any feeling be therein.

Of course, this does not mean that you are to abandon either the clear-cut use of your objective intellect or that you are to do away with the use of words, because both are very necessary to enable you to discern reality. But it does mean that you must in addition learn to use and to interpret the emotional language of feeling if you would avail yourself of the age-old experience and the invisible powers of your Subconscious Self.

In learning to understand, direct and use this unspoken language, you must concentrate your attention upon your emotions, your impressions and your intuitions, because these Are the symbols of the only language which your Subconscious understands. And these symbols are its only way of communicating with your conscious (objective) mind.

This ability to communicate with and to interpret messages from your deeper (subconscious) self is one of the most important things in the world to you. Remember, as we have told you before in this lesson, for countless ages this submerged (unconscious) self was the only guardian guiding the elementary beings of earth to food, to safety and to survival. Now, since the time unknown when these elementary organisms were some of there transformed into the more complete human beings, intellect (or mind) has assumed this guardian-ship, perhaps too exclusively.

So, because especially in modern life the Subconscious has been related to obscurity, because men have depended upon it less and less, this marvelous agency has relinquished its duties to the outer intellect generally, and has become silent and inactive. Hence far too often men flounder hopelessly in darkness unwarned of impending dangers and without guidance, because they are either heedless or ignorant of this unfailing "voice within," neither depending upon its guidance nor understanding its language.

But when this rather simple language of emotional "feeling" has been learned, and when we DEPEND upon the Inner Self for making known to us every condition important to our welfare, for unerring guidance, and for unseen power to meet emergencies, then this Subconscious giant will resume its activities in our behalf and will impart to us wisdom far above the limited knowledge of our objective, outer minds.

Your sympathetic nervous system can be developed into a state of surprising sensitivity to the vibrations, the impressions, and the intuitions by means of which your Subconscious can communicate with your conscious mind by constant practice of the simple exercises, forms, affirmations, etc., which we have given you in former lessons.

We would simply have you add to your habit of objective intellectual thinking, the emotional ("feeling") method of interpreting the world about you and...the worlds above and beyond. Try this little experiment— just check your own impressions, intuitions and feelings about people, events and circumstances with the truth about each of these as the future unfolds it. You will be more and more surprised at your own inner powers—powers you little suspected that you had

Thus you are opening an avenue through which your never-sleeping Inner Self can impart to your outer mind knowledge, warnings and guidance—ail of which will be priceless to you. So we would have you rely upon both intellect and emotional response (feeling) in all of your activities of life, for by so doing you are doubly armed.

It is little known how much Inspiration (as we call it) gains from the vast racial knowledge which is stored in the Subconscious Mind, nor now much healing, wealth and joy it can bring to us from its astral journeys. For the Subconscious Self does travel and in realms unknown to us consciously.

Again, perhaps all unconsciously to himself, the musician or the orator who sways audiences draws much of his power by "tuning in" to that same audience. So, when the orator or the artist is truly "receptive", he gains a tremendous power through the Subconscious thought-waves of his audience.

Lesson No. 23
PATHWAY TO HEALTH, WEALTH AND HAPPINESS

Fourth Gateway of The Temple Invisible, Being The Secret Instruction Taught by The Masters in White,.-Whose Sublime Precepts Are Now Exemplified in These Lessons.

Degree of Illumination

MASTERING THOUGHT—YOUR POWER INVINCIBLE

"The mission (purpose) of thought is to agitate, develop, enlighten and purify the human mind. The mind is a substance, and, like the body, is strengthened by exercise. Each faculty is susceptible of improvement or deterioration, and may be strengthened, perverted, neglected or weakened.

"Industry is a redoubling of the capital of the spirit. The Mind that lies fallow (unused) for a single day, sprouts up in follies that can only be displaced by a constant and assiduous culture. A man of genius even, is inexhaustible, only in proportion as he is always nourishing (expanding) his genius; both in mind and body, where nourishment ceases, vitality fails.

"Unless thought perpetually renews its youth and lifts a seeking eye afresh to the living light, decrepitude and waste befalls whatever it has achieved.

"How many live in the graves of their unemployed (thought) faculties! The soil of mind is rich and inexhaustible in resources. Mind has not yet been aroused; it has not yet declared itself. The superior (thought) faculties speak in silvery tones to that which is ordinary IN YOU, saying:

"Live worthier; be thou whole (healed), wise, rich, healthy and happy." Psychic Power.

Of the morning of thought Amiel wrote:

"Bathe, O disciple, thy thirsty soul in the dew of the dawn!" says Faust to us, and he is right.

"The morning air breathes anew and laughing energy into veins and morrow. If every day is a repetition of life (in miniature), every dawn signs as it were a new contract with existence. At dawn spiritual truth (thought), like the atmosphere is more transparent, and we, like the young leaves, drink in the light more eagerly, breathe in more ether, and less of things earthly. If night and the starry sky speak to the meditative soul of God, of eternity and the infinite, the dawn is the time for projects, for resolutions, for the birth of thought and action.

And it was W. V. Nicum who wrote these significant words:

"You can never tell what your thoughts will do

In bringing you hate or love;

For thoughts are things, and their airy wings

Are swift as a carrier dove.
They follow the law of the universe—
Each thing must create its kind,
And they speed o'er the track to bring you back
Whatever went out from your mind.

As we have impressed upon you in various former lessons, the most powerful energy in this world is mani-fested in the higher phases of thought. For it is the evolved, developed, focused energy of thought which demonstrates in every miracle, both ancient and modern. For it is through this developed energy of his thinking mind that man controls and directs countless other energies in the world about him, and is able to transform his environment through these other powers which he has made subservient to his thought.

THE ANCIENT WISDOM AND RELIGIONS TEACH COSMIC THOUGHT

Your power invisible lies in the mastery of thought—and this mastery is nothing more or less than the development of thought into cosmic consciousness, that is, the consciousness of your own inherent divinity.

Only this awareness can reveal the unknown to you, and unveil to you the occult mysteries. The mission of these higher lessons is to help to initiate you into this awareness.

While it is true that several oriental religions (including Christianity) have incorporated these occult mysteries into their systems of teachings under various ceremonies and symbols, still that fact does not make occult wisdom religious. For these religions simply include surviving remnants available to them in their systems in order to attempt to explain the psychic phenomena of man's spiritual (higher) nature. And these "surviving remnants" of the occult mysteries of the ancient wisdom of The Masters are generally incomplete and totally unrelated to each other, for no religion has the WHOLE TRUTH, only remnants. This is because the whole truth has remained securely hidden from all except the few proven Initiates and Masters in every age.

REMEMBER THESE SIGNIFICANT WORDS OF THE MASTER, CHRIST:

"And He said (speaking to the Twelve, His Initiates), Unto you is given to know the mysteries of the kingdom of God: but to others (the rest) in parables (symbols, allegories), that seeing they might not see, and hearing they might not UNDERSTAND."—Luke 8:10.

So, the mysteries of Christ's inner teaching was intended to be understood, ONLY by the Initiates.

The two greatest of the oriental religions, Mohammedanism and Hinduism, each of which is diametrically opposed to the other, are both founded upon mysticism, occultism, and both teach higher states of attainment which, in reality, are mental conditions approaching what we now call cosmic consciousness. But in each of these religious systems this attainment was to be found by following different pathways of understanding.

On the one hand Mohammedanism is a mystic monotheism—teaching that there is but ONE God, whom they recognize only by the name of Allah. On the other hand we have Hinduism, which is a pantheistic mysticism, so to the Hindus God is an all-powerful force and supreme Mind, neither of which exists as a personal being, but which work in and through all things, as inherent part of everything, and vibrating within all things on earth.

In the latter part of the 14th Century another oriental religion arose, founded by one Nanak, and this religion, called Sikhism, resulted from the mysteries, of meditation. The Sikh Bible known as the Granath teaches that there is but one true God, pictured therein as a supreme or fuling power which permeates all things, so here we find a touch of hinduism.

But The Granath further teaches that this one true God shall be referred to as "Sat Nam," (the true God), but shall ever remain nameless—neither Allah nor Brahma nor God—but only "true God." Man should not presume the familiarity of any more personal name.

The Sikh teachers, called "Gurus," taught that all worldly knowledge is transient, passing and unreliable, because they believed that this world, as we see it with our earthly eyes, (objectively), is an illusion.

They taught that the highest form of wisdom consists in knowing God, or rather, in becoming absorbed into the "consciousness of God" by which of coarse they simply meant Cosmic Consciousness. Actually, the Gurus were teaching the attainment of your power invincible through the mastery of thought.

Again here is where another religion, Sikhism, incorporates a part of the occult WAY into its teachings, because the Gurus instructed their Initiates into certain prescribed psychic ceremonies, practices and devotional meditation silence before (and by which) they could be absorbed into the God-Consciousness.

THE MOST ANCIENT WISDOM ASCRIBED TO HERMES

Turning now to the more ancient philosophy—the oldest recorded wisdom of the ancient world—we find the Hermetic Philosophy, which was the hidden system of philosophical teachings credited to one known as Hermes Trismegistus. "Trismegistus" is a Greek title meaning thrice great. This name will be somewhat familiar to you because we have quoted from his ancient words of knowledge and we have referred to his teachings in former lessons of yours.

There is some confusion as to the true identity of Hermes, whether he ever actually existed, or whether, as many authorities claim, he actually lived and taught in the ancient world long before Moses, before Plato and before the "Seven Sages." Whether he was legendary or not, we do know that the Egyptians, according to the Greeks, knew Hermes as one of their gods, Thoth. Dimly out-lined amid the shadows of the hurrying centuries many of the Masters of old seem masked as Gods, legendary figures, or as personified symbols. So, it would seem but logical that Hermes actually was one of the Masters in White, whose wisdom we now exemplify in our occult fellowship.

For the benefit of our most scholarly students, we note in passing that the name of this same Thoth, whom the Greeks later named Hermes, was found inscribed in demotic characters on the famed Rosetta Stone with the statement that he was the "Great-Great-Great," (the 'thrice-great').

The Egyptians in their temples pictured this "god," Thoth, with the body, of a human being; and the head of ibis, a bird found in ancient times wading in the marshes of the Nile.

Because much of the hidden wisdom taught is found only in the occult archives which record the story of Hermes, we should know more about this great Master Teacher of those forgotten ages. After all we must realize that Truth and Wisdom are ageless, so we find many, many of the teachings of Hermes as modern as tomorrow itself.

After all, we reaffirm the same simple but sublime truths taught so long ago by Hermes: that there is only one supreme system of laws controlling man and the universe—the God-Laws and that there is but one sublime Intelligence vibrating throughout the universe—The God (divine) Mind—and in due time destroying—incarnating and reincarnating endlessly upon an upward reaching spiral.

In, the most ancient Greek writings we find Hermes credites with being the great fountain of knowledge— the source of all revealed and of all hidden wisdom.

While the Greeks in their oldest records referred to Hermes as "the father of philosophy," the Egyptians in their most ancient literature called Thoth (Hermes) the god books (scrolls) claiming also that he taught men both to speak and to write, and credited to him the invention of numbers (the science of mathematics).

As you will recall, the ancient form of Egyptian writing was the heiroglyph (writing by means of Picture-symbols), but according to their archives Thoth originated script writing—a form similar in principle to our modern hand-writing.

"TRUTH OF THOTH"—SIGNIFICANT TITLE OF MANETHE

Three hundred years before Christ was born there lived Manetho, the great historian of ancient Egypt, and he was given the significant title of the "truth of Thoth." From this it is easy to understand that he, Manetho, was another of the Masters in White and that his mission was to teach the ancient wisdom of Thoth (Greek name, Hermes).

But, you may ask, what has this to do with me and with my studies?

Just this, and this means much to you—if you have followed our lessons and our instructions faithfully, you are now approaching very closely to the apex, or highest point, of our symbolic Triangle—Illumination. As we have intimated to you before, this course of study continues and perpetuates in an unbroken line this same ancient, occult knowledge of which Thoth (Hermes) was one of a. succession of Masters, who have transmitted this hidden, world-old wisdom of the unseen realms of spirit and mind.

Returning then to the enthralling story of the earlier days of the Masters who have transmitted these sublime truths to us, from the history of Manetho we learn that Ptolemy Philadelphus, who was then in charge of the Great Mystery School and the magnificent library at Alexandria, commissioned this same Manetho to gather all the unnumbered (countless) scrolls containing the ageless wisdom of the Egyptians for this Alexandrian library.

Among the tremendous collection of writings and scrolls which Manetho gathered and presented to Philadelphus in following out his mission, our records show. that the sacred books, (scrolls or writings) of Thoth (Hermes) were included, Among these our archives show that he, Thoth; wrote 42 "books," divided into six sections, as, for example, one about religion, one section devoted to astronomy, one on the art of writing, one on the science of mathematics, etc.

In passing it is interesting to note that in one of his works, entitled "The Shepherd of Man," Thoth states that God created man in His own likeness, and endowed man with powers and attributes similar to his own. Thus by more than three thousand years Thoth wrote first that very same statement which we find in our far more modern Book of Genesis.

Thoth is referred to by name again and again in the carved inscriptions upon Egyptian temples and monuments of the older dynasties. Some of these record that the great 'Mystery School of Thoth' was located at Khemennu. Later the Greeks renamed this city "Hermopolis, "that is, the city of Hermes.

Records state that this "Mystery School" occupied a "place on HIGH ground," and that "Ra," the sun, first shone upon that place at sunrise.

These most ancient records also explain that this 'Mystery School' presided over by Thoth (Hermes) at Kehmennu was the place where Initiation was conferred upon worthy candidates for the higher degrees of Egyptian occultism.

According to the same sacred Symbolism which our institution still follows today, these neophytes were taught The WAY by which they ascended to the heights ('mountain-top') of their own inmost minds, their inner (sub-) consciousness. And following the hidden meaning of this ceremonial of symbolic trans-figuration, when each reached the heights of soul-development, the SPIRITUAL SUN bathed them with the brilliance of Illumination.

Our researches convince us that Thoth, or Hermes, the Thrice Great, actually lived and was one of that goodly company of illustrious Masters who have preceded us and laid the foundation for our present institu-tion, which manifests today as their lineal successor. However, Thoth (or 'Hermes') was in reality not a "God", but a very great and wise Master of the Secret wisdom, who was born in that ancient capital of Egypt, Thebes thirteen hundred and ninety nine years before Christ was born, and it is recorded that he lived to a very great age.

"Thrice Great" indeed was the career of Thoth (Hermes)—first, he was the founder of the great 'Mystery School' at Khemennu, second, he presided at the initiation of Amenhotep IV as a Master in White, and third, and again he assisted at the initiation of the ruler who followed Amenhotep IV.

Such was the remarkable life of this illustrious sage whose sublime metaphysics, occult wisdom and philosophy have been blended with those of other Great Masters in your lessons.

These ancient initiations were called MYSTERIES, because they actually manifested, taught and dramatized those lessons of the higher wisdom concerning the mysteries of birth, life, incarnation, 'death', so-called, and realms beyond mysteries because the common mind of the untutored masses cannot comprehend their meaning.

Undoubtedly the most ancient of all mystery-initiations of which there is any present earthly record is the Egyptian Osirian, usually referred to as the Osirian Cycle, so-called because this initiation presented in dramatic form the birth, the life, the death and the REbirth of Osiris.

As far back as history goes, the Osirian Cycle was the first presentation of the concept of immortality in the world.

Many, many thousands of years ago in ancient Egypt there originated what authorities claim to be the oldest story in the world, called "The Tale of Two .Brothers." Biblical authorities agree that this story is reflected very clearly in the later tale of Cain and Abel in the Bible, remembering that the Hebrews were held captive in Egypt and so had every opportunity to learn the Egyptian legend of "...The Two Brothers."

But let us read with understanding the complete story as given to us in the most ancient Egyptian mythology (allegory), bearing in mind that each character and each deed or incident is a symbol, and too, a symbol of very deep meaning. And the allegory itself is interesting if not indeed enthralling.

"In the beginning" the Egyptian goddess Nut 'married' the Egyptian god, Geb, and of this union were born four children; of these two were brothers, Osiris and Set, and two were sisters, Isis and Nepthys.

LEGEND TELLS THAT OSIRIS WAS RULING GOD OF EGYPT. THE OLDEST LEGEND KNOWN TO MANKIND—

According to this most ancient allegory, one of these brothers, Osiris, ruled over all of Egypt as a "god." But he is pictured as a wise and beneficent ruler, for it is recorded that Osiris introduced a system of laws by following which the people of Egypt ruled themselves, and through Osiris they were taught building, art, irrigation, profitable farming, and under his kindly government the people flourished.

Also, the allegory says that Osiris endeared himself to the people and also brought religion to Egypt by teaching the multitudes to worship the gods.

Now, Set, the brother of Osiris, grew very jealous of the worship and the affection which the people lavished upon Osiris, and planned to take his brother's life in revenge.

And this was the cunning plan which Set hatched for his brother's undoing. Secretly Set secured the measurements of his brother's height, breadth, etc. Then Set secured skilled artisans who built for him a magnificent, carved chest, inlaid with gold and jewels, whose dimensions just fitted the measurements of the body of Osiris.

Now Set, with the aid of seventy of his retainers who were in the plot with him, caused a magnificent banquet to be given in honor of Osiris, who of course was present as the guest of honor. During the feast Set promised that he would make a present of the precious chest to any of the guests whom it would fit perfectly when he would lie down in it. Of course, each of the conspirators tried the chest thus, knowing the plot and that it would fit none of them.

Finally it came Osiris' turn to try the chest, and of course when he laid down in it the chest fitted him per-fectly—but the moment he was safely inside the plotters slammed the cover down and fastened it securely.

Thus, imprisoned in the chest which had become his coffin, Osiris was helpless, and the chest was then thrown into the Nile by the henchmen of Set. Finally, after reaching the sea, the chest was washed ashore at Byblos, in Ancient Phoenicia. With the passing of time, so the allegory relates, a huge heather plant grew around the chest, concealing it entirely, and in fact grew into a great tree.

The king of the land, seeing this great tree, commanded that it be cut down and fashioned into a column for his palace.

But meanwhile Isis, who had discovered this foul plot and the whereabouts of the body of her brother, Osiris, disguised herself and journeyed to Byblos, and removed the chest from the heather-like tree and returned with it to Egypt.

Freeing his corpse from the chest, Isis placed the body of Osiris upon the sands, and then one night while she was away Set, on a moonlight stroll, found the body of his brother. So vengeful was he that, flying into a rage, Set cut the body of his brother into small pieces and had these pieces distributed over a wide expanse.

Returning, Isis found out what Set had done, and her grief was terrible, But searching far and wide, she finally recovered all the pieces of Osiris' body and brought them together as they belonged. According to the allegory, Isis then restored life to Osiris by breathing into his mouth AND HE WAS RESURRECTED. Again Osiris was a living being, but now not of this earth, but of another and higher realm.

Remember this is the oldest story in the world. And this most ancient of all allegories teaches the continuity of life, or the concept of immortality.

In the rites of the ''Mystery Schools' of ancient Dekorah and Abydos, this allegory (which we have only briefly sketched for you here) was enacted secretly as a sacred drama for the instruction of those chosen neophytes who were to become Initiates. As this great drama was unfolded by degrees, over a space of perhaps many nights, the Kheri Hebs. (High Priests, Masters) instructed the candicates as to what was the inner meaning of each portion, or lesson.

Certain parts of this great drama were enacted upon huge barges in the moonlight upon certain sacred, hidden lakes.

According to the ancient Egyptian ritual Osiris was the symbol of the creative forces of the world and the universe, and he represented goodness, virtue, nobility in action, and the life that never "dies" (is never extinguished).

Of course, his Brother, Set, represented the destructive forces, evil incarnate, hatred, in fact, the absolute negative. (Perhaps he was "borrowed" to appear in our later Scriptures as the Devil?).

Thus it was shown to these candidates for Initiation so many, many thousands of years ago that while we cannot hope to always receive our just reward for noble lives and deeds upon this earth, there yet, remains an after-life. For Osiris was shown as resurrected, and enjoying an after life of glory within higher realms.

So, your noblest efforts may seem to be disregarded, but you, too, may prove to be a Master in disguise, even misunderstood and misjudged here, but you shall be raised in reward.

LESSON No. 24
PATHWAY TO HEALTH, WEALTH AND HAPPINESS

Fourth Gateway of The Temple Invisible, Being the Secret Instruction Taught by The Masters in White, Whose Sublime Precepts Are Now Exemplified in These Lessons.

The Degree of Illumination

ILLUMINATION IS THE VISION OF IMMORTALITY

"A vision of the future arises. I see a world where thrones have crumbled and where kings are dust. The aristocracy of idleness has perished from the earth.

"I see a world without a slave. Man at last is free. Nature's forces have by science been enslaved. Lightning and light, wind and waves, frost and flames, and all the subtle powers of the earth and air, are toilers for the human race.

'I see a world at peace, adorned with every form of art, with music's myriad voices thrilled, while lips are rich with words of love and truth; a world in which no exile sighs, no prisoner mourns; a world on which the gib-bet's shadow ones not fall; a world where labor reaps its full reward, where work and worth go hand in hand.

"I see a world without the beggar's outstretched palm, the miser's heartless stony stare, the piteous wail of want, the livid lips of lies, the cruel eyes of scorn.

"I see a race without disease of flesh or brain—shapely and fair, married harmony of form and function— and, as I look life lengthens, joy deepens, love canopies the earth; and over all, in the great dome, shines the eternal star of faith." Robert G. Ingersol.

Illumination is the vision of Immortality, and illumination can only be found upon the Pathway of Faith.

As a student who is now receiving this final lesson in the Degree of Illumination, you will now realize very clearly that it is not the purpose or the mission of our teachings to either deny or to supplant your religious beliefs and conviction insofar as your beliefs envision immortality, or the continuity of life.

Rather our mission is to help you to contact the psychic world, and the spirit realm within, and thus we establish your own religion more firmly within your belief, because we give you a greater perspective and a broader foundation for that religion.

So it matters not at all in your progress whether you accept literally or spiritually the doctrine of one religion or another, whether you believe in one limited human life or in many reincarnations, you will undoubtedly agree with us that LIFE IS CONTINUOUS. We certainly cannot conceive of life as being an isolated, aimless, purposeless freak of creation.

Instead of this, we see life as a manifestation of God, in whom and from whom is all life, and the higher the plane upon which we live that life the more fully we share in the essence and in the existence of God. From the God-Source comes the Soul, in the 'mystery school' of this earth-life that Soul develops by experience— this earthly journey (or journeys) then being but the Soul's mystic preparation for its return to God.

To use this world is a transitory (passing)experience during which WE reside in transitory physical bodies.

So this transitory period which we term human life, whether the Soul dwells upon earth for one or many incarnations, is but a segment of our entire existence, and we cannot look upon that segment as being unrelated to Cosmic Life or as being purposeless. Therefore, the petty limitations of your present physical life seem of small importance when contrasted with the tremendous concept of your endless, continuous existence.

Nor do we agree with those gloomy philosophers who would have us believe that this personal, living Soul which we each know as "I" is limited to our span of physical life. What comfort, what advantage or of what purpose would any belief in immortality be, unless that endless life be that of the Self, of the "I" which we know, which we are ?

No, the God-Law has decreed the everlasting conservation of energy and of matter, and your objective realizations, your experiences, and the wisdom you have gained upon the Pathway, all of these are imperishably stored in your Subconscious memory, all of these have become attributes of your Soul, and they shall not be erased.

Yet, as to the condition or the location of the future life it is certainly given to no man to know in detail, and in these realms even psychic comprehension (Illumination) fails to return with man-made words which can give to us an understandable picture. We realize that our present physical lives are bounded on all sides with limitations, the faculties of our material bodies are dull and often undeveloped for, as we have shown you in other lessons, science tells us of colors far beyond the range of your dim eyes to see and of sound so high and so low that your dull ears can register not even an echo of such vibrations.

LIFE AND IMMORTALITY TWIN CONCEPTS OF RELIGION

Unhappy is the lot of the man who has built his life entirely upon material values, for then that man values these material things above everything else, forgetting that his own physical life among these material values is transitory. When wealth is made a god, then riches prove as limited and as passing (transitory) as is the physical body of a Midas.

What must be the terror which the rich man feels when he faces the inexorable parting from his material 'possessions!' This was the thought of the poet, Blair, when he wrote:

"How shocking must thy summons be, O Death!

To him that is at ease in his possessions;

Who, counting on long years of pleasure here,

Is quite unfurnished for that world to come!"

You would hardly agree that life is merely a chemical process would you? Of course not, Then that invisible, that vital "something" which entered into your unborn physical body to transform you into a living, individual, personal being was Soul—Life—Mind—which is the essence of God.

How then was Religion—and we use the word here to signify the ways by which men have sought to know the Unknown, God with its twin concepts of Life and Immortality, born in the mind of mankind?

According to the most scientific authorities, ever since men developed the ability to think, ever since men discovered the world within themselves, they have not only investigated their material surroundings, but they have striven desperately to find some clue as to the destiny of those who fell asleep and never been man's most tremendous problem.

Return now with us mentally across the numberless ages to the infancy of the human race, back to the days of elemental (undeveloped) mankind, and there mayhap we shall find some of the earliest ways in which man first became dimly conscious that within him there existed a living Soul.

For instance, somewhere in those primitive days man became aware that in his dreams, while sleeping, his memory told him that he seemed to be vividly active in his waking pursuits, such as fighting, fleeing from danger, fishing, hunting, mating, etc. Yet waking he would find that he had hardly moved from the place where he had fallen asleep. The memories of his dreams seemed just as real to him as the actual events of his yesterdays.

What could be more natural then that his first dim awareness that within himself existed a super-self which not only never slept but which could project his personality into scenes, activities and experiences apart from the every-day functions of his physical body? From this it was but a step to a somewhat vague belief that there was another, a mysterious Self within himself which was the REAL "I"—the thinking Mind-Self, the "Soul".

So, when primitive man saw his human companions one by one fall "asleep" and never waken (die) was it not very natural that he should come by gradual stages to conclude that in this "long sleep"this thinking, dreaming, real Self of his fellow-men continued to exist, perhaps upon other planes, just as in dreams?

Such were the simple beginnings of the Ancient Wisdom and of its outer reflection, religion.

So, as to the Ancient Wisdom and religion, time alone hides their beginnings from us in detail, because these concepts were born countless ages before the first page of history was ever written—aeons before writing was even known upon earth. With the beginning of history, however, we find heralded from age to age outstanding Masters whom the Cosmos seems to have endowed with a mystic inner vision and minds apparently divinely gifted. And further, not only were these Masters the seeming recipients of intuitive wisdom, but in each of them the God-Consciousness vibrated in their very thoughts.

Such were the Masters of Wisdom named Christ, Buddha, Osiris, and Pharoah Amenhotep IV, Zoroaster, Plato, Aristotle and a host of others who shine illustrious in the annals of men. However, not all of the applied knowledge comprising the Ancient Wisdom was revealed, but much was developed throughout the ages from such simple concepts as the one concerning dreams which we have outlined above.

No, neither man's occult nor his scientific knowledge dropped from the skies like rain. For much of the Ancient Wisdom was mined from the deep tunnels of experience by men who suffered and tolled to unearth these riches. It took numberless slow moving centuries to develop this Wisdom into coherent form, and all this time it was hidden from the masses under supposedly sacred or religious symbols, which were only monuments to preserve and to perpetuate this occult knowledge for the Initiates and the Masters who would follow.

For not only was this majestic knowledge secreted from the understanding of the ignorant, but we know from our records in our own Arcane sources that there were times in the earth's history when this Secret Wisdom was lost in terrific upheavals, and later rediscovered and restored through its eternal symbol.

THE GREAT PYRAMID MARKS ANOTHER RESTORATION

Yes, according to the ancient Akashic records there have been several restorations of the Ancient Wisdom, and the Great Pyramid at Gizeh is an enduring monument to one of these remarkable periods. This mysterious land of Egypt has gained worldwide reknown for the wisdom of its Masters during the dim and distant days of antiquity. But it is curious to note that this treasure of occult knowledge then seemed to disappear from Egypt—apparently lost from that land.

In previous lessons we have explained to you much of the hidden lore of this ancient wonder of architecture, so we need not discuss that phase of this tremendous edifice. But our purpose is to impress upon you the fact that it is a monument to the certain re-discovery or restoration of the Ancient Wisdom at that particular time in the world's history.

According to ancient history it is significant that the arts and sciences, the professions and trades, the mathematics and the knowledge of astronomy of which this remarkable temple is a silent witness were entirely UNUSED BECAUSE THEY WERE UNKNOWN in Egypt even a short hundred years before it was built. Before the Great Pyramid there is no evidence that the Egyptians possessed any of the tools, the instruments or the machines which must have been used in its construction. Nor is there any evidence that the Egyptians had either the exact knowledge of masonry or the engineering skill to quarry, transport and to lift each huge stone into its precise position in the Pyramid.

Again, marvelous mathematical exactness is shown in the proportions of the Great Pyramid, and its measurements proclaim a deep and perfect knowledge of higher mathematics—and none of these engineering skills or mathematical attainments is to be found in any -building, structure or temple ever erected in Egypt or anywhere else before this time!

Authorities generally agree that this Great Pyramid at Gizeh was built during the reign of the Pharoah Cheops about three thousand years before the birth of Christ. And there it yet stands today, a mute and magnificent monument to the mystic Secret Wisdom of those who planned and erected it—combining arts, and sciences, wondrous engineering and marvelous symphonies of higher mathematics in ageless stone.

Coming from another and perhaps some remote and unknown land of the mysterious past, this tremendous knowledge (the Ancient Wisdom) was symbolized in this magnificent temple by strange Masters in White, whose unseen presence is exemplified today in our teachings, of which you are now an Adept, an Initiate.

But from whence this occult secret wisdom came, no man KNOWS today. For nowhere upon the face of the earth as it appears now can be found previous building monuments or temples to tell of so great culture and learning.

However, according to our arcane records, there is a seemingly world-old and incomplete legend, whispered to us across the thousands of years in fable and in strange traditions, that such an Ancient Wisdom did survive the wreckage of an unknown civilization which flourished in wealth and grandeur upon some vast continent which sank beneath the waves of the ocean.

You will remember that Plato in his dialogues speaks of a land beyond the "Pillars of Hercules" which was swallowed up by the sea as told to Solon by Egyptian priests.

THE WHITE BROTHERHOOD UNITED BY THE ANCIENT WISDOM

From time immemorial that strange fraternity, known as the 'Great White Brotherhood,' has been bound together as The Masters who guarded this treasure of the Ancient (or Hidden) Wisdom as a sacred trust, even as we guard the same occult trust today.

Throughout the world, and in various ages, the Brothers in White can be traced in monument, in temple, in writings and in symbolism and ceremony, often obscured by time and ignorance, but always recognizable by the Initiates.

For example, among the many ancient hieroglyphic inscriptions which have been discovered and deciphered in Egypt, there is one thousands of years old which relates the story of one of the ships of old which, having lost its way at sea finally found a strange, far-away country to the East where there lived an unknown people of tremendous wealth, a marvelous culture and a height of power and civilization undreamed of among the Egyptians themselves.

So, love of the occult wisdom and the sacred trust of preserving it for unborn peoples was the unbreakable bond that held the Great White Brotherhood inviolate through all the ages of time: And not only was this occult Brotherhood an historical fact, but a fact that has been held as a noble ideal among men. Witness the book by

Sir Francis Bacon, "The New Atlantis," in which he tells of a "House of Wisdom" on an unknown island where these Thinkers (Initiates and Masters) lived in secrecy and in seclusion to guard well and truly their treasures of the hidden knowledge.

So there is every evidence that the Ancient Wisdom was brought into ancient Egypt less than a hundred years before the Great Pyramid was erected under their direction by The Brothers in White some Five Thousand years ago, and it is accepted by certain scholars that this cloistered brotherhood was descended in some remote lands from the surviving Masters who dwelt aeons of time before in "lost Atlantis"—Plato's "land beyond the Pillars of Hercules."

It is also passing strange to note that the Hebrews have a similar tradition, which would seem to indicate that this occult wisdom was entrusted to their keeping in their most ancient times. In fact, the Hebrews have certain books (descended or copied from their olden scrolls) which they claim contain the ancient (secret) wisdom in hidden form. These works are called the Kabbalah, which is a Hebrew word meaning "Tradition."

Besides this, there are many Hebrew scholars among their authorities who claim that the Hebrews received a divine and a secret treasure of knowledge, which was never to be either written or spoken except by certain Initiates, and then only in symbols, unintelligible to all save the trusted priests, prophets or Masters. The Hebrew tradition is that God spoke to Moses concerning this secret wisdom, saying:" These things shalt thou make known—and these shalt thou hide."

Whether or not you choose to believe that God did impart this ancient wisdom directly to Moses, still the historical evidence does point to the possibility that the ancient Hebrews were at some dim and distant time entrusted with the secret wisdom—or a portion of that occult knowledge.

When we study the true Kabbalah, we can hardly dispute this evidence.

It is, of course, self-evident to any Initiate who examines the Kabbalah as it exists today that some time during the darkness of the middle ages the portions of the ancient wisdom which it originally contained were obscured, garbled and largely changed into a meaningless jumble of symbols and incomplete allegories which purported to teach a sort of unbelievable "magic."

Yet enough of the true Kabbalah remains in remnants scattered here and there through these mysterious writings to prove that the original, the authentic Kabbalah was indeed a deep philosophical explanation of the creative God-Law and the Divine Plan of Life in this world.

It is interesting to note that the title of the most ancient "book" of the Kabbalah is the Sepher Yetzirah, which is Hebrew, meaning the "Book of Creation, and Hebrew scholars claim that Abraham was its author.

Probably the most significant "book" of the Kabbalah is the book entitled the Sepher Dizeniantha, meaning the "Book of Concealed Mystery," because this is the book which claims to reveal "the secret (ancient) wis-dom," which begins with the words, "This is the book of the equilibrium of balance," (or of divine harmony, oneness).

Of course, according to the ancient wisdom, just as we teach today Perfect living, perfect healing and perfect happiness can only be attained through harmony, balance, or equilibrium with-Nature, with Man and with God.

From the deep and philosophical truths which we find in the Kabbalah, although often obscured and often shining dimly in certain evidently original passages, it appears that the "secret (ancient) wisdom" of the Hebrews originated from the self-same White Brotherhood, whose history is often obscured by the mists of time and the disappearance of whole continents, from whence came the ancient wisdom of olden Egypt, and of every other ancient root-race.

CONCEPT OF IMMORALITY—DIFFERING WORDS, ONE MEANING

Many and seemingly different are the great root-religious—and yet through every one shines the WAY OF THE MASTERS—that WAY taught by the more ancient wisdom by which man can realize his oneness with God.

However, the answer to the questions of Immortality is worded differently in different root-religions, but you will find that the underlying concept has the same meaning in all.

Listen first then to the Mystic words of Christianity:

"In my Father's house are many mansions."

"When this corruptible shall have put on incorruption, and this mortal shall have put on immortality, then shall be brought to pass the saying that is written, "Death is swallowed up in. victory!"

Next, listen to Buddha:

"Earnestness is the path of immortality, thoughtlessness the path of death.

"That individual in this world who reflects right thoughts who uttereth right. words, who doeth right acts, who is learned and virtuous here in this brief life—he after the dissolution of the body, goeth to heaven."

And Confucius says:

"The bones and the flesh moulder below and, hidden away become the earth of the fields. But the spirit issues forth and is displayed on high in a condition of glorious brightness."

And Hinduism strikes this keynote:

"In the heaven-world there is no fear, leaving behind both hunger and thirst, and out of the reach of sorrow, all rejoice in the world of heaven."

Taoism teaches that death is the pathway to our true home:

"To know Eternal Law is to be Enlightened. Not to know it is misery and calamity. He Who knows the Eternal Law... possesses of The Eternal, he endures (lives) Forever. Life is a going forth, death is a returning home.

"He who uses (walks with the aid of) the Eternal Light returns to the Eternal's Enlightenment, and does not surrender his person to perdition."

Zoroaster teaches:

The World Hereinafter shall be the worst world for the wicked, but the best thought (world) for the righteous. The Wise Lloyd with Dominion and Piety shall give us welfare and immortality in accordance with the Right by His Holy Spirit."

Says the Koran Mohammedan);

"Thou shall in nowise reckon dead those who have been slain in the cause of God. Nay, they are sustained alive with their Lord—(Saith the Lord.)"

And now in conclusion, we stand together upon the height—that mountain peak of occult mental and spiritual Illumination toward which we have journeyed together—you, the Initiate, and we, your guides. So Hail! and Farewell!—in these beautiful words of William Cullen Bryant:

"Thou go not like the quarry-slave at night,
　　Scourged to his dungeon, but sustained and soothed

By an unfaltering trust, approach thy grave,

Like one who wraps the drapery of his couch

About him, and lies down to pleasant dreams."

SOURCES

1.   1. Practical Metaphysics, M.C. Hutchison (unpublished).
2.   2. Practical Metaphysics, Barnett, Mathilda J. 1889.
3.   3. Practical Metaphysics for Healing and Self Culture, Mills, Anna W., Mrs. 1896.

BACK COVER MARKETING COPY

The works of Dr. Hutchison came into my possession about twelve years ago. As I read them, immediately I could recognize their utility as a mechanism for personal and spiritual development. You can realize throughout the various lessons of the work that they are very old. In fact, it was ancient when it came into the possession of Dr. Hutchison. You can conclude this from the language of both Dr. Hutchison and the various masters that instruct throughout the text.

I mention the age of the work in the previous paragraph in order to bring to the attention of the reader to modern day movements, namely the many yogic and spiritual schools of thought that emphasize transmission meditation. They all focus upon the AUM mantra as a mechanism for the transformation and improvement of the self and of world conditions.

We are told basically, that mankind stands as the precipice of determining whether he will advance into a greater union and understanding of his place as a unit of the absolute on this planet or whether he will degenerate further into racial, tribal conflict and war. It became important for society to attune to these god frequencies (AUM mantra) for his mental and spiritual growth. For many, this will be a difficult task, since they didn't grow up with this form of meditation as a family tradition. My answer to this impediment is simply this: "Judge by the fruits of the spirit". If the individual experiences positive results within his personal life; then he will have reached a state in his awareness where he can emphatically say that, "I am one with the heaven born".

BACK COVER

Self-Mastery is a work in practical-metaphysics and self-empowerment meshed in the tradition of the enlightened works of authors such as Anthony Robbins, Gary Zukoff and Deepak Chopra. It attempts to bring man to the realization of the fact that the truth and happiness in which he so desperately seeks can't be found outside himself but within. Not only does it tell man where to find his true self (his derive heritage) but it gives him a road map and direction of how to get there. For this is an age in which man will truly be his own priest, his own teacher as it always is and in all things there must be a focus to guide the student to his desired goal. This is what self-mastery does. It guides the student to the discovery of certain indisputable truths that will cause him to dispose of long held social programming and erroneous beliefs that the world presents to him as absolute and beneficial. I would like to end this note with a statement about belief.

Belief alone doesn't result in anything tangible. It requires knowledge or experience to support it. Let me illustrate this fact by an old story that I once heard. There once was a student that went to his master in the pursuit of wisdom, he approached him and asked, "Master what holds up the world? The master thought about it and replied, its elephants." The student reflected on this then asked, "But what holds up the elephant?" The master replied, "Its elephants all the way down."

23170718R00257

Printed in Poland
by Amazon Fulfillment
Poland Sp. z o.o., Wrocław